TALKIN' WITH YOUR MOUTH FULL

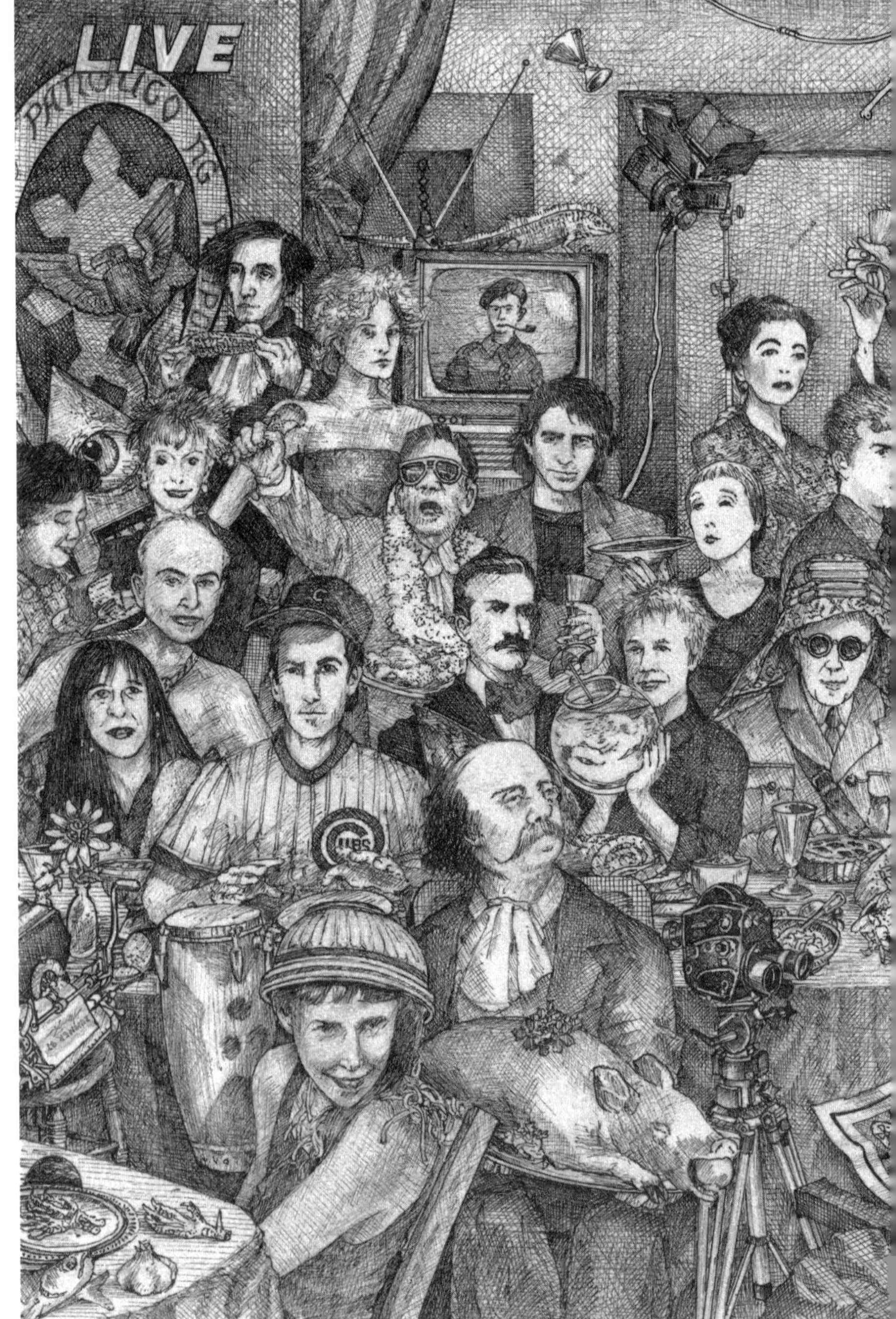
LIVE
CUBS

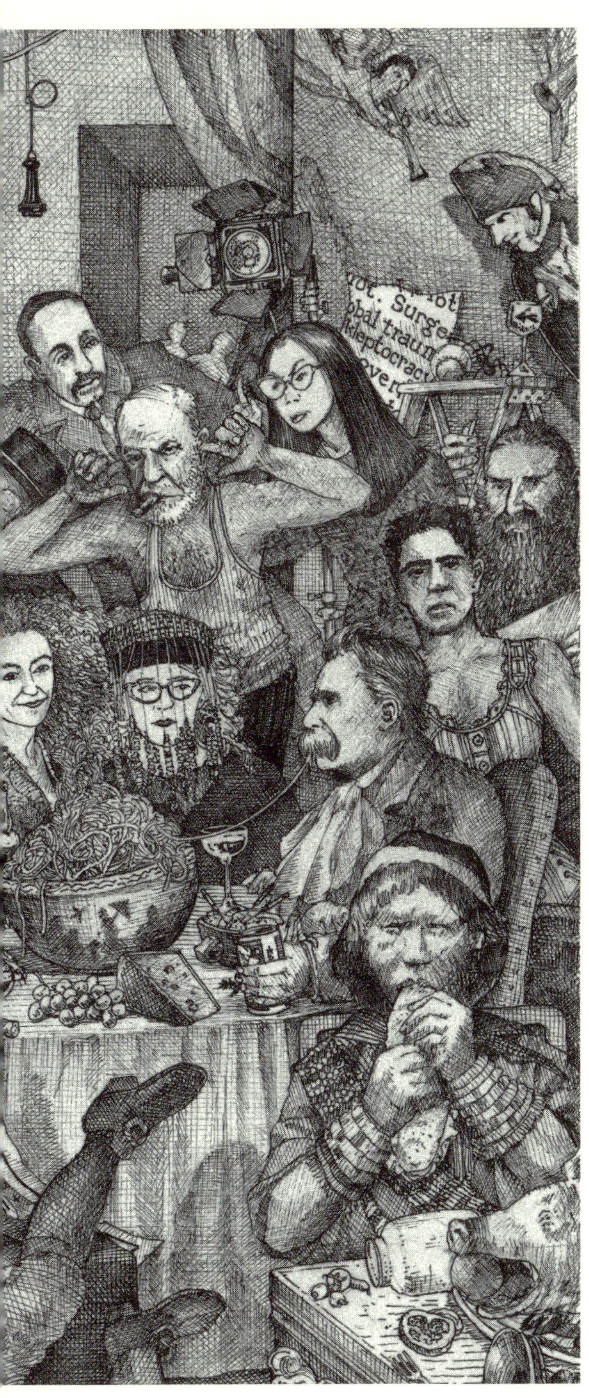

TALKIN' WITH YOUR MOUTH FULL

Conversations with the Videos of Steve Fagin

Edited by Steve Fagin

Duke University Press

Durham and London 1998

©1998 Duke University Press
All rights reserved
Printed in the United States of America on acid-free paper∞
Typeset in Stone Serif, Rockwell Medium, Helvetica,
and Bodoni Book. Designed by Mary Mendell
Frontispiece and key by Thomas Zummer, 1997
Library of Congress Cataloging-in-Publication Data
appear on the last printed page of this book.

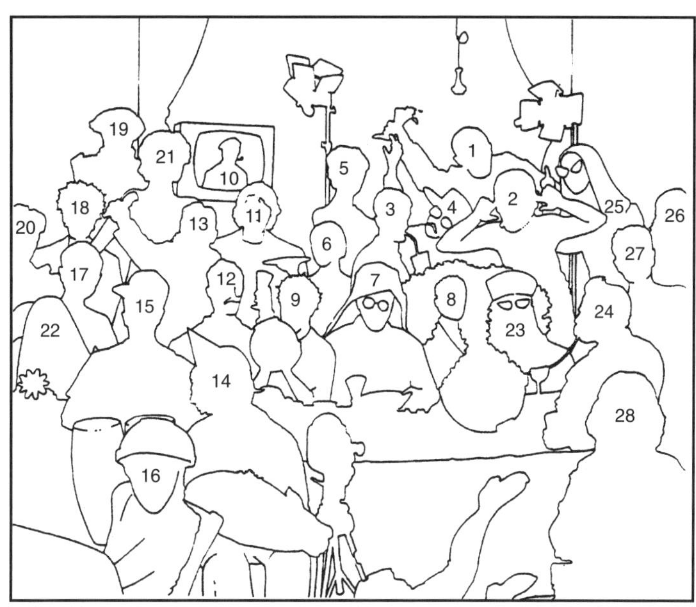

1 Rainer Maria Rilke
2 Sigmund Freud
3 Peter Wollen
4 Mark Rappaport
5 Joan Crawford
6 Constance DeJong
7 John Welchman
8 Bertha Jottar
9 Constance Penley
10 William Horrigan
11 Andrew Ross
12 Raymond Roussel
13 Ferdinand Marcos
14 Gustave Flaubert
15 Barry Gifford
16 Leslie Thornton
17 Ron Vawter
18 Pat Mellencamp
19 Alexis de Tocqueville
20 Imelda Marcos
21 Lou Andreas Salomé
22 Ivone Margulies
23 Anya von Bremzen
24 Friedrich Nietzsche
25 Trinh T. Minh-ha
26 Thomas Zummer
27 Gregg Bordowitz
28 Unidentified Quechua Man

Victoria Gill, Vicente Rafael, and Leslie Dick had a better party to go to; Vivian Sobchack is on vacation; and Steve Fagin and Margaret Morse are at the ball game.

Contents

Acknowledgments

Inept as I am, most of the editorial work for this book was done by a series of excellent coworkers. Andrea Slane, Liza Johnson, Nina Menendez, and Victoria Gill have indulged my impatience with their great patience. Most of the contributors also served the double duty of nursing me during the project. Of those, I would like to single out Constance Penley and Andrew Ross for their hours of sage advice in the face of my incessant whining and whinging.

My work on this book was partially supported financially by an Academic Senate Grant from the University of California at San Diego, and was supported intellectually by Duke University Press editor Ken Wissoker.

As for the existence of this book at all, I would like to thank Peter Wollen. Although I must confess I was a very bad student of his, he was truly a great teacher of mine, and whatever commitment I have to the joining of ideas, ethics, and art I owe to his great example.

Victoria Gill Foreword

When I was invited to interview Steve Fagin for the introduction to this book I balked because I had never seen any of the videotapes whose scripts you will find here. Further, my candidacy was unlikely for other reasons. My academic training is in French literature and literary theory; my master's thesis was on a French crime novelist. I work as a freelance editor on projects destined for such publishers as Simon and Schuster and Crown Books as well as on American crime novels translated for Rivages/ Noir and screenplays intended for major studio production. *The Baseball Encyclopedia* sits on my reference shelf next to *L'Argot chez les vrais de vrai;* I have one foot in the door of l'Université de Paris and the other stuck firmly in the round file of popular culture. "That's fine," said Steve. "But you can't see the tapes until the introduction is finished." Now I know why. He wanted a book that could stand on its own. And this book appeals to readers who may be familiar with Ferdinand and Imelda Marcos without having seen the videotape he made about the fall of their regime. There's something here for everyone—from the Home Shopping Network and Don Larsen's perfect game for the Yankees in 1956 to Flaubert's Orientalism and the love of Rilke and Nietzsche for Lou Andreas-Salomé.

The book you hold in your hands is multiple. It contains the scripts to five videotapes as well as critical essays about each. But Steve Fagin has invited a varied group of artists, writers, academics, curators, and activists to contribute, comment, intervene, interrupt, improvise, or generally riff out on his ideas. Why? The answers go straight to the heart of his project as an artist.

He knew that the scripts would assume a different identity on paper, but rather than have them function as "just a souvenir program of a more interesting event—not that I'm against souvenirs—adding the interruptions and other texts gives the book a sophisticated performative side, a fresh sense of discovery. "I do not know a notation system," he says, "that would reconstruct the script as interestingly as a box score, which has its own life, does a baseball game. Since I couldn't find a notation system of that level of beauty, I wished to produce another thing."[1]

Steve Fagin has no interest in creating art in the traditional romantic sense of the individual artist-hero suffering lonely torments in his room or studio, trying to set down a vision that he alone can render: "I do my artwork not to be that person. I find it tacky, shabby. You become an artist only when you give up that identity. Otherwise, you're just another neurotic." His work always involves others, both in the practical sense (production) and in the sense of intertextuality (Rilke, Nietzsche, Joan Crawford, Flaubert, Freud, Roussel, Andreas-Salomé, and Ferdinand and Imelda Marcos are all points of departure in the tapes). Thus Fagin disrupts the unity of his own authorial voice by constructing the book as a conversation and subverts his own "authority" (as well as traditional notions of documentary "truth") by placing scripts in a nexus, an intertextual field, of related or challenging contributions—a vor-text.

Not being alone in his own book is consistent with Fagin's way of working. The pleasure of a shared project organized around the intensity of an ethical commitment—"not as a good deed but as a performative life"—is part of what motivates him. Mayakovsky and his circle (as depicted in Victor Schlovsky's book of the same name) are an inspiration to him, although he is quick to disclaim any comparison ("in no way *whatsoever* do I have a fantasy of being Mayakovsky"): "To me, Schlovsky's book is a kind of exemplar text because it invokes the reason to be an artist—the passion of life, its constrictions, tragedies, hopes, ambitions, irony. To me that's more important than having a 'good art career.' I wanted to make a book that evoked participating in such an artistic-intellectual world. To make a book that's like the proceedings of an academic conference at which papers were given is to create something stillborn. Better the transcription of one good dinner party with passionate conversation."

Another parallel with Mayakovsky is the nature of the goals Fagin has for his work. "The projects we do are overambitious, utopian—and unlikely to be realized successfully. For example, right now I'm working on a project about Cuba, taking on impossible questions: to find a way to talk about Cuba that doesn't separate out into antagonisms, moralize around certain accepted ideas, or keep on asking Cold War questions. I'm taking a stalemate problem and trying to invigorate it, to bring it to life from another angle. You've got to be stupid to do this! It's like being a diver or a high jumper—I pass up all the medium-scale problems. But the way I work is to throw people into something that excites them. Then, after the excitement wears off or the delirium fades, comes the interest in finding out what excited you—the responsible questions, like, What were you doing? And that yields to the pedagogical demand to want to know why. But I believe in accepting your obsession and making it into a good idea later, rather than starting with a good idea. Unlikeliness is a noble challenge. . . . In fact, you could say that the way I work is by entering improbable territory in a reckless manner."

This helps us understand why Steve Fagin didn't want to simply produce a safe book of scripts with pictures. As Stuart Hall remarks, texts are both a source of meaning and "that which escapes and postpones meaning."[2] Just as the videotapes refigure historical events by presenting images and narratives from multiple sources, Fagin chose to resituate the scripts in his book by placing texts from diverse sources around them, provoking a different kind of looking, a different kind of reading, and creating (in Hall's phrase) "a site of representation and resistance."

"There is a simple book in here," Fagin insists, "a layer of the book that's absolutely traditional. You can read it straightforwardly; there are critical essays about each script, and so forth." To use a musical analogy, there are "standards—you'll find 'Melancholy Baby' and 'My Funny Valentine.'" But, as he points out about his invited collaborators on the book, "I had an all-star band, and I didn't want to have them just keep time. I wanted to give 'em a fuckin' solo!" That the solo might turn out to be a counterpoint to his own theme, or take off in a very different direction rather than serve as accompaniment, was fine with him. "Sometimes the most interesting relation is one of repulsion, not attraction; for example, the pieces by Minh-ha and Ross stray far from my text, and I like this about them."

On the experimental level, structuring a book like this mimics daily life, in which there are always distractions: the telephone rings while you read, a football game murmurs on TV from the next room, the neighbor's little boy asks interminably repetitive questions of his father while they weed the garden outside your window—a thousand narratives compete for your attention and get it, without your getting a chance to say yes or no.

Structuring a book like this also mimics real reading. The French novelist Daniel Pennac, best known for his crime fiction, recently wrote a book about reading that seems to anticipate Fagin's method;[3] it concludes with a list of the ten inalienable rights of the reader: (1) The right *not* to read. (2) The right to skip pages. (3) The right not to finish a book. (4) The right to reread. (5) The right to read anything whatsoever. (6) The right to *bovarysme* (reading to gratify one's own senses or fantasies), "a contagious textual disease." (7) The right to read anywhere. (8) The right to pilfer. (9) The right to read aloud. (10) The right to be silent.

As Steve Fagin says, "People's attention span varies; they skip, they cheat, they move around, they find a picture they like, they stop and daydream. The book supports, implies, that kind of readerly bad faith, which I would never call transgressive. . . . Any reading of the book will inevitably come back to me and my work as the central topic—perhaps like the bad relative who keeps showing up for dinner, you just have to deal with me because there are other people there you're interested in. You might read it in a way that situates me as an obstacle or an annoyance. I don't see that as a bad way of reading; I don't see why everything should read like a good detective novel or a coherent legal argument. These are very beautiful forms at their best. But we live in a world where there's so much information put in front of us simultaneously. . . . I like the idea of a slalom-course read, even though it may not have the same simple ecstasy as downhill skiing. That's the way I would read the book, myself. It's important to acknowledge that that's the way most people read. This book has that programmed into it; it's designed for a society that has a cracked literacy. In fact, all my work is about that."

And so is this book. Frankly, my advice to the reader is, Treat this book like a cocktail party where you have the good luck to be invisible. No one cares what you are wearing, and you can eavesdrop on whomever you wish for as long as you want. Since a lot of people are talking at once, there will be interruptions and cross-talk; one speaker may drown out another, and someone else will be so sharp you steal her lines to use yourself. You will find some people amusing, some inspiring, some dull. Some you will make a note to look up later, while other guests may make you wonder who was crazy enough to invite them. You will know Steve Fagin —he's the one talking with his mouth full.

Steve Fagin and Victoria Gill
Introduction

Victoria Gill: Why did you choose to do a book about your work now?

Steve Fagin: Both my work and the world around it have been through a rather interesting series of transformations over the last ten years, and I thought it would be useful to have some hard-copy documentation of this. Also, my work in video always had a strong desire to be a book. I often imagine myself as someone raised in a postliterate society, a visual culture, feeling a bit blind, wishing I had lived in the age of the book—trying to figure out how these ancient texts were constructed, but able to get to the written only through the screen of the image. I've been trying to stick my hand through a TV screen and pull out a book, like a rabbit out of a hat. So my work always wanted to be a book, but a book in a kind of interrupted fashion, a certain obstacle-laden course, a slalom run through images both constructed and found, being pushed uphill by a voice. And I did very much want this voice to appear in written form. Now that there *is* a book, oddly enough, I have the inverse problem—because you now have to try, like Max Fleischer drawing Koko the Clown, to animate the images, to pull the images out of the book!

V. Put the rabbit back into the hat and pull it out the other side. . . .

S. Yes. This was the initial energy, curiosity, and surprise element that I wanted from the book—to see if I could do such a thing. And it came to me that the book would be better as a conversation around a series of things I had done. Instead of pretending that this book was a perfect analogy for the tapes, I decided I would reconstitute another project as a spin-off or cottage industry based on the work I had already done. I was moving from the second-most unpopular cultural form, art video, into the most unpopular, a book of scripts, of words substituted for images.

The first of these genres, video art, most people find as pleasant an experience as a trip to the dentist, simply because nobody knows how to watch it, and don't make any cracks about laughing gas. People are very aware of how to watch movies; you sit back, the movie washes over you, you have your popcorn, and so forth. But TV is a very different experience: you have your remote control in your hand, and you're drinking bourbon and talking on the telephone and walking around your apartment. Cinema and TV are both very powerful in the specific lack of attention they require. With video, people think they know the type of no-attention to give. It's in a museum, so you treat it like the painting and sculpture—you skateboard through on your way to brunch, you rush to get to the museum cafeteria before they run out of the Thai-lemon-basil-arugula-confit sushi rolls you've heard so much about and they're even low fat.

The other "problem" genre is scripts. Even when they're by directors about whom you'd say, "I'd die to see their scripts," like Fassbinder or Godard, when you actually get the books, you put them at the back of your shelf, and no matter what other odds-and-ends books you get in the mail, you keep reshuffling the scripts so they're at the back of the shelf. So to do this project was, in a way, to find some space that people would enjoy circulating in. I decided on a type of conversation model around the work. This was also decided because I wanted to avoid the hagiography, another subcategory of artists' books I personally hate—by the time you're on page 30, you absolutely hate the artist, even if you didn't hate him or her to begin with. Clearly, this book has that side to it; it has its Ptolemaic conceit, with the interviews and critical articles and scripts. But I think there are enough interruptions and interventions to take it to another space, where it's across writers. The writing is all meant to interrupt, all meant to enter an overlapping conversation.

Someone talking to me recently about new technology said that email is conversation, and I said, "My idea of a conversation is two people talking at the same time with their mouths full." I wanted the book to feel like that: interruptions, interventions, people hijacking the text, going in their own direction, sometimes looping back, sometimes not. So the ideas are a generative field, where people can jump in—like a double-dutch jump-rope game where they can reinvent steps and things like that. It's also like jazz, in which musicians have solos, do their thing, and can either come back to the melody or go off into deep space—bon voyage, be sure to send a postcard, it's always nice to get some mail.

V. I was going to ask why you laid the book out as you have—so that, instead of being in the foreground, your principal works, the videotapes, are flattened into a collage element and then modified or altered by the presence of the other texts.

S. A lot of my initial interest in doing this production work was based on the rebus-like structure that I think knowledge works itself through—the combining of images and ideas, fragments, sounds, texts—and to leave the path of learning as part of the learning process. And that relates to the method I used for this book. There's a pleasure to that passage, and it allows a lot of side doors—sometimes you step on something, and I've left the option to exit through a side door into another world of thought. It's a magical world of countless treasure troves; obviously, Lewis Carroll comes to mind. And I wanted to lay that out and allow it to figure and separate as it wished, both in terms of my video work and in terms of the book itself.

V. Where does this book fit in the "plot summary" of your career?

S. It's maybe in *search* of a career, I don't know! . . . I've always felt that my work fell in between various fields. I actually did start off trying to do more traditional academic theory. I had a really wonderful instructor, Peter Wollen, and people always say, "Oh, you were a student of Peter Wollen's?" They have this perplexed look on their faces, and I say, "He was a wonderful teacher, but I was a bad student."

I used to think of saying that my work is a bridge between this field and that field or between theory and practice, but that metaphor only evoked the *Bridge at San Luis Rey*—collecting all these people on a bridge, and then it collapses! But the work has always simply been in uncharted territory, trying to find its way, trying to connect ideas from one field to another. And that effort to find its way—to see what devices, whether theoretical or popular cultural or interrogative in terms of interviews, would allow you to refigure a new space or new understanding—it's that side of the notion of independence and experiment that interests me.

V. How would you suggest that readers make their way through this text, assuming that they can't sit down and read it straight through? Is there any map or itinerary you'd propose? Like many of your future readers, I have *not* seen the videotapes.

S. To me, the advantage of the book form itself is potentially its interactivity. Perversely, interactivity in the new technologies, like Internet and CD-ROM, strikes me as klutzy and full of too much waiting. Books are interactive because they permit people to start anyplace and reconstruct the text according to the series they choose; also the touch of books can be quite erotic. I think this book does invite those options as well as that of skimming a cluster of interesting writerly interventions by people who have made other important contributions to cultural discussion. It also has a picture-book quality as well as a tele-novella-biography-interview quality, so I think it depends on what kind of channel surfing you wish to do.

I would surely not assume that anyone would read the book from the beginning straight through; that's not its intention. But it is in that form, and if you resist that assumption of the way something should be read, that's part of the childlike pleasure of reading it your own way. I come out of a cultural background in which how to read something was a bit of a problem. Although I was raised in American schools, I also had to go to Hebrew school, in which you read the book the opposite way. I would always ask myself, Now, which way am I supposed to read that book? And that sort of possibility is really a pleasure in itself.

V. You've enlisted the help of a lot of peers, artists, and collaborators, not just in the production of the tapes themselves, but also in the production of this book. You've asked certain people to contribute texts that take off tangentially from some element in the tapes or comment somehow on an aspect of them. So it looks to me as though you would situate your work in terms of individuals rather than positions.

S. In many ways the book, for me, has the pleasure of memory of people that I've worked with and been influenced by.

I really did grow up in this baby-boomer, Mother Goose neighborhood in Chicago in which there were all these apartment buildings and tens of thousands of kids rushing out of the buildings—a fairly secure neighborhood, not a troubled neighborhood, but in terms of European ethnicity quite mixed. There'd be so many kids you wouldn't even play with the kids from the next block—it would be like across the border. And so I always have grown up in this sort of conversation. As a kid, I never understood why anyone would want his own room; that wasn't even an appealing idea. Noise and interference, conversation happening and ideas developing—this terrain of being part of something inhabited has always been part of my spirit. When I moved to the Bay Area in the late seventies, the day Dan White assassinated Harvey Milk and George Moscone, I became involved in a community of intellectuals whom I have continued to see as my ideal audience, and many of them have contributed to this book.

Among that group are Maggie Morse, Trinh T. Minh-ha, Andrew Ross, and Constance Penley; Barry Gifford, whom I knew from Chicago but reconnected with in the Bay Area and with whom I shared a boyhood obsession with baseball; and Mark Rappaport, who was a visiting professor at San Francisco State for a brief period. Occasionally, I'd take these newfound friends, one at a time, to the Oakland A's baseball games, where I'd introduce them to this side of my personality. They would always be surprised that I had this whole other community.

This is very much the way I always saw myself—as going back and forth, mixing and matching between an American urban popular culture base and an American but strongly Left and independent or experimental intellectual community that worked both in media and in the academy. So I've always tried to keep all these things alive and afloat. I've had the good fortune of friends and people I admire to make me keep my head above water, at least for a minute.

V. So they were a survival network, but do you also see them as being your lucky charms?

S. I definitely feel that having them in the book is a type of protection for it, and it's one of the reasons I wanted them in. However, I also tend to do that in my art-making practices; I include a lot of things because I see them as magic or protection, and then I have to justify them—try to combine them in ways that are interesting or make sense. But usually the initial gesture of including them is because I see them as talismanic figures. I have to make sense of it at another level, and that's always where my creativity comes in—at the level of combination and syntax, not at the level of facing the blank page or facing the blank canvas. That's not for me.

V. Can you tell me a bit more about the people who were involved with you in making this book? Why were they chosen? Because I've also heard you say, "Don't assume you have anything in common with anyone."

S. I said that? It's like I always say to Barry Gifford: "For a guy who never listened to anyone you really write great dialogue." I think the inclusion of all the people involved came about because I had a strong respect both for the work they did and for the way they tended to drift into other communities than those where they precisely earned their livings. Going back to the school experience, I would say that the most important professional intellectual figure for me was and still is Peter Wollen. I have always felt he is someone with a strong sense of politics, but politics in terms of tactics or a can-do attitude; he is someone who easily moves across high theory to popular culture. He has always had a fantastic curiosity about everything and the courage to explore both ideas and things that are not on the agenda for intellectuals. He really did give me a sense of an ambition of what an intellectual cultural figure should be like, one that still maintains a sort of North Star force for me.

V. Most of the people you've collaborated with on this book have some kind of academic affiliation or training—with several exceptions, like Constance DeJong, Barry Gifford, and Gregg Bordowitz. Thus, the question arises, What about the role of the academy? As a support, as a source of collaborators, as an audience. . . .

S. What I wanted to do in this book was to connect a sort of horizontal line of cultural work because I think that there's too much of this "you work in this academy, you work over here," when what I think is important is to construct a popular front. Clearly, the book is meant to cover a cluster of people who work over a broad range. At the time the book was generated, Greg Bordowitz was working at the Gay Men's Health Crisis Center, and his work was activist, although he comes from a very strong tradition of anarchists and Marxist intellectuals, and his work since then has been moving in that direction. But I've always wanted to continue a conversational front from activism through artists and then to people working in, say, novels and then the academy. To create a refigured object that knots together those people, and tries to deemphasize the particular institutional accreditation of their work, and constellate them into a mobile front of cultural participants. It's the horizontal connection from activist through artist and writer to academic, and seeing the alliances across them, that I think is interesting—not burying oneself within one's institutional frame.

To work within an institution can itself be positive. I am not simply an anarchist or a hippie, but I am interested in the spaces in between. So both the book and my life, hopefully, have tried to cut across activists—people like Bill Horrigan, who's a curator; fiction writers like Barry Gifford, Leslie Dick, and Constance DeJong; filmmakers like Mark Rappaport; academics like Vivian Sobchack, Pat Mellencamp, Ivone Margulies; artists like Bertha Jottar, who was cameraperson on *Zero Degrees Latitude*; and so forth. This is what I want to be: on the move and in conversation. That's my professional credo. I believe that all the participants in this book are already, in their own multiple activities, contributing to this ideal.

V. You teach at the University of California, San Diego. What about your own role in the academy?

S. Two of the contributors to the book, John Welchman and Vicente Rafael, teach with me and are part of my support group at the school. For many people I respect—some of them included in the book—the academy is the place they do their work; they've found it a productive, energetic part of that work. I often find myself much more ambivalent than my colleagues. I would say that I'm a very reluctant member of the academy. My strongest sense of my role there is in relation to individual graduate students—instilling in them a commitment and ethics to enable them to go into a more professionalized role as artists or curators. I see it as an incubation period for eventual members of this other community outside the academy. People should always have only one foot in the academy. I always say that when you're in the academy, you're already half of a horse's ass. There's a sense of entitlement there that I resist. Obviously, the role of educator can be important, but truly, again, I'd say, Only *one* foot, not both feet. Unfortunately, the type of creature I want to be is an octopus. Sometimes I think I'm like Catherine Deneuve at the end of *Tristana,* limping on one leg back and forth, back and forth. . . . The one leg I'm left with is firmly buried in the academy.

The academy seems to set in motion a whole system of validation that becomes very cut off from other forms of exchange. It's not the elitism, it's the potential lack of outside relations that bothers me. The actual specificity and intensity of the labors and the space that allows people to do that are actually things that I appreciate. The idea of thinking that people in the academy are privileged because they have jobs and they're cultural workers is a very perverse dynamic. Not being underprivileged doesn't necessarily make you privileged. There's a lot of that type of bashing of the academy that I'm against.

As far as the book goes, I'd say that the tree doesn't fall very far from the apple—with the academy being the tree. So hopefully the book has some of that poison in it—when people bite it, they'll taste something between Eden and Snow White.

V. Stuart Hall remarks somewhere that what is mistrustable about the academy is its unfortunate tendency toward repetition, mimicry, or "destructive ventriloquism."

S. That happens when everything becomes part of *Rocky 9*—it becomes part of a sequel. I was lucky enough, or unfortunate enough, to be part of a series of major intellectual events in the late seventies in Edinburgh and Milwaukee. In the U.K. events, one felt the effort to align work done in many areas—journals, the production of art, television, activist and academic work. The ideas discussed actually were building toward a critical mass, and conferences were held on refiguring history, psychoanalysis, and the avant-garde. One might argue that it was precisely because of the inhospitality of the British academy to these new ideas that alternate spaces had to be found. Also, some members of this intellectual mafia were knockabout film fanatics who had been affiliated with the British Film Institute. But one cannot emphasize enough these efforts to construct a popular front. Then the show opened on the road—Milwaukee. They probably told Stephen Heath it was the Riviera of the Arctic Circle.

The United States seemed like a place where these ideas might find an institutional home—conferences, teaching jobs, books—as opposed to the United Kingdom, where these ideas had a burgeoning public life but, as I said, very little context in the academy. In the United States it went the other way round. The ideas were immediately absorbed into the academy and began a whole industry with standardization of product and a secure, eager market—which America, in its Tayloristic grandeur, is exceptionally good at. Surely, there were some intelligent people making worthwhile contributions, but there was a Tayloristic impulse driving the ideas into standardization, the lowest common denominator of product in the academy. Again, I think it's part and parcel of the American way to make something into a product. The academy's just another example of that.

Now, many people who work in the academy, some of whom have been included in the book, have been much more optimistic, resourceful, and effective as far as their role in the academy and its relation to other spheres is concerned. Clearly, cultural studies itself is meant partially as a corrective to the way *Screen* magazine's "high theory" entered the American academy. And this effort I applaud, but I must confess to a certain cynicism. When I was at the cultural studies conference at the University of Illinois a few years ago to show *The Machine That Killed Bad People*, I thought to myself, What's the difference between a film studies nerd and a cultural studies grad student? A leather jacket and a single piercing.

V. I also think there's a tendency to assume here that all intellectual work goes on in the academy, and that's just not true.

S. It's very hard not to have at least a toe in the academy. For example, in journals, they often start off staffed by very young people, for whom things soon have to be justified in terms of career. New York resembles London and Paris as a cultural capital, but the dispersal of intellectuals across this country—held together now only by the Internet, it seems—makes it easy for the reality of their lives to be the books and articles they publish, as opposed to the conversations and debates they have. That's partially a function of the dispersal of people from the capital to the edges.

But when you're in New York you tend to get drawn to another institution, which is the art institution. There, you get a lot of the academics crossing over into the art scene, which means that they imagine they'll get to go to better parties. I have a lot of friends who are academics, who are interested in the ideas manifested in my work, but they tell other people to come to my work because they think, "Oh, I'm going to be invited to an *art* party." And I've tried never to disappoint them.

Actually, I was initially very surprised at the reception of my videos in art venues because I had assumed that they were going to circulate more in an academic context or a literature context. But two weeks after I finished the tape on Lou Salomé (*Virtual Play*), the curator of the Kitchen, Amy Taubin, grabbed it up to show it, and then it was picked up by the curator at MOMA, Barbara London. So it was initially taken up by the art world.

This occurred at a time when the art world was hungry for theoretical ideas. Ironically, I was looking to escape from the confinement of those ideas into a zone that would allow for more free play, recombination, or fusion of them. As I was fleeing those ideas it was like Charlie Chaplin running into this parade of workers in *Modern Times*! I ran right into an art world that was desperate for the world I'd run away from, which was the academic world. And they took me on as someone who spoke those ideas fluently. During the ten-year period covered by the tapes, I tried to refigure that join between the art context and the academic context, each trying to get away from the fantasy that they intersect.

Also, because I did video and not film, I was more easily accepted in the art world. Because although my own cultural love was for the cinema, I was interested in producing video as a social object, in relation to television, and in terms of my sense of doing a low-tech type of project. The experimental film world was excluded from the art world—in fact, it was envious of video because it wasn't let into the art world as easily. On the other hand, it had self-determination; it was a small state, but at least it had its own integrity, like an old democracy. And in the film world—particularly in San Francisco around Steve Anker and the Cinemathèque and in New York around Mark McElhatton as curator and Jack Walsh as director of the Collective for Living Cinema—there were conversations that occurred where people argued about ideas, argued about autonomy.

In the video world, which I actually was not so much a part of, most of the arguments about autonomy in video related not so much to art practices as to agitational and propagandistic cultural projects, ones that were activist-oriented, meant for communities that wanted to use tapes to disseminate opinions. In terms of experimentation with ideas at a more conceptual level and their intervention into culture with either a big *C* or a big *K*—depending on your mood—video in its good side was an extension of conceptual work because conceptual artists were doing it. But then when it got legitimized as an art form—because it was being selected by museums and not by a self-determining art community—in fact it became a very sort of "avant-garde lite," like Bud Lite beer. Because in the end if you leave it up to museums to initiate judgment, they're usually going to choose decorative work.

When subcultures produce something that has intensity, that has a large degree of buzz and desire on the margin, whether it's fashion or music or art, the major institutions will come to it. That's the nature of the exchange; it's called a market economy. It has nothing to do with the good intentions of individual curators. They're just sitting in a different space and not participating in the same way.

A lot of my effort initially was to get academics and museum people to participate in a world related to video, books, and film— in terms of the issues I was interested in—*as full players* rather than as people who just heard about what was interesting. And I made a lot of effort to include and inform boards; for example, when I was on the video board of LACE in Los Angeles and the boards of the Cinemathèque in San Francisco and of Drift Distribution in New York, we worked on trying to form these alliances to get such people to participate from the first. The problem with both the museum and the academy is that they come in at a very late stage in the process.

V. I'd like to ask you about other strategies that govern your work besides people and alliances. What about the question of *places—here* versus *away* or *far away*?

S. I think the guiding principle of the work is that each piece has an imagination of another place, various eccentric and personal clutter in between here and there, and a large discursive screen between here and there.

Virtual Play is very much governed by the strategies around biography, as if Lou Andreas-Salomé were the king in a chess game—how you would move in order to capture the piece. It operates as if there were really someone playing on the other side, producing resistance, producing variation, and also threatening your own position. It was set up as a two-sided chess game in the guise of a biography. That was the strategy, with a strong sense of the space between the United States and Old Europe, between contemporary American postliterate space and the extraordinary cluster of people around Lou Salomé—Rilke, Nietzsche, Freud. A Chicago-Vienna tape.

I always think of two things in connection with that. First, the major producer of kosher meats in Chicago is . . . Vienna! And I think of Freud's joke, when he talks about the counterprojection of the analyst. He says that the analyst should look at the patients as a bunch of dogs racing around a track and that the doctor should not throw sausage on the track to distract the dog from his goal! Fortunately, or unfortunately, the tape is full of such distractions.

The next tape I did, *The Amazing Voyage of Gustave Flaubert and Raymond Roussel,* is very much structured around a major eye accident that I had and really living in a space of isolation and blindness, very dominated by music and moments of text produced in relation to vision. The piece is precisely at the epicenter of my desire to construct a novel by somebody who comes from a postliterate society, whose only knowledge of the novel is what's spoken to him about it, who tries to invent the novel without ever having read one. It's a postliterate creature trying to construct a novel through images, through text, turning pages . . . but he doesn't know how to read, or the books he opens only have pictures in them, things like that. And also I felt that Flaubert and Roussel related strongly to this space between image and writing, which I see as the umbilical separation that Barthes writes so well about—language and the mother's body, and the effort to crawl back into the womb.

I've always been inspired, as well, by Raymond Roussel, who simply wanted to be Victor Hugo; he wanted to be the most popular writer in the world. Yet only through affliction did he create experimental texts—not by ambition. I was so fascinated by Roussel's real affliction, his need to invent games to produce at all. Growing up in that cultural moment with the money he had, which was this exorbitant family wealth, pre–World War I, pre-income-tax wealth, he was able to take his everyday life and turn it into his dream. Of course that doesn't mean he turned it into a good life. It was a very neurotic life, which turned out actually to be nothing but isolating and self-destructive.

But Roussel's life also partially, perversely, relates to my take on the Marcoses [*The Machine That Killed Bad People*]. One of the things that attracted me about the Marcos family was just that they were able to turn their dreams into everyday life. I have a line in that script where it says that I prefer to see Imelda Marcos as Emma Bovary, except that Imelda Marcos actually was able to have her dreams come true. This idea of taking tawdry daydreams, movies, everyday life, American stuff, and then reconstituting it, was very attractive to me about that project.

Now that Philippine project forced me to address a very different set of questions than the Flaubert/Roussel piece. I do see the lives of Flaubert and Roussel as ending pathetically, driven into their privacy . . . no, their loneliness, using this loneliness to generate imaginary literary worlds—worlds whose literary skills I truly admire, but their wretched lives? Wait a second! I'm not going! Time out! Not me! No!

So I wished to redirect myself outward and use another side of my personality, a compulsive curiosity about politics and history, to try to write a history through other means, using the stylistics of infotainment television. To really work on the way the United States comes to terms with its xenophobia by proxy, a televisualized version of international relations, to initiate a discussion of the CNN-ification of the planet, I constructed an alternative network. It was one that did broaden the range and nature of the interviewers and interviewees, but it also addressed another issue: The question is not exclusively, Who is entitled to speak? but, How do we listen and watch? It is not only one-way streets that lead to solipsism; it is no longer true that all roads lead to Rome, but it *is* true that all roads do lead through Atlanta—it's what is called a hub city.

The Machine That Killed Bad People is not simply an abstract discussion of the formal problems of TV/global news/politics but an effort to tell of a specific relation, the relation between the Philippines and the United States. It is a history told in a very stylized manner and from a specific point of view. But I feel the piece has a very ethical and humble relation to this complex history. The idea of conceptualizing a project that starts here and circulates around another place, driven by this televisualization, strikes me as a conversation that we *all* should be having, not one that is restricted by ethnic identity or national boundary.

Zero Degrees Latitude was commissioned by the series "New Television" for a PBS screening. I wanted to do a piece relating to 1492 and the five hundred years of conquest, but from a different point on the compass. Dealing not with the relation of Europe to the Americas but with the relation between the United States and Latin America. When discussing the conquest, many historians had described what they perceived to be the affinities between Catholicism, one of the major engines of colonization, and indigenous religions. Both were so iconic, so expenditure-related, so able to find a place for the mother as a handmaiden of the deity— that clearly this allowed the conversion a natural bridge.

I never bought the seamlessness of this argument and wanted to address the question of religious/ideological conversion and a moment when the sculpture was not quite dry, so I turned to the very recent Protestantization of Latin America and the remaining indigenous people. Here is truly an odd couple—evangelical Protestant Christianity and these same icon-laden, ritual-bound *indios.* What unfulfilled desires lead them from the Amazon to bathe in this desert of a religion, born-again Christianity? The project led, much to my surprise, to an attempt to understand the role of sound and radio in the so-called age of visual culture.

The short I did [*Memorial Day (Observed)*] was commissioned by KCET; I was asked to do something on democracy, and I wanted to do it about the space between middle America and de Tocqueville. The short was intended as an introduction and an epilogue to a feature chosen by me; it is an accessory meant to complement, to change the tone of an already existing film. It plays best with *Sweet Smell of Success* but can play with many other features. I've seen the piece in its ideal form only once and was pleasantly surprised at how well it played with the feature. This short piece observes the observance of Memorial Day 1995 in Columbus, Ohio. It is meant to be an updated "acting out" of the wisdom of de Tocqueville. These are the great-grandchildren of the Americans that de Tocqueville observed over 150 years ago—living in an America that does not simply suffer from the absence of democracy but suffers in its heart and its heartland from the expectations of democracy itself. This piece is not simply about staying here but staying home, a very different concept. It is a piece about staying put. I've always been a bit confused by this expression—what does *put* mean? Anyway, the body may sit, but the mind still drifts.

V. So can all your works be seen as your way of moving through, or getting around, the dichotomy of insider versus outsider and answering the question of how spaces are traversed?

S. People are from specific places; they have passports and histories. To talk of no borders strikes me as corporate trans-national rhetoric, avoiding taxes and unions. Specific national identity is not a burial plot but a generating instance, subject to rather radical mutations. It's not that in the end you're not *from* a place, but it's only the first thing you say; it's not the last thing you say.

In critical debate there is often a series of equivalencies that collapse the different functions someone from the First World can play in the so-called Third World. You are, plain and simple, "the colonizer." Yes, you may be from the side of the colonizer, but the game is still in play—the function of your piece might change, go through transformation. We all have origins, but these are not our destinies. There is a generative quality, from the king to the military governor to the tourist. That you start at a bad point, and a bad place, is assumed. That you end in a bad place is only—you know, after you step in shit, are you going to stand in it, or are you going to wipe it off and keep walking?

Let's say that you're a tourist or that you're an ethnographer—yes, that carries specific baggage. But there's a certain sort of contact that's ascribed and a certain conversation that occurs. Not to come down on a position, to think you could have no identity that doesn't start in a single place, strikes me as more of a problem than assuming a bad-faith identity and trying to move. To think you have the power to simply empower others, that it's not part of the dialogue of mutual transformation, strikes me as doing more harm than good. So on one side is some hope; on the other side there's not. There's no guarantee. There is a degree of bad faith and corruption—but what else is new?

Independent documentary seems to me locked too much in the intentionality of the participants: either you endlessly reflect on your own position, or you simply hand the equipment over to the informants, the "natives," like they don't have better things to do than make documentary films. There should be more attention to what the piece actually has to offer: How does it transform the roles one plays? Are there wisdoms from bad-faith positions? I was just at a "doco" [documentary conference]—Australians abbreviate everything—and there was endless talk of the ethics of the filmmaker, and I responded, much to the horror of the organizers, that I didn't see that there was a priestly role for the artist; there is no grace in it. Even Stalin could make an interesting documentary. Well, at least I enjoyed the dance clubs in Melbourne, but not as much as Sydney.

V. As for other strategies that govern your work, I'd like to ask you briefly about one that's dear to my heart: baseball.

S. The notion of *home* and *away* comes into this—my ability to see the away position as an interesting one to have. And it's true that I did grow up in the friendly confines of Wrigley Field. I always think it's very odd—In Chicago, going to a ball game at Wrigley Field is an outdoor activity, it's what you do on a nice day. In California, people say, "What do you want to go to a baseball game for? It's a nice day!"

I am very partial to that idea of how you participate in something —as a noisy baseball spectator. It comes from growing up in Chicago with Barry Gifford, going to Wrigley Field and sitting in the bleachers, arguing about this, constructing a conversation about the archaeology of an event while you're witnessing it. Something does happen in front of you, but the nature of what you *do* is much more negotiable and archaeological.

One of the major things I loved about baseball is that it's one of the only zones that I could actually ever relax in. I could go to the

ballpark at 10:00 A.M. and stay there all day. It's not generated off
of a temporal model. I really do see baseball as a three-act play.
I'm very much of the purist temperament about that. Unless it was
the World Series, I would leave in the tenth inning. One encore! I'd
only give it one encore. The dramatic structure of baseball collapses after ten innings.

V. Does baseball fit in with the ludic aspect of your work?

S. In the Ecuador tape there's a moment when Cam's wife, upset
about not getting attention, says, "I didn't mind that his first love
was the Lord, but I did mind that his second love was baseball."
The text moves to try to understand a New Testament chapter and
starts telling that Biblical text in relation to the statistics that
George Sisler accomplished in the year 1922. In lots of ways that's
been my strongest interest in baseball—the sense of the quality of
what people produced and the actual discrete, unchallengeable,
immutable sense of it. The idea of these immutable standards that
baseball represents has the same function for me as figures like
Freud or Socrates. It's really the stature of their accomplishment
that I admire and the playfulness of their performance. (It's very
interesting to me that the only prize Freud ever won was the
Goethe award for writing.) It's the inspirational and poetic quality of
their performance—both baseball players and others—and then
the residue of that poetry. The residue in baseball, statistics, being
so precise that you could actually capture their poetry. We know
that defensively, with ballplayers, it's not the same thing; but
offensively—there's no arguing with Albert Belle's fifty home runs
and fifty doubles!

V. Although you may argue with Albert Belle! Or he may argue with
you! [Belle is famous for his bad temper.]

S. I don't think it's wise to argue with Albert Belle! It cost him the
MVP!

To me, the ludic impact is very strong, but I think it should rub
against something that clearly is at stake. The pieces that are very
ludic—the Lou Salomé tape and the Roussel/Flaubert piece—do
both generate out of personal catastrophes. One was a very radical, destructive, negative breakup with somebody I lived with for a
long time, and the other was my eye injury. So the ludic quality is a
very strong relation to these events; likewise, the ludic in the docu-

mentary pieces wished to rub against something real. The argument against the discursive nature of vérité is surely true, but
there actually *is* somebody there you're talking to, and the way
you have to negotiate the ethics around that in the construction of
the work is very important to my sense of documentary. In general, my relation to the ludic is that it has to actually engage the
risk of what it's stemming from and that it has to have a certain
sense of ethical responsibility to it. When it detaches into a second plateau of the ludic, I'm not interested. I've always had reser-
vations about Duchamp. The one piece of Duchamp I like is, I
think, the one where he takes his sister's book, and it gets rained
on, and it's left open to that page. That it's from his sister interests
me, that the glass [*The Bride Stripped Bare by Her Bachelors,
Even/Large Glass*] is cracked interests me: the ludic should always brush against a wound; there should always be a tender
spot.

Also, my relation to knowledge is similar. My work is often clus-
tered in the postmodern circulation of cross-ideas. The capacity to
mobilize ideas, to recirculate them, to take them and move them,
is important. But to me it cannot be like a game of checkers—it
has to be more like moving something that's rooted. You have to
feel the roots of the original ideas. And if you're going to evoke
Socrates, the level at which you evoke him should be worthy of
the source. There should be an understanding of that knowledge
and position *in* your work—not just notation as a point of reference.

Let me give you an example. Part of the reason I was driven to
do the Ecuador piece, *Zero Degrees Latitude*, is that when I finished constructing the piece on the Philippines, its original edit
was three and a half hours long. Even I knew it was way too long.
It was really about the flow of TV information, so I needed all
these different elements: infotainment, commercials, newscasters,
logos, and shopping channels as well as documentary footage. So
a lot of the documentary footage vanished. What resurfaced in the
Ecuador piece was a strong commitment to vérité, in order then to
recirculate it. But sometimes people have trouble with the piece
because it has a side that resembles a rooted documentary. And
then to see it *moved* — "Why, you can't move a rooted documentary and recirculate it with other discourses of dreams and autobiography! That's not what you do!" And my point is that that's ex-

actly why I want to do it. That's exactly what's interesting to me—
the relation of those elements and the way one tries to see
through them. Otherwise, I wouldn't bother. If we're going to be
Lola Montès in the trapeze act, let's do it with the safety net down,
not with the net up. If we're going to do this and be serious, let's
cut the net and go for it.

V. You did bring up Socrates and Duchamp, and I'd like to ask
about those tutelary figures in your work: Freud and so forth.

S. I've tried as hard as possible in my adult life to distance myself
from large big-bang ideas. I find the axiomatic quality of being so-
called Marxist or Freudian debilitating to my ability to think out of a
problem. I admire the intention to transform society, but to know
the answer ahead, as smart as Marx is, surely leaves no purpose
to the transformation. I'm interested in texts that come up with
surprising third acts, so I'm distrustful of the axiomatic, geometric
way of thinking. It's the speculative interventions of ideas, the way
they broke worlds, that interested me; likewise, when I talked
about film studies, or cultural studies, it's the breakthrough quality
of the ideas I liked. When they became standardized, I lost
interest. When people tell me I have to cover this, include that,
etc., I quote Johnny Mize, then first baseman for the New York
Giants. When told he had to hit only ten more home runs to break
Babe Ruth's mark of sixty home runs in a season, he replied, "The
only thing I *have* to do is die."

V. This seems like a good time to ask, What other kinds of
alliances and contexts do you seek for your work? We've talked
about baseball and movies. . . . Books? Ephemera, like pop
culture?

S. Ever since I had this massive eye injury, I've been very driven
by analogies related to music. It's a little like baseball, as I was
saying. . . .

V. It's unrepeatable. . . .

S. Yes. I've always been driven by the voice of that beauty.
Recently, I've been massively interested in Afro-Cuban music, very
interested in that polyrhythmic structure where you have basic
clave and people playing in relation to it, with the drum players
relating horizontally, the horn players relating horizontally, and the

piano connecting in between. Finding all this individual talent, which combines both horizontally and vertically, all going on at once and actually being driven forward within a coherent structure—as opposed to, say, free-form jazz, which I find too free-form and too solo-based for my taste. I've been very enamored of the accomplishment of these Afro-Cuban musicians, and it serves as an ambition for my work to be as rich as theirs, with as much depth.

V. What about video versus film? How does technology in general impact your work?

S. I'm very suspicious of aesthetics based on a fantasy of the new, of the future. When someone tells me about the future, I think he's either a shyster or a fool. Are these people willing to put a fifty-dollar bet down on what they predict?

I think it's odd that I came to be thought of as an artist in relation to video and technology because video, when I was in it, was still in this triumphant mode, being "the new technology." Good art pieces don't have such a clear map, a finger pointing in the direction of the future. They are much more apt to simply get sidetracked or lost entirely. I'm more interested in perceiving new technology as if it were a relic from a past civilization. I love the World's Fairgrounds in Queens, a place that promises the future and reeks of the past. It's more interesting to me to evoke a relation to the past with technology, to reinvent the past, than to imagine this technology as the royal road to some estate of future wealth, as a form of speculative investment. "Oh yes, I get it, virtual reality—real estate with no garbage or homeless people."

Video came to power on this notion of its being the future. But nothing ages faster than the future. Now video seems to be no longer the future, and it has very little past. Video never established itself on the same firm ground as film; it's been suspended from its role of being interesting as the "new technology." Because it's now been supplanted by something newer, it's almost vanished. If your only interest is as part of a futures market, I don't want to be around when the pork bellies are actually delivered; all these futures traders will have moved over to soy beans anyway.

Video was easily validated; it had a prodigy advantage that it never exploited. The early experiments, the initial improvisational work, were interesting as a continuity with conceptual art, but I have nothing but contempt for the kind of work done by the second-generation American video artists like Bill Viola and Gary Hill. I remember Raymond Bellour giving a lecture on ideas and media about Godard and Gary Hill, and I said, "Just like *Twins*—Arnold Schwarzenegger and Danny DeVito. Give me a break!" I think this whole thing was sold short—that's what happened in video. When the movie is made of its history, it will have the Bette Davis role in Aldrich's *Whatever Happened to Baby Jane.*

As I said before, independent film grew up as a willful, maverick, autonomous form in its aesthetic and theoretical side, whereas video's autonomy was more related to political activism. But its more novelistic and strong relation to itself as a developed form of complex cultural expression was initially short-circuited by its inclusion in an art world that was interested only in avant-garde lite—things that were decorative and an art community that was internationally based as a type of museum world. . . . If it's Tuesday, this must be Cologne; if it's Wednesday, it must be Lyon; and Friday we're going to Japan, so get ready for sushi for everyone.

And what you get then is a perverse realization of Murnau's universal cinema language—that is, *no* language because it has to circulate in so many countries. You also get short-circuiting of the development of the culturally specific and of any very strong linguistically, argumentatively, novelistically based form, in the name of this universal Nowheresville form of one museum versus another museum—which in the end are a bunch of Holiday Inns.

V. Well, then, what is there intellectually to be gained by using video?

S. I came to video with two major ideas of what was interesting about it. First, the TV side: you have a small box with a massive sound, you reach toward the box and energize it, and it's a very discrete, ethereal form of object. The Flaubert/Roussel piece is very much about that side. The other "television" side has to do with its only hypnotic effect, its pornography. Our palms sweat as we rub up against the shock of the present: touchdowns, earthquakes, revolutions, and. . . .

V. Shopping!

S. Right, home shopping! I wanted to develop those particularities of video. Continuing work in video is based exclusively at this point for me on the capacity to generate a low-budget project that would deal with complex cultural ideas. Also, I have a perverse negative relation to it, saying, "Film—almost any image is easy to watch. Video—hardly any." So any image you can construct in video that's worth watching is already an accomplishment, it's a straw-into-gold aesthetic, whereas commercial cinema could be seen as turning gold into straw.

I've never felt particularly ontologically attached to a material. That's got a lot to do with why my alliances cut across forms. I'm interested in what I see as committed, sophisticated cultural work that can be part of a larger access; and whether it comes in novels, or political activism, or academics—wherever you can get it, you grab it. You connect to what's alive and figure out how to make sense of it later. But when you know in advance where your "good sense" is, it's probably dead already—dead on arrival.

I've had the experience of growing up as a graduate student and witnessing the "hotness" of film theory, and the import of Continental theory within it, and realizing that it was interesting because you had a bunch of mavericks who no longer had a field— the British I talked about earlier, people like Peter Wollen, Stephen Heath, Laura Mulvey. They had to find a space, and it's their creative side that makes it worthwhile, not the inherent interest of film. I don't think there is an inherently interesting object. But there are people who are speculative in refiguring where their energy attaches. It happens because of personal obsession or because of a certain institutional restraint. . . . Or it *could* happen. Unfortunately, these things only last for around five years because of exhaustion, personal melodramas, and so forth. So it's a floating crap game, and you have to keep alert and call up Nathan Detroit and find out where the action is.

V. I'm leading you into a minefield here, but I'd guess that it's one you know your dance through pretty well: I'd like to ask you about art and artists, what the role of the artist is—both traditionally and as you see it.

S. In the late seventies and early eighties, there was very strong support, at least in the academy, for avant-garde artists. Critics and academics were coming to pay homage to these experimental projects and spending a lot of energy writing very complex, interesting texts to try to figure out what new knowledge was available in them.

Now I say this not about Peter and Laura particularly, because I thought they were very grounded and responsible in terms of an equal relation to artists and theorists, and a lot of my spirit of what I believe it should be like is based on them, but there was, in a certain male-oriented American avant-garde, a certain sort of self-indulgent guru/dauphin sense of what their work implied, assumed, or left dangling for you to figure out, and these artists functioned on the prophet model. In the period of my own production I've noticed a retreat from interest in certain experimental work in favor of popular culture work, which has its good side—opening up other than experimental texts for points of wisdom and cultural contact and political engagement.

So the artist has moved, in the ten-year period covered by this work, from being a prophet to being a panhandler. Now, in Soho, if you see critics on the street, they cross to the other side out of fear that you'll ask them to come to your show or write about your work.

And I understand the withdrawal from this assumption of the prophetic quality of the text and the notion that anything an artist touches, no matter how abstract or fragmented, implies everything that a critic might think. But that doesn't mean that there aren't texts that are interesting because of their complexity. Likewise, although it's true that much of popular culture and subculture generates all types of complexity, that doesn't mean that artists are exclusively poseurs.

I'm supportive of breaking down the mythos of the artist, but I'm supportive of breaking down all mythoi. Whenever I hear that "the artist is dead" or "the author is dead" argument, I always say, "Well, how about the critic's writing? Equal time for the critics!" I'm willing to admit that every text or art object is not like some Old Testament to be endlessly reinterpreted as if by some Talmudic scholar, but on the other hand it's not nothing at all, either. What about the critic's text? Why is your criticism of art-making not the same type of text? The artist is surely no more dead than the critic.

V. So would you situate yourself in any kind of avant-garde? Do you think there is such a thing now as an avant-garde?

S. People have compared my work to Ornette Coleman's *The Shape of Jazz to Come*, but I respond that I'm just looking to produce Ellington's *Reminiscing in Tempo*. I guess I'm not doing such a good job. I am personally not on the side of an avant-garde model based on the idea of shredding tradition: I'm pro-blasphemy and anti-ignorance.

The other thing I'm suspicious about with the avant-garde is this guarantee of what it's in front of. Clearly, the initial notions of the avant-garde, best emblematized in the Soviet Union in the twenties, assume that it's part of a larger social revolution that is just around the corner—it's a utopian model. With the recent collapse of the Soviet Union, and with the awarenesses around the Cultural Revolution in China or the massive destruction in Cambodia under Pol Pot—clearly one should not abandon the hope of overthrowing tyranny and authority, but to abandon every form of identity in the name of some single prophetic voice has proved in this century to be catastrophic.

I'm in favor of the capacity to overturn and shift traditions, but with humility and awareness of the possibility of one's own limits— not simply assuming that you're moving forward. It's crucial to perceive that critique and development can come from a 360-degree access—that there's no North Star, there's no simple past, and there's no simple future. One's sense of the future should always be built off variations of the wisdoms of the present and the past. There are rich traditions, and I'm on the side of those investments. Clearly, the political analogy—in terms of down with certain class structures and the idea that the proletariat is somehow the avant-garde of history—although it surely acknowledges an oppression that occurred, produces the potential for a damaging wake in its trajectory. And it's unclear to me that the trajectory is moving forward, even though it is overturning much crime. The correction of a crime does not inherently produce a noncriminal world.

V. Could you go further into, or closer up to, the question of what the French call *narratology*? How is it possible to tell stories in a world of multiple voices when narrative coherence has become untrustworthy?

S. I'm very fond of the Afro-Cuban model of the clave. You have this point of reference that you're playing around, and voices circulate, and sounds play off each other both horizontally and vertically. And there's a sense of their circulating within a system that can even be reversed, so you could play what would be called son-clave or rumba-clave. It's not even always heard in the music; it's heard by the practitioners. They are *in* it. Cubans have all these words for being born in it or not being born in it. A lot of the people I work with culturally are people I would say are born in clave—they have a certain awareness that I admire that makes me feel that I could play alongside them. And I don't want to underestimate them either—each of these people I feel committed to is extraordinarily ethical. It's not just their intellectual or artistic talent; it's a combination of the talent and the ethics. There also has to be a certain tension, and this tension should drive things forward; it's not the melody that holds things together but the rhythm.

V. Let's talk about identity politics and the cultural studies critique, about where you'd place yourself in this debate about who is entitled to talk about what and how.

S. The contexts tend to vary. I think we're in a very difficult period because we have a macro social circumstance in the United States of immense suppression and elimination of cultural differences. Here in California, for example, we have Proposition 187. It's very clear on a larger scale that the ability for some voices to participate in a self-determining way in dialogue has been very constricted. On the other hand, in the arts, which is a type of project that links up with larger sociological and political concerns, the debate is not exactly the same, and what constitutes productive dialogue is governed by different rules. Within the arts, the more mixing, the more dialogue, the more working on a position from beginning to end and from all different types of relations, the better. This does not mean that artists should not make alliances with larger communities, but their relation to those communities as artists is rather complex.

Historically, it's worked better if there has been an artists' wing in a political movement, like the Chicano movement, whose posters and murals have been a central part of the political project. But there is also a less urgent zone of inquiry, a workshop on questions, an arena that indulges the efforts to ask differently and eccentrically—if this is what an artist does, then I would call myself an artist. Societies need space for these seemingly self-indulgent pursuits. Otherwise—without historical exception—you end up with the eventual absence of different views and positions. I feel much more confident arguing about the disadvantages of a world that would not show support for what I do than I do arguing in favor of the immediate instrumental use of what I do. My work will not save the whales, but I don't see how it's going to hurt them, either.

I'm not asking to politically represent a certain state or a nation or even an interest group, but in terms of argumentation on the topic, there's a certain moment where there has to be some credibility given to the quality of the argument itself. It's clearly the case that certain stories can be complicatedly told and richly told from the point of view of one's personal history, and every opportunity should be given to allow that to happen, but people should not be excluded from having something interesting to say about a question just because they're not eugenically *marked* by the question. I think that's hideously dangerous, and there has to be a zone of acceptance of the quality of the argument holding its own on its own terms. I don't think we want to get into this endless debate where the proof of your argument is the size of your pain, where to prove that you come from the most underprivileged or marginalized context is to prove your statement. It might be the proof of your pain, but it's not necessarily the proof of what you say. That's too accepting of the initial marks of exclusion. The truth of what you say has to be negotiated, discussed, debated.

People intersect across different questions in different configurations, and part of the nature of the projects I do, including this book, is to open up roads of discussion and paths that one might have presumed didn't exist and to address seemingly dead-ended questions in a sideways and potentially constructive manner. The questions I address are not checkmate-in-one-move kinds of problems. I'm just looking to untie the knot. After that you can hang me if you like.

V. How would you characterize the difference, if any, between your project in the videotapes and your project in this book?

S. I don't see them as inherently different projects. I see them as having overlapping goals. The important thing to me is to see the reconfigurations that occur when you juxtapose different styles of discourse and you move across diary to academic article to script remnant to picture. What happens in terms of understanding a topic when such things are opened up in this way? I want to show passages and openings between these things—not simply their additive quality but the way they can reformulate and create a different object or understanding entirely. I find that so much of what we say and do operates under the parameters of "the grand dictionary of received ideas."

As I said earlier, the difference between the videotapes and the book is interactivity—the so-called user-friendly side. Now, when people think of video, they usually think it's interactive or at least is like some baby-sitter at least aware of their presence. My position about video is, perversely, No! It's not interactive! I don't want you stopping it! I don't want you redoing it! I feel bad arguing with people who like my work, which is already not that many people, but the ones who *do* like it say, "I want to take it home and look at it slowly, so I can look closely at this, that, and the other. . . ." My idea of my work in time-based art is that it's like a symphony. I really do think of it as this musical structure across time, with motifs, and how they come together, and there's a crescendo, and that's to me what's interesting about the tapes: their symphonic quality. What interests me in the book is its interactive quality: you can open it up and start reading from the back or the front, or read the interviews first, or read all the asides, or look in the index and make sure you find all the articles that don't even mention my name and read only those. My attitude is, Do not touch the tapes, but interact all you want with the book.

V. And how do you suggest we use this introduction?

S. Not as some simple set of instructions of how to put the book together, that's for sure. I know my own frustration and ineptitude when I get "any idiot can put this together" instructions with a new household appliance. I know I can't put the thing together myself, and I usually end up destroying the toaster, then borrowing a friend's.

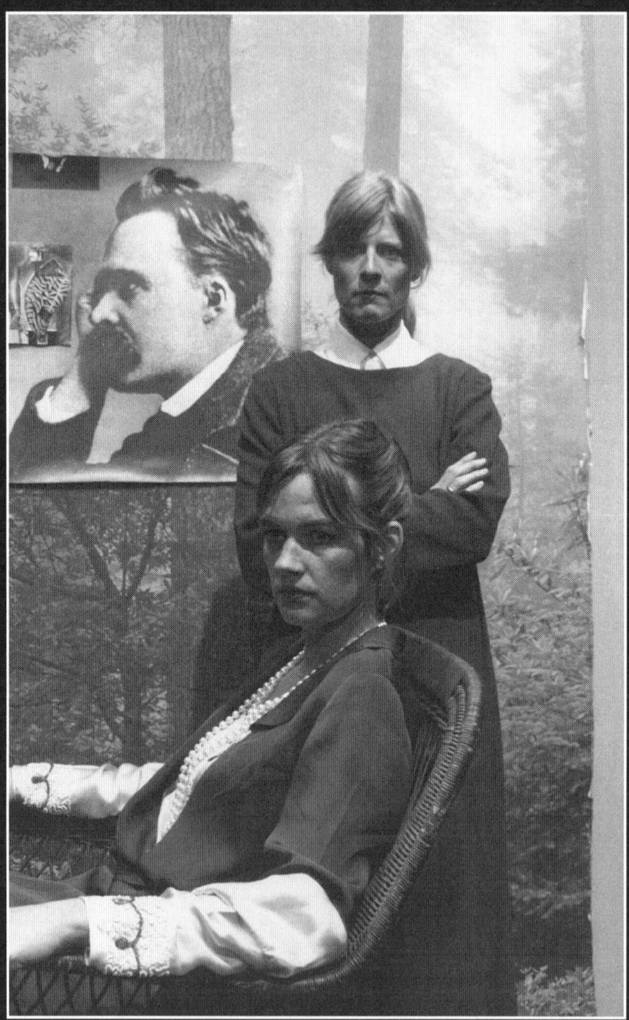

Lou and Elisabeth Nietzsche, from *Virtual Play*

Margaret Morse
Waking and Shaking

The Russian formalist Viktor Shklovsky called his unconventional writing about conventions in art "the knight's move." The title of Steven Fagin's eighty-two-minute videotape *Virtual Play* is another chess term, designating not a move but a type of chess problem. The goal of virtual play in chess is to get as close as possible, as elegantly as possible, to checkmate without achieving it. If the problem of postmodernism is "how to do without narrative by means of narrative itself,"[1] then Fagin's title is an apt analogy that indicates his solution to the problem as well.

Steven Fagin is a lecturer in film theory and history at San Francisco State University. *Virtual Play,* his first video production, has been well received in psychoanalytic circles. (It was shown at the 1984 Amherst conference on Lacan and at the International Conference on Psychoanalysis, Illinois State University, May 1986.) Its specific antecedents can be found in avant-garde film, namely, those films concerned with the act of storytelling itself. One could compare this video to the films of Marguerite Duras or Syberberg's *Unser Hitler* or the classic Ophuls film *Lola Montès;* one might even mention Michael Snow's *So Is This. Virtual Play* shares its concern with enunciation or performance with current video productions coming out of performance art as well, but, unlike that work, its prime concern is the problem of narrative.

The video does not offer a story in a conventional narrative form that can be recounted; rather, it is a presentation that can be read in a variety of ways, which change according to the viewer and the viewing. A rich field of associations is evoked across each segment of the tape. The connections between segments are not those of a traditional story or a sequence of events in some causal order. The links are more like those Freud described in dreams or like those memory theaters depicted by Frances Keyes, in which a memory and a place are arbitrarily associated. Furthermore, the associations and linked memories are patently false or out of whack—a major theme of the tape. Potential readings are announced (in voice-over) by the titles of various segments of the tape: representation, reminiscence, forgetting. Thus, the prime organizing feature of the video is not the story of its heroine, Lou Andreas-Salomé, who is there primarily as allusion, but rather the act of telling a story itself.

Lou Andreas-Salomé acts as a virtual point around which many conflicting stories can be generated from several points of view. The video is "about" her only in the most literal way—it is collected around her. There is no master position from which one can possess *the truth* or comprehend the story as beginning, middle, and end with *a* meaning. A traditional narrative would offer Lou as an object to be known, investigated, and contained. Here, she is but a shadow, a view of a fur collar (yes, it is probably significant in a Freudian sense), a hank of hair, or a woman playing a "Lou." Significant parts of the tape do not even refer to her, only to the prime concern of the video—representation itself. One needs something to represent, something to tell, in order to play "virtually" with representation and narration. In that sense, Lou is just an excuse for play. In another sense, however, she is an excellent focal point for linking together the relation between the advent of woman as subject and the kind of storytelling without a (male) master subject I've been trying to describe—a mode of narration that can be termed *postmodern*. The link is made not logically or causally in a metadiscourse but rather through more dream-like association and juxtaposition.

First, I will discuss how the video works as "virtual play." Then I want to add some historical notes about Lou Andreas-Salomé (1861–1937) that will suggest why she raises the "problem" of a multigendered subjectivity. I think of the "double direct monkey wrench" of the subtitle, another chess term, as applying to her and her effect on late nineteenth- and early twentieth-century (male) culture, although it could apply as well to the videotape's desired effect on narrative machinery. I will not, however, list the segments in the video—the "meaning" in the video is precisely not "in" a story reconstructed from the order of segments. Nor will I offer an overview; I would have to invent one against the very project of the video itself to do that.

Virtual Play is exceptionally rich both formally and in reference to ideas of current cultural debate. These ideas are not presented as such, that is, as metadiscourse; rather, they are realizations or embodiments. The play of visuals and sounds can be enjoyed sensually as well as for its allusive power. The visuals themselves are a multiple succession of quite varied short tableaux, each scene of which is itself packed with details. Narration and voices exist in yet another plane, adding more complexity.

What is virtual play? Almost a figure for desire itself—desire wants to keep playing—virtual play also has consequences for the chess game as a narrative. Ordinarily, a chess game privileges one chronological succession of events, like an Ariadne's thread out of the maze. Delays and interruptions may prolong the game, but its meaning is a retroactive result of the last move. In virtual play, the order of successful moves recedes in importance compared to the entire network of interrelations set in play. By eschewing closure, protagonist and antagonist become merely oppositional players, and the figures they form together are seen as pleasurable in themselves. Meaning is not *in* the resolution of the game but "floats over the text or beyond it."[2]

An image of transition to the frame story of Lewis Carroll's chess fiction, *Through the Looking Glass,* suggests the moment that recurs over and over again in *Virtual Play*—the moment of passage between the imaginary world *in* the chess game and the view on this side of the mirror of a cardboard schema with markers. In Carroll's book, however, the moment between "shaking" and "waking" is not depicted in the narrative or in the illustrations—it occurs between two chapters and between Tenniel's illustration of Alice with the chess piece in her hand on one page and her hand on the black kitten on the next. *Virtual Play* evokes this transition, this in between. Significantly, I misremembered which chess piece was in the Tenniel illustration. It is not the White King but the Red Queen who turns into a kitten after waking. Carroll was concerned with maturation and emancipation from the terrifying and arbitrary powers of the mother; the concern in this tape is more with the Name of the Father. The tape does not offer emancipation—how could it?—but it does unsettle the relation between the act of narration and the story into a kind of netherland trembling between the imaginary and the symbolic.

Rather than presenting realistic scenes, the tableaux of *Virtual Play* offer schemas and symbols of great variety—drawings, photos, postcards, toys, a cardboard Taj Mahal, a block model of Berlin, an undersea world (seen from the mermaid's point of view) of shells and shiny material on dry brown soil. In other words, the representational is visible as such, yet the charm of the imaginary has not faded. The sets remind us of ourselves as children when we could wish whole worlds into existence. They also evoke a certain admiration for an economy of means: low production values and high evocative power.

Childhood is an explicit theme of *Virtual Play*. In an opening sequence, a woman's voice over an exotic photo introduces the themes of the double of representation, the third term or the shadow of the real, and the position of the spectator. The "title sequence" consists of the hands of a young girl fingerpainting while the camera "fingerpaints" too. The child tells riddles while an offscreen "mother" prompts her to spell the words that will prove to be the themes of the tableaux that follow. She usually spells the words wrong—"Berlyn," "Veania," "Pompaii," "Perssia." Meanwhile, she writes the dedication to Lou Andreas-Salomé, curving the ill-fitting words around the paper's corners. We see the words upside down. At the end of the scene, the child introduces herself to us and asks, "What's your name?"

We as spectators occupy a number of positions: we are the hand, the mermaid, the "house" in a shell game, the director, the camera. We see the backs of chairs of a conversing Lou Andreas-Salomé and Anna Freud. But most often we are directly addressed as ourselves, as spectators. The sound track consists largely of narration and voices telling stories, anecdotes, and incidents over the image. There are scenes in which onscreen characters (Lou, Anna) or children or presenters do speak (a cooking lesson, a lecture on exposure times in nineteenth-century photography, or an exposition on memory techniques by a distant figure in an urban graffiti landscape). Voices throughout do not "embody" a person but tell stories; even the characters' voices are storytelling or "presenting."

There are two temporal realms the voices refer to in the tape: Lou's Central European intellectual society from the turn of the century to the 1930s and a present-day level of commentary on storytelling. The two levels are not separated; voices of the first level seem to know the whole story, beginning, middle, and end, and are also made to speak ironic self-commentary and theories belonging to a later age. Some voices are incongruous as well, that is, a Southern or a New York accent on a Central European figure or a French accent reading German. Sound effects mix modern traffic noises into the past; Lou's voice speaks to us via a telephone answering machine. This potpourri of voices, nomadic, disengaged from an origin, can bring the listener a kind of musical pleasure. One story Lou tells of her Russian girlhood illustrates a similar kind of pleasure: how the terrifying tolling of cathedral bells becomes desired as a "touch," signaling Lou's loss of faith and her emancipation from her father-lover, Gillot.

The mismatching of voices and times throughout is accompanied by the mistaken information these voices purvey. *Memory*, its fictiveness and inadequacy, is a recurring theme of the tape. The memory theater that links places and thoughts is mislabeled (*Pompeii* and *Vienna* share the same architectural drawing) or misremembered (a mock-up of Berlin is linked with streets utterly mismatched in the memory narrative). Not only memories are faulty; places are missing, or a "memory" qua postcard does not fit its place. (These postcard images are themselves mismatched, for example, a Walter Keane Mona Lisa.)

The most successful and memorable tableau pits Nietzsche's sister, Elisabeth, against Lou, with a Nietzsche poster as backdrop. Both women address us separately and at once, in a sort of dual voice like a German-accented rap record. But they take turns sitting closer to the camera, each successively garnering our primary attention. At one point Lou attaches a Lindner "voyeur" painting in the line of Nietzsche's gaze, then proceeds to tell of the beauty and innocence of her relationship with Nietzsche. At issue in the historical quarrel between the two women was the relation of Lou and Nietzsche—who tried to seduce whom, and who was hurt? Historians have discovered that both women actively engaged in revisions of the past, the most scandalous and well-known instance of which was Elisabeth's falsification of papers in her brother's name. In *Virtual Play* it is Elisabeth, who admittedly does not speak English, who expounds (in English) on the paradox of discourse as lie and the necessary discrepancy between the subject who speaks and the subject of the sentence.

The merging of the presentational or performative aspect of narrative and the (hi)story is but another aspect of this foregrounding of representation, without, however, dismantling the story and its pleasures. The discrepancies treated thematically "within" scenes include the mismatched, the misremembered, the ill fitting, and the out of phase. The greater web of discrepancies and commentaries is generated between tableaux; for instance, the lecture on exposure time in the nineteenth century was preceded by a scene of the famous photo showing Lou Andreas-Salomé crouched in a car, holding a whip to her team of Friedrich Nietzsche and Paul Rée. Who set up the picture? Whose idea was the whip? The much-debated issue of who asked whom to pose in 1882 recedes before the complicity of all in the representation. But, if it exists, this commentary is in a virtual space outside the text, in the mind of the spectator.

Contrasts and juxtapositions crisscross the entire tape. For example, a "TV" cooking lesson seemed weak in realization and fairly pointless at first viewing. In it, all the ingredients of a chicken dish are deemed injurious to "your" health, and the recipe and cooking are abandoned. The chicken, however, gathers associations with the overall theme of the video when, much later, Lou's voice tells of the fate of her favorite childhood chicken, evidently a "transitional object." I remembered a riddle from the child in the tape too (Why did the chicken cross the road?) and also a story in voice-over from the end of the tape about anthropologists, natives, and a "camera-snake." The snake story resembles a "chicken" story McLuhan wrote of several times. All these chicken/snake stories refer to a larger problem of storytelling in our self-conscious culture and bespeak a shift in the raw and the cooked in our cultural recipes. "Cooking/culture" references also occur throughout the tape. For example, in an early segment, a figure in "cook-nomad" garb offers postcards and toys in an illustration of a story peripherally "about" Lou Andreas-Salomé, seen in a Parisian café.

There are many unspoken references in the tape to theorists and historians from Benjamin and Freud, to Lacan, Foucault, Frances Yates, Benveniste, and Barthes, and more. A virtual bookshelf (or café?) of current culture is activated. There are also numerous visual and auditory allusions, among them the sound/image of films of Marguerite Duras, the camera of Michael Snow's *Region centrale,* and the symbolic circus with its heroine revolving like a wedding cake in Max Ophuls's *Lola Montès.* In *Virtual Play,* we have an indication of how pastiche[3] or a succession of tableaux in various styles can privilege paradigmatic oppositions as opposed to meanings that develop syntagmatically out of a succession of narrative elements. Many voices rather than a "master narrative" come into play.

Why is the tape dedicated to Lou? In *Virtual Play,* the body of Lou Andreas-Salomé and her displacements have but a fleeting representation as "real" women; instead, we see "empty" and ill-fitting copies. The interrogation of the heroine is actively avoided or interrupted (a telephone ring breaks into a résumé of her article on narcissism). The question Lou Andreas-Salomé raises for us in this tape is not posed by the body of her works or by a quest for truth in a biography rich in relationships (among them Nietzsche, Rilke, Freud, and Wedekind of Lulu fame) and disputed events (when, for example, did she lose her virginity?). The issue is rather the nineteenth-century antinomy of the intellectual woman, the woman as Subject. What happens to representation when the Other/other becomes a subject, too? In *The Second Sex,* Simone de Beauvoir makes the point that the image of woman is created from man's needs; she is the other pole against which he defines himself, not in mutuality, but as his alienated soul or nature, outside the struggles for existence. She is a double and a mediator who exists only for him; for herself, she appears inessential. Should she become a subject or an individual herself, man would lose that intermediary and find himself again between the silence of nature and the demands of other subjects.

In her own period, Lou unsettled record numbers of both sexes and all ages with a kind of double whammy. Perhaps the subtitle of this video is a reference to Lou's general operating procedures. According to one lover, psychoanalyst Poul Bjerre, "she had the gift of entering completely into the mind of the man she loved. Her enormous concentration fanned, as it were, her partner's intellectual fire. I have never met anyone else in my long life who understood me so quickly, so well, and so completely, as Lou did."[4] Another biographer attributes her fascination "for all who knew her, herself included," to her mind, "captivating beyond compare, stimulating beyond compare."[5] But that "male" mind was available in a female body, a perfect companion as an Other to mirror his, the Subject's, world. On the other hand, the captivated person would eventually discover the pawn to be a queen and himself only playing a role in her projection on the world, to be discarded when he no longer fit the rules of her game. Lou's privilege to occupy a "male" position was due to her unique economic and social position, as a brilliant and university-educated woman, a Russian general's daughter with the means (a family allowance), the narcissism, and the will to impose herself and her meanings on the world. In a period of many fascinating women, none could operate with such impunity behind "enemy" lines or leave behind such devastation.

Consider the situation of feminist and Lou's contemporary Hedwig Dohm, for example, speaking as an outsider for a general subject, woman per se. Or compare the brilliance of Alma Schindler, who sacrificed her own gift as a composer in marriage to Mahler and later to Gropius and Werfel. Even Bertha von Suttner, the governess who eloped with her much younger charge to the Caucasus and who later convinced Nobel to offer a peace prize, could not unsettle the male as subject in "his" own territory and prerogatives as Lou did. Lou is linked to the suicides of Paul Rée and Viktor Tausk, both among her many abandoned lovers; in *Virtual Play* this becomes part of a larger theme of "castration" in psychoanalytic terms. (The separation from the imaginary in representation is another kind of psychic castration.) Bjerre writes: "I think that Nietzsche was right when he said that Lou was a thoroughly evil woman. Evil, however, in the Goethean sense: evil that produces good. . . . She may have destroyed lives and marriages but her presence was exciting. One felt the spark of genius in her. One grew in her presence."[6]

Naturally, Lou as femme fatale would be regarded as "half-genius, half-mad," by one biographer who finds her demands for autonomy and disrespect for reality "freakish." I find her fiction frankly awful, and many years ago as a feminist searching for foremothers I disregarded her ideas about feminine destiny.[7] While scarcely a solution to relationships between the sexes, Lou's narcissism and her uncompromising demand for autonomy are precisely what make her available today as a symbol of woman as subject.

Lou is not the only double direct monkey wrench. In *Virtual Play,* the Taj Mahal, known popularly as "man's greatest erection for woman," is burned down at an unseen woman's hands. The girl-child gets off the "wedding-cake" merry-go-round and sabotages the description of her older companion on how to make a dollhouse[8] with ridiculous riddles (Why do elephants paint their toenails red?). The problem Lou poses is no longer a matter of havoc in individual lives but a cultural one: how to tell stories in a world of multiple voices. How to imagine a different way of structuring discourse? A new situation in representation is given account here, just after the loss of what might be called a symbolic system unified by one point of view. That transitional period between capture by the image and loss is obsessively (mis)remembered; the memories of one are out of phase with another. The tape is introduced by posing the problem of the double and the third term—but in my interpretation the jolt comes not from the Law of the Father but from the coexistence of other subjects.

Virtual Play resembles a description of postmodernism itself, but re-accented and revalued. Is it schizophrenia we see, a result of being too close to the sensual world,[9] or is it multivoicedness, heteroglossia,[10] a result of being just far enough away to hear the other as subject? I am not alone in suspecting that the phenomenon of postmodernism has some relation to feminism and issues raised by the "problem" of women as subjects. Many of the formal features of postmodernism are shared by "woman" as a cultural construction. The critical devaluation of postmodernism by critics such as Jameson, mourning the master narrative, can be seen as a reaction to the insistent voices of women in the last two decades.[11] *Virtual Play* takes account of a self-conscious cultural discourse on representation and, to its credit, the problem of sexual difference and the advent of the female subject. In the last tableau, the camera shakes almost imperceptibly—but the voice of the maker on the sound track asks, What if the camera were completely still? I am glad the camera trembles. *Virtual Play* is witty and encouraging of work on our present condition. Like Lou, it is plain of dress and fascinating in the ideas it sets in play.

Steve Fagin
Excerpts from *Virtual Play:*
The Double Direct Monkey Wrench
in Black's Machinery

Lou's Writing: Narcissism

Lou's husband Paul worked harder and harder to complete his magnum opus on Persian philology, but the harder he worked, the further he moved from completion because he was continuously adding to the beginning.

"I would like to discuss my work on Narcissmus, my most celebrated article 'Narcissmus als Doppelrichtung' was published . . . (*[phone rings]* . . . If you would like to leave a message) I would like to discuss my work on Narcissmus, my most celebrated article . . . (*[phone rings]* . . . He said, "Don't worry") I would like to discuss my . . . (*[phone rings]* . . . My entire family would go to the country every summer) I would like to discuss my work on Narcissmus, my most celebrated article 'Narcissmus als Doppelrichtung' was published in the official organ . . . (*[phone]* . . . Tonight, Ges, Serdez, Guardia, my wife will prepare Doogaf hav . . . *[inaudible, jammed]*) I would like to discuss my work on (*[phone]* . . . I covered my eyes and screamed, but over my cry I heard the most horrible tr . . .) I would like to discuss my work on Narcissmus, my most celebrated article 'Narcissmus als Doppelrichtung' was published in the official organ of the psychoanalytic movement, *Imago* . . . (I sat forlornly, helping the old woman sort freshly laid eggs. She said to me, "I know the . . .") I would like to discuss my work on Narcissmus . . . (entire family would go to the country every summer) I would like to discuss my . . . (If you would like to leave a message, wait until after the beep. You will have 30 seconds) I would like to discuss my work on

Narcissmus, my most celebrated article 'Narcissmus als Doppelrichtung' was published in the official organ of the psychoanalytic movement, *Imago,* in 1921 . . . (She said to me, 'I know the exact thing that
will cheer you up') I would like to discuss my work on narcissism . . .
[*phone*]."

Forgetting: Lou
If it is true that animals don't commit suicide, why did Brother Animal
and Pet Rée die?

Dr. Victor Tausk, physician, analyst, and lawyer, died late last night
from self-inflicted wounds. The specific cause of death was not as reported earlier, castration, but death from a broken neck and a bullet
wound through a temple. He tied the rope around his neck, and when
he pulled the trigger from his revolver, his neck fell, and the rope
pulled tight. Freud had written about Tausk that he would not really
miss him. He had long since been taken as useless, indeed a threat to
the future, and would long since have dropped him from the psychoanalytic circle if he hadn't been so close to Lou. When Tausk gave his
first paper in front of Freud, he mistakenly referred to Aristotle as master of Plato. Freud promptly corrected him. Once, instead of attending
a psychoanalytic meeting on the latest findings from Pompeii, Lou and
Tausk went off to a movie. Unlike Freud, they preferred the reflected
glory of the imaginary over the petrified remains of the symbolic. Lou
had referred to Tausk as a tender berserker. Tausk had thought of himself as a person so wretched that no one would sit at the same dinner
table with him. Tausk was born in 1879, one of nine children, and always hated his father's surname. His ambition was to be a universal
genius and besides medicine and law wrote plays and did charcoal
drawings as well as being a gifted linguist. Before killing himself Tausk
itemized his accounts down to the last penny and then relaxed with a
glass of slivovitz, his national drink. Dr. Tausk is survived by his two
sons.

Paul Rée, physician and philosopher, was found this morning by workmen after plunging to his death from a steep cliff in the upper Engadine. Whether the death was accidental or suicidal remain unknown. Although Rée worked the last fifteen years of his life as a doctor helping the sick and the poor, he is best known for his association with Friedrich Nietzsche and Lou Salomé, who called each other the Holy Trinity. He was born in 1850, the son of a wealthy Jewish Prussian landowner. His intense self-hatred was generated by his distaste for his Semitic heritage and appearance. Rée in fact found himself to be physically repugnant. Although considered a great philosopher, Rée was unable to secure an academic position. Rée's philosophy held life to be meaningless, and he always carried a vial of poison on his person. Although Nietzsche thought he was intelligent, he thought Rée was neither courageous nor imaginative. The happiest years of Rée's life were spent living a celibate relation to Lou in Berlin. They lived as brother and sister, and Rée referred to Lou as his affectionate little snail. When Lou became engaged to Carl Andreas, Rée severed all relation to Lou. Without saying good-bye, he departed, leaving a picture of Lou as a little girl behind, which she had given him. On the back of the picture he wrote, "Be merciful, do not search for me." Although Lou never saw Rée again, she would often dream of him. In one of her most lucid dreams, Rée appeared as an old fat man hiding behind a bundle of coats in a cloakroom. Upon being discovered by Lou, Rée smiled contentedly and said, "Don't you agree? Here nobody will find me."

■ ■ ■

Gregg Bordowitz

Dear Steve,

I am told that every day is a new beginning and another chance to be healthy. I wake up thinking, This is my day to be beautiful. The forecast says it won't be pretty, but it won't be a disaster. There's a drought in my state. Rain is welcome. Currently, I can wade in the reservoir without getting my ankles wet. It's all a question of resources.

Been thinking about the questions you posed to me after we watched the rough cut of *Fast Trip, Long Drop.* You asked me, "What's with all the Jewish stuff?" Before I could answer you added, "And what's a Jew? What's a Jew," twice emphatically. Were you implying through your emphasis that you think there is no answer to this question? Since then I have formulated some answers.

What's with all the Jewish stuff? In *Fast Trip, Long Drop,* I wanted to include Jews as part of the audience of the work, not merely by showing Jews; rather I wanted to address Jews. A fundamental operative assumption of the work is that Jewish philosophical thought informs every move within the work. Among the central concerns of the work is, What is the function of testimony? (What this has to do with the recent history of AIDS, the relation between my identity as a person with AIDS and my identity as a Jew, cannot be addressed here. It will have to wait.) What's a Jew? A Jew is the person who asks that question. Only the Jew is burdened with the task of explaining what a Jew is. Everybody else walks around thinking they know who the Jews are.

This is not to say that our preoccupation with defining ourselves originates within us. We define ourselves in answer to a
demand placed on us. By whom? Who wishes us dead? To com-
plicate matters, our enemies are both real and imagined. I think
the problem of Jewish self-loathing can be located at the center of
our burden to enunciate ourselves. I am what I am, but it's not who
you think I am . . . or is it? Our self-doubt is provoked by the
contested status of our identities as Jews. We are called on to de-
fend our identities against relentless prejudice. It's wearing.

At a very early age I was told by my grandmother, "There are
two kinds of people in the world, Jews and non-Jews. Don't forget
who you are." I have been told that I am my own worst enemy.
Sometimes, I am other to myself.

To solve the problem of self-loathing we must solve the crime,
Who killed Paul Rée? To consider this question let's start with
Schopenhauer and Nietzsche for insight into philosophical views
on suicide contemporary with Rée—views he must have been familiar with given that he was an intellectual with ties to Lou
Andreas-Salomé and Nietzsche. "As far as I know, none but the
votaries of monotheistic, that is to say Jewish religion look upon
suicide as a crime. This is all the more striking, inasmuch as neither in the Old or in the New Testament is there to be found any
prohibition or positive disapproval of it; so that religious teachers
are forced to base their condemnation of suicide on philosophical
grounds of their own invention. . . . They tell us that suicide is the
greatest cowardice; that only a madman could be guilty of it"
(Schopenhauer, *On Suicide*).

Remember the scene in Fassbinder's *In a Year of Thirteen
Moons* when Elvira, the transgender protagonist, stumbles on a
"bum" about to hang himself. He quotes Schopenhauer for Elvira:

Bum: If you want to know what people in general are worth
in moral terms, then look at their general fate. It is want,
misery, torment, death. Eternal justice reigns, and if it

weren't in general so worthless, then people's fate would generally not be so sad. In this sense, we can say that the world itself is one's world view. In any case, to understand suicide only as the negation of the will to live, as an act of negation, is to completely misunderstand it. Far from being a negation of the will, this phenomena is a strong affirmation of the will, since this negation means a denial of the joys, not the sorrows of life. The suicide desires life, but is just dissatisfied with the conditions under which it has come to him. He in no way, therefore, gives up the will to live; rather he merely renounces life, and destroys the outward appearance it has for him.

Elvira: I think you'd better do it now.

Bum: You can watch quietly.

The man hangs himself. (From the script of *In a Year of Thirteen Moons,* printed in *October,* no. 21)

The ideal informing Schopenhauer's views is Christian: "The inmost kernal of Christianity is the truth that suffering—the cross—is the real end and object of life."

Nietzsche had views on Christianity and suicide: "When Christianity came into being the craving for suicide was immense—and Christianity turned into a lover of its power. It allowed only two kinds of suicide, dressed them up in the highest dignity and the highest hopes, and forbade all others in a terrifying manner. Only martyrdom and the ascetic's slow destruction of his body were permitted" (*Gay Science,* no. 131).

He also had thoughts about Jews: "Too Jewish—If God wished to become an object of love, he should have given up judging and justice first of all; a judge, even a merciful judge is no object of love. The founder of Christianity was not afraid enough in his feelings at this point—being a Jew" (*Gay Science,* no. 140).

Both Schopenhauer and Nietzsche believe that Judaism was superseded by Christianity and that philosophy supersedes religion. Both use the figure of the Jew as the straw man for their arguments. Schopenhauer views Jewish thought as regressive in its relation to the Stoics. He observes that the "ancients" had no prohibition on suicide.

Pliny: "Life is not so desirable a thing as to prolong it at any cost."

Although Schopenhauer is against suicide—like the Jews—he develops what he considers to be a philosophically superior argument against suicide: "Suicide may be regarded as an experiment—a question which man puts to Nature, trying to force her to an answer. The question is this: What change will death produce in a man's existence and in his insight into the nature of things? It is a clumsy experiment to make; for it involves the destruction of the very consciousness which puts the question and awaits the answer" (*On Suicide*).

So Rée performs the clumsy experiment. Why? Was he too Jewish? Given the available philosophical options of that moment, did he have a choice? Perhaps, he should have read Spinoza. Nietzsche liked Spinoza:

> Proposition 10. An idea that excludes the existence of our body cannot be in our mind, but is contrary to it.
>
> Proof. Whatsoever can destroy our body cannot be therein, and so neither can its idea be in God insofar as he has the idea of our body; that is, the idea of such a thing cannot be in our mind. On the contrary, since the first thing that constitutes the essence of the mind is the idea of an actually existing body, the basic and most important element of our mind is the conatus to affirm the existence of our body. Therefore the idea that negates the existence of our body is contrary to our mind. (Spinoza, *The Ethics*)

Throughout the Jewish philosophical tradition, thinkers tried to come to terms with the problem of suicide. Apparently,

Schopenhauer and Nietzsche viewed only the Old Testament as the calcified body of Jewish thought to be chewed over and spit out. I included the Spinoza quote to introduce—within the context of the German philosophy quoted in fragments here—the idea that self-inflicted violence against one's own body can be externally caused. (No doubt, Freud would have much to say about this, but his contribution will have to come later, in subsequent conversations.)

By locating the violence behind the act of suicide outside the subject have we solved the crime? Is this solution a sufficient end to the problem of self-loathing?

I have solved nothing. Instead, I send you an index, a bibliography . . . a search. My mind is a drain clotted with quotes. Writing fills the page like a sink backing up. The faucet's running, and there's a shortage of clean water. I'm parched saving what's left in the bottle. I wonder how many microns filter my source. Forgive me, but "all Jews become mawkish when they moralize" (Nietzsche, *Gay Science*, no. 357).

A final thought. We're all treading water in a dead sea. Our drowning would be a relief, but to whom?

I'll speak to you soon.

Love, Gregg

■ ■ ■

When Nietzsche first met Lou, he went straight up to her, held out his hand, and said with a deep bow, "From which stars have we been brought together here?" Lou responded, she had come from Zurich. They both laughed.

When Nietzsche first met Lou, he went straight up to her, held out his hand, and said with a deep bow, "From which stars have we been brought together here?" Lou responded, she had come from Zurich. They both laughed.

Rilke and Lou: First Love

When Lou and Rilke first met, she was thirty-six and he was twenty-two. Although Lou had already been married several years and was constantly in the companionship of devoted admirers, Rilke was her first lover. Although this is a lie, it makes a wonderful story.

■ ■ ■

Leslie Dick
Lou: A Superficial Look

Women are considered profound. Why? Because
one never fathoms their depths. Women aren't even shallow.
—Friedrich Nietzsche, Twilight of the Idols. (1888)

The femme fatale is an anachronism. She no longer exists.

This is because women enjoy sex now, or they're supposed to, anyway. They're supposed to, by others, who listen out for the gasp, the sigh, the shriek or moan of pleasure. (Or there is the notorious case of the woman who laughed when she came.) Women are supposed to enjoy it, or at least they're supposed to try to enjoy it. Pleasure is part of what they are expected to expect, now, what they are expected to get out of sex. Whereas the classic femme fatale was sexless, pleasure free, although occasionally sexually active, as they say. She wielded power precisely because she was herself unencumbered, unembarrassed by the possibility of pleasure.

Lou Andreas-Salomé was amused and insulted when Friedrich

Nietzsche, and his friend Paul Rée, spoke of "concubinage," of "a two-year marriage, at most." Concubinage: cohabitation without legal marriage. Concubine: (in polygamous society) a secondary wife, usually of lower social rank, or a woman who cohabits with a man. Lou was not to be seduced. She was twenty-one, Nietzsche thirty-eight.

Nietzsche wrote Rée: "Greet the Russian girl for me, if that makes any sense: I am greedy for souls of that species. In fact, in view of what I mean to do these next ten years, I need them! Matrimony is quite another story. I could consent at most to a two-year marriage, and then only in view of what I mean to do these next ten years" (21 March 1882).

When Rée realized that he didn't really want to share Lou with his friend, he repeated these words to Lou. Subsequently, Lou shocked Nietzsche's sister, Elisabeth, by speaking openly about this, about the possibility of concubinage. They were together in Bayreuth for the first performance of *Parsifal,* Elisabeth (somewhat comically) functioning as Lou's chaperone, at her brother's request. Lou gallivanted around, going to parties and, Elisabeth later claimed, showing off the notorious photograph taken in Lucerne, boasting about her relationship with Nietzsche and Rée.

The photograph shows Lou crouched in a cart, holding a whip decorated with flowers, with both Nietzsche and Rée harnessed to the cart with ribbons. A backdrop depicts the Alps; dry leaves are scattered at their feet. Some books emphatically state that it was Nietzsche who composed this mise-en-scène, others that it was Lou. In any case, the anecdotes about the making of this photograph throw dramatically into question what is meant by Nietzsche's famous line, "You are going to women? Do not forget the whip!" (*Thus Spoke Zarathustra,* pt. 1, 1883).

While critical of the "immorality" of his philosophy, Elisabeth Nietzsche thought of her adored brother as devoid of sexual thoughts or feelings. Lou, insubordinate as ever, and not insensitive to the irony of Elisabeth acting as her chaperone, insisted

that men are all alike, "men all wanted only that." Lou Andreas-
Salomé said something like, I could spend a whole night in the
same room with him and not get excited. Or, "I could sleep in the
same room with him without getting worked up." Or, ". . . without
insurgent thoughts." Depending on the translation.

At least that is what Elisabeth Nietzsche, appalled at a girl of
twenty even thinking such things, said she'd said. When she realized that she really didn't want to share her brother with Lou, she
repeated these words, to him, and to various others. She bandied
it about town, so to speak, thereby making it more or less impossible for Nietzsche to pursue his plan, to carry out Lou's proposal
of discreetly, chastely living together.

It was a complex accusation to make, Elisabeth's accusation,
to repeat these words to Nietzsche. As if to frighten her ob-
sessionally secretive and reclusive brother by presenting Lou as
someone out of control, someone who'd talk about these things
anywhere, to anyone, someone who spoke openly about sex. And
at the same time to convey the other message, as if unintention-
ally, to offend her brother's amour propre by providing irrefutable
evidence that Lou didn't even fancy him, anyway. She could share
a room with him and not get excited.

In another place Nietzsche writes of the necessity for concubinage if we are to attempt a marriage of equals: if we want to
converse with the women we marry, if we want to raise children
with them and take them seriously, then we must have somewhere
else to go for sex. "Marriage," he wrote, "according to its highest
conception as a friendship between the souls of two human beings
of different sex, in other words, as it is hoped for in the future,
concluded for the purpose of begetting and educating a new generation—such a marriage, which uses the sensual, as it were,
only as a rare means to a greater end, probably requires, I fear, a
natural aid: *concubinage*. If, for reasons of the husband's health,
the wife should also serve for the sole satisfaction of the sexual
need, then the choice of a wife will be decisively influenced by a

false consideration that is contrary to the aims suggested; the production of offspring becomes accidental, and a good education highly improbable. A good wife—who is supposed to be friend, helper, bearer of children, mother, head of the family, manager, and who may even have to stand at the head of her own business or office, quite apart from her husband—cannot at the same time be a concubine: generally, this would be asking too much of her" (*Human, All-too-Human,* no. 424 [1878]).

Nietzsche himself couldn't attend the opening night of *Parsifal* because he'd fallen out with Wagner. Wagner let it be known that he thought Nietzsche's blindness had its origin in sexual perversion. (Nietzsche was at this point "seven-eighths blind.") Nietzsche believed that Wagner had implied that he was homosexual and broke off the friendship. In fact, Wagner had meant that Nietzsche was a compulsive masturbator.

Nietzsche was the first important writer to use the typewriter. The machine had originally been invented for blind people, to enable them to write legibly. (Subsequently, Henry James dictated his late novels to a [female] typist, as he walked up and down the room, which is one reason why his sentences are so beautifully constructed and so nearly interminable.) Paul Rée was given the task of bringing the typewriter from Nietzsche's mother's house in Germany to Nietzsche in Genoa, just before he met Lou, and managed to break it on the way. Later, Nietzsche compared Rée's breaking the typewriter to his treatment of other things he'd attempted to deliver intact and failed to, such as Lou. He wrote: "As for the typewriter, it is on the blink like everything weak men take in hand for a while, be it machines or problems or Lous" (27 April 1883). There is other evidence, however, that the typewriter broke down at certain critical moments; for example, it was just after he'd typed the sentence about "a two-year marriage" in the letter to Rée that it "refused to go on performing—wholly enigmatically" (23 March 1882).

Lou's idea was a parlor and two bedrooms, or, if Nietzsche were included, if it really was to be a "Holy Trinity" after all, three bedrooms. For a brief period it looked like she was going to live with both Rée and Nietzsche, in Paris, probably. They would study natural philosophy together. And, apparently, it was Lou's idea: this open, unconventional, chaperone-free domestic arrangement that nevertheless excluded the possibility of sex. Lou wrote later, in old age, that at that time she'd had a dream, in which she had seen "a pleasant study full of books and flowers, flanked by two bedrooms, and, moving to and fro between us, comrades in work, a cheerful serious circle" (*Looking Back* [1932]).

"Concerning Vienna," Nietzsche wrote Lou, "it is now my wish to be set down like a piece of luggage in a small room of *the* house you want to occupy. Or next door, as your faithful friend and neighbor F. N." (18 June 1882).

As it was, she broke Nietzsche's heart. They knew each other for only about six months, in 1882, and during that time spent a total of less than four weeks in the same place, mostly two or three days together here and there. Lou broke Rée's heart too, although they did indeed set up house, chaste, sharing a parlor, in Berlin, for three years. There they entertained other freethinking intellectuals, like themselves, although it seems that there weren't any other women in this group, none that anyone took note of, anyway.[1]

The first time Lou met Rée was in Rome, in March 1882, at the home of Malwida von Meysenbug, a feminist idealist, where he rushed in unannounced one evening. Rée had arrived directly from Monte Carlo, where he'd lost all his money, and had to ask Malwida for a loan to pay his travel expenses. At that time Rée always carried a vial of strychnine with him, in case of an impulse to suicide. He was Nietzsche's friend, and, immediately convinced by Lou's extraordinary conversation, he was already discussing probable sites for the intellectual ménage à trois (Genoa,

Vienna, Munich, Paris) before Nietzsche met her on 25 April. It was at this point, the moment of possibility, that Rée wrote Nietzsche about Lou, and Nietzsche wrote back to him, of a "two-year marriage," and Lou wrote Gillot, her first (unconsummated) lover, who had written to her expressing his grave concerns about her plan. (Lou's mother had implored him to intervene.)

Lou replied, "You also write: you had always thought of this sort of wholehearted devotion to purely intellectual goals as a 'transition' for me. Well, what do you mean by 'transition'? If any other goals are supposed to stand behind it, such as would make one give up the most magnificent and most hard-won thing on earth, namely freedom, then I want to stay forever in the transition, for I shall not give that up" (26 March 1882).

Lou broke Rée's heart by marrying someone else, Fred Charles Andreas, noted philologist and scholar, who had mastered Greek, Latin, Pahlavi (the language of Zoroastrianism, whose prophet was Zarathustra), Sanskrit, Old Norse, Aramaic, and Hebrew, in addition to Javanese, Dutch, German, French, the Scandinavian languages, English, Hindi, Arabic, Turkish, Armenian, and a large variety of Persian dialects. Lou was twenty-five, Andreas forty. They were happy together, for forty-four years, until death parted them, yet the marriage was never consummated. Lou had decided on this well before the wedding, and she never wore a wedding ring.

(The first time Marie Bonaparte left Freud in Vienna to rejoin her family, she left her wedding ring behind. When Elisabeth Nietzsche married Bernhard Forster, the famous anti-Semite, and left Germany for the Aryan colony he had founded in Paraguay, she discovered on the ship that she had left her wedding ring behind.)

Lou finally lost her virginity at the age of thirty-five, probably, with a doctor called Zemek, although some writers prefer to believe that she kept herself to herself until she met Rainer Marie Rilke, when she was thirty-six. Lou spent a good deal of time with

Zemek, over the years, as if this relatively unprepossessing figure was just the ticket, so to speak. Their relationship was "mainly sexual," although she didn't write about it. And she had to deal with at least one pregnancy, which she seems to have aborted, in Vienna, or perhaps it ended in miscarriage. (Freud subsequently implied that Lou's relationship to Vienna and psychoanalysis was in part connected to the child she lost there, whether by abortion or miscarriage.)

During and after the long relationship with Zemek, Lou had a number of other affairs, falling into bed with all sorts of people, consistently, over a period of thirty years. She went on breaking hearts—by delivering the goods and then withdrawing, returning to herself. (As a young woman she'd managed it by precisely *not* delivering the goods and sticking around.)

Writers who are sympathetic to her say that Lou was careful not to enter into a sexual relationship until she was in such a position, professionally speaking, that there could be no danger of subordination. Rilke was twenty-one when Lou met him; Zemek was twenty-seven. By that time she'd written two novels as well as the first book-length study of Ibsen, and the first book-length study of Nietzsche (vehemently denounced by Elisabeth, needless to say), and a large number of stories and articles.

When Lou was fifty, she took up psychoanalysis, and it occupied her intellectually and practically for the rest of her life. By all accounts, she was a good analyst, although she herself was never analyzed, unless a series of intense yet informal conversations with Sigmund Freud count. At his time, it wasn't unusual for (wealthy) women to take up psychoanalysis in order to take possession of their own sexual pleasure; as Marie Bonaparte said, she had come to Freud in search of "the penis and orgastic normality" (*sommaire d'analyse*, 10 November 1925). There she encountered other women around Freud, notably Ruth Mack Brunswick and Freud's daughter, Anna. Hectic conversations ensued between Marie Bonaparte and Ruth Mack Brunswick on masturbation techniques, celebrating the promise masturbation offered of independence from husbands, lovers, or indeed Freud himself. In a sense early psychoanalysis was all about women talking openly about sex and sexual pleasure, for the first time. Or talking openly to men about sex, talking to Freud about sex. Or talking to each other.

Freud loved Lou because she was the personification of female narcissism. Elisabeth Nietzsche saw her as another kind of avatar: "My brother's philosophy *personified:* that raging egoism which knocks down anything in its way and that utter want of morality" (2 October 1882).

After the debacle in Paraguay, Elisabeth devoted herself to creating a cult of her brother, opening the Nietzsche Archives initially in a downstairs room of her mother's small house in Naumburg, and later moving the archives to an enormous house outside Weimar, remodeled by Henry van de Velde and financed in large part by the Swedish millionaire Ernest Thiel, who was, ironically enough, himself Jewish.[2] Many famous intellectuals paid homage to this shrine, as Nietzsche's writings had become very influential and very widely read during the First World War. Thiel withdrew his support when Hitler came to power, but Elisabeth had no difficulty in finding other sponsors. Indeed, the high point of her life was when Hitler himself paid her a visit, in 1935. Elisabeth is best known now for freely editing and rewriting Nietzsche's late work and especially for her shameless forgeries of Nietzsche's letters, in order to misrepresent her brother as an anti-Semite like herself. In reality her brother wrote her about his rage and despair at her engagement to "an anti-Semitic chief," adding, "It is a matter of honor with me to be absolutely clean and unequivocal in relation to anti-Semitism, namely, *opposed* to it, as I am in my writings" (25 December 1887).

When Lou encountered psychoanalysis, she saw narcissism as her vocation. It's unclear whether Freud so to speak gave her this task—the narcissistic woman, precisely *not* "in search of the penis and orgastic normality," would, of course, illuminate narcissism. Possibly, Lou took it on herself, always hoping to show that everything we are derives from the "fertile soil" of an original protonarcissism, a "good" narcissism that we can't get enough of. And the bad traits associated with narcissism, vanity, self-absorption, sexual frigidity, etc., are the result of a narcissistic deficit, a wound or blow to that primary narcissism. She and Freud argued about it for years, but there's no doubt he regarded her as the perfect type of narcissistic woman, in some sense an ideal woman.

It seems odd that he should have sent his daughter, Anna, to Lou for analysis when he was worried that she would not be able to overcome her "father fixation" in analysis with him. As Freud well knew, of all the people Anna might have consulted, Lou was virtually guaranteed to reinforce this syndrome, as she herself shared the very same fixation, on her own father and on Freud. In the event, Lou celebrated Anna's attachment to Freud as infinitely more satisfying than any *normality* could ever be—and Anna, like Lou, and like Elisabeth Nietzsche, too, was destined to live the rest of her life as a memorial to the great man.

What was best about being Anna's analyst was the way it positioned Lou as somehow "like" Anna's mother (and therefore Freud's wife) yet also "like" Anna's sister (and therefore Freud's daughter). But Lou had already had a long and thrilling (and wildly unconventional) life when she became Freud's devoted disciple, and her submission to psychoanalysis (in a way that she *never* submitted to Nietzsche's philosophy) did not preclude a series of love affairs, often with other psychoanalysts, notably Viktor Tausk.[3] Anna, however, was only twenty-two when she gave herself to psychoanalysis, and, while it is possible that she had a sexual relationship (much later) with her life partner, Dorothy Burlingham, it seems unlikely.[4]

It is pleasant to think of those years as a time of female conversations, outrageous conversations: Lou and Elisabeth, on "insurgent thoughts," and later Lou and Anna, on Anna's childhood fantasies of being beaten. (Lou herself recalled intentionally breaking rules as a child in order to elicit punishment in the form of spankings administered by her father.) Conversations between Marie Bonaparte and Ruth Mack Brunswick, who later became a junkie and died after giving a dinner party in New York for Marie Bonaparte, having fallen in her bathroom and fractured her skull. Marie Bonaparte and Anna, Anna and Dorothy. (Anna spoke in place of Lou, delivering by proxy Lou's required lecture for membership to the Vienna Psychoanalytic Society in 1922, the same year she herself won membership by presenting her paper "Beating Fantasies and Daydreams," in which her own experience serves as the case in point. Anna later said that she could never have written it without Lou.)

In 1916, Lou wrote "'Anal' and 'Sexual,'" an essay that won Freud's heartfelt enthusiasm. In it, writing of the primacy of the anal, Lou postulates that the caregiver's first expressions of disgust at the baby's shit—"*Pfui!*" or, "*Ugh!*"—constitute the infant's body as divided, split between a (fantasized) "clean" self and a (fantasized) filthy body. Lou's theory of primary narcissism was deeply scatological; she saw the "fertile soil" at the root of all experience as a shitty oozing mess, a mess that elicits this originary exclamation of disgust that begins the process of individuation, of separation from the body and bodily *jouissance.*

Lou describes the intensely policed border between anal and sexual as purely artificial, culturally imposed, and proposes this first repression, of anal pleasure, as the moment when the child is propelled into subjectivity. Lou then makes her most extravagant claim, that in women the vagina is only "taken on lease" from the cloaca. That is, as a site of penetration, the vagina is in some sense only a representation or simulation of that first experience of border crossing, the experience of defecation, and the penis is therefore only a stand-in for a piece of shit. That Freud quoted this text approvingly is one more example of his absolute repudiation of essentialist or biologistic theories of femininity. Freud vacillated and contradicted himself, inevitably, working and reworking psychoanalysis, yet Lou's idea of heterosexual intercourse being, so to speak, "taken on lease" from buggery is a truly thrilling example of an anti-essentialist position.

In a letter to Lou, in November 1882, when things were falling apart, Nietzsche wrote: "You had something further to say to me?—I like your voice best when you are requesting. But this is not heard often enough.—I shall be studious.—Ah, this melancholy! I am writing nonsense. How *shallow* people are to me today! Where is there a sea left in which one can still really *drown*? I mean a person. My dear Lou, I am your faithful F. N." (8 November 1882).

Later, in *Thus Spoke Zarathustra,* written the year after the split, Nietzsche wrote: "Surface is the disposition of woman: a mobile, stormy film over shallow water. Man's disposition, however, is deep; his river roars in subterranean caves: woman feels his strength but does not comprehend it" (*Thus Spoke Zarathustra,* pt. 1, 1883).

Lou herself noted, after a long conversation with Freud, that she had not come to psychoanalysis to untangle "mix-ups between depth and surface" (diary, 2 February 1913). Yet ten years later, when Freud made friends with Marie Bonaparte, he told her: "Lou Andreas-Salomé is a mirror—she has neither your virility, nor your sincerity, nor your style" (*sommaire d'analyse,* 14 December 1925). At least Marie Bonaparte said he'd said that. She made a note of it in the journal of her analysis. It makes a good story.

Can we approach the femme fatale as a problem of surface and depth? The narcissistic self-sufficiency of the femme fatale is complete, entire, and therefore depthless, like a reflection in the mirror or a film of oil on water. Yet Lou did not see things this way;

mud between the toes, running barefoot through the forest, she felt herself to be tremendously profound.

Women have always been accused of shallowness or superficiality, yet Lacan suggests that there isn't anything else to be: "As Gide says in *The Counterfeiters*, there is nothing more profound than the superficial, because there isn't anything profound" (seminar book 2, sec. 13 [1954–55]). If femininity is itself a masquerade, as Joan Rivière, another early woman analyst, proposes, and if narcissism is inherent to women, as Freud repeatedly insists, then possibly Nietzsche was right; women aren't deep, or shallow, but a mask, a surface, like a mirror, or a screen, like oil on water. We might also argue that the narcissistic position is the only position of power available to women, the only position that entails a certain degree of autonomy, a certain self-centeredness. Yet what does it mean to say, as Freud apparently did, that someone *is* a mirror? What we see in the mirror has a coherence we feel ourselves to lack. Not unlike the femme fatale.

Lou's sexual relationships tended to last exactly nine months and were characterized by an extraordinary attentiveness to the lover for that precise period of time. (They said that they felt profoundly and immediately "understood" by Lou, all of them.) Yet she was fugitive; she sidestepped attachment and broke it off after nine months, as if giving birth to herself.

In her memoirs, written in old age, Lou contemplated the notion that she had never experienced the three forms of love that are characteristic of women's lives. She had never had a child or a "real marriage," nor had she experienced the "sheer eros-bond." These three encounters with others are, in a sense, to be expected of women, yet they eluded her, or (more precisely) she persistently eluded them. Staggeringly self-possessed, she did exactly as she pleased.

In the last analysis, possibly, Lou got it wrong. Her narcissism was less a fertile soil than a shiny surface; in some sense, for her, other people were like water off a duck's back. Yet it was essential to her, this narcissism, for it was this very quality, this *not even shallow*, that made possible her lifelong refusal to relinquish that "most magnificent and most hard-won thing on earth, namely freedom."...

■ ■ ■

[*In Russian.*] Fellow members of the Russian émigré community of Berlin, tonight we are very pleased to have with us two distinguished visitors, Lou Andreas-Salomé and Rainer Maria Rilke. [*In English.*] They have just returned from a visit to our home country and will tell us how our homeland has responded and changed in this the first year of the twentieth century. I would like to first say a few words about our visitors before we get on with the presentation. Lou Andreas-Salomé is now quite celebrated, but her star will soon fade, and eventually she will be remembered not for her own work but for the fame of her lovers past and future. On the other hand, her present companion, Rainer Maria Rilke, now unknown poet who is madly in love with Madame Andreas, will eventually, [*in Russian*] for no financial gain, [*in English*] be thought of as one of the great poets of all time. And although he will always adore her, their relationship will end tragically. [*In Russian.*] Please hold all questions to the end.

Everyday Life: Photography
It would have been easy to have dedicated this section to Brecht. To have dedicated it to Walter Benjamin, a true brother of Andreas, Rée, and Tausk would have been a noble gesture. Instead, it was decided to be perverse and dedicate the section to Nietzsche, of whom Lou said that he had a total incapacity to come to terms with everyday life.

[*Text continues with Larry Parks talking about photography.*]

The Body: Feet
While traveling in the East, Andreas learned to live like the ancients,

that is, before the distinction of man and beast had been made. He would awaken at daybreak, strip naked, and test the scent of this dog by trying to sneak up to it and go unnoticed. Andreas taught this skill to Lou.

Child Patient: Deep Structure

At Freud's suggestion to make a little more money, Lou took on a young girl as a mail-order patient. I wonder how the transference was established?

[*Little girl reads comic.*]
To memories I shall ever be true. To persons, never.

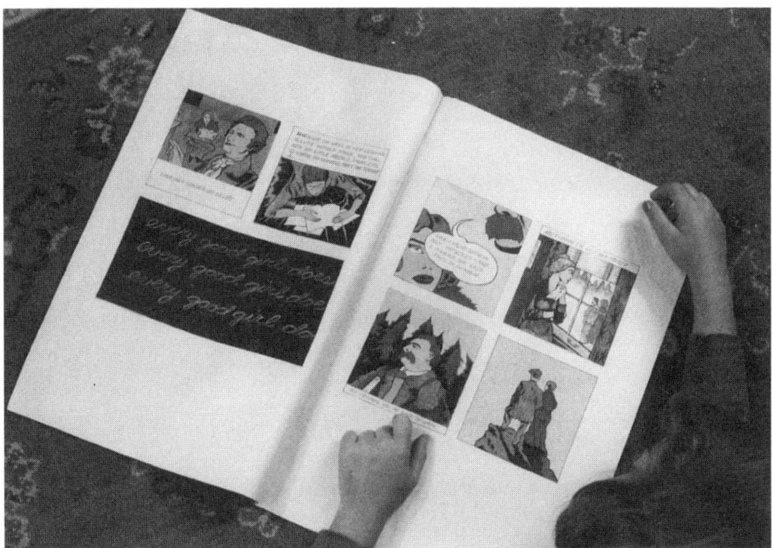

"Lou's Life Deep Structure," from *Virtual Play*

Places: Vienna

If there were to be a section on Vienna, it would have been inspired by Lou's remark. When she and Freud would go on their late-night strolls through Vienna, Freud would treat the city as if it were a patient and psychoanalyze it.

Everyday Life: Cooking

A labyrinthine man never seeks the truth, but only his Ariadne.
[*Cooking dialogue follows.*]

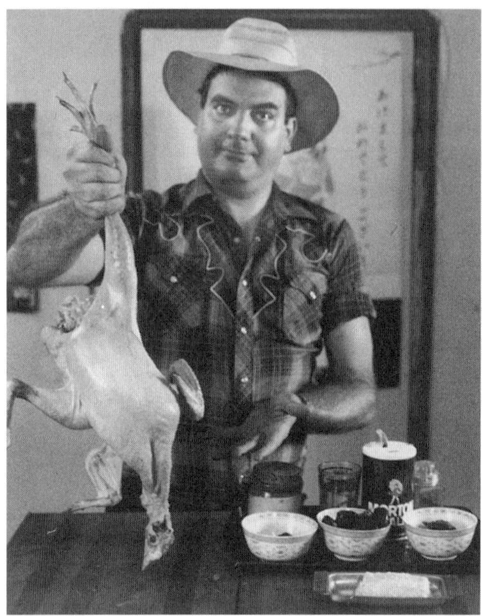

Jim Pomeroy cooks
Lou's favorite, from
Virtual Play

Lou's Writing: God

When I was sixteen years old, I lived in St. Petersburg, and I was studying at the time under Guillot, who was an eminent scholar of religion. . . .

Everyday Life: The Wickedest Man in Vienna

Oh Zarathustra, your fruits are ripe, but you are not ripe for your fruits.

The Body: The Ear

A belief forgotten nowadays but preserved in the traditions and legends of the Catholic church is that the conception of Jesus by the Virgin
Mary was brought about by the introduction into the ear of the breath
of the Holy Ghost.

Although Lou would never talk in Freud's Wednesday session, he often
would come over and whisper and whisper in her ear. [*With stutter.*]

Lou's Writing: Love

Everyone displays two contrasting tendencies: to amass and to bestow goods, to assert and to surrender. Two tendencies interact at bottom, as if another secret longing underlay both. . . .

[*Male voice.*] I am Karl Krauss, and although you've probably never heard of me, I am more important to the Viennese intelligentsia than Schnitzler, Freud, and Wittgenstein rolled into one. I am editor of the literary review *Die Fakel,* and I'm a fierce critic of almost everything. At this very moment I am negotiating with that great Hollywood producer, Harry Cohen, to make a film on my life. He wants George Sanders for the lead and Ophuls to direct. I prefer Jimmy Stewart to star and Capra to direct. Here are some examples of my caustic wit: Christianity has enriched the erotic meal with the hors d'oeuvre of curiosity and spoiled it with the dessert of remorse. No one under the sun is more unhappy than the fetishist; he pines for a boot and must content himself with a woman.

Forgetting: Rée and Tausk

Love always has its afterglow; a rather tender cast is thrown. All the rough edges have receded. The darkness is near, but this pleasant glow, the twilight of the imaginary, is still quite warming. When the darkness does come, it is welcome because it signals the end of pain. But the end of sight does not mean the end of vision because the object will have its revenge for letting things die. There emerges out of the darkness a pornographic nightmare that heralds the Götterdämmerung. The whole image repertoire collapses; the edifice is brought down. But, unlike for Samson, for you this apocalyptic collapse includes no revenge. Because there is no one present to witness the destruction of the Philistine temple, for history has ended.

Coda

The anthropologists and semioticians had kindly relented to the natives' request to shoot a few roles of film. . . . [*Continued.*]

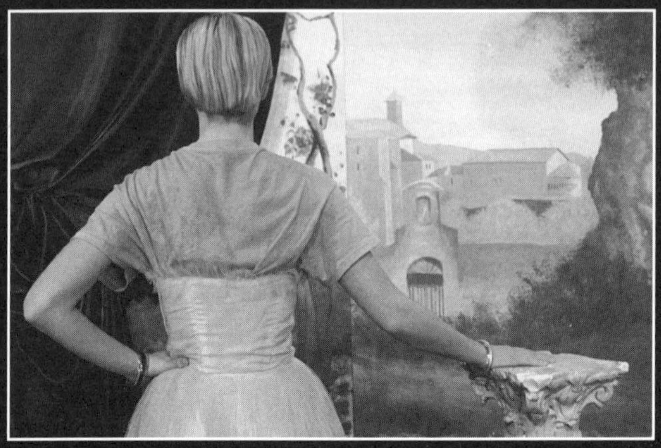

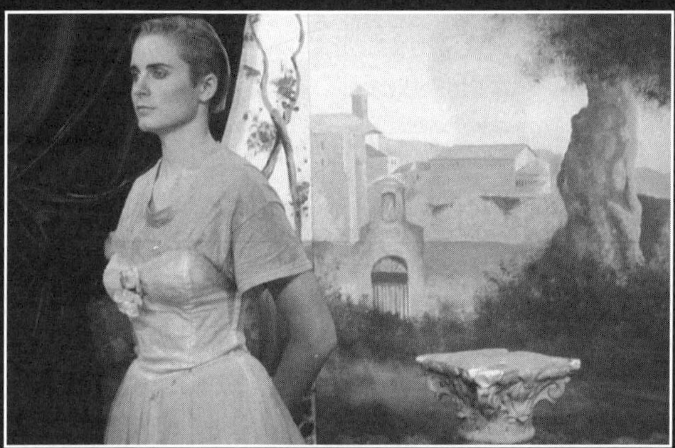

"Museum of Copies," from *The Amazing Voyage*

Vivian Sobchack
The Occidental Tourist:
Steve Fagin's Virtual Voyage
for Armchair Travelers

It seems likely that the outside world never broke through into the universe he carried within him, and that, in all the countries he visited, he saw only what he had put there in advance, elements which corresponded absolutely with that universe that was peculiar to him. . . . Placing the imaginary above all else, he seems to have experienced a much stronger attraction for everything that was theatrical, trompe l'oeil, illusion, than for reality.—Michel Leiris (of Raymond Roussel)

Often during work on the piece I felt trapped, as if in a coffin, digging through treasures, cut off from their function in exchange, being led by a voice, the sound track, that I thought would get me out of the trap. But, on hearing the voice, I knew it was just telling me over and over again, in different tongues, that I was trapped and would never get out. The tape is a mock journey, desperate, amused.—Steve Fagin

Hale's Tours and Scenes of the World, or *Meet Me in St. Louis*

"A mock journey, desperate, amused." In 1904, at the St. Louis Exposition, Hale's Tours and Scenes of the World began commercial exhibition. Gustave Flaubert had been dead for almost a quarter of a century. Indeed, his life completely predated the cinema, even as his inner eye was protocinematically obsessed with detail. Steve Fagin was not yet born and so had not yet imagined his *The Amazing Voyage of Gustave Flaubert and Raymond Roussel,* a postcinematic and impossible pairing of the successful French novelist with his less successful, but equally obsessive, countryman. In 1904, however, Raymond Roussel was twenty-seven years old and—if we would have it that way—could have overcome his increasing reclusiveness to wander about this American World's Fair, passing Esther and Tootie without a comprehending glance, escaping the crowds and an impending nervous attack by taking refuge in the false railway carriage that used the new mechanical medium of projected motion pictures to simulate scenic travel to exotic, Other, places.

Fagin's surrogate—an unseen and sole male narrator, a writer whose book has the same title and project as Fagin's video—"free" associates around "secretive" words not his own: friend, look, hypnosis, kill, *and narrativizes toward a summary whisper: "You're being hysterical, making a spectacle of yourself." Recognizing the story he has seemingly created, he tells us it's "a real-life melodrama bracketed within the making of a fun-filled musical,* The Pirate, *about hypnosis, with Garland and Kelly." If Fagin can take these liberties (it's a trait that save him from repetition, confinement, death—and the video from pretentiousness), then so can I. Thus, I am going to evoke another fun-filled musical,* Meet Me in St. Louis, *with Garland (if lacking Kelly) bracketed within the making of a real-life melodrama about hypnosis, hysteria, and spectacle—for I can see Raymond and Gustave doing a "turn" together, waving their canes and straw hats, hermetically sealed in a bourgeois parlor, singing falsely but purely about being in exotic climes, "Under the Bamboo Tree." (Roussel, in fact, thought "his greatest triumphs were the mimicking of the music hall entertainers of his day in front of his family" [Fagin].)[1]*

Inside the fake railway carriage going nowhere, what did Raymond see out the window that was really a screen? "In all the countries he visited, he saw only what he had put there in advance." The stay in each country was very short (perhaps, on average, only 2.7 minutes), but the whole voyage lasted a good twenty to twenty-five minutes and made several stops liberated from a geographically necessary itinerary. One list of offerings, for example, "showed fourteen Hale's Tours titles, all of them photographed in foreign locales. These included Tokyo, Canton, Switzerland, Ceylon, Hanoi, Mount Cerrat, Vesuvius, Agra, and Frankfort."[2]

Bits and pieces. A collage of countries, cities. Gustave must have taken the tour, too. And Fagin. His surrogate tells us, "My book is still only in fragments, and those are scattered: notes in boxes mixed with dirty laundry lists crumbled in coat pockets, and an outline, lost, last seen on top of train schedules, but underneath stale cheese. The writing causes me to struggle, like a beast of burden. I carry the collective weight of a previous century, my back almost broken by its priests, donkeys, and pianos. I tire easily, but push on. At least I know the chapters of my book: Flaubert, Roussel, the Imaginary, their mothers. But where do I begin?"

Flaubert and Roussel: two male writers obsessed with their mothers, two travelers whose mock odysseys disposed the world into "scenes," two occidental tourists drawn toward exotic lands who never dared look the Sphinx in the eyes. Certain primary historical "documents" tell us that the languid Flaubert—who died when Roussel was only three years old—

wanted "to stay in and watch the world like a moving diorama" (Fagin). And that, "when Roussel traveled, he always kept the blinds drawn" (Wollen). Theirs was an oblique, and intensely solipsistic, form of spectatorship.

Thus, temperamentally, they could easily have shared the faux railway journey offered up by Hale's Tours and Scenes of the World, blindly looking out the window at the prearranged screening of their Imaginaries, each dreaming their own language machines for making all the short bits and disconnected pieces of exotic landscape cohere into a coordinated geography, a resolved narrative. In 1904, when Hale's Tours first appeared, "the use of film for storytelling purposes had hardly begun," we are told. "Indeed, up to this time, many films were never seen projected onto screens at all, but were seen in peep shows of the Kinetoscope or Mutoscope variety in penny arcades." And those films that were projected were "scarcely more than a novelty, momentarily doomed to occasional end-of-the-bill performances at vaudeville houses." Lasting only about ten to fifteen minutes on average, the program consisted "of several brief 'turns' or 'bits' of a comic, dramatic, informational, sports, scenic, or novelty sort."[3]

Vaudeville? Bits and pieces? Brief "turns" and "'bits' of a comic, dramatic, informational, sports, scenic, or novelty sort"? Wait a minute, they're all here. Comic: *The Punch and Judy debate between the Señor Wences–like hand puppet and the disembodied voice on the tape recorder about the copy versus the simulacrum moderated by the woman who literally in-forms both.* Dramatic: *The "stand-ins" for Roussel's legs, reeling and writhing in suicidal agony/bliss on a floor, near a bed.* Informational: *The unseen female narrator with an Italian accent who gives the biographical facts, who contextualizes, whom we ridiculously trust because she begins by telling us: "Opera buffa, farsa, opera comica, melodrama burlesca. The world has changed, like Donizetti without Lucia. History no longer repeats, in the manner of Marx, first tragedy, then farce. Now, it is simply one farce after another."* Sports: *A remembrance of things past perfect: Yankee pitcher Don Larsen's perfect World Series game (and, hey, Steve, I was really there in the stadium, I can testify perfection really happened once).* Scenic: *Exotic ethnographic footage from the land of Propp. And an ocean voyage,* 20,000 Leagues Under the Sea—*in a fish tank, with a blue plastic sea monster and several small goldfish.* Novelty: *Well, there are the hysterical interludes provided by unknown women, but I really liked all those bits and pieces of Méliès-like films with their cardboard sets, indecipherable action and desire, their magic tricks and trips.*

Fagin tells Peter Wollen in an interview: "I think Méliès is an extraordinary figure, and the whole phenomenon of 'primitive cinema' and tableau structure is something that's very interesting to me. It's a tremendously rich tradition, surely more interesting than things that have been done recently. Except for 'Pee Wee's Playhouse,' which is great." Using tacky tableaux, fictional diaries, paintings turned into playing cards and table coverings, oblique narrational and musical commentaries, pretend postcards and letters, references to art historical and popular icons of high and low culture, reductively funny dramatic "reenactments," strange and estranged footage from old movies, and myriad condensed and displaced female voices, Fagin attempts to grasp the impossible voyage of Raymond and Gustave as a vaudeville "chaser," as the "bits" and "turns" of a "primitive" cinema that—passing through Hale's Tours and Scenes of the World—will eventually resolve itself into the nauseous repetition of an imploding language machine ("invented" by Roussel) and the bourgeois narrative ("novelized" by Flaubert) to become the "classic" Hollywood cinema we all hate to love (or so we say).

That Roussel and Flaubert could never actually have traveled together (or met each other at a showing of Hale's Tours) is an irrelevance—for, whatever their respective idiosyncrasies and the great variance in their literary "success," they are fellow travelers. It is this perception of their cranky affinity, their common implosive existences as "bodies without organs," as "bachelor machines" who do not really want to go anywhere but back to "Ma Mère" and "La Mer," that fuels what little narrative organizes *The Amazing Voyage of Gustave Flaubert and Raymond Roussel.* (The video often returns to a "stand-in" for Roussel's mum—a cheerleader of sorts, doing a strange and funny dance on the beach, the ocean breaking behind her as she breathlessly talks in parables and baton-twirls a bundle of sticks about.) Fagin muses to Wollen: "The work of Roussel and Flaubert, so invested in writing as a substitute for a maternal absence, trying to fill the space in ways diverting but always insufficient, is much of the terrain of the work." Writing to their mothers, writing in stead of their mothers, writing their mothers, these two European men (with Fagin along for the ride)—unseen, unspeaking, unspeakable—tour an orientalized Imaginary that passes through the defiles of the occidental Symbolic.

What do these three blind men, these three blind mice, all blindly see through the blinds, on the moving diorama, on the window/screen of this sealed faux railway carriage showing of Hale's Tours and Scenes of the

World? Having put their eyes out, they see Mother, Madonna, the Femme Fatale, the Sphinx, the Orient. They see only what they have already put there in advance. They see everything and nothing. Writing of Roussel's *Locus Solus,* Michel Foucault could be reviewing Raymond and Gustave's amazing voyage: "What treasure is silently pointed out here and there, only to be withdrawn the moment it is proffered? All these scenes are like spectacles, since they display what they show but do not disclose what is in them. They have a radiance in which nothing is visible."[4]

"I felt trapped, as if in a coffin, digging through treasures, cut off from their function in exchange." Who is speaking? In 1906, as cinema moved on its way to narrative fulfillment, leaving Flaubert and Roussel behind and Fagin ahead, *Variety* speculated on the declining popularity of Hale's Tours: "With the closing of the summer comes what eventually will mean the last of what are known as 'Hale's Tours.' Little success has followed the car enclosed picture machines. The rocking has caused the women to remain away after the first visit, and the difficulty in securing sufficient scenic views has been another reason. Close confinement also contributes its share of disagreeable features."[5]

But enclosed pictures, imaginary scenic views, confinement, rocking, are precisely what appeal to Flaubert, Roussel, Fagin. Three blind mice. See how they run. Speaking to Wollen about the video's stalled Oedipal trajectory, Fagin reveals its simulated journey as "organized around a personal incident, a very horrible eye accident . . . and a series of operations. The male narrator in the tape, someone in exile, running away, a very different amazing voyage, tries to fight off the pain of blindness in order to tell this tale of Flaubert, Roussel, the Imaginary, their mothers."

Now, Voyager, or Letter from an Unknown Woman
"Flaubert, Roussel, the Imaginary, their mothers," the narrator/Fagin says. *"Ah, yes, the mothers, the daughters, the women, . . ." I say.* "The writing causes me to struggle, like a beast of burden," the male narrator says. *"The writing causes me to struggle, like a breasted being," I say.* "I carry the collective weight of a previous century, my back almost broken by its priests, donkeys, and pianos. I tire easily, but push on," he says. *"The rocking has caused the women to remain away after the first visit," I remember.* "At least I know the chapters of my book: Flaubert, Roussel, the Imaginary, their mothers. But where do I begin?" he asks. *"You begin with who gets fucked," I say.*

And he does. Before the voyage, before the beginning, before the title that tells us we're actually on our way, Fagin begins the video with a *Quaestio de virginitae*—the Latin phrase for an interrogation about virginity. Extreme close-ups of a woman's face (the "stand-in" for Roussel's mother), engaged in responding to an offscreen woman's questions. About who fucked whom—he, her? she, him? About the first time she fucked—when? where? About whether it hurt—no? yes? About whether she bled—yes? no? Accused again and again of laying and lying, narrating different stories, the woman finally says to her interrogator: "I confess, I lied." And when her offscreen questioner begins again: "When was the first time you fucked?" she smiles slightly and responds, "I've never been fucked."

La Giaconda. We've always been virgins. We've always been madonnas. We've always been fucked. In some cases, however, the rocking of the fake railway carriage has kept us away after the first visit, the first fuck. Let's not forget that, in Letter from an Unknown Woman, *Joan Fontaine makes a first—and last—visit to a version of Hale's Tours. As expected, she doesn't get anywhere. Virgin, fucked woman, mother, madonna—Jourdan pushed her away after the first visit so that he could travel and play that damned piano (hauled by two priests and a donkey), and then he forgot her. Let's not forget that Fontaine insists that nothing in life happens by chance. Thus, it is not by chance that everything that happens to her of any importance and drama (her adolescent move to Linz that takes her away from the object of her desire, Jourdan leaving her alone and pregnant, her son going on a trip and fatally contracting typhoid fever) happens as a result of train travel. Waiting on the platform for the lover, the son, who never return from their circular, self-absorbed, and loopy odysseys. A titled section on the tape: Penelope's song. The song that is not—but grounds—narrative.*

When Wollen asks Fagin "why there isn't a single male character who appears directly on the image track," Fagin responds that, in the tape, "the feminine is that which allows the bachelor entry into the imaginary, but the feminine is not the imaginary." *Thank God, Steve, I needed that. But you could've fooled me.* It is true that I would describe the "stand-in" women (even the one who gets an argument from her own Señor Wences hand) as seeming cheerfully free from the constraints of the hermetically sealed reveries they enact. They're all fresh-faced, contemporary in dress and manner, down-to-earth about carrying out and yet distancing themselves from the tasks the director has asked them to perform. They provide, as Fagin puts it, "the hint of the real that causes the narrative to flee and latch onto whatever will keep it afloat."

Afloat? It's an ocean voyage now, is it? We're back to the sea, are we? *Ma mère. La mer* (where the "stand-in" for Raymond's cheerleader mama cheers him on to the densest of narratives). Dearest Mama, *ma mère, la mer*—it's the sort of homonymic play that sets Roussel's language machines and poetic voyages off. And Fagin goes along for the ride. He tells us: "The images are animated from beyond the dead; they reek of the symbolic. Anyway, I don't see only woman but a bachelor machine driven by the sound, the wind, and moved by the image, the sail."

"I felt trapped, as if in a coffin." "Close confinement also contributes its share of disagreeable features." Daughters have their problems with their mothers, too. I feel trapped, as if in a narrative. This particular voyage is constituted—like Roussel's, Flaubert's, and Fagin's, like Proust's, Breton's, and Cornell's—through the process of re-membering fragments and inhabiting images in the modality of post-Romantic yearning, skeptical desire. It is no surprise that in contrast to the fresh-faced women who seem to escape the mournful and sonorous songs sung by Flaubert, Roussel, and the narrator by virtue of their cheerful banality, their lack of mystery, we watch movie stills of Crawford in *A Woman's Face* and *Johnny Guitar,* Dietrich in *The Shanghai Express* and *Morocco,* mutilated as they are re-membered. Writing of Roussel's *Locus Solus,* Foucault might well have been writing about Fagin's *Amazing Voyage* when he suggests that the work "requires a 'second navigation' around the objects, scenes, and machines, which are no longer treated as marvelous games in space, but become narratives crushed into a unique, fixed figure (with little temporal bearing) and indefinitely repeatable."[6]

As a woman spectator trapped in the dreamworld of Western narrative, I would prefer to enter the mise-en-scène of this ocean voyage as that fixed figure (not nude) descending the ship's staircase to the main deck—every eye fetishizing in close-up my neatly turned, silk-stockinged, spectator-pumped legs, every eye rising only to frustrate its desire to know me better against the barrier of my hat brim. When finally revealed, I would have Bette Davis eyes. I've gone on a voyage, a "second navigation," too—away from the mother who never wanted me toward a motherhood not of this woman born. I first navigated the staircase in her house—plump and spinsterish in black orthopedic shoes and bushy eyebrows. If I'm trapped in narratives of self-sacrifice, I'd rather do it this way—svelte, noble, smoking. "Oh, Jerry, why ask for the moon when we have

The Occidental Tourist, or *Around the World in 80 Days*

Thus we are Oriented. The occidental tourist locates himself in relation to the East (and to "woman"), where the day dawns and the Sun rises, toward the Orient, where excessive (and feminine) description is perceived as overwhelming narrative's ends, and—if you're a Western male and think that way—thus cheats death. Just like the photograph. Just like the museum. Toward the video's end, struggling with this writing, suffering from "too much light," his eyes drooling, the male narrator tells us, perhaps, a single "true" fact about the connection between Flaubert and Roussel: "In writing, they had shared only one adventure, a trip to a museum. A pilgrimage to see a great work of art." "Flaubert," he says, "wrote mostly of breakfast. . . . The museum he referred to as a junkyard. The great work of art is mentioned only by name, *The Painted Bride.*" "Roussel," he goes on, "thinks the museum to be a zoo, but the work of art thrills him. He calls it *The Painted Veil* and writes about the thousand and one Arabian nights."

Too much coincidence here—precisely the act of association, the precise act of association, the act of precise association. Fagin's, the narrator's. Mine. The Painted Bride. *Duchamp enters the picture with his bachelor machine of the* Large Glass. *On one side Flaubert and Roussel, on the other Greta Garbo— followed by Marlene, again walking on the desert (as if it were water) in high-heeled shoes. The* Painted Veil. *Probably an odalisque or harem scene, but also a 1934 film directed by Richard Boleslawski—with Garbo as a neglected Western wife carrying on a tortured and adulterous affair in Hong Kong. Two years later, Boleslawski made* The Garden of Allah *in early Technicolor, its Algerian desert a painted one, a studio desert hermetically sealed—Charles Boyer playing a bachelor machine "holy man" and Dietrich the femme fatale who desires him.*

The narrator ends this particular reverie by relating a fable about a painting competition between Zeuxis and Parrhasios, the latter the winner by virtue of having been smart enough to paint a veil. "If you wish to fool a man," he tells us, "you paint a veil, and he will surely ask, 'What's behind it?'" "There is much in the piece," Fagin tells us, "about veiling, unveiling." There are many veils on this amazing voyage. Some are literal—sensuous silk scarves in vibrant color both providing and covering the image, pulled away in a manner reminiscent of the beginning of old MGM movies. Some are displaced as sheets stained with virgin blood ("When was the first time you fucked?" "Did it hurt?" "Did you bleed?"), some as shrouds stained with bachelor machine blood ("A virgin already stained and a son already bloodied," Fagin tells Wollen). Again, the Large Glass.

In the room the women come and go, speaking of. . . . No, not of Michelangelo, but of exotic ruins and oriental places. Posed so as to stand—as if in a museum—behind that heavy green twist of rope that cordons off spectators from the paintings that are indecipherable substitutes for their real objects of desire, these Western women speak of touring in old capitals and famous old ruins, shopping for local artifacts, taking snapshots, and of what they will do next: "Tomorrow, after a special visit to an ancient artists' village to see their own delicately painted tombs, continue on to the awesome Valley of Forgotten Hope. And, for those who wish, a short hike, with fabulous views, over the cliffs, to Queen Lodedapuris's temple." Where do we go on this Hale's Tours and Scenes of the World? Where the veils are. Listen to some of the imaginary names of the postcards we see and the places we hear: the Taj Mahal; Eusapia and Edoras; the desert by camel or horse; *India Song;* "Empire of Flora"; Lutha ("famous for its museum, which houses paintings and sculpture worthy of Mount Olympus," and where originality is forbidden); the land of Propp; *The Naked Jungle;* Tamar; *20,000 Leagues Under the Sea;* the desert, with Rimbaud in Abyssinia and Harrar; *Morocco;* Orfeno ("a country obsessed with mourning"); Silha (where Gustave and Raymond are "befriended by other tourists from home"); Saknussen; the Baraciusan desert (where Gustave sighs and remarks: "I don't much care for the landscape . . . , except for the mirages"). An Orientalist atlas to sit alongside that Chinese encyclopedia.

"This used to be an oasis, they said. I do not know. I cannot find it on my map." These, the exotically accented words of an Arab woman who has removed the purple veil covering her face. Standing behind the green rope of the museum, she muses in a foreign tongue and then in English: "My itinerary is the inverse trajectory. I come from the East and am always moving West. . . . To steal into the heart of the capital, I've found a new identity. From the remnants of civilization, I've created my disguise. C'est la ruse de sauvage."

To stay fixed in the Western male eye as an oriental odalisque or to flee in exotic disguise to the occident? To stay in a land of mirages, of painted deserts, or to wander about the mirages and paintings of Western museums. What a choice! There's no escaping the Western Imaginary. Better, perhaps, to hook up with these accidental, occidental, tourists who, nonetheless, know in advance (since they've put it there) what they will see out their windows and in their travels. And if Gustave and Raymond won't have me (since, so as to disguise myself, I've removed my face veil and my mystique), perhaps Phileas Fogg will. Always uptight, always well heeled, he's not quite the bachelor machine he dreams himself to be—thanks to Allah, he's not a writer, and he never mentions his mother. Around the World in 80 Days. *From West to East, with that other sauvage in disguise, Passepartout—he a Mexican in the ruse of a French man-servant, me an Arab woman in the ruse of Shirley MacLaine (she disguised as the Indian maharani, Princess Aouda), the landscape-disguised studio back lots where Mike Todd built streets, cities, railway stations, and jungles to meet the specifications of his own imaginary geography. Raymond is tempted to join us. Not only does he appreciate the complexity of the simulation, but Jules Verne is his favorite writer. (On the video, in the fishtank,* 20,000 Leagues Under the Sea, *Gustave writes to his mother: "If he mentions Jules Verne once more, I'll scream.")*

"Where is all this travel taking us?" Wollen asks. On a "series of wanderings" and "home," Fagin replies. Rather than Ulysses, it is Verne (whom Roussel thought the greatest writer in history) who provides "the meta-tale for the nineteenth-century voyage"—with his enterprising inventiveness in mechanically realizing those imaginary trips to the moon, under the sea, and around the world. While Verne never admitted to having a model for Phileas Fogg, in 1870 a Boston businessman almost toured the world in eighty days—and in 1892 had gotten it down to sixty. His name—are you ready?—was George Francis Train.[7]

"We end up," Fagin says, in "a library of the voyage with many different types of analysis: personal stories, geographic descriptions, political conquests, ethnography, etc., all stacked next to each other under the card-catalog topic *the amazing voyage*. Also, there is an effort to confront the post-Romantic imagination, of which Flaubert and Roussel are such a strong part. To join the work being done within the critique/discussion of Orientalism." A section of the video is titled "Requiem for Sight: India Song." The Italian female narrator (the one we trust) tells the following tale: "As a child, Raymond had accompanied his mother to India. They had rented a private yacht, special for the occasion. One dawn, after many weeks of travel, she was awakened by a sailor whispering in her ear, 'Hurry! Come see! India by first light!' She quietly scurried topside. The captain proudly gave her his spyglass and pointed. She looked, just for a moment, returned the glass, and said, 'Do not dock, turn round, turn round.' The captain had no choice. A few moments later, Raymond awoke. He had missed India."

Whose story is this? I want to know the mother. Sensible, she probably thought she was being. But she created desire. The next night, at sea, I dream that Raymond dreams of a song, befitting the banality of occidental male desire: "Where the veils are, someone waits for me." At the door of the video (after the first ambiguous fuck and a pop-up book whose pages summarize in caricature the tableaux we will see later) is a painting of a turbaned black man: Gérôme's The Guard of the Harem. *He holds an archaic axe and stands in front of the door. Keeping what's inside a secret—like the veils. Passepartout has the key and Princess Aouda the secret, but no one really wants to enter. That would put an end to desire and to writing. Raymond never sees India. Mother knows best.*

Foucault says of Roussel: "All his machines function at the inferior limit of resurrection, on the threshold, where they will never turn the key."[8] The trustworthy Italian female narrator says of Gustave: "He would be overwhelmed by an image. A dwarf wearing a large blue silk turban, arms folded, sword at his side, standing in front of him. His knees would tremble. Of his childhood, he couldn't think past a large wood door, he, on the outside, knuckles and knees bruised and bleeding. The door was unmoved." It was the door to his father's study. "Raymond Roussel died," the trustworthy Italian female narrator tells us of his mysterious suicide, "at the Grande Albergo Delle Palme, room 226. It was connected by a door to the adjoining room occupied by Charlotte Dufrenne, his lifelong celibate companion. Their custom was to keep the door unlocked. He dragged the mattress, which represented a superhuman effort, to the ad-joining door. It was like he had died on the bachelor side of the Large Glass. The door was locked." "If," as John Ashbery notes in his introduction to Foucault's *Death and the Labyrinth,* "it seems possible that Roussel did bury a secret message in his writings, it seems equally likely that no one will ever succeed in unearthing it. What he leaves us with is a body of work that is like the perfectly preserved temple of a cult which has disappeared without a trace, or a complicated set of tools whose use cannot be discovered."[9]

The Magical Mystery Tour, or
The Adventures of Baron Munchausen
The turbaned black man standing guard at the door and over the secrets of the oriental harem. "The barbaric Turk . . . battering at the gates of 'the town,' which is never named, but you might be tempted to call it Western Civilization."[10] The kind of story you write (and whether you can write it all) depends on which side of the Large Looking Glass you're on—and whether you can pass through to turn and face the Other.

In 1895, Wells wrote *The Time Machine*—which allows its hero, "the Time Traveler, . . . to slip like a vapor through the interstices of intervening substances and travel into the future."[11] In 1895, Louis and Auguste Lumière opened their Cinématographe in Paris, allowing viewers the same privilege. Fagin's surrogate, the male narrator, has a question—one for Flaubert and one for Roussel. "For Flaubert: From someone afraid to even meet its glance, is it really true that one's greatest triumphs are in front of the mirror? Or is this said to fuel the passion of a narcissistic lover? For Roussel: A lover of children's plays, parlor games, cheap imitation. Why didn't you ever go to a movie? I imagine your comfort in the dark, close to the luminous screen, laughing: Langdon, Lloyd, and Stan Laurel."

Is it again mere coincidence? Musing about Fagin's Amazing Voyage, *about Raymond and Gustave, and Verne as author of the metatale for the nineteenth-century voyage, I go to see* The Adventures of Baron Munchausen. *It is "the late eighteenth century. The Age of Reason. Wednesday." Hardly different from the late nineteenth century when it comes to amazing voyages, I think. Or the late twentieth. Did Terry Gilliam subvert Verne—and Wells? Or did Verne and Wells forge the subversive baron's itinerary? Neaten it up with rational machinery; repress the old rutting goat to whom reason meant nothing. Verne and Wells used technology to get their heroes around and off and into the world, the baron imagination and desire. (Méliès used all—and Verne and Wells.) Nonetheless, here in the late eighteenth century is Phileas Fogg's hot-air balloon—but made with ladies' silk and hardly scanty panties. Here's* A Trip to the Moon—*all simulation, detached heads, and personified constellations: is Méliès a forger too, or is it he who has been copied? And here's* Journey to the Center of the Earth—*where the baron discovers Botticelli's Venus and a foundry for nuclear warheads. What century is this? Whose text is this? Whose imagination? With all the copying and quotation, the boundaries blur. We could be in Fagin's video. Gustave and Raymond are near. Here, also, is a trip* 20,000 Leagues Under the Sea—*instead of Verne's submarine or Fagin's fish tank, we have Pinocchio's whale (living quarters inside). Yet there's the oriental harem and (Méliès again!)* The Terrible Turkish Executioner.

What goes around, comes around, someone's mother used to say. Clifford Irving—forger and "co-star" of Welles's (not Wells's) *F is for Fake*—is asked to write a magazine review of *The Adventures of Baron Munchausen* because, he says, "almost two decades ago I trampled on proper reality (or real propriety) by claiming that my tall tale about Howard Hughes was his autobiography."[12] The amazing adventures and voyages of Gustave and Raymond are also the recording of imaginary autobiography, true forgery, real illusion, trompe l'oeil. "I assure you my adventures are true," says the baron—furious at the theatrical travesty being done them in the late eighteenth century, in the Age of Reason, on a Wednesday.

This is "Pee Wee's Playhouse." Fake waves and sea serpents. Tacky scenery. Quotation. Patent copies. A great deal of hysterical running about. As Fagin explains, with admiration, to Wollen: "an infantile character amid lots of color, and objects, and silliness." Fagin is more Pee Wee than Roussel. He is not European but American. And he is very funny, very silly. Raymond's precise and imploded writing machines inspire him. By the psychic and symbolic machinery Fagin builds does not compulsively reproduce and repeat itself. When Wollen suggests he uses Roussel's system "in the American way. Pragmatic and can-do," Fagin responds: "In the American way. I cheated and made it vulgar!" It is Fagin's sense of humor and metaphor that keeps him in the land of the living—that is, the place where special effects come from Woolworth's and sounds of the world interrupt a self-obsessed writer's hermetically sealed reverie in an aquarium, *20,000 Leagues Under the Sea*. Compared to the carping beauty of Flaubert's account (to his mother) of his undersea voyage with Raymond in which they encounter "fathomless grottoes, at whose bottoms will be heard horrible stirrings," and are "confronted by terrifying octopuses who intertwine their tentacles like a living thicket of serpents," Fagin gives us the wonderful banality of goldfish and a blue plastic sea monster. Indeed, if Fagin had gone so far as to put an underwater vessel in the fish tank, one expects it would have been a model not of the *Nautilus* but of the *Yellow Submarine.*

Rather than evoking the precise and solipsistic inventions of Roussel (or the visionary mechanical ones of Verne), Fagin's creations remind us of Tom Swift, Buster Keaton, Rube Goldberg, and Ernie Kovacs. His language "machines" are surprisingly functional but also imaginatively make-do and humorously reductive. Hardly the grandiose absolute worlds constructed by poor, mad, brilliant, imploded Raymond, Fagin's virtual worlds are cheaply made, comfortably tacky, and cheerfully meant to undermine the pomposity and elitism of all his higher aspirations. As Margaret Morse puts it, "the representational is visible as such, yet the charm of the imaginary has not faded. The sets remind us of ourselves as children when we could wish whole worlds into existence."[13]

Against Fagin, I think, "Poor Roussel." Yes, the representational is visible as such, but there is no childhood in Roussel's imaginary. Foucault tells us: "His work as a whole . . . systematically imposes a formless anxiety, diverging and yet centrifugal, directed not toward the most withheld secrets but toward the imitation and the transmutation of the most visible forms: each word at the same time energized and drained, filled and emptied by the possibility of there being yet another meaning, this one or that one, or neither one nor the other, but a third, or none."[14] We all had treasure boxes as kids, didn't we? Sort of mini-museums. Strange things inside, unnamable and secret. These things had no sentimental value— kids have little sentiment. But they had "thinginess"—were odd and fascinating in their very existence as objects, as bits and pieces of the world that held secret meanings we didn't particularly care to decipher. They could mean anything, nothing, everything. They meant a lot to us. And did not make us anxious. Strange but pleasurable assemblages—Cornell boxes without tops, open to the present rather than the past. "How did you accumulate all the objects?" Wollen asks. "I usually steal them from people, borrow them," Fagin replies. "There are people who won't let me into their houses when I'm working on a project; they say, 'Uh-oh, he's back again, hide all the objects, he'll take everything!'"

"An infantile character amid lots of color, and objects, and silliness." "Pee Wee's Playhouse." *Raymond and Gustave have no place here amid the silli-*

ness, poor things. They are far too serious, and their play is feeble, if intense. In this playhouse, the baron asserts his amazing adventures as true. Passepartout and Princess Aouda mimic Phileas Fogg. Fagin sorts out objects, and I finally touch my face with the sensuous silk of veils.

Offstage, offscreen, the male narrator broods as he writes: "Eggs, toast, and bacon. I smell breakfast, yesterday's, rotten, still sitting. I'm haunted by a chapter, unnamed. Their fathers—who were they? I hesitate and then rush to say men like all others. . . . Their fathers were more. They were impossible. At least their mothers spoke to them. A tongue taken from an image, cracked and luminous. The sons sat attentively, rubbing against the speech, misunderstood, but warming. Their fathers never spoke, so images were found to replace them. But the sons were loyal. They were bright, too bright. The images were only seen in their shadow. Sometimes large, others small, this shadow hounded them, like a ghost. Afraid to turn round, sensing more than they knew, they walked head down. Fearing this would cause delay, they always arrived early. I pull the curtain—broad daylight. My eyes recoil, and I draw the shade." These are the video's last words.

Gustave. Raymond. I've known too many loyal sons. They never look me in the eye. Their eyes recoil, and they prefer that I draw the shade, put on the veil. At least I speak to them—but what I really want to say remains unspoken, unspeakable. "Down with Freud, your father," I want to say. "And Up the Sandbox." *"Down with the Blue Meanies," I want to say. "Fagin knows. We all live in a* Yellow Submarine." *He can borrow—but not steal—my objects any time. Together, complicit, we can wish whole worlds into existence.*

Peter Wollen
An Interview with Steve Fagin

Peter Wollen. How did you first get into video? I guess there is always a shadow to that question: Why video rather than film?

Steve Fagin. The shadow that film casts is quite long. In fact, sometimes I feel like Cary Grant, in *North by Northwest,* pursued by an ominous, noisy thing casting a large shadow on the flat landscape. I really wrestled with the option of doing the Lou Salomé project on film, but it didn't seem to fit. The financial demands of film are tremendous. Both the Salomé and the Roussel and Flaubert pieces would have cost twenty to thirty times more in film than in video. I wanted to work cheaply to show that good work in time-based art could be done inexpensively, out of one's piggy bank. Sometimes I feel I'm Rumplestiltskin trying to weave straw into gold. Other reasons for working in video related to a general sense of film's losing its experimental edge; this is especially the case with the feature in the United States. Yvonne Rainer and Mark Rappaport remained positive examples, but so many other filmmakers have crossed over into something called deconstructive mainstream cinema, which I distrust immensely. Also, the format of video production really turns me on. The indulgence of improvisation, the ability to work off the monitor— things just feel so resilient. I guess in the end I always think of cinema in terms of Bazin's story about rushing to the set of *To Catch a Thief* to watch the master at work, only to find the crew eagerly working and the great Hitchcock sound asleep. In addition, at least in the experimental venues, there no longer seemed to be a place where something could really happen. I remember reading about the splash Snow made in the mid-sixties with *Wavelength.* Video still seems to have events—the World Video Festival in the Hague and the American Film Institute Video Festival—where everyone is. Of course, the same people appear in both contexts. I was amazed at how few people constituted the world of video validation. I didn't mind seeing them over and over again; I just wished they had changed clothes between Holland and Los Angeles.

P. I have a follow-up question on the specificity of video. In your tape we see backdrops, close-ups, ECUs [extreme close-ups], miniatures, a very shallow space with bright, saturated colors, not very many camera movements, a preference for frontal shots and for "low-altitude" top shots. Was this a visual strategy that you thought about in advance? Or did it evolve? Did you find yourself adapting to the medium? Do you think the medium has that sort of aesthetic specificity?

S. When I decided to work in video, I sat down and watched a lot of MTV. In fact one New Year's Eve I sat home and watched all one hundred top rock videos.

P. But music videos tend to have three-dimensional sets. They have a deeper space.

S. That's when they are originally shot in film. When shot in video, they're extremely flat. I came to the conclusion that visually video combined two or three traditions from painting and very little from film. One is a postimpressionist sense of space, like Cézanne's. Two is obviously a pop use of color, which comes out of video's/TV's formative years. And three is an ability to overlay materials and spaces from different traditions, which pushes the work in two directions: toward a collage aesthetic derivative of someone like Rauschenberg, and a Byzantine sense of space attached to early Madonna-and-Child icons. But the two-dimensionality of my work relates to the fact that I have sight in only one eye. When people ask me why my work lacks the third dimension, I tell them I don't believe in the third dimension, only the second and the fourth.

P. You mean the fourth dimension in Duchamp's sense?

S. This emphasis on two-dimensional space also relates to specific issues that grow out of the projects. In the Salomé tape there's an interview with a photography historian who discusses how the nineteenth-century portrait always used flat backdrops. And there's the picture of Salomé, Rée, and Nietzsche used in the tape that has such a backdrop. So fake flat backdrops are used in a perverse sense to respect the nineteenth-century photograph, which that culture used to authenticate itself. It's my gesture toward "realism." Also, the flattening out of space allows me to juxtapose objects from different materials to produce a synthetic but rather uniform space, one similar to a rebus, where areas of people, pictures from books, and writing overlap, producing a zone of exchange among them. There's also an effort to animate the museum diorama. I believe it was Michelet who remarked that after his visit to the natural history museum in Paris, as a child, he felt history had come to life, and this inspired him to be a historian.

Duchamp's glass became very important to me, and it related to several different ideas: a space more conceptual than retinal; the third dimension as a fold between the second and the fourth, appearing only as a shadow; the sense of a bachelor/bride relation in the piece. But in terms of specific video aesthetics, what interests me is the sound/image relation and how different it is from film. In cinema, even in an extreme example like *Earthquake,* in "Sensurround," where the sound is literally above, below, and behind you, it still feels firmly rooted in the screen in front of you.

P.   What about the "dimension" of sound?

S.   I have never bought the arguments about Duras and the voice-off. In the cinema, at least at the level of enunciation, one never feels the voice is offscreen. And ironically, in regard to Duras, for me the work is quite childlike, things speaking, the water, a bridge, a tree, and so on. Video is very different; technically the sound in video is better than the sound in film, and the image in video is small. One's attention can be pulled off the image, toward sound and the space in between; the darkness becomes quite active. My aesthetic is based on that possibility, where you have a sort of Cornell box waiting, unavailable, tacky, flat, that you reach toward, and the sound is very full and energizing. The sound shocks the image to life, like Frankenstein's monster.

P.   In most people's minds there is probably a contrast, a tension, between video, which is regarded as ultracontemporary and high tech, and the subject matter of your tape: the web of references to the late nineteenth century, a lost prevideo age, Roussel, Flaubert, the photographic backdrop, the optical toy, the museum diorama. How do you see this working—this curious juxtaposition of a contemporary medium with Victorian and fin-de-siècle material?

S. There's a quote from Nabokov that I like, that the future is the obsolete in reverse. On one level it's similar to my respecting and using fake backdrops, to dealing with the historical distance between me and the nineteenth century by using my own authenticating machine, TV. On another level, Europe and the nineteenth century are posed as an unavailable other, which needs to be put through secondary revision, American popular culture, so that we can have anything to hold onto at all. Nineteenth-century Europe as the dream, and America as the daydream. Also, the project is posed in relation to the novel, but with TV as intermediary. I produced a makeshift machine using found objects to stand in for the novel, working as a sort of twentieth-century Robinson Crusoe using whatever bric-a-brac was available.

P. Doesn't the machine function as an emblem of the late nineteenth century: Edison's optical machine, the "machine" of academic painting, Roussel's bizarre textual machines? And you look back at them from the new electronic age?

S. There's a machine in *Impressions of Africa,* cumbersome, but able to tell the weather perfectly. After many generations of prosperity, the culture grew tired of the practical side of the machine and concentrated on its aesthetic qualities instead, admiring its elaborate construction. After several generations, they had entirely forgotten how to read it to tell the weather. Eventually, the culture was overrun by storms and drought and, on the verge of extinction, tried to recover the lost art of reading this awkward objet d'art. But instead of trying to decode the top half, which was the relevant half, they concentrated on the bottom, reading a few badly scrawled, meaningless marks left in the sand. My relation to the nineteenth-century novel is like this, a relation to the bottom half.

P. I'd like to zoom in on Roussel and Flaubert, "fathers" who specialized in the exotic. Why—let's start with Roussel—why him?

S. As usual with an obsession, I've forgotten the initial impetus. I think I was attracted to the level of detail by which he is known to us, how many times he changed shirts, the fact that he never traveled to places he had been to as a child, never opened letters, was afraid of germs, etc.—all these seem so much a part of his reputation. But, on the other hand, there is so little written that can be considered comprehensive biography; this surely overlaps with my interest in Lou Salomé. They both seemed to be infinitely generatable at the periphery, transparent at the edges and totally opaque at the center. There is a void at the so-called core.

P. When Roussel traveled, he always kept the blinds drawn.

S. All these sorts of details stuck in my mind and are repeated in the piece. There is also in my piece a lot of *Locus Solus,* which I thought to be spectacular. Its relation to language, representation, its weavings of story into myth, with language blocking up and backfiring, producing lots of images, but failing to depict a world; the more the language describes, the more the images fall apart. It is fabulous, and I wanted to unravel its writing process and psychoanalytic makeup, to deconstruct it and at the same time reproduce a double of it, an invocation.

P. Did you use Roussel's system of composition, which he explains in *How I Wrote Certain of My Novels*? Owen Land works in a Rousselian way in *The Marriage Broker Joke according to Sigmund Freud,* and I used techniques derived from Roussel in *Crystal Gazing.* Or were you more interested in the projection of an exotic "other," the obsession with machines, the weird personal details?

S. All of the above. I really had trouble writing; and the level of ecstasy, then withdrawal, then system that allowed Roussel to start writing very young, then stop writing altogether, and then begin working in a systematic way, was something that intrigued me. I decided to work from theoretical texts, or movies I liked, or baseball games I had gone to; I would take notes of these things, then leave the so-called original material aside, and several months later pick up the notes and write stories from them. I found this comforting in the sense that I already knew I had something I loved. I had a grid to work from, so I didn't have to face the empty page, and it allowed me to produce combinations of words and story twists that I don't think I would have otherwise.

For instance, there's a story I told about books. The first book, *Empire of Flora,* is the title of a Cy Twombly painting. He interests me tremendously. A line, some scribbles, color, and then a title like *The Veil of Orpheus.* I feel two ways at once about Twombly's work. It is about gesture, the painter's hand, etc. and then like an archaeological object full of hope of a lost civilization restored but charred almost past the point of recognition. Much of my work strives toward this sense of being both very close to some origin and full of death. So I say that Cy Twombly's father pitched in the major leagues, and I like baseball, so the names are those of baseball teams, and then you have Angel, Tiger, Cardinal, Twin. . . .

P. Now I get it.

S. And then *Cy* becomes a switchword, becomes *sigh,* and *Cy Young,* the name of the award in baseball given to the best pitcher. . . .

P. This makes it hard for the European viewer. . . .

S. Yet people often say that it's too European, not American enough. But basically I feel the work is very American and situates Europe in a particular way. So the writing process is in the spirit of Roussel, but I didn't submit totally to the system. I used it as inspiration.

P. In the American way. Pragmatic and can-do.

S. In the American way. I cheated and made it vulgar!

P. Let's turn to Flaubert—the novelist, the traveler, the decadent. Do you see Flaubert as the double of Roussel, or is there a difference between them?

S. There's a quote from Sartre that I use: "Why Flaubert? Because he is the imaginary. With him we are at the border, the barrier of dreams." One should remember that Sartre chose Flaubert over

Robespierre for his magnum opus on the construction of the subject. For me Flaubert was a rich relative—with all the advantages and disadvantages of the literary validation withheld from Roussel. Initially, I came across Flaubert while researching travel to exotic lands. I was impressed by his letters and also his relation to Maxime Du Camp, his traveling companion. His story is told in the received ideas section. The way Du Camp, the first photographer of ancient Egypt, would talk of Flaubert: of his languidness, his wanting to stay in and watch the world like a moving diorama. This led me to put Flaubert and Roussel together as traveling companions. The mood between them is a bit carping. First came the idea of a traveling companion, then the idea of the companion relating to the way that Roussel wrote—with two words that sounded the same, taking the second meaning, the lesser meaning, and spinning the story off of that. So Flaubert somehow became the greater meaning. And then I read the Sartre book, which. . . .

P. You're telling me you read the whole of Sartre's book?

S. I read a bit and thought, "This is good enough to read a bit more." *Yale French Studies* printed fragments from one of the unpublished volumes—exactly the kind of mystery, the "missing archaeological link," that really attracts me. Sartre was important to a generation of Americans just before my own—I think of "like, beatniks" snapping their fingers and quoting Sartre, a phenomenon I was never really part of. And I was overwhelmed by the way Sartre constructed Flaubert's infancy from so little information; the stories he created were so spectacular and so cold. It's actually the only text in my piece that appears literally copied.

P. With "nauseating repetition," as you say in the tape.

S. The other source was *Bouvard and Pécuchet,* a novel about two people's. . . .

P. Bric-a-brac. An assemblage of bric-a-brac.

S. Yes, and the emphasis on copying, and the privileging of books in an effort to master the real. Also the sense of being lost in an infinite regress of quotation that eventually leads back to the beginning, simply copying. After the project, I came across a wonderful article in *October* by Douglas Crimp on the museum and ruins, which I thought a great companion piece to the tape.

P.   There are two other important "virtual" characters: Flaubert's and Roussel's mothers. Now we are getting further into the Oedipal lineage.

S.   After the Lou Salomé tape I was quite lucky to have several very bright people become interested in my work. At a conference on psychoanalysis a friend of mine presented a paper on my work; since he knew that the original title of the piece was *The Everyday Life of Lou Andreas-Salomé,* he discussed it in relation to Freud and Lefèbvre. But, right before the talk, someone told me of an analysis that my friend had arrived at but would not present in his paper: that my work was all about breaking up with my girlfriend. Well, the Flaubert/Roussel piece is organized around a personal incident, a very horrible eye accident I had and a series of operations. The male narrator in the tape, someone in exile, running away, a very different amazing voyage, tries to fight off the pain of blindness in order to tell this tale of Flaubert, Roussel, the imaginary, their mothers. . . .

The work of Roussel and Flaubert, so invested in writing as a substitute for a maternal absence, trying to fill the space in ways diverting but always insufficient, is much of the terrain of the work. The mothers are stand-ins, mannequins brought to movement, somewhere between two worlds, madonna and [the pop star] Madonna. These images as North Stars guiding us into this prison of the imaginary. Often during work on the piece I felt trapped, as if in a coffin, digging through treasures, cut off from their function in exchange, being led by a voice, the sound track, that I thought would get me out of the trap. But, on hearing the voice, I knew it was just telling me over and over again, in different tongues, that I was trapped and would never get out. The tape is a mock journey, desperate, amused. In some ways I would have preferred to be Lautréamont—more hostile—or even Céline, but the piece comes out more like Cornell. Several sections on the sound track, especially the one called "Penelope's Song," and the last section, where the sons are figured in conical mirrors, directly lay out and address the dilemmas of this trap. It is a bachelor journey, very sad, like the ones of Roussel and Flaubert. The effort is to pose questions not from the point of view of the hysteric, asking, "Am I a man or a woman?" Much of the work of contemporary film theory has focused on this question, but from the point of view of the obsessional, who asks, "Am I alive, or am I dead?" And the world feels much different if you think, "I am dead."

P.   To what extent do you see the "imaginary" as being on the side of the "feminine"? Perhaps I am asking why there isn't a single male character who appears directly on the image track, but posing the question in a theoretical way.

S.   In the Flaubert/Roussel tape the feminine is that which allows the bachelor entry into the imaginary, but the feminine is not the imaginary. The opening credit, of Gérôme's rigid guard standing in front of the opaque door, the sound of the sea bleeding through, cut to the stand-in for Roussel's mother wearing a red dress, holding a stick, guarding the ocean, dancing while she narrates the story of her son's journey, the telling never completed, broken across the tape. The tape ends with her at attention, head bowed, stick forward parallel to the sea, then the credits. Gérôme's guard returns, repainted, garishly, but unfinished, as bad Hawaiian music plays on the sound track. The painting is a fraud, Gérôme's forged signature at the bottom is only crudely imitated; the painting, unlike the work of Gérôme, has a poor sense of perspective. For me at least, as just another reader, this is not the meaning of the piece that I find especially interesting. What interests me is the piece's mobility, its evasiveness, so to speak. I think of psychoanalysis and Oedipus and remember what an uninteresting story it is. What interests me is not its deep meaning, but the fact that it's in the unconscious, subject to displacement, condensation, and the absence of negation. In its telling one can see the unconscious at work/play. My two pieces have a complementary quality. The Salomé tape is organized around the woman but is distilled through Nietzsche, Freud, Rilke, Rée and, most importantly for me, Victor Tausk. The Flaubert/Roussel tape takes the men as the organizing figures but images the feminized. Also, unlike the way Propp associated the Oedipus story with the coming of patriarchy, the tape—the section called "The Land of Propp"—tries to trace matriarchy's coming to power. So narrative in the tradition of *The Thousand and One Nights* becomes, from the side of the female, associated with the suspension of death.

P.   Steve, I'm going to interrupt you. You know, I've written about Scheherazade. Her narration takes place in a setting that served as a screen for the projection of orientalist fantasy—by Flaubert and by Gérôme, two of the "patrons" of your tape. Within the context of nineteenth-century Orientalism, you could interpret the tape as a succession of almahs or odalisques, confined by the images of the harem guard, which occur at the beginning and the end of the tape. So even if the "symbolic" is associated with matriarchy, the "imaginary" could be given a patriarchal reading.

S.   I don't see the tape as coming from the place of the sultan, but perhaps from that of the sultan's son.

P.   You mean the child who was brought up in the seraglio but has been excluded and looks back with regret to a lost paradise?

S.   Yes, this is the sadness of the piece—its destiny. If I knew nothing else when I began the piece, I knew that there would be this inversion, and this is specifically dealt with in the last sections of the tape, most densely in the one called "Dying in Front of the Large Glass: The Perfect." The music: the Shangri-Las singing "and that's called sad" over and over again, mixed with Bellini's *Norma.* The images, domesticated versions of Orientalism: Ingres's odalisque turned into a couch, Gérôme's Napoléon turned into a footstool, and the Sphinx now a lamp—what an odd notion of ready-mades! And Magritte's *Human Condition* joined at the horizon line of sky and sea by a baseball game, Don Larsen and Yogi Berra, hugging, after the perfect game. The voice track: talking of Roussel dreaming of heaven, imagining Dante, but finding only street names, monuments, and medals, "it was perfect." This is the only image in the tape that is perfectly still.

P.   But not silent.

S.   Often there is a vulgar separation, posing image on the side of the imaginary, language on that of the symbolic. One should remember that for Freud the separation is between word presentations and thing presentations. The tape is a game of cat's cradle interweaving the imaginary and the symbolic. Language and image are appropriated as need be; the game is always reset by the impossible, the hint of the real that causes the narrative to flee and latch onto whatever will keep it afloat. The images are animated from beyond the dead; they reek of the symbolic. Anyway, I don't see only woman but a bachelor machine driven by the sound, the wind, and moved by the image, the sail.

P. What about the veil? This seems to be a very overdetermined image. It stands for the East and exoticism, it clearly connects to the harem guard, and then it also relates to the bride and thus to the bachelor; and, in addition to that, you tell the story of Zeuxis and Parrhasios toward the end of the tape, the story of a successful painting of a veil as a demonstration of trompe l'oeil.

S. Yes, there is much in the piece about veiling, unveiling, etc. To answer, I guess I should say a bit about meaning. When asked about the resemblance of his process to Sherlock Holmes's uncovering an enigma, getting at the heart of a story, telling the true meaning, Freud recoiled and said he thought his work not like Holmes's at all but like that of Schliemann, the man who uncovered Troy. The emphasis is in laying out, restoring things to their place, not interpreting. This is my ambition. Whether I'm right or wrong is not the point. Readings are always a question of timing anyway.

The veil in the piece has two sides, one marked by red paint, which stands for both the blood of the Virgin and the stain of the son, the Shroud of Turin. A virgin already stained and a son already bloodied. A friend commented that the piece seemed to be constructed around Catholic envy, and there *is* a way in which Catholicism has a place for the mother that Judaism does not. Not a correct place, but one to start discussing. Between the two sides is a lining, the paste of royalty, depicted through purple satin, then displaced through a shawl worn by the Madonnaesque singer. The unveiling also relates to a turning of pages, relating the piece to reading and, in general, a series of unwrappings. But then there is the retort in the section organized around a series of packages, making exotic sounds: if unwrapped they would no longer be a gift. I guess at its most abstract the veil suggests the way the obsessional relates to his or her object of desire. It is as though a thin veil stands between him or her and the loved object, almost like a pane of glass. The tape is an exhuming, something that the nineteenth century was obsessed with. Death is necessary for the obsessional to act. There's a famous psychoanalytic story about the obsessional's always imagining people to be dead so that he or she can pay his or her condolences. Maybe the piece is a condolence card.

P. Talking about regret and exhumation, I was struck by the number of traces of cinephilia in the tape. There are citations of many great classics: *Lola Montès, The Barefoot Contessa, Johnny Guitar, Morocco.* Old favorites. How do you see cinephilia now in relation to the "imaginary" and to video?

S. Cinema is in some senses a tremendous inspiration. Part of the advantage in working in video is that it allows a more distant relation to the cinema. It becomes another arena of loss. I often say, very willfully, about the Lou Salomé tape, that it's my effort to remake *Lola Montès,* and I'm sorry I couldn't do any better. One of the sections people like the most in that tape includes Elisabeth Nietzsche and Lou Salomé arguing about the status of language and truth. It's inspired by the sequence in *Johnny Guitar* between Sterling Hayden and Joan Crawford.

P. "Tell me lies. Tell me you love me." Godard takes that scene word for word in *Le petit soldat.* But it's as if you had shrunken the cinema into the video box of tricks. Giant images become scaled down into a world of postcards, playing cards, shells, tiny objects, toys, miniatures, all these diminutive things. Let's discuss this question of scale. I saw the TV set as an aquarium or a dollhouse. And then I related this to the Cornell boxes that are alluded to intermittently through. . . .

S. I think you want to produce an anthropomorphic scale for video that would have more potential for identification. By reducing things to a certain size you are allowing an exchange. As when you make hands participating in some activity the actual size of your own hands. In some senses, ironically, when things are small, parts of your body seem the right size. So it's a way to engage the body actively, a bit life-size. Also I think there's a way in which whatever information you have in front of you can function as the full field. So you can have a picture of the Eiffel Tower that has the force of the actual thing for a second. Then when you pull back and see it's just a postcard, it's thrown into cultural relief, becomes kitsch.

P. It's another kind of trompe-l'oeil effect.

S. Yes.

P. How did you accumulate all the objects?

S. I usually steal them from people, borrow them. There are people who won't let me into their houses when I'm working on a project; they say, "Uh-oh, he's back again, hide all the objects, he'll take everything!" I've also been very lucky to have people work with me who are able to make some things. But most importantly I've had a great producer, Jack Walsh.

P. The other cinema you cite is that of Méliès. Like Roussel or Lou Andreas-Salomé, he was also a fin-de-siècle figure. He also used backdrops and tricks of scale and dreamlike props.

S. I think Méliès is an extraordinary figure, and the whole phenomenon of "primitive cinema" and tableau structure is something that's very interesting to me. It's a tremendously rich tradition, surely more interesting than things that have been done recently. Except for "Pee Wee Herman's Playhouse," which is great.

P. What's that?

S. It's a Saturday morning TV show with an infantile character amid lots of color, and objects, and silliness. You've never seen it?

P. No, no. I never had Saturday morning TV. Cornell used to collect trick films, didn't he? Méliès and Zecca. I was struck by the insistence of Cornell, not only the boxes, but the procession of female figures, which, with Cornell, begin with Lind and Malibran, with nineteenth-century opera, and then descend to the twentieth-century cinema, to Rose Hobart, Hedy Lamarr, and Sheree North.

S. Much of the relation to Cornell is a ruse. A woman I lived with for a very long time, Aimee Rankin, does these wonderful boxes—unfortunately, we don't talk. Often my work is an exchange with hers; she makes a comment about Masaccio, I respond; she says something about *Turandot,* I give a different reading. A rather expensive form of letter writing. But I guess it's better than arguing. On the other hand, a ruse is a very serious thing.

P. A different topic: the traveler's tales, the ethnographic footage, the imaginary land of Propp. Where is all this travel taking us?

S. In some sense both pieces are organized around Ulysses, whom I see as the patron saint of chutzpah. I looked in Freud for reassurance and was stunned that he had never written about Ulysses. Anyway, the organization of the voyage home and the series of wanderings is important, both personally and structurally. Also the way Ulysses becomes the metatale of telling, narration, in the West. So Joyce becomes a major influence. In the Flaubert/Roussel tape, Verne's becomes the metatale for the nineteenth-century voyage. After all, Roussel thought Verne the greatest writer in history. What we end up with is a library of the voyage with many different types of analysis: personal stories, geographic descriptions, political conquests, ethnography, etc., all stacked next to each other under the card-catalog topic *the amazing voyage.* Also, there is an effort to confront the post-Romantic imagination, of which Flaubert and Roussel are such a strong part. To join the work being done within the critique/discussion of Orientalism.

P. When you talk about this very complex web or mesh of allusions and threads of metaphor and metonymy, do you see it as a web that has some kind of a center or direction? Or do you let it grow haphazardly through a free play of signifiers?

S. Sometimes I think of the way things hold together in a rather mundane way. It's as though you've gotten up in the middle of the night, gone into the kitchen, turned on the light, and opened a drawer to find an empty center with all these cockroaches at the edge. You feel like closing the drawer, but instead grab at them to restore them to their place. Often when people think of how things connect, they think of the symptom. There's a real meaning underneath, sweep the symptom to the side, and get to the bottom of it. But Freud himself remarked that he was bringing the plague. So things get connected from so little and can turn in almost any direction. The Western disciplines of the dead—archaeology, geology, etc.—pull so much together from so little. From a bone we get a dinosaur eating ferns in a swamp. The object found is used to constitute discourses on origin, legitimacy, and custom. And this is what so many stories in the tape use as their methodological base. There is a quote I like of Cornell's: It's not that things so close feel apart that's the problem but that things so far apart fit together so easily.

Another issue of organization is very important to the piece, and this is a distinction that I would draw between Duchamp and Cornell, both so important to me. Much of the aesthetic of Duchamp is on the side of the ludic, the game of chess, and we know to what degree chess is a synchronic event; it doesn't need to know the move before. On the other hand, so much of the play structure of Cornell is modeled on the fort/da game, a waiting for the mother to return. I see my own work as closer to Cornell's. It's very important to me that it was the American movers who broke the Large Glass, made *marmalade* out of it, as Duchamp said, using a word that doesn't exist in French. All this relates to the tape's prelude, the interrogation of virginity, very direct, set off in tone from the rest of the tape, which is sublimated and childlike. The interrogation is followed by the pop-up book that, in the tradition of the prelude, introduces all that follows. The body of the tape has a very symmetrical structure, rhyming both on micro and on macro levels. Then there is the male narrator, the backbone of the piece, holding it together but turning it inside out.

P. The chess player can be figured as an automaton, as a bachelor machine. But this idea of the bachelor. . . .

S. There's a very eccentric book by Craig Adcock on Duchamp and nth-dimensional geometry, in which he traces Duchamp's last piece, *Etant donnés,* back to Gérôme's *Guard of the Harem,* discussing the door in great detail. Within my work there is an antimony between doors and veils. The bachelor with a door in front of him sees a bride with a veil, who imagines she must be imprisoned by the veil instead of, like him, a solid door. This difference is represented and narrativized in many ways, ranging from the section on Flaubert's being locked in his father's study through the retelling of the Zeuxis and Parrhasios legend.

P. I think of Duchamp's bachelor more in terms of "nauseating repetition," the spectacle of repetition. The nineteenth century becomes the site of this spectacle.

S. For the twentieth century to have doubts about what it is missing.

P. Then there's the repetition of the image, the idea of the museum of the copy, that the tape keeps coming back to.

S. I was very interested in pursuing nineteenth-century modes of producing images. One of the major aspects of this involved the journey to Rome, where one would simply copy other images. There was even a museum of copies. It was thought that a good copy was better than a bad original. I was also fascinated by Gérôme's Orientalist work. I did some research into his work process and was interested to learn that people generally comment on his paintings' *fini,* their extremely finished surface construction. The image that was in front of Gérôme was in fact an extraordinary collage. I show the way the paintings were constructed in one of the stories in the tape: there's a bunch of bric-a-brac, a woman there, a fake backdrop, a photograph, clothes brought back from the original place, and objects that he more or less always used. It's a very eccentric combination. I was intent on reproducing *that* space rather than the finished space of the painting.

P. In dwelling on copies, did you want to get into a discourse about postmodernism?

S. I did once, but now postmodernism is an overused idea, it's become too fashionable, so it's hard to go back to it. It's the same with the issue of the simulacrum versus the copy.

P. That's a section that works very well, the dramatic knockabout debate between the finger puppet and the tape recorder.

S. The person who performed it, Valerie Manenti, is very good, and she really worked very hard on the ideas. This section also relates to Roussel's being a mimic, his thinking that his greatest triumphs were the mimicking of the music hall entertainers of his day in front of his family. As a child I was always impressed by ventriloquism; in the United States there was someone named Señor Wences, who performed with a hand puppet and a box. My tape runs the Deleuze piece on Plato through my memory of Señor Wences. It's meant to be a good illustration of Deleuze. You start with a Cornell box, and you substitute an image of a gremlin; I think of the movie *Gremlins;* the gremlin is the image of the simulacrum. . . .

P. This is the sequence with an altered facsimile of a Cornell box?

S. Yes. I think the gremlin is the perfect idea of the simulacrum. And so a debate ensues between the copy and the simulacrum, sort of substitutions of substitutions. The ideas of the simulacrum and the copy are taken directly from Deleuze. I'm hesitant about Baudrillard's work. Actually, I think Baudrillard should become a painter—you know, "This is the real Baudrillard, see, there's the signature, if all you want to do is illustrate my ideas, here's my signature, this should be worth something."

P. I think he's probably becoming a gremlin.

S. I don't think he's interested, though. To return to the question about postmodernism: I think the style comes to me from growing up on TV and always filtering things through an ethnic specificity. I have a hard time reading poetry because it sounds to me like it comes out with my own accent, a Chicago accent. I have been resistant to reading much of the literature on postmodernism, though I think that even by scanning and trying to avoid it, I have probably read the equivalent of several books. Even when you avoid it, you see three words each time, and I've seen so much on it.

P. Like the person in the Godard film who worked at the check-out counter in a bookstore and always glanced at the first and last pages while wrapping the books. I was interested in raising the question of postmodernism because I wondered whether quotation, repetition, copying—whether all these things were necessarily pervaded with nostalgia and regret.

S. If one is presuming that wholeness can be restored, that's one thing; but if one is willing, more in the tradition of Benjamin, or Barthes, or even Nietzsche's best texts, to hold pridefully onto the fragment and use it as a critical fold, a tactical relation to the future. . . . The effort to bind it always has to be undone.

P. You used this term *fold,* and I'm not quite sure. . . .

S. Cooking! Like when you fold in egg whites; when you make a soufflé you whip up the egg whites, then you fold them in so they keep their identity, though they're integrated completely with the other ingredients.

P. But my question was going to be about repetition. There's another aspect to it. One of the main features of your sound design is the use of loops.

S. Yes, I use the sort of circularity and delirium attached to loops to pull away from the imaging. I also tried to set up a series of repetitions in order to provide that sense of security one gets when things are repeated. You have, then, both sides of the rollercoaster ride—delirium and the return to the point of entry.

P. There's a kind of aural bric-a-brac: snatches of pop songs, bits of opera, found noise. . . .

S. The sound has a perspectival space that the image lacks. A rather eccentric space combining pop music, ambient sound, and opera, but it has a semblance of perspective, as in Escher. I work very closely with William Davenport on the tracks. They take months, and I'm very pleased with his input into my work. For me the pieces are sound entry pieces. The ear is the one organ that doesn't close, so everything begins with the ear. Unlike cinema, which grows out of the fantasy of its own origin as image without sound, video had sound from the beginning. In fact I think of TV, historically, simply as deposing the radio. It's a stand-in for the radio, which was so comforting a part of the American past. Think of Woody Allen's *Radio Days.* From my own past, I remember Sunday mornings, the only time I ever noticed that my parents slept together, because they would sleep in, door closed. I would sit in front of the radio, Sunday funnies sprawled in front of me, and let the radio animate them for me. I've never read the Sunday funnies since; they make no sense to me without the sound. In my own work the sound is an anchor, which is a bit different than anchorage; if you hold on too tightly, you'll drown.

P. You refer a lot to childhood memories of radio and TV. How do you see the tapes fitting into the landscape of video art?

S. One of the issues is long work versus short work. People readily understand the difference between short stories and novels; they know they are organized around different principles. In film you have a distinction between the short and the feature. But in video you have, "Oh yes, you're the guy who makes the long tapes." And so I've made a real effort to intervene in video, to push away from the notion of video as moving wallpaper, toward something that might have to be looked at more than once. I've also been interested in shifting the space of exhibition to one where people might have to pay to sit, would commit their time.

P. Turn it into cinema.

S. No, turn it into a machine like the cinema, but with a different aesthetic.

P. How do you see your work in relation to museums, which are really the dominant space for video?

S. I think of the "Tristan und Isolde" section in Buñuel's *L'âge d'or.* I see the image as a severed hand twitching on a kitschy, fake pedestal, very small, and the sound as a high school band version of Stravinsky's *Rite of Spring* played very loud, and the audience sitting attentively. Assuming the image as central, but being torn to the edges by the sound, even to the point of erotic delirium (perhaps a bit wishful). Anyway, I'm very thankful for the support I've gotten within the video world. Many of the curators have tried to accommodate video's particular demands, to give the best viewing context available within their institutions.

P. And how do you see the audience? Because the dollhouse, Cornell-box scale of the TV monitor in some way determines the scale of the audience as well.

S. In many ways video is more on the side of painting, for which there's not really an audience, but rather a kind of connoisseur-ship. If you had a gallery opening, and Mary Boone or the Saatchis walked into your gallery and said, "This is wonderful," and they were going to circulate or buy your piece, it wouldn't matter, in terms of validation within the institution, what anyone else thought. In place of a functional audience, video has an audience of connoisseurs.

P. There's no box office.

S. I look at it as an advantage in a way because it allows me to experiment, to work at the edge, which I don't think I'd be able to do if I had to work in a forum that wasn't supported in this way.

P. Yet, in a way, there is a mass audience. I read somewhere that the attendance at museums was now greater than that at sporting events. It's not implausible. Museums are open all week. There are many new ones being built. They have lines around the block. The throughput must be immense. But it's an audience that just comes in and feeds through, pausing for a moment, moving on, stopping, skipping whole rooms, and so on. How do you create that fixed look, that attentive look, that you're talking about when it goes against the whole grain of museum spectatorship?

S. One could argue that cinema has that same problem in the museum, it's not just video. But on the other hand. . . .

P. I don't want to put cinema in the museum. I would much sooner it was in other kinds of spaces. But video art doesn't seem to have many alternatives.

S. I'm trying to work from what's there, to figure out a way to have it work. On one side I'm trying to work with the notion that the image *isn't* compelling. But when I try to organize a screening in alternative spaces, the thing I try to do is set up a system, perhaps like five very good monitors in a circle with thirty people around each monitor—nobody does window-shopping among monitors—and the sound coming from outside through large speakers. One of the advantages of having an art form based on connoisseurship is that it allows you to experiment and take risks, and the history of much of what passes for experimental exists initially under a very protected patronage. So I think what I do is look at this as a license to be experimental.

P. Do you think video art in general has that license?

S. I think that one can take that license. Because of the demands of the museum and of broadcast, video often functions according to a middle-brow aesthetic that I don't like. I do like some of the work done in video; I like the work of John Adams in England, and the installation work of Tony Oursler is fantastic. I like Paper Tiger's work very much—informal, alternative, and cheap. Video provides several different formats for doing interesting and creative work, and I'm using some sort of license, and other people are using others.

P. We've talked about museums and the conditions of exhibition. What about the discourse that surrounds video? Do you see problems or constraints there?

S. The curators are the people who produce and are often the critics as well. This leaves very little room for the separation of estates. Video is an art form raised on pluralism as opposed to partisanship. And traditionally, at least where I come from, the cinema is based more on partisanship; there's a healthy disrespect for other people's work, and you argue and work out positions and alliances across differences, not according to the pretense, I'm OK, you're OK. That upsets me.

P. Is that because the video world is too small?

S. It's because it's developed as a sort of network, which probably relates to its smallness and the need for friendship. I don't know the history well enough, but coming to it at this moment in time, that's the way it feels.

P. When you talk about partisanship in the film world, isn't that connected to the role of film theory as a partly prescriptive force? There isn't any pressure of video theory in the same way.

S. I want to insist very strongly that one of the reasons I'm doing video is to run away from film theory. At a certain moment film theory felt very much like it had lost its exploratory and speculative dimension and had settled into a series of axioms in response to which you get people writing papers: "True or false: *Desert Hearts* is an embodiment of female desire."

P. "Undecidable."

S. "Undecidable." So it began to feel that theory had become a sort of Discourse Police over practice, which I think has now spread to the art world. So video struck me as a place where I could produce in an atmosphere of exploration and risk.

P. You see the theoretical culture as a kind of constraint, rather than as liberating?

S. I think it's switched its function in both the art world and the film world. There is a cross-examination of the text for correctness so that you eventually lose any sense of speculation and risk taking.

P. I think maybe you're trying to have your cake and eat it too. You can't have the liberating side of theory without the constraints. And certainly you can't have partisanship without prescription.

S. Everything has its imaginary, even film theory. And for film it's the Soviet Union in the twenties, where there was a high level of partisanship.

P. That was an extremely constraining discourse—as well as liberating.

S. At what level?

P. Look what happened.

S. I don't think you can say, "Look what happened." I'm talking about the polemics surrounding LEF [*Left Front of the Arts*], not Zdhanovism.

P. LEF was under pressure from the various proletarian groups and tendencies as well as from more universalist currents; look at Trotsky's critique. After Lenin's death, the art world became inextricably caught up in inner-party struggles. The collapse of LEF and Mayakovsky's suicide took place at the end of a long period of intense theoretical and political struggle over the correct line.

S. Yes, but I think the flow of energy between creativity, risk taking, and speculation within both writing, which is called critical, and production, which is called artistic practice, was very rich at that time. Also I feel my work and other people's work, including yours and Trinh T. Minh-ha's, have been trying to produce a Northwest Passage, an open-ended relation, where one sees both sides as being creative and speculative. Criticism at its edge, Barthes, Blanchot, Benjamin, and certain filmmakers, Godard and Marker, cross over—perhaps not dissolving the border but allowing one to travel freely, without a passport.

P. I agree with that. Without a passport.

S. I don't think that video criticism is lacking its Christian Metz; it's lacking its Jonas Mekas.

P. I would have thought it was lacking something other than either of these.

S. I'm talking about partisanship, championing, saying that something is important.

P. Mekas was a partisan for independence and experiment, but within that boundary, very pluralistic. I think that's probably the situation with video now. People see themselves as partisans for video as such. What about the relation to television? You've talked a lot about television, how you sat there watching the Winky Dink show all the time.

S. I mentioned Pee Wee Herman, but I did watch the Winky Dink show. You used to put this Saran Wrap piece in front of the screen, and it was up to you to connect the bridge so Winky Dink could go from one side to the other. I really liked that show.

P. There's all this childhood investment in television. And now here you are with video. How do you see its relation to television?

S. I have a hard time watching TV, except for news and sports—assassinations and touchdowns—where I think something's happening. Otherwise, I begin to hyperventilate. Again, I see television as something that is pushing from behind and allows me to produce and organize things in a way that is probably different from those people who have only a high-culture background. But I do not at this moment in time see my work as an intervention in TV.

P. Would it ever be possible to see it in that way in the United States?

S. I think Paper Tiger is good. To work on cable, work at your own density, push your own issues, feel that if you produce something interesting, people will come to it, is important. But the level of compromise in relation to the institutions of PBS. . . . I have not seen anything coming out of that tradition that interests me.

P. I find the audience for TV even more scattered and abstract than that in museums. Obviously, there is an audience out there, watching. But inchoate and ephemeral. Here one minute, gone the next. It's just the inverse of the museum: throughput of images instead of throughput of viewers.

S. For me video culture is more like a cell group. Like Freud: if he sells a hundred copies of *Interpretation of Dreams* in ten years, what's important is who reads it and what they do with it. I've concentrated on people who could do something with it, people who will come to it, to the edge. The center will collapse because enough people will move from the center to the edge. There's more of an effort to conquer the edge than the center.

P. A kind of microcultural politics.

S. Yes.

P. Enough questions. Let's switch off. Can we still catch Pee Wee Herman?

Steve Fagin Script of *The Amazing Voyage of Gustave Flaubert and Raymond Roussel*

Transcription by Christine Tamblyn

ACTION	IMAGES	NARRATION	AMBIENCE
#1	#1 Title: *Quaestio de virginitae.* (This is a Latin phrase for an interrogation about virginity.)	#1	#1
#2 **Sync sound.** **Stand-in for Roussel's mother:** Yeah, I fucked him. **Female voice, offscreen:** You're a liar. **Stand-in for Roussel's mother:** The first time I fucked? **Female voice, offscreen:** That's what I asked.	#2 The scene begins with an extreme close-up of the eyes of the Stand-in for Roussel's mother. The camera pulls back to a shot of her entire face. She moves so that the camera angle varies by 180 degrees. Sometimes she faces the camera; at other times	#2	#2

Stand-in for Roussel's mother: I thought I already answered that question.

Female voice, offscreen: But you lied. When was the first time you fucked?

Stand-in for Roussel's mother: I didn't lie. The first time I fucked, I was seven-teen.

Female voice, offscreen: Where was it?

Stand-in for Roussel's mother: It was in the back seat of a car in the driveway.

Female voice, offscreen: What time was it?

Stand-in for Roussel's mother: It was sometime during. . . .

Female voice offscreen: Did it hurt?

Stand-in for Roussel's her right or left profile is to the camera.

mother: Yes, it hurt.

Female voice offscreen:
Did you bleed?

**Stand-in for Roussel's
mother:** No, I didn't bleed.

Female voice, offscreen:
How old were you?

**Stand-in for Roussel's
mother:** I was seventeen.
His name was [beeped out].

Female voice, offscreen:
What did he look like?

**Stand-in for Roussel's
mother:** He was tall, about
six-four, blond hair, green
eyes.

Female voice, offscreen:
Did you fuck him, or did he
fuck you?

**Stand-in for Roussel's
mother:** I fucked him.

Female voice, offscreen:
You're full of shit.

Stand-in for Roussel's

mother: No, I'm not. I fucked him.

Female voice, offscreen: When was the first time you fucked?

Stand-in for Roussel's mother: When was the first time I fucked? I was twenty-one.

Female voice, offscreen: Liar!

Stand-in for Roussel's mother: I was twenty-one, really.

Female voice, offscreen: Where was it?

Stand-in for Roussel's mother: It was in my bedroom.

Female voice, offscreen: What time was it?

Stand-in for Roussel's mother: It was about 8:30 at night.

Female voice, offscreen: Did you bleed?

Stand-in for Roussel's mother: Yeah, I did.

Female voice, offscreen: How old were you?

Stand-in for Roussel's mother: I was eighteen.

Female voice, offscreen: Who was it?

Stand-in for Roussel's mother: His name was [beeped out].

Female voice, offscreen: You're a liar.

Stand-in for Roussel's mother: Yeah, I am. I confess. I lied.

Female voice, offscreen: When was the first time you fucked?

Stand-in for Roussel's mother: I've never been fucked.

#3
A black-gloved hand opens the cover of a pop-up book.

The black-gloved hand turns over the first page of the pop-up book.

#3
The cover of the pop-up book has a hand-drawn landscape scene. The first page of the pop-up book contains a crudely painted image of a rustic pastoral scene with a hut in the distance. A blue drawn backstage curtain is in the left foreground of the painting. A female artist wearing a T-shirt with a prom dress over it pops out of the centerfold. She stands on an ornate, elaborately sculpted pedestal. The second page of the pop-up book features the surface of a table with dishes of standard American food spread out over it. The pop-up is a cooked turkey on a platter being held by an elderly woman wearing an

#3
Voice-over of Italian female narrator: Opera buffa, farsa, opera comica, melodrama, burlesca.

The world has changed, like Donizetti without Lucia.

#3
Woman's voice singing operatic aria from Verdi's *Force of Destiny.* Tape looped segment of Cole Porter song repeats.

apron. An elderly man
stands behind her. He holds
a carving knife, which is
plunged into the turkey.

The hand plunges the
detachable knife into and out
of the turkey depicted in the
pop-up book illustration.

On the knife are printed the
words *Rhetoric of the Image.*

History no longer repeats, in
the manner of Marx, first
tragedy, then farce. Now, it is
simply one farce after
another.

The black-gloved hand turns
over the second page of the
pop-up book.

The third page of the pop-up
book contains the pop-up
image of a dark-haired
Arabic woman who wears a
blue veil. A rope of the type
that cordons off paintings in
museums is drawn across
her figure, so that it, too,
pops up. In the background
are two indistinct paintings.

Sounds of a siren and a
parrot saying "hello" are
mixed with the looped
Cole Porter song.

The black-gloved hand turns
over the third page of the
pop-up book.

The fourth page of the pop-
up book is a painting of the
sky over an ocean that is a

cheap imitation of Magritte's *Human Condition.* To the left a bathroom sink is painted into the foreground. On the right is a raised canvas, resting on an easel. The painting on the canvas is a continuation of the scene of the ocean and the sky in the background. Above the canvas's surface is a movable wheel, which also has the same scene depicted on it, along with a black arrow.

The black-gloved hand turns the wheel to reveal a rendering of the Sphinx.

The black-gloved hand turns over the fourth page of the pop-up book.

On the fifth page of the pop-up book is a pop-up of a woman sitting in a chaise lounge looking through binoculars. She is viewing a

#4	#4	#4	#4
painting of the Taj Mahal, depicted as though it were a slide being projected on a portable screen.	The title of the tape *The Amazing Voyage of Gustave Flaubert and Raymond Roussel* appears over Gérôme's painting *The Guard of the Harem.* This image of a turbaned black man, who holds an archaic axe and stands in front of a cryptic inscription in stone, has been colorized with a video paintbox.		

#5	#5	#5	#5
Sync sound. The Stand-in for Roussel's mother dances on the beach, hitting different parts of her	The Stand-in for Roussel's mother is framed in a medium shot against a background of the ocean	**Sync sound.** *The Stand-in for Roussel's mother narrates breathlessly while she is dancing:* I've just	Ambient sound of wind and waves.

body rhythmically with a
bundle of sticks.

and sky. She wears a strapless orange dress.

received a letter from my son,
and he writes of a wonderful
dance troupe whose performance included twirling
sticks, whirling movement,
and clacking sound. Although
my son didn't much like the
dancing, he was fascinated by
the rhythmic intensity of the
drummer, who sat, as if in a
trance, to the side of the
dancers, never once looking
up, either to look at the
audience or the dancers.
Afterward, he, my son, that is,
went up to the head of the
troop and asked if he could
meet the drummer. The head
of the troop hesitated. . . .

#6
A game of solitaire is played
by a pair of dismembered
hands. The nails on one hand

#6
A close-up of a flat surface
covered with an anamorphic
picture of Flaubert. The cards

#6
Voice-over of male narrator:
Like travelers before me, I
have arrived in a village

#6
Looped sound of male voice
laughing, from Verdi's opera

are painted red. The nails of
the other hand are un-
painted.

in the game of solitaire are
from a deck showing a series
of classical nude paintings.
The camera keeps moving in
closer on the spread of cards.

whose name I do not wish to
remember. I have hidden in so
many. I'm a fugitive, although I
have committed no crime. The
villages read like a list in
Michelin: Illhausen, Vienne,
Eugenie Les Bain. But my map
is not marked by sumptuous
repasts, but by pain and
productivity. My path is
erratic, always doubling back.
Lurching to the side, I circle
around the periphery, fearing
only death waiting at the
center. As I flee, I have one
pleasure. No, it brings me no
pleasure, but occasional joy.
My writing. A book. *The
Amazing Voyage of Gustave
Flaubert and Raymond Roussel.*
Their journey has remained
hidden, a mystery.
I will unveil it. But my book is

The Masked Ball.

still only in fragments, and those are scattered: notes in boxes mixed with dirty laundry lists crumbled in coat pockets, and an outline, lost, last seen on top of train schedules, but underneath stale cheese. The writing causes me to struggle, like a beast of burden. I carry the collective weight of a previous century, my back almost broken by its priests, donkeys, and pianos. I tire easily, but push on. At least I know the chapters of my book: Flaubert, Roussel, the imaginary, their mothers. But where do I begin?

The last card to be turned up is a depiction of Gabrielle d'Estres and the duchesse de Villars, by an unknown artist. The two women are portrayed nude from the waist up. One touches the breast of the other.

#7

Title: "Dying in Front of the Large Glass: THE COWARD." The camera pans across Magritte's painting *The Human Condition* in extreme close-up. Scrot's portrait of Edward VI has been inset into the Magritte painting.

#7

Voice-over of Italian female narrator: Raymond Roussel died at the Grande Albergo Delle Palme, room 226. It was connected by a door to the adjoining room occupied by Charlotte Dufrenne, his lifelong celibate companion. Their custom was to keep the door unlocked. He dragged the mattress, which represented a superhuman effort, to the adjoining door. It was like he had died on the bachelor side of the Large Glass. The door was locked. On the floor below, Wagner had written *Parsifal.* Roussel had written of a suicide, restaged, no repeated as a

#7

Loop of Leslie Gore's song "It's My Party" mixed with a musical loop from Verdi's *La traviata.*

theatrical performance at 8 and 10 P.M., matinees on Wednesdays. Immediately prior to his death, the victim wrote two words on a slate—*bleached* and *recto*—and signed the name *Francois-Charles Cortier.* Then, beneath the first *c*, which was as yet unprovided with its appendage, he quickly drew, with the ease of long habit, a curved serpent in the required position to serve as a cedilla. Immediately prior to his suicide, he wiped the slate clean. The audience thought him to be a coward. There were no performances on Mondays.

The camera pans across a man's bare feet. He is lying face down on a bed.

Son vil—the coward—Addio fiorito asil di letizia e d'amor dempre il mite suo sembiante

Con strazio atroce vedro
Addio fiorito asil non
reggoaltuo squallor! Fuggo,
fuggo, son vil. [This Italian
quotation is from Puccini's
Madame Butterfly.]

#8

#8
Postcard of Masaccio's
Expulsion from Paradise.

A hand puts down a postcard
of Joan Crawford's scarred

#8
**Voice-over of Italian female
narrator continues:** I will
never find refuge from this
torment. I am running away,
running away. I am a coward.
Pinkerton abandons his
Ariadne. Son vil. The unmen-
tionable has been uttered.
The stench should resonate.
How to say such words? With
conceit? Hypocrisy? Bravado?
That is to play the part with
honor. Cowardice should be
performed with grand
treachery, whispered
teneramente.

#8
Musical loop from Verdi's *La
traviata* continues.

face from the film *A Woman's Face*. A cut-out image of Eve from the Masaccio painting, wearing a dress, has been pasted on top of the original photograph from the film.

Sound of violin warming up.

Voice-over of American female child narrator:

Dearest Mama,

Unfortunately, we have been caught in the middle of a border skirmish between Eusapia and Edoras. Gustave says, if we were home, England would take Eusapia, the Russians would take Edoras, and, in retaliation, the French would get themselves slaughtered in the neighboring mountains of Chelm.

One thousand tender thoughts,

Title: "Line of Received Ideas."
The title is keyed over an image of three young women standing together with their arms linked. Behind them is a backdrop with postcards of Washington, Lincoln, and the Taj Mahal on it. The woman stands behind a rope of the kind museums use to cordon off paintings. Behind her is a backdrop with a representation of Abraham Bosse's *The Masters of Perspective* on it. The drawing shows a man with exaggerated perspectival lines coming together at the focal point of his eyes.

Sync sound.
One of the young women speaks: Yesterday, we arrived in the new capital by mid-afternoon and were met and escorted through arrival formalities. After lunch, we traveled through the old capital, bargaining for jewelry and hand-tooled leather goods in the grand bazaar.

Cut to a middle-aged woman, who reads from a piece of paper, which she holds at arm's length: I was the first to record this now famous ruin, almost, that is, through my now well-known photographs and travel diary. On first sight, the wonder had been completely swallowed by the desert, except for the tip, and that stood half covered with bird droppings. I supervised its unveiling and was appalled to discover near the base that it had been desecrated, scarred. A Christian name had been clumsily scratched onto the surface, like the markings on a childhood school desk. I raved in print about this sacrilege. Who could have committed such an egotistical act? Years later, while attending a party, an old acquaintance came up to me, saying how she had just returned from this great sight, and wanted to tell me that the desecrator's name had been scratched away, but another had been etched over the uneven surface of the ruin,

Cut to another middle-aged
woman, who stands in profile
against *The Masters of
Perspective* backdrop.

and that name was mine. I am
here to erase that name. [This
passage is based on Maxine
Ducamp's *The Great Ruin*]

*Cut back to the three young
women with the linked arms.
The middle girl speaks:* Today
was a fine day to just relax, or
stroll around the Great Ruin,
explore the desert by camel
or horse, see local villages,
etc. Christman Eve at the
beautiful Great Ruin Sound
and Light Show.

**Voice-over of American
female adult narrator:** After
turning right at the waterfall,
he arrived at the Great Ruin.
The Great Ruin is a mirror
with two sides. These two

sides are separated by a
partition invisible to the eye.
Although these two sides
reflect one another, their
incongruence is strong.
Although the reduction of this
incongruence can be imag-
ined, it will never be seen.
But this does not mean that
the two sides will be separated forever. However, it is
wise to allow oneself to be
enamored by each in their
turn. Unfortunately, you are
forbidden to take pictures of
the Great Ruin. But you are
free to photograph people
watching. [This passage was
derived from Lyotard.]

*Cut to the young women
standing with linked arms.
The one in the middle speaks:*
Tomorrow, after a special

The three girls begin to
giggle and huddle together
conspiratorially.

Cut to an Arabic woman with
a purple veil covering her
face, who stands in front of
The Masters of Perspective
backdrop. She resembles the
painting of the veiled woman
in the pop-up book.

visit to an ancient artists'
village to see their own
delicately painted tombs,
continue on to the awesome
Valley of Forgotten Hope.
And, for those who wish, a
short hike, with fabulous
views, over the cliffs, to
Queen Lodedapuris's temple.

Sync sound.
*The veiled woman uncovers
her face and begins to speak:*
This used to be an oasis, they
said. I do not know. I cannot
find it on my map. . . . *The
woman begins to speak in a*

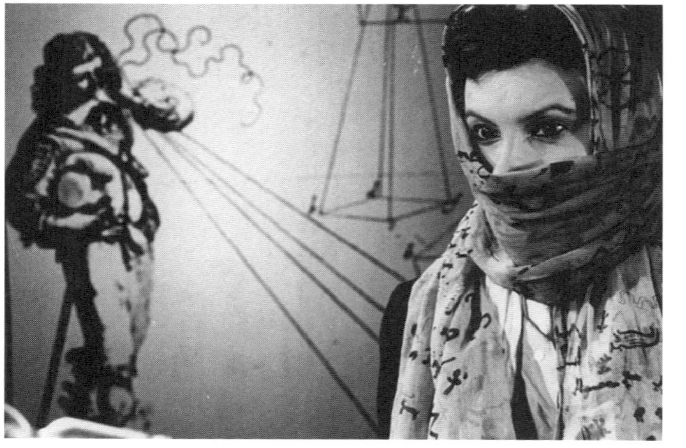

"Line of Received Ideas," from *The Amazing Voyage*

foreign language, then resumes in English: My itinerary is the inverse trajectory. I come from the East and am always moving West. My city is burning behind me. When [Arab military leader] landed with his men in 3013, he burned all the ships that had carried them across the waters. Then he assembled his men by the light of the burning ships. [. . .] The men had but one choice. The burning ships and the water lay behind them. Ahead, enemy territory. To steal into the heart of the capital, I've found a new identity. From the remnants of civilization, I've created my disguise. C'est la ruse de sauvage.

#10	#10	#10	#10
	Title: "Requiem for Sight: INDIA SONG." The title appears over a movie screen. Then the shadows of two hands form shapes, which are projected onto the screen. The camera slowly pans to reveal that the Stand-in for Roussel's mother is sitting in front of the screen, making the shadows.	**Voice-over of Italian female narrator:** As to her son's request, Raymond Roussel's mother, née Marguerite Moresu Chalson, of a bourgeois family of some prominence, was buried at high noon without shadow. She was lowered into the ground, then slowly covered by dirt from toe to head. The casket had been made special for the occasion. Over her face, there had been built a glass skylight. Her son had wanted to watch her, till the very last moment.	Loop of music from Marguerite Duras's film *India Song*.
The Stand-in for Roussel's mother turns away from the screen and looks into the camera, while beginning to get up from the chair. Fade out. The Stand-in for Roussel's			

mother picks up an antique
3-D viewer that has been on
the table next to her, inserts
a picture into it, and looks
through it. Then she turns
away from the camera to face
the screen again. She
continues to look through the
viewer.

Voice-over of Italian female narrator: As a child, Raymond had accompanied his mother to India. They had rented a private yacht, special for the occasion. One dawn, after many weeks of travel, she was awakened by a sailor whispering in her ear, "Hurry! Come see! India by first light!" She quietly scurried topside. The captain proudly gave her his spy-glass and pointed. She looked, just for a moment,

returned the glass, and said,
"Do not dock, turn round,
turn round." The captain had
no choice. A few moments
later, Raymond awoke. He
had missed India.

#11
A book with the title *Giovanni
Bellini* on the cover is placed
on top of the anamorphic
painting of Roussel. The book
is opened by a hand, and the
pages are turned. The book
contains a series of paintings
of the Madonna and Child.
The book is closed and
removed.

#11

#11
**Voice-over of male narra-
tor:** Books. I think of the poor
village schoolmaster, without
a library. Leafing through the
catalog for an upcoming
book fair, his hand passes
longingly over the unread
titles: *Don Quixote, The
Divine Comedy, Hamlet.*
Unable to purchase them, he
writes them himself. Then my
first book, the pages, one
yellow, another without lines,
still another from newspaper,
eight in all, on the cover

#11
Loop of whistling sound from
Gary Lewis's song "Save Your
Heart for Me."

scrawled *Empire of Flora.* On the inside, seven words: *angel, royal, tiger, twin, cardinal, brave,* and *sigh.* The words in pencil, almost hidden among pages of scribble-scrabble: yellows dripping, blotches of red, spirals here and there, held together by glue. Written under banishment, it marked my return, not like a poet, but a warrior, triumphant, casting a shadow, proclaiming, "I have written my story." Finally, a great writer, 83, now blind, confiding to a tape recorder, "I'll tell you a secret. I still go on buying books. I still fill my house. I feel the friendly force."

#12	#12	#12	#12
As in scene 5, the Stand-in for Roussel's mother dances on the beach, continuing her narrative.	As in scene 5.	**Sync sound.** *The Stand-in for Roussel's mother narrates breathlessly, continuing from scene 5:* Not wishing to insult someone who was traveling with a letter of introduction from the governor. The warrior, it seemed, came from an almost extinct tribe, who, sensing their demise, had vowed only to speak in their warrior dialect, which allegedly included some rather fierce gestures. This particular warrior had taken a bride from a neighboring island, and although she couldn't speak the warrior dialect, she had, after many years of cohabitation, gotten the basic gist of it.	As in scene 5.

#13

#13

The scene begins with a close-up of Masaccio's painting, *Expulsion from Paradise.* Then the camera shifts to the side to show a postcard made from cut-out figures of Adam and Eve. Eve reclines on a chaise lounge. Adam is fleeing from her, his head in his hands. They are pasted over a newspaper photograph of an airplane, captioned "Of TWA Flight 547." A hand-tinted old silent film begins. A title is keyed over the film: "Museum of Copies: Inspiration." Maidens in togas dance around the front of the facade of a classical temple. An intertitle from the film appears: "The Kiss of Love." Two women descend a stone staircase

#13

Voice-over of American female child narrator:
Dearest Mama,
We have just left Lutha, famous for its museum, which houses paintings and sculpture worthy of Mount Olympus. Here, originality is forbidden. The age of great art has passed, and the responsibility of modern art is to imitate. There are two museums, one for old work, where only patrons may enter, and occasionally an

#13

Loop of general ruckus noises, such as the sound of gym shoes squeaking on the floor.

and pause next to a statue.
One of the women tosses a
bouquet of flowers over the
statue.

The other woman places her
bouquet at the statue's feet
and then kisses the statue on
the lips. A man suddenly
comes to the top of the
staircase and catches her
doing this.

artist of extraordinary promise, so they can copy the
masters, seek inspiration. In
general, artists copy from
copies. New copies are shown
in the other museum. Though
it is open to the public, only
critics attend. Being guests of
honor, we were allowed access
to both museums. Since
leaving Lutha, Gustave has
been overwhelmed by
melancholia. He sits idly for
hours, chastising himself,
saying, "How stupid to be
saddened by statues." Then he
will abruptly shift moods,
laughing maniacally, saying,
"Only ostriches can digest
stone."
One thousand tender
thoughts,
Your loving son,
Raymond.

The female artist's face is filmed in profile, in front of a green curtain.

The female artist is shown with her back to the camera. She wears a white low-cut chiffon gown, with a green short-sleeved T-shirt under it. One hand is on her hips, and the other rests on a classical style sculptural pedestal next to her. She faces a backdrop consisting of a painting of a rustic ruin and a green

Sync sound.
The female artist speaks:
Well, we couldn't find it. We looked from hill to hill, and in rooms full of paintings from the same time, I mean century. Even the lady behind the counter agreed, what a beautiful painting, although she was talking about another. Well, the painting wasn't there, but the space was. There was a crack to mark its absence.

curtain that frames its left edge. She resembles the pop-up book painting in scene 2.

There is a cut, so the female artist is facing the camera, which zooms in to frame her face more tightly.

Cut to a close-up of the female artist's face, as she looks into the camera.

Surely, the painting would have covered it. After he had shown us the painting, he agreed, what a shame, instead of all this academic stuff. Well, we got our money back, we thought because we said we were artists. But, afterward, I realized that it was because he thought we had come a long way to see it. So we left with the memento of an unseen image. We paid more for the copy than it costs to have a peek at the real. At least, we can have it forever. Would I have preferred an instant of the

real, or should I be satisfied
with this copy, though I can
keep it forever?

#14

#14

A close-up of a hand resting
on a globe. The continent of
India is framed so that it
appears in the center of the
screen. A title appears over
an overhead shot of a table
setting: "Requiem for Taste."
On the bachelor's side of the
table setting (identifiable by
a postcard size depiction of
the malic molds from
Duchamp's *Large Glass*)"the
edge of the plate is visible.
On the bride's side (identifiable by a postcard size
depiction of the bride from
Duchamp's *Large Glass*) is
another plate, flanked by
silverware.

#14

**Voice-over of Italian female
narrator:** Crawling on all
fours, without speech, little
Gustave heard everything.

#14

Cut to the globe, which spins behind a close-up of a hand.

Cut to the camera panning across the bride's side of the table setting. A still from the movie *The Shanghai Express*, is on a plate that is surrounded by a ring of cut-up carrots. On another plate next to it, Jacques de Gheynll's painting *Poseidon and Amphitrite* is surrounded by a circle made of crackers. The camera also reveals a conch shell, a Norman Rockwell painting of Thanksgiving dinner, a map, a

As a small child, he had been allowed entry to his father's study. The books were heavy, maps bright, and the desk he thought to be cold. All were eaten. His mother, a smile creeping to her lips, would tell of her naughty little child, locking himself in the study, laughing at the window. She had reluctantly called for his father. Later, every time Gustave knocked, pain would rush to his hand, and he would be overwhelmed by an image.

photograph of the couch in Freud's examining room, a Viennese dessert, and Heartfield's collage *Adolph the Superman Swallows Gold and Spouts Junk.* A very brief cut interrupts this pan. The image is of blood or red paint dripping on a white shroud.

After this abrupt insert, the shot of the spinning globe alternates with the pan across the table setting.

A dwarf wearing a large blue silk turban, arms folded, sword at his side, standing in front of him. His knees would tremble. Of his childhood, he couldn't think past a large wooden door, he, on the outside, knuckles and knees bruised and bleeding. The door was unmoved.

Four naked white female dolls laid on a blue surface

Voice-over of male narrator: Four words, hastily

Sound of general ruckus, including breaking glass.

are filmed from overhead.

A hand enters the frame,
covering the dolls with hand-
colored pictures of Charcot's
Hysterics from Salpetierre.

written on separate scraps of
paper, sealed in an enve-
lope, the exterior meticu-
lously marked *care of the
Prince of Moscow.* Roussel
didn't even write letters, only
postcards. The sealed
envelope brought on a
phobic reaction. Who knew
what had been entombed?
Maybe it's a joke? I remember a story. At his funeral, a
group of close relations
huddled. One whispered,
loudly, his epitaph should
read, "Here lies a drug-
crazed homosexual scrib-
bler." They all tittered. I
return to the sealed words:
friend, look, hypnosis, kill.
How to make them mine?
Forget myself, then use them
in a story. She knew they
were going to kill her. They

This sound occurs periodi-
cally throughout the rest of
the scene. Shouting male
voices and a screaming child
can be distinguished out of
the din.

There is a cut to a hand-colored photograph of Little Richard, the rock and roll singer.

had been close friends since she was a little girl. They had adored her, called her their heart's desire. Now, she cried out, "The flames are spreading, save me." They look on passively as she tugs on coat sleeves, begs at petticoats. They whisper, "You're being hysterical, making a spectacle of yourself." They turn away, ashamed. I recognize the story, voodoo, a real-life melodrama bracketed within the making of a fun-filled musical, *The Pirate*, about hypnosis, with Garland and Kelly. I look at my story. Four new words jump out: *heart, desire, spectacle,* and one unseen, *conversation.* A smile sneaks to my lips as I say, "The words are the same, but

The camera pans to show four women sitting in a row, singing lines serially. Sometimes they sing alone and sometimes simultaneously. They are hysterics, being orchestrated in a hysterium.

One woman has bleached blonde hair and sunglasses. Sometimes only the women's mouths are visible in close-up shots as they sing. Another woman wears a piece of fabric around her head and has long dangling earrings. A third woman is blonde and wears a purple dress with a large bow at the collar. They make hysterical gestures as they sing their lines.

different. They are close relations."

Sync sound.

One of the women sings, her voice wavering: I want to be your friend. Won't you come over for a cup of tea? But first, let me tell you. Just don't look at me.

#15

A hand pulls aside a red cloth to reveal an image and then covers it again.

#15

The image that is revealed is a "*Michelin* map of pain and productivity." An arrow points from a section

#15

#15

labeled *productivity* to one labeled *symbol*. Cutouts of sunglasses and a lounge chair are pasted on top of the map.

#16
As in scenes 5 and 12, the Stand-in for Roussel's mother dances on the beach, continuing her narrative.

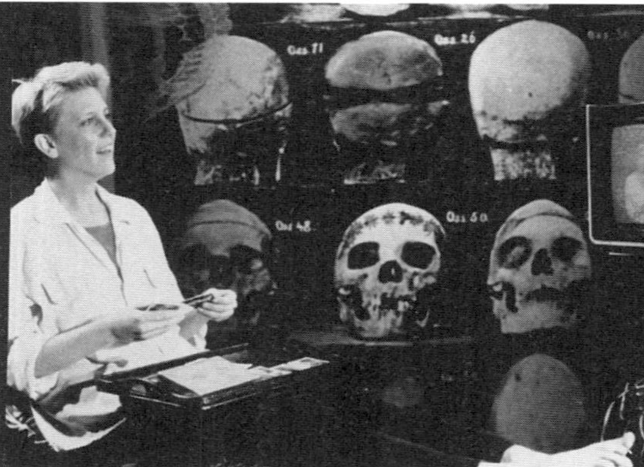

"Home of Nauseating Repetition," from *The Amazing Voyage*

#16
As in scenes 5 and 12.

#16
Sync sound.
The Stand-in for Roussel's mother, continuing from scene 12: "Well, surely, I can speak to her," my son said. "Not so easy," said the head of the company. "Although she is quite gifted in languages, speaking four major and three tribal dialects, she shared a language with only one of our dancers, who neither you or I can understand." "Well, I guess that's the end of it," my son said. "Not so fast," said the head of the company.

#16
As in scenes 5 and 12.

Title: "Flaubert the Infant: Home of Nauseating Repetition." The camera pulls back to reveal a backdrop of images of skulls decorated in a domestic fashion. There is a Norman Rockwell painting pasted on the surface of the TV set screen. The Stand-in for Flaubert's mother sits in a lounge chair in front of the skull backdrop. A brief image of a woman's legs and feet, wearing fashionable patterned stockings and boots, pacing across a linoleum-tiled floor, is inserted here.

Voice-over of Italian female narrator: It has been written of Gustave's mother, Caroline Flaubert, née Fleuriot, that she had the saddest of childhoods. It was almost like a novel. Her parents, madly in love, had eloped. Her mother died giving birth to her, the father ten years later. She saw her childhood mourning as a repudiation. People would rather die than take care of her. She loved her own sons, but not tenderly. She adored the tasks and accoutrements of mothering: diapers, swaddling clothes, the cradle. This love without tenderness is called absolute devotion. Gustave was born between two deaths. His parents

Sync Sound.
The Stand-in for Flaubert's mother speaks as she plays cards, but what she is saying is barely audible.

Cut to the playing cards with the paintings of nudes on them being laid out on top of the anamorphic portrait of Flaubert. In the remainder of the scene, the shots of the Stand-in for Flaubert's mother playing cards, the pacing legs, and the spread of nude playing cards alternate.

overprotected him to mask their resignation. For his mother, he was dead from birth. She guarded him against death, while inflexibly awaiting its arrival. He was nursed in the family apartment at the Hotel-Dieu, commonly referred to as a cemetery for the living. His father was the head doctor. Their hallway was a thoroughfare. Each morning, the public dead were dragged through. Their basement housed corpses, and in the amphitheater adjacent, limbs were dissected. The living quarters themselves reeked with the aroma of phenoil and decomposition. No one lives there anymore.

In half a century, the grand-
sons have finally accepted
what their grandmothers had
always told them. This was
no place to raise a family.

. . .

Constance DeJong
For Steve Fagin Who Made
The Amazing Voyage of Gustave Flaubert and Raymond Roussel Whose Fathers and Mothers . . .

Mother will never see the place where I live. She is too frail now to climb the steps, three flights of stairs to the top of the house where I live, the entire floor an apartment behind a narrow door, grimy and years smudged and with a lock so flimsy any pistol-brave man could break right through. Brave. Mother is too frail to face the journey that would lead to the narrow door, a journey involving cars and at least one airplane, involving roads and airport, travelers and vehicles moving on schedules too daunting for an eighty-three-year-old body that can travel only at the speed of sound, her voice every Sunday on the telephone. . . .

And for her eighty-three-year-old eyes unclouded now by a laser's beam, there are pictures, my amateur snaps of the apartment—especially of the so-called living room with its contents, a careful composition of things and more things occupying the territory.

In this occupied territory I am (as yet) no prisoner confined to a four-walled world. Through the smudged, narrow door I come and go, arriving and departing on no schedule fit to other travelers. This where I live for the time being, which I don't call "my" apartment, this place is no destination for the voyager seeking to see the world . . . though there is a world in here. . . .

Oh, how big I am next to my favorite little blue cup. Oh. Not such a big girl in the faux Scandi chair that was once the bad-girl seat turned to face the wall in the corner of my parents' living room. Oh. How did Mr. Carroll get in here?

The only looking glass in my living room is seldom central to the composition, a maroon-colored box sitting on my dead father's table. It's my thirteen-inch Sony Trinitron with its inert black glass screen that electricity coaxes to light, life.

How big my little Sony is now that these thirteen inches belong to Steve Fagin, now that his *Amazing Voyage* animates inches and flatness and the contained space of a box with things and more things that belong together only here. *Here* is where the dead and the living and the inanimate overlap or coexist. Or, *here* all things —including sound and language—are elements carefully composed, made to come together, to come apart. Or, elements *here* are details of an investigation that is fingering shards of memory, shuffling in a drawer, a receptacle that harbors a world of sorts; or the world of physical spaces occupied by bodies and objects is seldom referenced *here*. Or, the space of *here* is shaped by memory and imagination and other activity that might be called mental. And if only the word *here* was as definite as four-letter words in our language that drive a point home. Or, if only the separate categories I've made—things and activities and spaces—could now mix together as fruits of a different feather. . . . But, no, my metaphoric silliness fails to conjure Steve Fagin's shifting and shuffling around of elements made to live multiple lives, shaped along no single line of inquiry, never delivering the tidy resolution that is the true fiction of order and certainty. And never mind about how big my little Sony is now that this paragraph studded with *or*'s and *if*'s is a trail of crumbs long sentenced to a point of no return. No, Lewis Carroll will not be seen again here.

I see S. F.'s voyage as someone, as Mother, anyone might first see my place . . . see pieces of a composition, fragments, not the whole thing hanging together. Once, twice, three times I've sat and watched. And still the voyage is a passage of time, a movement I can't hold together, gather into one location in my mind as does the author, who knows each small and large element, what and where it fits: ". . . most densely in the [section] called 'Dying in Front of the Large Glass: The Perfect.' The music: the Shangri-Las singing 'and that's called sad' over and over again, mixed with Bellini's *Norma*. The images, domesticated versions of Orientalism: Ingres's odalisque turned into a couch, Gérôme's Napoléon turned into a footstool, and the Sphinx now a lamp—what an odd notion of ready-mades! And Magritte's *Human Condition* joined at the horizon line of sky and sea by a baseball game. Don Larsen and Yogi Berra, hugging, after the perfect game. The voice track: talking of Roussel dreaming of heaven, imagining Dante, but finding only street names, monuments, and medals, 'it was perfect.'"[1]

Perfection. With experience, a past, some so-called education, I can perfectly well identify, recognize this and that element of the *Amazing Voyage*. Shall I name the parts, some bits and pieces you perhaps have seen or not seen for yourself? Or would you rather skip to the good parts? Because without prior knowledge the act of recognition is less cozy, less a salve massaging the little self who does so like to know and know. Because without names, the identities perfectly well known, the act of recognition is more startling, more engaging—a knock-knock on the psyche, or perhaps the heart, some chamber that taps out a message in a quickened pulse that continues to sound, send out waves. For examples: a ring of cookies on a picture plate, a group portrait of unknowns, one of whom is "conducting" under a portrait of Little Richard; two baseball players hugging/dancing; fake jewels dangling among goldfish; thatched huts, bleached villas, landscapes I've never visited, never seen before. . . . But this is only a list; the waves do not arrive in the shape of words.

Shapes. My little maroon Sony sits on a low, rectangular table that, like so many objects that once belonged to the now dead, now belongs to the living—the passage of things a long biography of objects that are aging at a different rate than the past and present owners, than the bodies that come and go. So here is my present body moving through a couple of compositions, one made by me, one by Steve Fagin, the living room and the maroon box. Oh, not the containers, silly. The contents, the contents . . . the two compositions belonging to a process that never ceases to intrigue and attract. It works like friends and lovers who venture to know through fragments of the selves arranged to approximate a whole with parts forever unknown, out of reach, beyond grasping. . . .

Love? Why not mention it? Since compositions are loving acts, mindful acts, entailing work and deliberation and loads of ideas, received and less received.

Three women in the *Amazing Voyage* represent received ideas, three among the many beautiful women pictured in colors and singing and saying, and surely S. F. loves women, colors, singing, and saying. . . .

The final say. Does it belong to men, to Gustave Flaubert, Raymond Roussel, these childless men writing of places and objects and mothers? . . . These childless men are not, I think, not Steve Fagin's way of representing Father, though without a body, without an image of these childless, talking, writing men. . . . Oh, the power of language.

And so with no men in sight, with Gustave and Raymond appearing in voice only, in sound and in words, Steve seems to be saying to me that language lives beyond the corpus that is aging and dying at a rate more rapid than the objects that linger on, linger on through successive lives. The *Amazing Voyage* seems to say: language is witness that survives. So comes the unspoken message: in the late twentieth century the witness is located not only in pages turning, in books, but in these boxes that Steve Fagin and electricity coax to life. So here's to boys and men without faces or bodies, a succession of voices, a broken line running through. . . .

Oh. The music. One cannot forget the music, the fragments of culture, pop, and *operandpop.* The sound track spikes the inner ear of we who have occupied our rooms and theaters and our cars, listening, acquiring a collection of memories. To my ears, these sounds of music selected and assembled for the *Amazing Voyage* do not operate like the video's spoken fragments of writing. These sounds of music are not exactly language's system of association and memory. And ignorance has a role to play too. So let us play . . . dodge the direct blow, the KO of ignorance for a little shadow boxing; a little, glancing knock from the osmotic process, the process through which culture seeps into us, into that maroon box temporarily housing the composition of Steve Fagin. *Here*—not knowing which opera, which girl group, which specific name to attach to the general recognition of opera and teen time, is not exactly ignorance, not quite a blow that flattens us.

Most objects are silent. Even now the little thirteen-inch realm is a dead black screen again. Now Steve Fagin's passing "contents" emit their half-life in my head, perhaps in the room where particles of information continue to radiate, trapped in this place where my Sony sits on the table of my father too dead to ever again polish the slab of rosewood; too dead to ever again treasure its dark glow, its surface, a place to locate his silent objects . . . his fake Picasso ashtray, his. . . .

His stereo is missing. It played music in the night, only music, smoky and sultry, no words, no radio. And now his rosewood table supports that inanimate object made by Sony, that occasionally benign object. Because at times it is not television, is not receiving the broadcast, but is connected to other realms. So thank you inventor of the VCR; my little Sony now released from imprisonment in one TV world. Thank you Steve Fagin for amazing voyaging, of scale and detail, and this your brain-born thing . . . your loving composition.

So where in all these sentences, where are the individual insights, the treasures I have gleaned, the places I have visited from my couch now that my body no longer in the living room is in some place of pleasure received? So where is the stuff that knowledge is made of?

Oh, isn't that each of ours to . . . isn't that the Shangri-Las I hear? Another lingering emission from the *Amazing Voyage*, the Shangri-Las repeating, repeating, "and that's called sad." Hey girlfriends, you make the past collide with the present. You remind me . . . my aging body is not connected to pasts I never lived through save in this way, in this registering of S. F.'s, G. F.'s, R. R.'s compositions all lovered together. Hey. Maybe there's something like a future for these aging bodies, if something like electricity or love coaxes us to life, to voyages again . . . and that's called dying?

(Hey girlfriends, am I dead?)

(Hey, S. F., on a fifth viewing I saw I was mistaken; I saw R. R. and G. F. reflected in a looking glass for a moment, like a knock-knock on the psyche. . . . I think I know who's there.)

■ ■ ■

Sync sound.
The volume is raised so that
the speech of the Stand-in
for Flaubert's mother is
audible.

**Stand-in for Flaubert's
mother:** Aunt Mamie looked
at the note. I just went back
over and sat down and kept
watching the game because
I didn't know if Aunt Mamie
was really going to acknowledge the note or not. Then
I could tell that she was
starting to get a little irri-
table. She started saying
snide things about Aunt
Mertie's card playing and
how Aunt Mertie really was a
lousy cardplayer. The other
ladies in the room knew that
something bad was going to
happen.

Female voice, offscreen: What card game?

Stand-in for Flaubert's mother: Pitch. Ten-point pitch.

Female voice, offscreen: What's pitch?

Stand-in for Flaubert's mother: Don't ask me any details about pitch because I don't know. That's why I'm playing solitaire, because I don't play pitch. They never could take the time to teach me.

Female voice, offscreen: Is that some kind of Baptist game, pitch?

Stand-in for Flaubert's mother: No, the Baptists would never have allowed pitch. That's why Grandma Mary never played, because she's a devout Baptist, and

she never laid her hand on a
card.

Female voice, offscreen:
Grandma Mary's the mother
of Mertie?

**Stand-in for Flaubert's
mother:** No, they're all
sisters-in-law. They were all
married to the brothers, to
these three men who were
brothers. So they're all
sisters-in-law. They've known
each other for fifty years.

Female voice, offscreen: So
where were the husbands?

**Stand-in for Flaubert's
mother:** The husbands were
dead. They're not around
anymore.

#18	#18	#18	#18
In the silent film, some men in oriental costumes push a	Old hand-colored film. A title appears over the first part of	**Voice-over of male narrator:** I awake—4 A.M. Or	The sound of "Um Kalsoum," an Arabic singer, is mixed in

fat woman into a contraption made out of a barrel. They then light burners mounted on the contraption, and it ascends into the sky, like a rocket. In actuality, the film is shot indoors, on a stagey-looking set. The barrel travels through mock outer space. A large star appears in the sky with the head of a woman at the tip of each of its points. Then several women fall from the sky, waving their arms as though they are mimicking the motion of the falling stars. Several strangely costumed men fall from the sky, making swimming motions like starfish. Next, the large head of a man also appears in the "sky." A stream of women gushes from his

the film: "The Conquistado-res."

should I say I am awakened by pain? I'm frightened by the dark, but hear myself laughing. To avoid the pain, I try to write and think of a famous novelist. "Writing is the second most painful thing in the world," he says. The naive reporter falls into the trap and asks, "Then, why do you write?" "Because not to write is the most painful." I try to concentrate on Flaubert and remember yesterday. I had been so enthused. I had stumbled across something from their voyage, a remnant from Flaubert's niece, Caroline. "Take it away," she had told the junkman. "Who cares? What's the difference? Just get it out of here. Pay me

faintly with the narration.

mouth cavity. The original men and the fat women launch the barrel rocket again. This time it lands in a pool of water. They drag the woman out of the barrel and revive her with a pump.

anything." Somehow, from her hand to mine it passed from refuse to relic. I pay dearly. Sometimes, my eagerness gets the best of me. Now, it is no longer yesterday, but not quite tomorrow. I watch it over and over. Is it fiction? A travelogue? A home movie? I have trouble concentrating. The pain, again. The avoidance spreads. I no longer think of Flaubert and Roussel, but Cortez and Montezuma. Not an exploration, but a conquest. I decide to pursue what's called working through. At the end, Montezuma relays to the Spaniards, "You can have everything in my kingdom. Just grant me one request.

Don't look at me." The Spaniards think it to be a jest and don't reply. The next day, Montezuma kills himself. I think back to the beginning. The small renegade invasion party, the Aztec empire. Contrary to popular belief, the Aztecs are quite sophisticated in modern warfare, especially in what comes to be called reconnaissance. They have a network of spies relaying back to the capital every movement and gesture of the foreigners. An encyclo-pedia is compiled, and a secret weapon is built, specifically to throw the enemy back into the sea. The Aztecs march confi-dently into battle, waiting for the perfect moment to

bring forward their machine
of destruction. The moment
arrives. Cortez is sighted.
The weapon is brought
forward. It is Cortez's
double, the beard, the hand
movement, down to the
glance in the eye. Even his
horse has been cloned. The
Aztecs wait confidently for
the Spaniards to turn from
the double and flee in terror.
Instead, without breaking
step, they advance. The
Aztecs are shocked, and the
small invading party
conquers the massive
empire. My thoughts are
broken. I write a note:
history has been decided,
and difference will never be
the same. I chuckle. The
pain has subsided.

#19

#19

A postcard of Joan Crawford from the movie *Johnny Guitar* is on top of Masaccio's painting *Expulsion from Paradise.* Joan Crawford wears a white prom dress. Cutouts of musical notes have been pasted on the *Johnny Guitar* picture.

#19

Voice-over of American female child narrator:

Dearest Mama,
We have been sunning ourselves on Poliarcopolis pond. Gustave constantly complains about the air. He says, "But it is for the ocean that the tempest is made. Ponds, when they are stirred up, only give off unhealthy odors.
One thousand tender thoughts,
Your loving son,
Raymond.

#19

Sound of a triangle being played.

#20

As she talks about the dance, the Stand-in for Roussel's mother strikes a series of stylized dance poses.

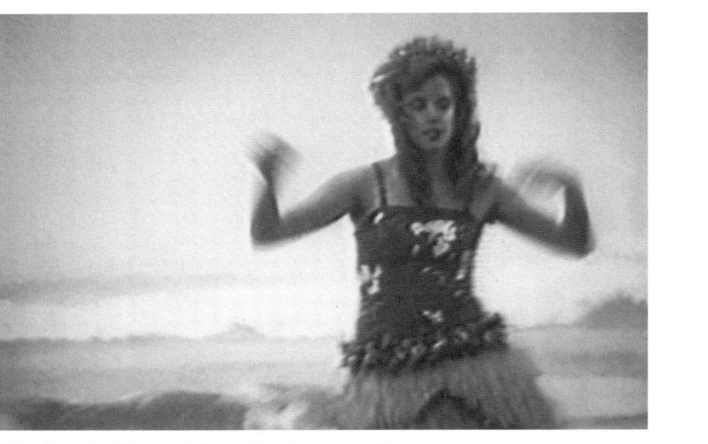

"The Land of Propp," from *The Amazing Voyage*

#20

The Stand-in for Roussel's mother stands on the beach, with the ocean behind her. She wears a dress with a floral-patterned bodice and a grass skirt.

#20

Sync sound.

The Stand-in for Roussel's mother speaks: My son has sent me some rare photographs. They come from the land of Propp. They are all that remains of the founding legend of this culture. The pictures document a dance. They are a series of poses from the dance with some notes on their backs. Nobody remembers the story or tune or dance. These fragments are all they know of their history. The notes tell of a king, a prince, a maiden, and an abductor. Something was stolen and after great hardship was returned. Who went searching, what was stolen, and by what means it was returned, all are a mystery. We do know the maiden became queen because there was a death and the lineage is now in her name. Whether she married the king or the prince is a mystery. But these limits don't stop the people of Propp from carrying on with a full feeling of origin, legitimacy, and custom. Each year, they hold a festival with a competition to select a song, dance, and tune to go along with the poses and notes. The only limit on the competition is that no one born during an ascendent moon can compete. Popular legend has it that the abduction took place during this period. After the festivities, a winner is selected by voice

vote, and the new legend is
dramatized for all to witness.
Then the people of Propp
return to their villages to live
a new myth of origin,
legitimacy, and custom, until
the following year.

#21
A hand pulls aside a purple
cloth to reveal an image.
Then another hand holds a
magnifying glass over
portions of the map that have
been revealed.

#21
The image that is revealed is
the "*Michelin* map of pain
and productivity" from scene
15.

#21
Voice-over of male narra-tor: Twenty questions. No,
three wishes. Don't be
greedy. I haggle with myself.
If only I could have talked to
them. What would I have
asked? I make a list, become
judicious. How unlike me!
Yes, I'll be fair. One question
for each. Two remain. They
surprise me. For Flaubert:
From someone afraid to even
meet its glance, is it really
true that one's greatest

#21

triumphs are in front of the mirror? Or is this said to fuel the passion of a narcissistic lover? For Roussel: A lover of children's plays, parlor games, cheap imitation. Why didn't you ever go to a movie? I imagine your comfort in the dark, close to the luminous screen, laughing: Langdon, Lloyd, and Stan Laurel. I rip up the paper. The questions are unworthy: one trivial, the other ponderous. One question remains. Which is which?

#22

#22
After a fadeout, there is a shot of a piece of purple fabric. A title appears over it: "Museum of Copies."

#22
Voice-over of American female adult narrator:
Ma Mere,
What a relief! A respite from golden flowers being blown by gentle spring breezes,

#22
The sound of a triangle being played is mixed with the narration, along with Muzak and the noise of breaking glass.

A hand pulls back the fabric
to reveal a corner of the
Michelin map. Cut to another
clip from the "Museum of
Copies" silent film that
appeared in scene 13. One
of the gowned women pulls
aside a theater curtain in
front of a backdrop depicting
a stage and a columned
building. Then she ignites
the flame of a ceremonial
torch. The scene shifts to a
large group of women doing
a dance, using long pieces of
fabric as props. They lift the
fabric above their heads,
like a canopy.

white sand beaches lazily
lapped by morning surf. The
fresh air was choking me.
Finally, I can breathe—art.
Last night, we were invited to
a salon. Raymond stayed
behind to write. It felt just
like home. Forty-five came,
and forty-three talked of a
single painter. The air
vibrated—not just whispers,
or even rumors, but gossip.
One sensed the nearness of
great art. A respected banker
insisted the model's cos-
tumes had been taken off the
body of a dead lover, preserved in a chest, only to be
worn for the paintings. An art
historian scoffed, the landscapes were hardly more
than copies, taken from
photographs, in a manner

similar to our camera obscura. I turned right and overheard a gray-haired gentleman reluctantly insist, being a close friend of the artist, that the decors are ludicrous, slapped together from whatever bric-a-brac happened to be nearby. I lurch in one direction, then sway in the other, trying to overhear every remark. I feel my arm being gently pulled, and I am drawn by my hostess toward the balcony. She insists the night air will do me good. Once away from the others, she whispers, "Don't listen to the bunch of them. The paintings, they're done exclusively from memory. The artist is blind."

Red paint is poured on a large piece of white paper. Then yellow paint is poured on top of the red. Next blue is added. The female artist, wearing the white prom dress and the green T-shirt, her hair protected by a rubber bathing cap, dives into the paint. It covers her dress. She spreads the paint around on the paper with her hands, mixing the colors together. She revolves in circles on her hands and knees, saturating her dress and limbs with paint, and then stops abruptly.

Hours later, I find myself back in the hotel, Raymond still sitting at his desk, shades drawn, paper tilted so. I try to tell him of the evening, but he insists, "Ten more minutes." The page in front of him has two words on it, but as to his habit, he sits in front of it daily for three hours, to the minute. What a fine little clerk he could have been. After ten minutes, I burst, but he hardly listens, and then interrupts to tell of a play he had written and taken to Amsterdam at great personal expense: full orchestra, sets, and cast. At 8:00 exactly, the play began. The massive auditorium had but one distant spectator, sitting right-side rear. The performance was given with gusto, and upon its completion, Raymond mounted the stage, thanked his audience, and after a deep bow, refunded their money. I asked if the tour had continued. He responded with incredulity in his voice, "After a command performance?" Anyway, please don't berate me again. I promise to send Caroline's birthday present soon. I just want to find something special.

Ton petit nou nou qui t'embrasse fort,

Gustave.

#23

Cut-up pictures of the movies *Morocco* and *A Woman's Face*. This is followed by a shot of swaying palm trees from an ethnographic film and a brief clip of a woman's mouth from the hysterium in scene 14. Then the shot of the palm trees recurs, interspersed with brief close-ups of the eyes of the Stand-ins for Flaubert's and Roussel's mothers and the women's mouths from the hysterium. There is a short excerpt from scene 9, showing the Arabic woman as she removes the veil from her face. Other shots of exotic locales from the ethnographic film are also mixed in.

#23

Voice-over of male narrator: Day's residue. Something avoided. To write on Roussel's *Impressions of Africa*. Something done. To daydream. I wanted to go to a movie, a Hollywood movie, in the style of Breton and Vache, to go in at the middle, make the images mine, then leave. But the movie is too compelling. I stayed to see it twice. It was called *A Woman's Face,* with Joan Crawford and Conrad Veidt; the others didn't really matter. It was about mad love, much better than anything by Breton. Roussel had described the surrealists as a trifle obscure. What a lovely comment, both too much and not enough at the same time. The movie—Crawford and Veidt making

#23

The sound of Muzak is mixed in faintly with the narration.

love, how ecstatic, in the American style, all at once and nothing happening. One side of her face, no longer scarred, but still veiled, now by a gauze light—foreplay. The other, dominated by a smoldering cigarette, denouement. And he, Conrad Veidt, in the foreground, graphically on top of her, playing the piano, fucking. Then they talk of a child, not an heir, that they will kill. At night, I dream of paintings in the orientalist manner, one by Renoir. A little red-haired girl and a slave. Another by Gérôme, a fair-skinned nude, also with red hair, but a woman, being washed by a black maid. But I don't see the images, but only hear them speak. The red-haired woman of Gérôme speaks with the child's voice of

Renoir. She talks of a movie, *The Naked Jungle*, with Eleanor Parker and Charlton Heston, which she in a child's voice eagerly describes: "Charlton Heston has this plantation with a brand new grand piano in the Amazon jungle. He buys Eleanor Parker and is disappointed to find out she's not perfect, like his piano, unused. Then Eleanor Parker tells him he knows nothing about pianos or women. They both play better after they've been broken in. Then they talk about the jungle, and he says the jungle is wonderful because it is the only thing that grows through its own negation. She says, that's a bunch of rubbish, and the only reason he's in the Amazon is because he's a soul being driven to death by romanticism. Well, near the

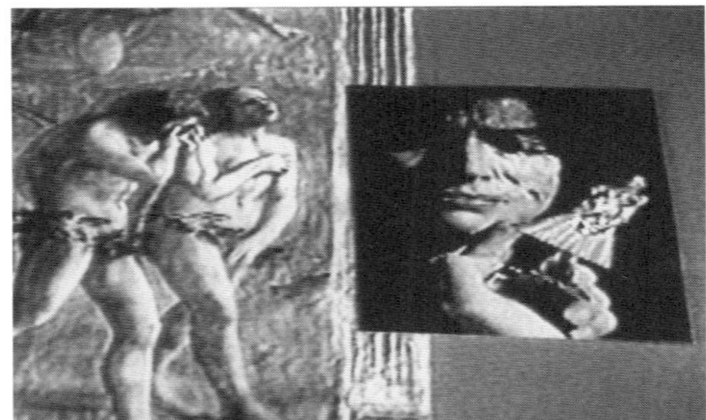

Collage based on *A Woman's Face*, directed by George Cukor, from *The Amazing Voyage*

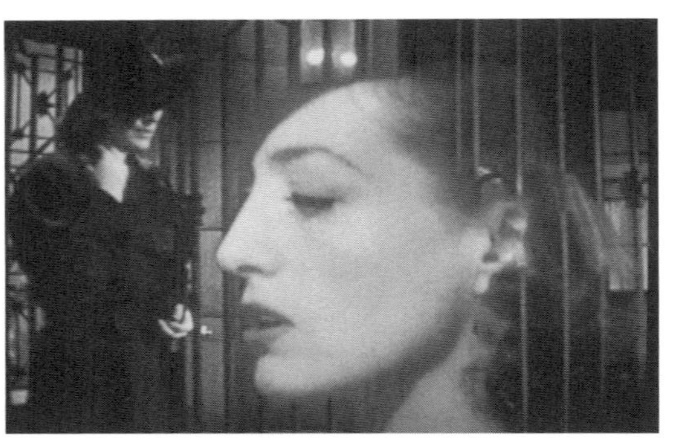

Still from *A Woman's Face* (1941), directed by George Cukor

end, they kinda fall in love, and he says, my heart is throbbing, and she says, I don't know if I love you or am only pretending, but it doesn't matter because there is no difference between a pleasure imagined and one brought about by chance." The slave interrupts and asks, "How does the movie end?" The Renoir child, speaking through the Gérôme bather, says, "An army of red ants eats the entire Amazon jungle."

Mark Rappaport A Woman's Face

Speaking of *A Woman's Face*. . . . Well, of course that's as good as the old-time comics' shtick, apropos of nothing, segueing into "speaking of mother-in-laws. . . ." Howls of laughter. If I break in here to talk about *A Woman's Face* (1941) directed by George Cukor, it's because (1) in the last few years it's become one of my favorite movies, (2) I was surprised to learn that Steve also loves it—even though we rarely agree about contemporary movies, we are in complete accord about the past—and (3) I hope to be doing, in the not-too-distant future, a film/video about the face and the fetishization of the star as icon, a work in which *A Woman's Face* will probably be the centerpiece. So basically I'm availing myself of these pages to try to work out some ideas and articulate some still inchoate thoughts.

The Story

She, Anna Holm (Joan Crawford), her face hideously scarred by a childhood accident, takes revenge on the world by becoming a gangster. She runs a blackmailing ring out of a restaurant she owns. (Don't ask who does the cooking, shopping for food, paying the bills. The restaurant is just a pretext to get the story rolling and is soon forgotten. Apparently, in a restaurant you can comfortably rummage about in your paying customers' overcoats and come up with some juicy tidbits that they'll pay you a lot of money to have returned. The restaurant as setting for such seedy activities will be replaced in movies of a similar ilk, in only a few years, by the psychiatrist's office—for example, Nightmare Alley [1947], a much more fertile hunting ground for incriminating information.)

At the restaurant she meets Count Barring (Conrad Veidt), a suave sleazeball. To suggest how sleazy he is, he has a foreign accent in this otherwise accent-free Hollywood movie. It's some kind of sign that he's some kind of bad. He also plays Chopin when he is alone. He turns out to be very bad indeed. He pretends not to notice that she is disfigured and treats her as graciously as if she were, well, a beautiful woman. She falls crazy in love with him. It becomes clear later in the movie that it's more complicated than that. She has been erotically awakened by Barring, the only man who has ever treated her courteously, that is to say, as a woman. She becomes his sex slave.

Since this is 1941, and since this is MGM, the codification of such a complicated arrangement has to be drawn with a very fine line, almost but not quite to the point of invisibility. Every time she wants to back out of some evil doings that he is planning, all he has to do is touch her arm, and she is like putty in his hands. Her badness, however, can be cured—by making her beautiful the way she was always meant to be. *He* is rotten to the core. And beyond. In an otherwise empty concession to the period in which the movie was made, he clearly is soon to be a Nazi, although the word itself is never spoken. His political philosophy, however, is unnecessary information in this melodramatic environment that doesn't really require grounding in contemporary realities.

On one of her blackmailing expeditions, Crawford is blackmailing a beautiful woman, so she ups the asking price—beautiful people should have to pay for their beauty, as we will soon find out. Anna/Joan, trying to leave the scene of the crime, sprains her ankle. As chance would have it, the blackmailing victim's husband is a renowned plastic surgeon. When he sees Anna/Joan's face, he falls in love with the possibilities of what one can do to a face like that. He and his wife, the woman Anna/Joan came to collect from, agree not to prosecute her, although each for entirely different reasons.

The doctor sizes up Crawford's face the way a potter might look at a lump of clay or a hungry man a buffet table. As the doctor (Melvyn Douglas) so gamely puts it, "It would be a shame to send a scar like that to prison." Unlike anyone else in Anna/Joan's life, he realizes what she has always known and what we the audience intuit, that she *is* her scar. There's none of this inside/outside dichotomy. You *are* what your face is. If you're deformed, clearly your physical appearance mirrors your soul. If you're beautiful. . . . Well, there you are. The challenge clearly excites him. He takes her on as a pro bono patient. The blackmailing plot, in case you're wondering, falls by the wayside. Drop whatever plot complications you don't need when you no longer need them. Perhaps that's what happens when thirteen writers (Donald Ogden Stewart gets a credit, Christopher Isherwood doesn't) who never get to sit in the same room cobble a script together.

More of the Story
After her operation, she becomes—*voila!*—Joan Crawford. Here's her chance to become a person every bit as good as her face is now beautiful. As her Pygmalion (or is he her Dr. Frankenstein?) says, I don't know what I've created. Is it a Galatea or a Frankenstein's monster? We will soon find out. Any bets?

It is after her operation that she agrees to be involved in some nefarious plot that Conrad Veidt has cooked up. If his scheme is carried out, she will be tied to him forever. At first she resists, but when he takes her by the arm (clearly her erogenous zone), her will dissolves. I think this is as far as we have to go with the plot proper. The rest of the film really belongs to another movie. For those who insist on knowing, Crawford kills Veidt rather than let him kill his four-year-old nephew whose governess she has become, and Douglas falls in love with Crawford, his perfect creation.

The Triumph of Local Color
The film is set in Sweden, primarily because the film it's based on, *A Woman's Face* (1938), directed by Gustaf Molander with Ingrid Bergman in the Crawford role, is a Swedish movie. Hollywood,

ever on the lookout for new exotic locations (even if they're all simulated on the back lot), sets the movie in Sweden, although there's nothing intrinsically Swedish about it. So, in order to justify the Swedish names, we're treated to a lot of local color, including peasant songs, Swedish (I'm only *assuming* mind you, but I'm prepared to take MGM's word for it) folk dances, including Crawford in a dirndl and a hat that the Old Dutch Cleanser girl would kill for.

All these surface trappings aside, however, it's the story of a bad girl who becomes a good girl. The disfigurement that made her bad permits her for the first time, when it's removed, to feel real love (instead of that horrible sex stuff) and to fall in love. Feminists please take note: the bad guy, Conrad Veidt crypto-Nazi, loves her "as is." That she is damaged goods doesn't bother him at all. On the contrary. It excites him. Douglas, the Pygmalion of plastic surgery, the good guy, loves her because of what he has been able to turn her into—that is, a beautiful woman, the woman of his dreams. But what really excites *him* is that she is a beautiful woman who knows a thing or two about the darker aspects of life. He has known beautiful women before but none who've walked on the wild side. What's interesting and peculiar about this film is that Joan Crawford is the star and presumably everyone who went to see the movie at the time it was made came to see the new Joan Crawford vehicle. They/we get the shock of seeing Joan scarred. It is built up like a great star entrance. First we see her shadow looming large on the wall, then we see the untouched left side of her face, then we see! . . .

A Little Digression

Unlike the Swedish movie on which it's based and, I'm assuming, the French play on which *that* is based, *Il y'était une fois* by Jean Croisset, this film is told in an elaborate set of flashbacks. Considering that it's a forties movie, that may not seem all that extraordinary. But considering that it's 1941, that *is* interesting. That was the very same year as *Citizen Kane*, which reinvented, for those who wanted or were able to use such an invention, the Hollywood narrative. Movies with a frame in the present and multiple flashbacks told by different characters were not yet in the Hollywood vocabulary as they were to become in post-Kane Hollywood.

In fact, flashbacks were to become a relatively common technique in film noir. (Think of *The Killers*, flashbacks interrupting flashbacks, *Mildred Pierce*, *Double Indemnity*, *Ruthless*, *Detour*— the list is a long one, and I'm only throwing out the first titles that come to mind to suggest how pervasive it was, although it was equally pervasive in Joseph Mankiewicz's films, *A Letter to Three Wives*, *All about Eve*, and *The Barefoot Contessa*, none of them noirs.) But not in 1941. Not yet. And certainly not at MGM, Louis B. Mayer's studio where glamorous stars languished in gorgeous gowns by Adrian. That was the glossy studio where no shadows lurked, where the only noir on the set was deliberately placed there by the cameraman. But, in 1941, not only were there no films told within this elaborate Chinese puzzle structure, film noir had not yet been born, invented, made, or given a name.

What makes this movie even more unusual is that, until Crawford and Douglas get cracks at the bat, the flashbacks are all by supernumeraries, minor characters who are not essential to the action—minor characters who can tell only as much as they know and no more, who can report only from a very limited perspective. It's as if Hamlet's story were indeed told by Rosenkrantz and Guildenstern. Even Nelly Dean in *Wuthering Heights* is more central to the action than some of the characters who tell Joan Crawford's story.

The Striptease as Art Form

It's already forty-five minutes into the movie. I know because I can look at the digital readout on my laser disc player. We've only seen the scarred Joan Crawford. The new Joan Crawford has been pulling her wide-brimmed hat over her newly reconstructed face. She no longer, as well she knows, looks like Quasimodo. So why are she and the camera in cahoots with this coy behavior? Anyway, forty-five minutes into the film, in Joan's flashback, we finally get to see Crawford as we and her audience of the time knew her. For the first time we see the right side of her face. This elaborate Hollywood striptease may or may not produce the desired effect. Since we already know, from past experiences, what our star looks like, what *is* being revealed? Are we supposed to gasp? Or what? And aren't there plenty of well-documented stories about actresses (Claudette Colbert, for example, and Audrey Hepburn when she was getting older) who insisted they be photographed only from certain angles?

But this is a familiar strategy in the "new life via plastic surgery" film subgenre—Humphrey Bogart in *Dark Passage* and Rock Hudson in *Seconds*. (If you can think of other examples, let me know.) The postop character becomes the familiar face that we've paid our price of admission to see. However, the unveiling of the face becomes a ceremony that is so ritualized that it parallels the more elaborate Catholic sacraments. These films, however, should not be lumped together with a sub-subgenre of this admittedly finite genre: the plastic surgery film, in which the patient unwittingly assumes the identity of a criminal or murderer or gets to look exactly like another character in the film. In any event, the unveiling of the face serves two purposes—suspensefully prolonging as long as possible actually seeing the outcome of what we already know and fetishizing the star face we were expecting to see anyway when all the unwrapping is done. In a sense we are reminded how truly *hard* it is to look like Crawford or Bogart or Hudson, how much *work* is involved. When the doctor first volunteers to operate, he tells her, "I warn you now. It'll be pain. Agony." Yeats said it, too: "To be born woman is to know— .../That we must labor to be beautiful." Just substitute *movie star* for *woman*.

I had this idea that it was like delaying an orgasm or something like that, not letting us see her new face. It's the kind of stuff that Hollywood is really good at. Five hundred shots of Joan's surgically enhanced face shot from different vantage points, with a mirror obscuring her newly operated side, until the audience is screaming as one, "Let's see it already!" Even the Ingrid Bergman version prolongs the moment of revelation quite skillfully, but without the finesse with which Hollywood has turned torture and calculated manipulation into an art form.

The complicated flashback structure also serves the same purpose. It delays the moment of release so that the revelation of the face becomes an apotheosis of screen stardom. Instead of having untold opportunities to fall into the star's face—which certainly has to be one of the implicit purposes of the close-up—we are continually denied the privilege of seeing it. Similarly, the convoluted flashbacks keep us away from that moment of the film as long as possible, until there is no way out. We must see that face, or else the movie can go no further.

Monstres Sacrés *and Other Monsters*

In a way, it's the same strategy that is used in horror films. At first you show only a little flash of monster. A quick cut here, a partial view there. You reveal the whole thing only when it becomes absolutely necessary, when the audience is despairing of ever seeing the monster or starting to think that it's been hoodwinked, that the budget never allowed for a full-scale monster. *That*'s when you cut to the monster. The delaying tactic in revealing either monster *or* movie star is conflated in Jerry Lewis's *The Nutty Professor* (1963). In a Jekyll-and-Hyde role, Jerry, the nutty professor of the title, an insecure, bespectacled nerd, drinks the forbidden concoction and turns into his alter ego, The Monster. We see any number of shots of peoples' responses to this creature. Gasps of horror, shocked faces, grimaces of repulsion. The suspense is intolerable. Finally, cut to—The Monster. It's Jerry Lewis as Buddy Love, lounge singer extraordinaire, replete with brilliantined hair, a powder-blue polyester suit, and pinky ring to go with. The Monster is Jerry Lewis–as–Dean Martin, his former straight man, lounge singer extraordinaire. It is also Jerry Lewis as we know him to be, when he is not playing infantile spastics. It is, in short, the film debut of the real Jerry Lewis.

After Crawford's "unveiling," it's a downhill slide into tired melodrama—the second part of the film. Interestingly enough, from this point on, with very minor interruptions, the story unfolds in a fairly straightforward manner. There's no more need to tease the audience. Crawford has turned into a good girl and will certainly thwart the evil intentions of Veidt, who was only good for sex anyway. Now, with Douglas laying claim to what was his all along, falling in love with the beautiful woman he created (talk about male narcissism!), we know how it's going to end.

The basic premise, by this point, has been forgotten—the face as a metaphor for the soul behind it. And, when the very last shot comes, you only wish it had been a long, creamy close-up of Joan, to send you away wondering if what you see is in fact what you get, if there might not be some doubt or a hint of darkness in the initial premise. Perhaps evil can and indeed *does* lurk behind the beautiful facade. Any noir film worth its noir salt would have flirted with that idea. But, even if it is protonoir, *A Woman's Face* was made well before noir directors understood more fully the implications of their material. Just imagine what Preminger might have done with the same story. Even the title of his *Angel Face* (1953) gives us a clue ("Face of an angel, soul of a devil," screams the ad copy).

But, in *A Woman's Face,* it is the concept, not the movie, that becomes an extended metaphor—the tortuous, convoluted road that becoming a star icon and a gorgeous face has to take to achieve its well-earned goal—audience adulation and box-office divinity.

Speaking of Croisset *and* Flaubert and Roussel. . . .

■ ■ ■

#24	#24	#24	#24
	A postcard collage, with its background a newspaper photograph headlined "Fatal 'Dance of Death.'" Over it are pasted dressed versions of Adam and Eve from the Masaccio painting and a table laid out with food and place settings. The postcard is on top of a reproduction of the Masaccio painting itself.	**Voice-over of American female child narrator:** Dearest Mama, We are in Tamar, and things are buzzing. Revolution is in the air. There are two claimants to the throne. Tomorrow, there will be a tribunal, and one will be chosen. Gustave says, revolutions are always going strong since every new government promises to put an end to them. One thousand tenderthoughts, Your loving son, Raymond.	Sound of bass warming up.

#25	#25	#25	#25
	A close-up of a facsimile of Joseph Cornell's *Medici Princess Box,* with the princess replaced by a	**Sync sound.** [Dialogue based on Deleuze's ideas.] *A woman speaks in an artificially high-pitched voice:*	

gremlin from the movie of the same name. A title appears over the image: "The Copy versus the Simulacrum."

The camera pulls back from the collage to reveal a woman manipulating a hand puppet, pretending to make the puppet speak. In response to the "puppet's" question, the hand puppet punches the "play" button of a tape recorder, and a voice on tape speaks: "My sibling rival—I do believe you overvalue appearances."

Come in, come in. You see that image over there? That guy's a fake. I've looked him inside out, upside down, all over, and I haven't found as much as a cheap designer label on that guy. I'm telling you, he's not worth the cardboard he's made of. *Addressing the gremlin:* Hey, you pervert, what have you got to say for yourself?

The puppet interrupts: I'm no sibling of yours. *The puppet presses the stop button and continues:* Holy Zeus, me! You're the one who likes the way things look, and I don't see why. You're the ugliest thing I ever saw in my life. What have you got to say to that, huh? Big shot!

The hand puppet punches
the play button again, and
the voice on tape speaks: "It
is you who go on and on
about authenticity. Anyone
can see you look nothing like
the original."

The puppet pretends to write
on a piece of paper, hum-
ming a wordless tune.

The puppet mutters: I hate
you. Oh, I hate you! *The
puppet tries unsuccessfully to
punch the stop button again.
The puppet finally hits the
button and retorts:* What!
Holy Zeus! You dirty sophist!
Don't you know resemblance
is a matter of internal
correspondence? Of course,
you wouldn't know anything
about that, you empty box,
you soulless piece of metal.
Look at this!

Now, that's soul for you!
Look, I've been holding out
on this, but here's the big
secret of my success. Come
here, look at this.

Look at this, simulacrum, I'm
attached to the original!
What do you say to that?

The puppet points to the
woman's shoulder.

The puppet punches the play
button on the tape recorder.
The voice on tape answers:
"You've been falsely representing yourself."

"You're only five fingers on a
hand."

"You have no independent
status."

"Without dismemberment."

The puppet interrupts: I
haven't been falsely representing myself.

The puppet retorts: Well,
they've done me good so
far.

The puppet protests: I move
around quite freely on my
own.

*The puppet punches the stop
button and shrieks:* What!
Dismemberment! Dismem-
berment! You didn't say
anything about dismember-
ment. There's nothing in

The woman's other hand
picks up the script from the
table, and the puppet
examines it.

The woman punches the play
button on the tape recorder
with her free hand: "As I was
saying, without dismemberment, you aren't part of the
world of representation at all.

here [indicating the script]
about dismemberment.

I am taking a train, I'm
getting out of here. *The
woman addresses the puppet
in her own voice:* Hold on!
Hold on! Let's just hear what
he has to say.

The puppet explodes:
Dismemberment! It gives
me the creeps just to think
about it. Well, I could do
without you, too. You're just a
sore loser. *The puppet
begins repeating the words
of the recorded voice,
mocking them.*

[The tape is drowned out by the noises the puppet makes.] The collapse of authenticity by changing the model from sameness to difference." The puppet pushes the stop button.

The puppet carps: Shut up, you big. . . . *The woman interrupts in her own voice, addressing the puppet:* OK, hold on a second, OK? Look you two, let's remember. . . . *The puppet begins to repeat her words, mocking them in the same way. The woman reprimands the puppet:* Hey, knucklehead, that's me you're imitating there. Let's remember who's running the show here. I'm the author here. Besides, what do you want from a copy? Of course, he's misrepresenting himself. Let's just stick to illusion, OK?

The voice on tape replies: "All right, all right already." Then the puppet pushes the stop

The woman continues: Look, I didn't want to barge in here,

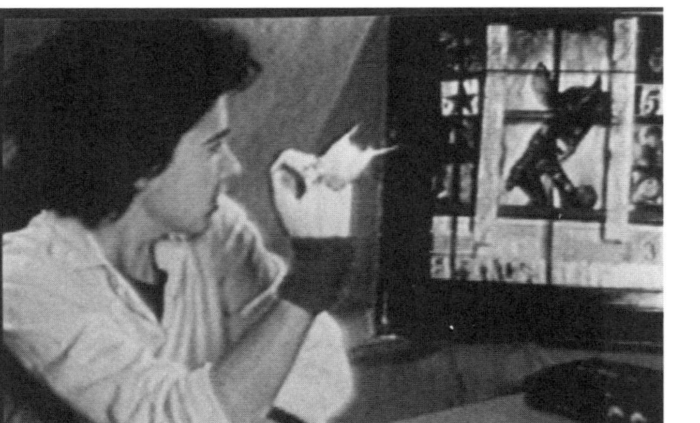

Valerie in "The Copy vs. the Simulation,"
from *The Amazing Voyage*

The puppet punches the tape
recorder's play button, and the
voice on tape says: "If you

but where would I be without
my little buddy, the copy?

The puppet interrupts to sing:
My savior! Love and mar-
riage, love and marriage.

The woman proceeds:
Besides, if we did what you
did, simulacrum, and
destroyed the model of
sameness, we'd destroy the
model of otherness, or
difference.

The puppet interjects: Yeah,
and then where would you
be, big shot? What have you
got to say to that? Come on,
come on.

want to be the sun, so be it. As for me, I'd rather be the moon because it shines at night when you really need it. As for the sun, who needs it to shine when it's broad daylight?'' The puppet pushes the stop button and silences the voice.

#26
As in scenes 5, 12, and 16, the Stand-in for Roussel's mother dances on the beach, continuing her story.

#26
As in scenes 5, 12, and 16.

#26
Sync sound.
The Stand-in for Roussel's mother speaks: Not wishing to insult someone traveling with a letter of introduction from the governor. . . .

#26
As in scenes 5, 12, and 16.

#27

#27
A close-up of the interior of a fish tank.

#27
Voice-over of American female adult narrator:
Ma Mere,
If he mentions Jules Verne

#27
Ruckus sounds, including a hammer pounding, a rooster crowing, a horse whinnying, a phone ringing.

once more, I'll scream. No, I can't scream. My ears ache too much, from having to listen to Raymond over and over again. Or maybe my anguish is due to this extended undersea voyage. Two agonizing weeks, which sounded so tranquil in the travel brochure, petrified shrubs will dart here and there in grimacing zigzags. Fish will rise up in masses at your footsteps, like birds surprised in the tall grass. You will pass through deep holes, fathomless grottoes, at whose bottoms will be heard horrible stirrings. Your heart will leap to your mouth as you are confronted by terrifying octopuses who intertwine their tentacles like a living thicket of serpents. The originality of Roussel's repetition doubles the anguish. He doesn't go on about the sea, but about the ice and the cold, of John Hateras and a tundra of red snow, which each spring produces streams of blood. The captain who braved the Arctic without a coat, and by now I know the section in Verne by heart, "'Oh, the question of clothing is trivial,' replied the doctor. 'What's the use of putting warm clothes on something that cannot generate heat? That would be like trying to warm a piece of ice by wrapping it in a woolen blanket.'" Anyway, soon it will be over. As you requested, I am sending you some rare gems for your collection. Yes, I

Cut to another view of the underwater fish tank. On the back of the tank is a picture of a red ant lifting a huge object. Pieces of jewelry float in the tank.

know, I teased you and
called them just a pile of
rocks, but if they please you,
my anguish will melt away.
Love to Caroline.
Ton petit nou nou qui
t'embrasse fort,
Gustave.

#28

#28

A hand holding a scissors is cutting up photographs. One photograph is from the film *Morocco*. Another is from *A Woman's Face*. The hands arrange the cut-up fragments into a replica of a Magritte-type painting. The background surface is a shroud with a red stain on it, resembling either paint or blood.

#28

Voice-over of male narrator: Hardly a picture. My mind saturated by an empty image, Rimbaud in the desert. His travels in Abyssinia and Harrar are published by the Geographical Society. They're a huge success, and a second edition is planned. It awaits his picture. They write, asking for a photograph. He absentmindedly ignores the request. His career is ruined,

#28

Fred Astaire singing a Cole Porter song. The words are "Soon, you'll be without the moon." This alternates with Ella Fitzgerald singing another Cole Porter song, "You're the Top."

his work never solicited again. I change, from emptiness to disguise. Fantômas, master criminal of deception, created by Souvestre and Allain. Under the pressure of their triumph, the public demands a new episode weekly. They conspire. Each will write separate chapters. The work is coded. If written by Souvestre, the word *néanmoins* appears on the first page. If by Allain, toutefois. The words mean the same thing, "nevertheless." I have so few images of either. Flaubert and Roussel prove so hard to capture. Perhaps, like Juve pursuing Fantômas, I should change tactics. No longer chase, but lie in wait, catch them by surprise, lurk in their dreams.

#29

A series of postcards are laid on top of the Massaccio painting by a black-gloved hand. The first is Joan Crawford in A Woman's Face with the cutout of Eve wearing a dress pastred on it. The second has a background of a photograph of an airplane from a newspaper. Adam and Eve from the Massaccio painting are pasted on it. Eve reclines in a loungechair. The third is of Joan Crawford wearing a white prom dress from Johnny Guitar. Musical notes are on top of it. The fourth is of a newpaper photo, headlines "Fatal Dance of Death". Over it are pasted dressed versions of Adam and Eve and a table laid out with food and table settings.

#29

Voice-over of American female child narrator:
Dearest Mama,
No time to write.
One thousand tender thoughts,
Your loving son,
Raymond.

#29

The sound of a piano being played.

All these postcards have appeared in the tape previously. A new postcard is added, but its appearance onscreen is not long enough in duration to distinguish its features.

#30

#30

A surveillance camera randomly scans a globe of the moon. The area labeled *Mare Cognitum* is visible. Cut to an overhead shot of a bed. Next to it is a pair of legs wearing pants, writhing on the floor. The rest of the body is not within camera range. A surveillance camera scans the scene in a mechanical rotation, back and forth. Finally, the legs stop moving.

#30

Voice-over of Italian female narrator: Proust de la nuit. How sweet! Tropposdolcinato. Proust of the night. What do they know of the night? Roussel was born nearby. Their families traveled in the same circle. They even corresponded briefly. Think of Proust, head propped just so, comforter pulled snugly, coffee still warm. His is the art of memory, pulling the dream

#30

Sound of dripping water, associated with scenes of torture (i.e., "Chinese water torture").

back to the dawn. At first,
Roussel scribbled madly,
days at a sitting. Later, he
would writhe on the floor for
months, unable to write a
single word. Finally, he
invented a system. A good
session yielded five words.
Chapters would take years.
He had begun writing in
ecstasy and ended without
joy. His is not the art of life,
or even of death, but of death
reheated, feigning life,
death, dreaming. Language
supends death twice over.
Before the first—Proust. And
after the last—Roussel. If you
want to know where the sun
goes at night, just watch.

#31
As in scenes 5, 12, 16, and
26, the Stand-in for Roussel's

#31

#31
Sync sound.
The Stand-in for Roussel's

#31
As in scenes 5, 12, 16, and 26.

mother dances on the beach as she narrates.	As in scenes 5, 12, 16, and 26.	*mother speaks:* Not so fast, said the head of the company. It just so happens I can understand a bit of the pidgin gesture subdialect the dancers have invented to communicate among each other, and I can translate it to you.	
#32	#32 A graph of Flaubert's horoscope fills the screen. The "*Michelin* map of pain and productivity" is uncovered when a red cloth is pulled aside. A corner of the	#32 **Voice-over of male narrator:** Notes to notes. Fragments to fragments. My hand trembles as I write. Why Flaubert? Because he is the imaginary. With him, I am at the border, the barrier of dreams. It's not that he despises a practical life; he doesn't even comprehend it. To dream of wanting to be a writer is to dream of a future dream. On his mother and niece? What a strange	#32 The sound of a bass being picked, played at the wrong speed, and mixed with a loop of Gary Lewis singing "Save Your Heart for Me."

dynasty of Carolines, whose first and last members murdered their mothers. And on the beloved Emma? The entire problem is the value left in her. If she had nothing, death would not be necessary. I stop. I hold the pan too tightly as I think; to copy a writer near nothing is to add a great deal. You are left with language, minus courage.

map with a primitive camera drawn on it is on view. A case containing a miniature pair of opera glasses is opened by a pair of hands. The opera glasses are removed. The fingernails of one of the hands are painted red. The fingernails of the other hand are unpainted. The hands replace the opera glasses in their case; they cover the map again with the red cloth.

#33

A hand lights three vigil candles.

A pair of hands enters the image from the left, replacing the flowers in a vase adjacent to the vigil candles with flowers of a different color.

#33

The vigil candles appear in front of a poster. The bottom corner of the poster is visible. It is labeled *European Paintings: The Metropolitan Museum of Art.* As the camera tilts up, the rest of the poster is revealed to be a composite image. The bottom is

#33

Voice-over of American female adult narrator:

Ma Mere,

Last night, eating vegetables and rice, I knew I was missing you. Me, who loves chewing the bones and eating the marrow. How I used to make fun of your finicky habits. And

#33

Mexican music of a generic variety is mixed with a fakey Japanese string instrument being plucked.

Gérôme's *Pygmalion and Galatea.* The top is a movie placard of Ava Gardner in a Mexican jacket with Humphrey Bogart, from *The Barefoot Contessa.* The camera pulls back so that a movie being projected to the right of the poster also becomes visible. The movie contains scenes of terrorism, ruins, dinosaurs, and volcanos.

now I find myself recognizing you in my voice saying, "No, just vegetables, preferably green ones, with rice, brown rice." Unfortunately, once again, I'm ill. This time, it's too much sun, so I only go out at night. But the wind howls, so I don't go too far. We are in Orfeno, which the guide tells us is a country obsessed with mourning. Everyone wears black. This strikes me a bit odd. I remember reading that Orfenoans were immortal. I query our guide. He laughs and remarks, "Yes, they are immortal. But it's not for themselves that they mourn, but for what *you* call nature." Still unclear, I ask him to describe this nature. He rattles off a list: flowers, trees, streams, birds, books, buildings, fish, fowl, films. He waves his hand and says, "Et cetera, et cetera, et cetera." Later, we learn that the Orfenoans mourn in two distinct manners, what they call diurnal and nocturnal. Each assumes a complete and distinct lifestyle. The other tourists at our hotel endlessly repeat the same stale joke, "You meet any Orfenoan, and he's as different as day and night." Raymond laughs, each time. Even our guidebook has two different translations for each of their words. Let me read a column. By day: *Gérôme, ruin, India, requiem, touch, glass.* By night: *Bellini, copy, opera, farce, red, bride.* I'm totally confused, but assume it's because I only go out at night. But Raymond,

The poster is replaced with another poster. This composite image is made from the bottom of the movie placard from *The Barefoot Contessa* and the top of Gérôme's *Pygmalion and Galatea.*

who has yet to leave the hotel, claims the culture to be totally transparent. He says that, for the Orfenoans, life isn't death, but nearby. It's the same as death. Anyway, I hope little Caroline has gotten over her cold, and give her my love.
Ton petit nou nou qui t'embrasse fort,
Gustave.

#34

#34

A postcard of Rita Hayworth in the film *The Lady from Shanghai* is on top of Masaccio's *Expulsion from Paradise.* A cutout of Everett Sloane replaces Fred Astaire on the postcard.

#34

Voice-over of American female child narrator:
Dearest Mama,
We are in Silha and have been befriended by other tourists from home. They say Gustave is like Balzac, that he looks at nothing but remembers everything.

#34

One thousand tender
thoughts,
Your loving son,
Raymond.

#35

A hand puts a cut-out tear, a
large ear, and a bra in the
appropriate places over the
painting of the Madonna in
the Bellini book. The book is
covered up by the red-
stained shroud. Then the
image of a purple cloth
fades up and fills the scene.

#35

The camera zooms in on the
book of Bellini paintings,
which rests on top of the
anamorphic picture of
Flaubert.

#35

**Voice-over of male narra-
tor:**

I awake, I must get some
sleep! Tomorrow I travel, but
my eyes ache, I feel lost. I try
to fill the time. I start with a
void, then a wish. Someone is
waiting for me. I relax, and I
feel moisture, turn and feel
soft skin, then I hear rustling.
Each sense struggles to
produce a fragment. A
picture is needed. Things are
named. The moisture turns to
tears. Turning yields the
breast and rustling the ear,
but the shapes are gaped. I
reach out and only feel

#35

A loop of Fred Astaire
singing "ha, ha, ha" from the
Cole Porter song "They All
Laughed at Christopher
Columbus."

197

darkness. I connect things.

The title "Penelope's Song" appears over the purple cloth. There is a cut to the linoleum floor the legs paced across previously. A purple scarf lies crumpled on the floor.

I don't even have to look, but as the picture takes form, I lose my sense of time, the price paid for covering the gaps. I feel dizzy and no longer know whether the image is half built or in ruin. Things stabilize. I construct a fantasy. No, not one, but an endless string. Each time I send them out, they seem different, but somehow they return, they feel the same. I return to Roussel. He preserves his mother perfectly, like a side of beef, frozen and cut into fragments. She stands proudly, sometimes coyly, between void and sign, running first one way, then the other. She serves as

The sound of the Stand-in for Roussel's mother whistling "Save Your Heart for Me" is mixed with the "ha, ha, ha" loop.

The stand-in for Roussel's mother appears. She is filmed from overhead. She wears a blue chiffon prom dress and carries a valise. She puts down the valise and picks up the purple scarf, wrapping it around her like a shawl. Then she turns the valise upside down and dumps a lot of objects out of it. These objects are things that have already appeared in the tape, such as flowers, playing cards, etc. She faces the camera and sings off-key: "Walk along the lake with someone new. Have yourself a summer fling or two. But remember I'm in love with you, so save your heart for me." There is a fade-out, and a lining, devoid of her own speech, but near to meaning. Her circulation is limited, an occasional foray out. He imagines her in a pastiche. He laughs. Burlesque and vaudeville are preferred. Her son holds tightly. She loves me because she is waiting, and I know she waits because I am alone and in pain. This perverse logic he calls maternal love.

a close-up of the Stand-in for Flaubert's mother appears, shot from overhead, against the tile floor background.

Sync sound.

Stand-in for Flaubert's mother: I just received this great letter from Gustave.

Female voice, offscreen: Come on already, get to the point.

Stand-in for Flaubert's mother: Well I'm trying to get to the point.

Female voice, offscreen: Hurry up!

Stand-in for Flaubert's mother: It's telling about this weird land. . . .

Female voice, offscreen: Can't you tell it any faster?

Stand-in for Flaubert's mother: Yes, I can! It tells

where all meaning is carried from the intonation of the voice. Yes, yes, yes, like Chinese. Well, anyway, I have.

. . .

Female voice, offscreen: Get to the point of the story.

Stand-in for Flaubert's mother: I have all the traditional folktales of the culture with me. There's just a problem. The tape he sent, which was supposed to demonstrate all this, got lost in the mail. But they're great, so I'm going to tell them anyway. There's these two mothers, who're sitting in the tropics, luxuriating around a swimming pool, like one of those Miami Beach scenes. One mother starts telling the other mother, "My life's a *michaya*, and it's all because of my son. Anything I want, he gets me. He's got me a condominium with a view, a new convertible. He got me a sofa with slipcovers so the velour won't get all *smutzig*. Just the other day, he bought me a new mink coat. I said, 'Save your money for when you're married. It's too warm here anyway.' And he said, he's such a *shaneshatodah,* he says, 'Keep it. So when you open the closet door, the maid can see it.'" The other mother, she starts getting really perturbed, and she says, "Ah *fah*. That's nothing. Your son's a *nitchdukite*. My son's a *mensch*. He pays a hundred dollars an hour just to talk about me."

Female voice, offscreen:
That was the most thinly

veiled anti-Semitic story I
ever heard.

Stand-in for Flaubert's mother: That's not anti-Semitic.

Female voice, offscreen: I dare you to tell another one.

Fade out to black.

Cut to the Stand-in for Roussel's mother who continues with her song: When you're all alone, far away from home, someone's gonna flirt with you. I won't say it's wrong, if you go along. Just don't fall for someone new. When the autumn winds begin to blow, and the summertime is long ago, you'll be in my arms again I know, so save your heart for me. *When she finishes singing, she whistles the same tune. Cut to the Stand-in for Flaubert's mother, filmed in close-up against a background of linoleum tile.*

Stand-in for Flaubert's mother: How do you know that our Lord came from the chosen people?

Female voice, offscreen: What, are you kidding? Was this written by Martin Luther or something?

Stand-in for Flaubert's mother: Let me finish it.

Female voice, offscreen: I'm telling this story. Just be quiet. How do you know Jesus was Jewish? He was over thirty, he still lived with his parents, he was supposed to go into his father's business. . . .

**mother and female voice
offscreen:** *Speak simultaneously, interrupting one
another:* He went into his
father's business. His mother
thought he was God. And
she thought that he thought
she was a virgin.
Fade out to black.

#36

Several gifts, including a fan,
a pine cone, and brightly
wrapped packages, are
tossed on the ground. Hands
pick up some of these gifts
and shake them. The hands
keep placing the gifts in front
of the camera, stacking them
hurriedly, and then removing
them.

#36
The screen is black.

#36

**Voice-over of American
female adult narrator:**
Ma Mere,
Finally a gift worthy of
Caroline! I've just put it in
the post. I'm sure she'll
adore it. How I happened on
it, c'est vraiment amusant. It

#36
Audio excerpt from the radio
show "The Shadow." After the
introductory music, a deep
male voice says, "Who
knows what evil lurks in the
hearts of men? The Shadow
knows."

Sounds of general ruckus,
including breaking glass.
The volume of this sound
track obscures some of the
verbal narration of the voice-
over.

was in Saknussen. Our guide had told us of their central market, at the edge of the city. Raymond, of course, stayed behind with his two favorite books. No, not Loti, or Hugo, or even the exalted Verne. These are authors that inspire him. In his daily writing, he sits with two dictionaries, *Larousse* and what he calls its superior, *Bescherelle.* What a fine little librarian he could have been. Anyway, the market was dazzling. Not a row of stalls, which by now I've become accustomed to, but a series of stages, each partially covered by rich velvet curtains. My guide asked me to choose one. My breath taken, I just closed my eyes, spun around, and pointed. We moved past the curtain, joining a children's puppet performance in progress. At its completion, a grandly clad usher took a ticket from one of the spectators and gave her one of the props. My guide informed me that she had purchased a gift. The object was elaborately wrapped and, when shaken, made a rather eccentric sound. The gift was never to be opened. I asked our guide about this custom, and he said with surety in his voice, "If the package were to be opened, it would no longer be a gift." Anyway, I'm sure the one I received will make Caroline swoon. I do hope, to my instructions, everything on my desk has been kept

exactly as I left it. I could not
go on thinking it had
changed.
Ton petit nou nou qui
t'embrasse fort,
Gustave.

#37

A hand pulls aside the purple
cloth to reveal another
segment from the "Museum
of Copies" hand-colored
silent film. The film begins
with an intertitle: "Poison.

#37

The image of the purple
cloth fills the screen. A title
appears: "Museum of
Copies: Validation."

#37

**Voice-over of male narra-
tor:**

An odd form of blindness.
Too much light, and my eyes
drool, uncontrollably. Dark
glasses reduce the pain but
don't increase my vision. I
decide to write, blindly. In
writing, they had shared only
one adventure, a trip to a
museum. A pilgrimage to see
a great work of art.

Flaubert wrote mostly of
breakfast. The marmalade
reminded him of dates,

#37

Sound of squeaky gym shoes
hitting against a floor.

United in Death." A man and
a woman dressed in toga-like
costumes are in front of a
backdrop depicting a
classical building. She
dances for him and then falls
to the ground. He reacts with
hysteria and then snatches
up a goblet and drinks it.
Another woman enters the
scene. He points to the
woman who has swooned
and then swoons beside her.
Cut to a close-up of the face
of the female artist. She
wears dark glasses. The
camera pulls back to show
her image is being reflected
in a mirror. On the other side
of the screen is a painting of
a rustic landscape and a
green velvet curtain. The
camera finally reveals the

coconut, and plum. He
thought it to be marvelous.
The museum he referred to
as a junkyard. The great work
of art is mentioned only by
name, *The Painted Bride.*
Roussel thinks the museum to
be a zoo, but the work of art
thrills him. He calls it *The
Painted Veil* and writes about
the thousand and one
Arabian nights. A fable
comes to mind. A competi-
tion between Zeuxis and
Parrhasios, who can paint the
better picture. They work out
of each other's sight, each
drawing on a separate wall.

Parrhasios finishes swiftly
and furtively sneaks toward
the other wall. He can't
restrain his laughter. Zeuxis

real female artist facing her mirror reflection. She wears a T-shirt and a strapless prom dress. The female artist walks offscreen. She reappears, carrying a rock, which she uses to smash the mirror. The camera then pans across the painting and focuses on a close-up of the paint-stained prom dress from scene 22, suspended from a hanger. The camera zooms out to show the entire set again.

had painted grapes. They bear little resemblance.

His laughter is broken. Birds gather and pick at the grapes that bear little resemblance. Overhearing the squelched laughter, Zeuxis triumphantly approaches and says, "Surely, I win. See the birds, they are fooled. Let them be the judge." They walk toward Parrhasios's wall, and Zeuxis looks. Seeing only a veil, he impatiently asks, "Let me see what you have painted behind it." The combat is over, and Parrhasios is declared the winner. If you wish to fool a man, you paint a veil, and he will surely ask, "What's behind it?"

#38

A postcard is placed on top
of the poster, with the written
side facing up.

The postcard is flipped over.
The other side shows Fred
Astaire and Rita Hayworth
dancing. They are in evening
dress.

#38

The backdrop is a poster
from the movie *The Earth
Stood Still*. A woman wearing
a red dress in the poster
resembles the Stand-in for
Roussel's mother in her
scenes on the beach.

#38

**Voice-over of American
female child narrator:**
Dearest Mama,
We have been crossing the
Baraciusan desert for what
Gustave describes as an
eternity. He repeatedly gives
a deep sigh and remarks, I
don't much care for the
landscape of Baraciusa,
except for the mirages.
One thousand tender
thoughts,
Your loving son,
Raymond.

#38

Vague outer-space-type
music.

Barry Gifford
In Search of the Big Perfect

On October 8, 1956, Don Larsen's father was working as a clerk in Hink's Department Store in Berkeley, California. The elder Larsen would rather have been at home or in a bar watching on TV while his son pitched game 5 of the World Series for Casey Stengel's New York Yankees against the Brooklyn Dodgers, but the store manager refused to give Larsen *père* a day off or to allow him to listen to the game on a radio.

Not that Big Don (he was six-four) was expected to do much that day. During the regular season he'd won eleven games, lost five, with a respectable 3.26 earned-run average. He was twenty-seven years old, in his fourth major league season. Two years before, in 1954, he had compiled a record of three wins and *twenty-one* losses for the Baltimore Orioles, a team that lost an even hundred. Interestingly, Larsen's Yankee teammate Bob Turley, who was scheduled to start game 6 of the '56 Series, had also been on that terrible Baltimore team (he won fourteen and lost fifteen). Nobody, certainly not Turley, anticipated what Don Larsen would accomplish in game 5.

"Larsen had started the second game," Turley recalled, "in which we took an early 6-0 lead, but Casey took him out when the Dodgers rallied in the second inning. That made him really mad, especially since we ended up losing 13-8. Don was a drinker, and he went drinking every night after that. . . . Larsen didn't know he was pitching until he came to the Stadium that day. He'd slept only about a half hour the night before."

I was ten days shy of my tenth birthday when I watched Don Larsen working without a windup—which Rube Walker, the third-string Brooklyn catcher, said threw off the Dodger's timing—pitch the only perfect game in World Series history. Larsen was a gangly, ugly guy, kind of a pinhead with elephant ears. Along with Don "The Sphinx" Mossi of the Cleveland Indians, Don Larsen was preeminent among major leaguers in the Department of Unfortunate Features.

Coming in, the eighth of October didn't add up to perfect for Larsen: Big Don was pissed off at Stengel and badly hungover, and his father couldn't even listen to the ballgame. But he had a good fastball and a heavy breaking ball, and, as Les Moss, a catcher on that miserable '54 Orioles team, remarked, "Larsen was a happy-go-lucky guy. . . . Nothing could depress him. He wasn't depressed when he went 3 and 21. . . . He would have been the same if he lost 51 games."

Attitude had a lot to do with turning this particular trick. That, plus a live arm and Don's decision to pitch from the stretch. Putting his arm above his fogged-up head made him dizzy, so he threw off his right hip, meaning that in the mid-to-late innings the ball broke in on the Dodger hitters from the notorious left-field Yankee Stadium shadows.

After home plate umpire Babe Pinelli called strike 3 on a high pitch to pinch-hitter Dale Mitchell, sealing the *perfecto*, most everybody watched catcher Yogi Berra race to the mound and leap into Larsen's arms. I watched Mitchell wheel in disgust and yell at Pinelli, who rapidly headed south. It had been a bad call, the crowning occurrence of what Mahayana Buddhists describe as dependent arisings, and the final nail in the coffin of the Big Perfect.

■　■　■

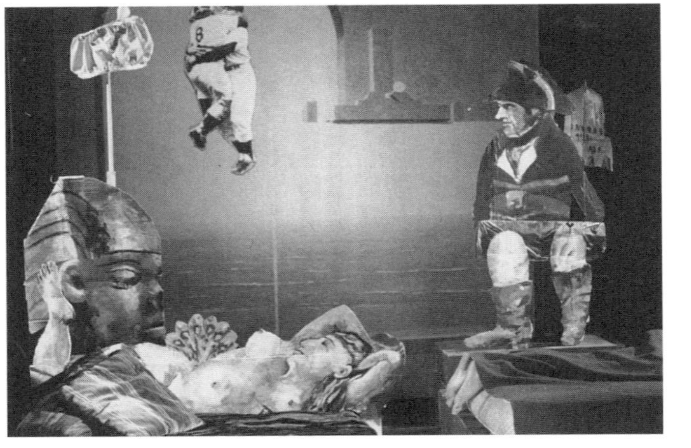

"Dying in Front of the Large Glass: The Perfect,"
from *The Amazing Voyage*

#39

#39
A composite image including
a reproduction of Magritte's
painting *The Human Condition,* orientalist furniture,
Gérôme's painting of Napoléon, and Ingres's *Obelisk.*
Inset into the background is a
photograph of baseball

#39

#39
A loop of the words "And
that's called sad" from the
Shangri-Las' song "You Can
Never Go Home," mixed with
music from Bellini's opera
Norma. Thus, there is a
displacement from the

player Don Larsen playing his perfect game in the World Series. Over this background appears the title "Dying in Front of the Large Glass: THE PERFECT."

Voice-over of Italian female narrator: Raymond Roussel died at the Grande Albergo delle Palme. Room 226 was connected by a door to the adjoining room occupied by Charlotte DuFrene, his life-long celibate companion. Their custom was to keep the door unlocked. He dragged the mattress, which represented a superhuman effort, to the adjoining door. It was like he had died on the bachelor side of the Large Glass. The door was locked. On the floor below, Wagner had written *Parsifal.* Roussel had

painter Bellini to the composer Bellini.

The sound of breaking glass is added to the mix.

written of a poet's death and his journey to heaven. He had dreamed of Dante, but found neither Beatrice nor Virgil, but street names, statues, monuments, and medals. It was perfect. Turnandot; Te lo do, Principessa e perdo tutto! E perdo tutto! Persino l'impossible speranza! Le gatemi! Tormenti e spiasmi date a me! Ah! Come offerta suprema del mio amore! She will not give his name and dies gladly for love. The composer dies without writing another word. The opera is finished by Franco Alfano and performed at La Scala on 25 April 1926. The third act is interrupted. Toscanini lays down the

#40	#40	#40	#40
	The anamorphic image of Flaubert fills the screen.	baton and says, "The opera ends here, because at this point the maestro died." The performance is aborted. On succeeding evenings, it is conducted as we now know it. He is named, loved, and allowed to live.	Loop of laughter from Verdi's *Masked Ball*.
	A conical mirror is placed next to the image momentarily. Cut to an anamorphic image of Roussel.	**Voice-over of male narrator:** Eggs, toast, and bacon. I smell breakfast, yesterday's, rotten, still sitting. I'm haunted by a chapter, unnamed. Their fathers—who were they? I hesitate and then rush to say men like all others. This leaves me unsatisfied. Their fathers were more. They were impossible. At least their mothers spoke to them. A	

A conical mirror is placed next to the image momentarily. Cut to the same conical mirror, next to the image of Flaubert, revealing the image's normal configuration.

tongue taken from an image, cracked and luminous. The sons sat attentively, rubbing against the speech, misunderstood, but warming. Their fathers never spoke, so images were found to replace them. But the sons were loyal. They were bright, too bright. The images were only seen in their shadow. Sometimes large, others small, this shadow hounded them, like a ghost. Afraid to turn around, sensing more than they knew, they walked head down. Fearing this would cause delay, they always arrived early. I pull the curtain—broad daylight. My eyes recoil, and I draw the shade.

#41

As in scenes 5, 12, 16, 26, and 31. the Stand-in for

#41

As in scenes 5, 12, 16, 26, and 31.

#41

#41

As in scenes 5, 12, 16, 26, and 31.

Roussel's mother is on the beach. She completes her dance and bows.

#42

#42

The credits appear over the same Gérôme painting, *The Guard of the Harem,* that appeared in scene 4. The painting has been repainted with a video paintbox.
The credits are:
Written and Directed by Steve Fagin. Produced by Jack Walsh. Sound Design by William Davenport. Edited by Jack Walsh. Director of Photography—David Baker. Sound Recordist—Heather Presley. Sound Engineer—William Davenport. Creative Consultant—Valerie Menenti. Art Director—Lynn Sachs. Assistant Art Director—Leslie Alperin. Still Photography—Margaret Hussey. Camera Operators—

#42

#42
Hawaiian string music.

Ethan Van Der Ryan, Lynn Kirby. Lighting—Heather Hansen, James Hill. Production Assistants—Ethan Fagin, Greg Grieve, Sarah Haberfeld, Rebecca Long, Joyce McKee, Adam Moss, Crosby McCloy. CMX Editor— David Weissman. Additional Dialogue—"Copy versus the Simulacrum" —Valerie Manenti. "Notes to Notes" and "Home of Nauseating Repetition"—J. P. Sartre. African footage courtesy of Trinh T. Minh-ha. Additional Artwork—William Alick, Gervais Tomkin, Nouraman Manoucheri, David Owen. Narration— J. M. Svendsen, Monica Gazzo, Joy Berry, Sarah Haberfeld, Tamara F. Cast—Kathleen-Marie Shelton, Valerie Manenti, Heather Hansen, Rebecca Long, Bushra Azzouz, Amy Levine, Sharon McGowen, Fern Renville, Lisa Simon, Dana Sachs, Lynn Sachs, Crosby McCloy, Margaret Morse, Margaret Hussey, Laverne

Terrace. Special Thanks—Peter Adair, Haney Armstrong, Jeanne Wolff Bernstein, Eric Bauersfeld, Bonnie Kane, Mark Rappaport, Leslie Thornton, Department of Cinema, San Francisco State University, Margaret Morse, Wendy Pappas, August Coppola, Barbara Klutinis, Jim Pomeroy, Ellen Zweig, Film Department, San Francisco Art Institute, Gifford Family. Off-line facilities provided by Adair Films. CMX subsidy provided by Bay Area Video Coalition. This project was funded by a grant from the National Endowment for the Arts. This project was funded in part through a Western States Regional Media Arts Fellowship awarded by the Rocky Mountain Film Center, Boulder, Colorado, in a program funded by the National Endowment for the Arts and the American Film Institute, with additional funds from the California Arts Council.

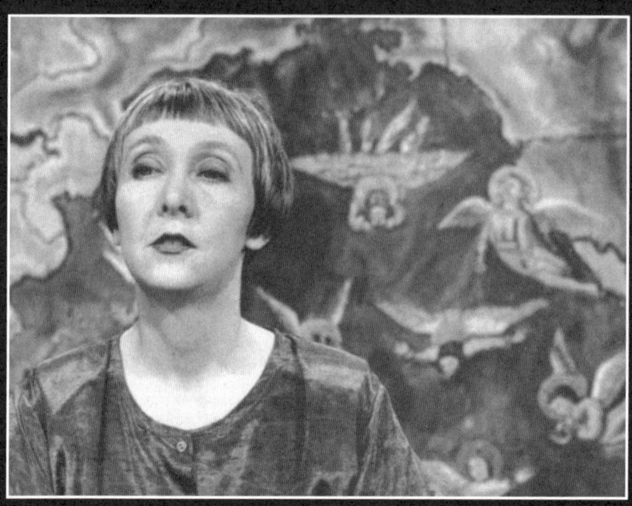

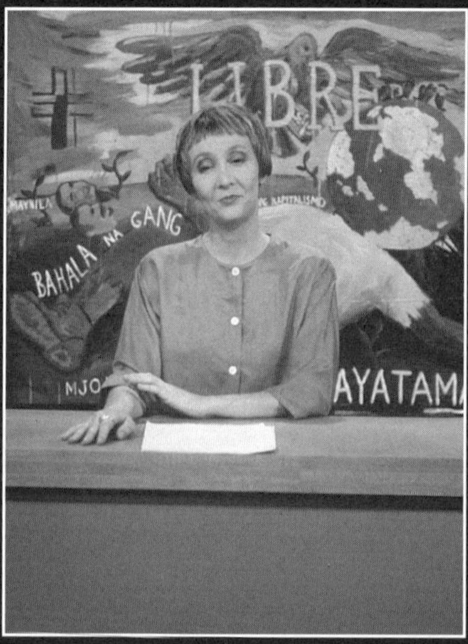

"Constance DeJong, Newscaster," from
The Machine That Killed Bad People

Patricia Mellencamp
Disastrous Events

The Machine That Killed Bad People, a 1990 videotape by Steve Fagin, is a rendering of catastrophe (the collapse of the Marcos regime) and scandal (Imelda's spending sprees and government graft). Avant-garde formalism meets the techniques of CNN and syndicated TV, unraveling network news coverage of the Philippines.

After the snap election of 1986 in the Philippines, Marcos's opponents Juan Enrile and General Benigno Ramos, in alliance with Cardinal Sin and Corazon Aquino, were jousting for power—with General Fabian Ver on Marcos's side. In one of the many extraordinary clips interwoven in *The Machine That Killed Bad People,* Marcos went on live TV, hoping to be picked up by the U.S. networks. In a family melodrama right out of *Dynasty,* Marcos played Lear in a season-ending cliff-hanger climax. Imelda and other family members framed him while children clambered onto Imelda's lap and wandered in front of the president/grandfather. The scene was informal, almost casual. This tone was undercut by General Ver, from stage right, wearing his combat fatigues, issuing growling, guttural reports of outside chaos and awaiting Marcos's commands to action. While the scene was staged, Ver's interruption of Marcos was very transgressive, akin to Schwarzkopf interrupting Bush.

The long and rambling TV appearance (like Nixon's tortured farewell press conference), orchestrated for U.S. television and politicians, was a simulation of mastery now in chaotic decline. Technology failed Marcos just as neocolonialism had served him. Fagin describes these fifty minutes as a "drama of duration: the untelling of a dictatorship. . . . TV had been reversed and now power flowed upstream. A dictator under surveillance, television stripping the emperor bare. A whole nation watched a machine hand out its own justice, as spectacle toppled before the wrath of the real."[1]

The differences between U.S. and Filipino TV conventions and the chasm between the industrialized United States and the agricultural Philippines are startling. A high-tech electronics clashes with a low-tech colonized culture, revealing a time warp. Marcos had become an impersonation, a mimicry kowtowing to U.S. power rather than outwitting it. Video, imitating syndicated studio style and replaying live TV clips and home movies, *reveals* rather than represses cultural, political, and economic differences.

The struggle for power was electronic, mediated by colonialism—U.S. politicians and the CIA in lockstep with corporations and journalism. This intervention has been economically and psychically internalized within Filipino culture, where, in spite of everything, America still means superior. All sides courted the seal of U.S. media approval and legitimacy—a pipeline to U.S. support. (Stanley Karnow reports that, in 1985, Cory Aquino had met Abe Rosenthal of the *New York Times;* reputedly, Rosenthal found her "vacant."[2] Afterward, she played poorly in the *Times,* which cast a pall of personal ineptness over her leadership that still persists.) To cover the events of the 1986 election, the TV networks had fielded crews and celebrity anchors. The elections were perfect TV fare— gossip and catastrophe as prime-time political soaps. Marcos would be interviewed on CBS only by Dan Rather. General Ramos and Marcos appeared on *Meet the Press,* with Marcos declaring: "I don't believe President Reagan would ask me to step down."

The equally strenuous job in the United States was to convince Reagan to depose his old friend, which, after assurances of U.S. asylum, finally occurred indirectly. Imelda and Ferdinand "show biz to the end . . . with a retinue of sixty . . . left the Malacanang palace, after singing a farewell duet, `Because of You.'" They flew to Guam and then Hawaii. "Once aloft, Imelda began to sing 'New York, New York.'"[3] The show tunes, like the Marcoses' group performances of them, are transformed in *The Machine* from a U.S. media joke into signs of cultural difference, the Filipino tradition of minus-one singing, imported from Japan, for which Imelda had a real talent. Her singing transfixed Lyndon Johnson, who was also fascinated with her young beauty, as were the U.S. media in the late 1960s. After Cory Aquino was inaugurated, it was all Reagan's advisers could do to convince him not to visit the Marcoses in Hawaii—no small task given his commitment to the couple.

Before his decline, Marcos had alienated the ruling families in the oligarchic culture, including the business community and the Catholic church, his early supporters. These powerful families shifted their allegiance to Cory Aquino, who represented the old oligarchy that Marcos had dispossessed.[4] Karnow argues that his economic failure, virtually bankrupting the country, more than revolutionary or reform fervor, resulted in his deposition. In many ways, nothing has changed; given the role of kinship as the cornerstone of the political system, change could occur only if the powerful families relinquished, or were dispossessed of, their land, the source of their power.[5]

Armed with an introduction to a family clan tied to the intelligentsia, Fagin traveled to the Philippines on a three-month journey. This experience of culture shock infuses *The Machine,* which unravels a complex history of colonialism, whether government, corporate, or psychic. For Homi Bhabha, colonialism functions within the contradiction of recognition and disavowal of "racial/historical/cultural differences" that places the "colonized [as] a fixed reality which is . . . entirely knowable and visible." He calls this "a complex articulation of the troops of fetishism."[6] That Fagin takes fetishism literally in the shopping channel inserts and the rape machine at the end is not insignificant. In addition, he doesn't minimize, as does Bhabha, that in Freud's construction it is the woman's body that is the source of the fetishistic disavowal for the man. For Freud, "woman" embodies contradiction.

There is a snug fit between Bhabha's model of fetishistic disavowal and colonialism—wherein race is visible and clearly not a secret (like Foucault's repudiation of Freud's repression hypothesis, arguing instead that the secret that is sex/identity is loudly proclaimed)—and the defining logic of U.S. television, which also operates via overt, declared contradictions, a logic of both/and rather than either/or. Like colonialist discourse, TV overtly speaks with a forked tongue, declaring its contradictions, unlike cinema, which is more seamless. Unlike Freud's fetish, for TV and colonialism there is no reassuring object. *The Machine* reveals the mechanism of all three fetishes—the woman, the colonial subject, and television—as logics of contradictions.

The unbelievable scene of hands-on surgery in the fourth section, "Tourism," stages this psychic mechanism. This is shocker, drop-dead footage of "Alex Orbito, Faith Healer and Travel Agent" from Manila, who doesn't want to promote his mystical talents, only heal. With Fagin's voice outside the frame lending veracity, there is an uninterrupted shot of hands-on stomach surgery on a middle-age, middle-class American woman. She lies on Orbito's desk; the camera zooms in on her body as his hands create a gaping wound with red fluid, then its resuturing and cleaning. She sits up, perkily smiles, and testifies: "This man has saved my life twice. . . . It doesn't hurt; it feels good." This scene is an assault on Western surgery and a challenge to both fetishistic disavowal and the truth of vision. The woman's testimony is linked to tourism and the tape's shopping channel re-creations, which also include comments from happy customers.

Imelda, a central figuration, no longer serves as an easy target, a cultural joke of bad taste, a cover-up for real corruption. Rather, she is a leftover, a symptom, the result of colonialism—neither Filipino nor American, without identity yet so well known as a celebrity caricature. Fagin gives her a fictive identity, that of a tragic heroine of the late nineteenth century. Neither is the blame placed singly on Marcos. The strands of power—visible and invisible, audible and inaudible—are full of anomalies and cultural difference, yet replete with greed and covert acts turned corrupt and personal.

The Machine embodies two models of time and history: successive, moving chronologically from Marcos to Aquino, and simultaneous, doubling back like memory or shock. The collision of the everyday with shocking or catastrophic scenes culminates in an extraordinary, macabre performance at the end: the bloody coupling/rape of the Filipino emblem, an eagle, by a Cyclopean U.S. phallic rocket/dollar—a perverse, violent, fire-breathing machine. The metaphor of rape is staged earlier, over a Filipino woman's body tended by surgeons, lying on top of a map of the world, a body that has replaced the corporate station logo, KSKY, which has a bleeding eye in its last letter. Rape is literal in the child prostitution trade near the U.S. military bases. The Cyclopean eye/phallus/money machine reminded me of Bhabha's description of the colonizer: "Their governance is overwhelmed by . . . an exciting pleasure . . . which might turn into a Cyclopean policy."[7]

The tape stages what Graham Pechey calls "the theater of history," a strategy of decolonization, with a critical relation between performance and writing.[8] Fagin's technique is rigorously thought out. He rips off abstract formalism, commercial TV tactics, cinéma vérité, guerrilla video, performance art, and acting methods. This bricolage, of familiar, mundane techniques combined with high-art formalism, unsettles the relation between person and actor, the real and the simulated, the documented and the re-created, the historical and the experiential or personal.

Super VHS, shot in handheld vérité style with the color removed, is used in two recurring conversational tableaux: the first, an activist land reformer and priest meeting with constituents in Ilocas Norte, Marcos country; and the second, a dinner-table interview with an activist lawyer, his articulate wife, and a former political prisoner. These clearly privileged sections retain the liberal to Marxist politics style of cinéma vérité (including "real" locales) and raise deeply serious, straightforward issues: the presence of U.S. business and military bases.

A variant of this handheld, black-and-white format is the granular Fisher-Price video or toy footage (reminiscent of avant-garde films) of Ron Vawter as Alden Pyle. This toughly sensitive reporter/agent is closeted in his hotel room, reading or writing about events; his experience is mediated, fantasmatic. Pyle is a condensation of Vawter, the ex-Marine and off-Broadway actor, Fagin, and Edward Lansdale, a CIA operative in the Philippines and Vietnam. The simulated and the real elide and collide; history is impersonated.

Lansdale was Oliver North's hero and the model for the characters of both *The Ugly* and *The Quiet American.* In the first novel, he is Colonel Hillendale, anti-Communist crusader. In the second, by Graham Greene, he is Pyle, teaching democracy to the peasants to "resist the Communist menace." Lansdale, who died in 1987, wrote, "I took my American values into these Asian struggles." Karnow argues that "the clue to Lansdale was his youth in the advertising trade."[9] Vawter/Pyle also suggests a Jack Smith performance in a Ken Jacobs film or Martin Sheen going nuts in his hotel room in *Apocalypse Now.* This Fisher-Price footage is shot (by Leslie Thornton) and edited in tight, fragmented images, bound in further by a black matte frame.

As Pyle writes and reads, the text, which is shown in lettered, broken close-ups, is also heard. "Under the Marcoses this place was a kleptocracy. Imelda would go into Tiffany's on Fifth Avenue, a Unesco check made out to the Philippines neatly folded in one of her native bags. . . . Now, like a character from *Dawn of the Dead,* she haunts the malls of Hawaii."

The "I" of Pyle's text is the "I" of Fagin's experience, an alter ego acting out fictive history. Critique and autobiography are presented as performance more than documentary experience. Regarding his introduction and the taping of the coffin of Marcos's mother:

> When I first arrived, I thought it to be my good luck. Drop the right
> name, doors, now even coffins opened. Everyone seemed to know

one another, and they were so closely knit. . . . That's what an oligarchy feels like. The wake . . . longer than a miniseries but not quite
long enough for syndication. The paid mourners, the mother in state,
well lit, just enough flowers to fill the frame. The Right had become
so accessible. Once arrogant and removed, they saw their last hope as
American television. The Left, on the other hand, was cautious.
Maybe their image would be seen by the vigilante death squads, perhaps you're in the CIA, oh yes, a concerned writer. Know an issue in a
weekend, and show it in a thirty-second balanced featurette. . . . I
insisted the camera should shoot directly into the casket. . . . The
sequence was shot a second time. A retake. What did I expect? The
corpse to blow its lines, to blink, to sneeze? Only the camera made
death feel near.

We see Marcos's dead mother, who bears an uncanny resemblance to her
son, preserved and waiting, later.

A handheld camera brushes over the items on Pyle's desk. This inciden-
tal detail is reminiscent of the throwaway newspaper item that first attracted Fagin to this project. It described "the objects left on Ferdinand
Marcos' desk the day he departed from the Philippines. . . . An exploration of the objects left behind, on a day that would prove to be historic,
could function as insight into the configurations of power, the random
and the everyday."

This personal image reminds me of the CNN reporter covering the
1989 earthquake in San Francisco (coincident with Fagin's editing; like
this tape's conclusion, catastrophe was linked to baseball), asking the
now-homeless standing outside their collapsed apartments to describe
what they had taken when they fled or what they would retrieve during
their fifteen-minute visitation before demolition. To Fagin's not surprising good luck, Marcos "took the gold bullion rather than the home movies," which Fagin "accessed." While copying TV technique, we are not
held in by conventions of flow or narrative containment. Rather, we are
displaced within a chain of associations where one catastrophe slides into
another or, just as unexpectedly, jumps back, like the flash of personal
memory. Time, like history and disaster, is a series of unexpected simulta-
neities.

Connie Lansdale is the anchorwoman, played by Constance DeJong.
This condensation of DeJong, Connie Chung, and Edward Lansdale embodies TV grammar, linking segments and contents. She reports the

weather and the price of Filipino commodities. Her intonation is undifferentiated, an affectless monotone. Her "professionalism," a lack of emotion, is in high contrast to the dramatic performance of Vawter. Behind her are bizarre, Giotto-inspired murals of Christian allegories. She exists in a satellite studio suspended above the earth, completely removed from any social context. Her intonation, English, and TV non sequiturs are superimposed on the world, flattening it into sense, eradicating differences. Like TV, Connie smooths over any disruption by failing to notice any difference.

Given that network TV news studios are increasingly run by remote-control cameras, with computers picking up satellite feeds from around the world that are then stored in memory banks for instant access, they can be anywhere and don't need anyone to be present; anchors can be keyed in (like being beamed aboard the *Enterprise*). The network valuation of being on the scene is an old-fashioned realist (Baudrillard) claim, one that denies the very electronic technology enabling the broadcast or point-to-point transmission—an interesting contradiction. Although we couldn't see either Koppel or Rather in Iraq in August 1990, they were *there,* as their voice broadcasts informed us.

The postproduction mix of hard-core TV graphics and flashy but commonplace editing linkages subverts the visual and aural grammar of TV flow. These linking and packaging techniques of logos, promos, phrases, IDs, and graphics (which grab our attention, promise a future, and erase memory) are crucial for TV continuity and normalcy; they are devices that we ignore or endure. In nonplussed manner, these visual and spoken connectives can link the weather to an assassination, an artificial cause-effect illogic. Fagin fills these empty markers with conflicting content, forcing them to "mean" differently. These repetitions lack redundancy, unlike TV. While many references are immediately recognizable, over time they assume an intellectual complexity they didn't initially warrant. TV's intricate grammar has been deformed through what Eisenstein called vertical and intellectual montage and revised by language.

The TV precursors are neither the networks nor PBS but programs made for syndication: the Home Shopping Channel, "America's Ten Most Wanted" (and other re-creations of sensational events), magazine format shows like "Entertainment Tonight" and "Inside Edition," and particularly CNN, the cable news channel. The alternation of techniques resembles channel zapping; the return to the same scene with different commentary suggests instant replay, multiple viewings, or time shifting. The shopping channel re-creations, miniature compositions hawking compact discs, necklaces, or cellular telephones, are commodity tableaux with spiders, snakes, and frogs in the mise-en-scène—scenes that illustrate Bhabha's analogy between the fetish and colonialism. A long-fingernailed hand caresses the glitzy merchandise, while on-the-air telephone chats with TV viewers meld into accounts of the graft of Marcos cronies. The consumerism of shopping, like Imelda's shoes, is peanuts compared to official graft.

"Hello Shoppers. Welcome to 'Some Are Smarter than Others.' Our featured shopper is Marcos crony Herminio Disini, who masterminded the fattest single contract ever landed in the Philippines: the Westinghouse nuclear power plant in Bataan, built on a site subject to tidal waves, five miles from a volcano and twenty-five miles from three geological faults. Disini was paid a commission by Westinghouse of $50 million dollars. Disini companies became in charge of civil works, engineering, communication, and insurance. . . . [The project] eventually cost $2.2 billion. Remember to stay home and shop. If you ever want to get a taste of what it would be like if World War III broke out, go to a shopping mall between now and Christmas."

The lowly shopping channel turns to critique, to style that can be filled with alternative content. TV's lack of connection between random events and its brevity of items begin to hook up and make sense. Voices are dispersed, wrenched from a single, authorial viewpoint. Power is no longer a one-way street, on the side only of the colonizer. The tape "reconstructs a process of cultural resistance and . . . disruption, by writing a text that can answer colonialism back."[10]

Along with catastrophe, the tape circles around gossip and scandal, particularly in the second section, "The Marcoses." The focus is on Imelda. A patron of the arts with an affinity for other wealthy patrons, she hung out with the Whitneys, Rockefellers, and Fords, courting celebrities and politicians with her dazzling entertainment. Her famous friends, including the pages of *Women's Wear Daily,* abandoned her in the end; her taste, formerly stylish, soured to tacky, excessive. "I have surpassed Cinderella," she declared as she invented a fairy tale of a life that included singing for Irving Berlin and meeting Douglas MacArthur. She was, as the tape so poignantly remarks, "more like Emma Bovary, an ambitious girl from the provinces who had dreams that were symptoms of her century. The difference, Imelda's dreams came true. First as daydream, and finally as nightmare."

As official culture revised it, Imelda's life resembles a soap opera, perhaps starring Joan Collins. After facing Marcos's myriad and public sexual affairs, for which Benigno Aquino was also famous, she "buckled under the pressure and flew to New York to consult a psychiatrist—who prescribed tranquilizers and advised: Either quit Marcos or adapt to his lifestyle. She adapted . . . but she was never fully stable. Her subsequent shopping binges and insomniac soliloquies plainly reflected manic [or addictive] tendencies."[11] Thus, like so many women, she was tranquilized and adapted, explaining her shoe closet—a compulsive obsession so typical of addiction (as in Valium).

However, like Emma Bovary, the fairy-tale princess was not always a joke, not always "stout and a bit blowsy" and "tacky." In 1966, *Life* compared her to Jackie Kennedy with Eleanor Roosevelt's energy, while *Time* praised "Marcos' dynamic, selfless leadership." It is as if Imelda froze in that earlier and happier image—wearing one of her many sixties/seventies formal gowns to her 1989 hearing in New York, held in a Jackie time warp, surrounded by mocking media, alone, pathetic, sad rather than funny. Women must scrutinize the objects of men's jokes, often, like Freud, at (rather than about) women's expense.

Karnow's take on Imelda is typical; she is ridiculous, out of control, grotesque, just like an aging woman. He dishes out the gossip: "Arriving in Tokyo, Rome or Paris, she would buy racks of clothes and trays of diamonds. . . . She squandered $12 million on jewelry in a single day in Geneva. . . . Bloomingdale's opened especially for her on Sunday."[12] The abandoned loot, like the conclusion of *Citizen Kane* and her shopping sprees, is displaced in the tape onto parodies of the shopping channel and government greed.

The Machine opens with an image of the televised assassination attempt on Imelda in 1972—a clip that was played as a continuous loop for hours on Filipino television. Section 2 features home-movie footage of Imelda's birthday party. In a setting resonant of a U.S. country club, the partygoers sing show tunes; Imelda takes the microphone and the singing lead. She is sweetly gracious, very beautiful, the center of attention and adoration. The scene will return, with a different text—like the obsessive return to key moments in catastrophe coverage or key plays in sports, trying to understand events by repeating them, piling on diverse interpretations or facts.

At this point, the performance of DeJong as the anchorwoman takes on texture and resonance. She becomes more than an impassive connective fixture shuffling papers and tells parables about Imelda. The first is of Maria Malibran, the opera singer, who had been forced to sing the role of Desdemona in Rossini's *Othello*. Like Emma Bovary and Lady Macbeth (and their obsessions or addictions), Imelda takes on fictive and tragic/pathetic stature. The words cue us to the novelistic dimensions of the text and to the paucity of language on TV, blanded into a delimited uniformity. History, story, and allegory blend, retaining a nineteenth-century flavor.

Then the words referring back to her assassination footage: "Imelda arose, the morning after the assassination attempt, in the manner of the hysteric who, after a hectic day of being beaten, tortured, and defeated by her symptoms, awakes refreshed. . . . Later in the day, still resting, watching the events in an endless loop on the television, she remained perplexed. Why had Ver's security, standing by, not rushed to her rescue? Ver politely explained, his men had wished to remain out of camera range to give her center stage." The third tale is Imelda's own fairy tale: "Imelda sang to Berlin 'You Are My Sunshine.' She had been told this was the anthem of the American liberation. Despite Berlin's praises, Imelda decided not to pursue a singing career." Imelda's life as fantasy, as Hollywood movie, suggests another reason for the close affinity with the Reagans.

After shots of the very famous shoe and dress closets and another shopping-channel insert, the tape returns to Marcos on formerly live, but now dead, TV, followed by a visit to his mother's funeral and a look inside the coffin, staging Vawter's earlier words. Dona Josepha looks exactly like the aging, ill Marcos, then holed up in seclusion in Hawaii. The visit reminds me of the *National Enquirer* paying relatives for photographs of Elvis in his coffin. Even the tabloid was astonished at how many family mourners complied. The winning photograph became headlines. In this mise-en-scène of sensational kitsch, more than death or grief, the camera goes into the coffin for a close-up. The mother's death scene, reminiscent of the son's TV appearance, is framed by ironic logos and pop music.

The relations between TV and tourism are clear. This is not, however, a tracing of the West superimposed over another culture, resulting in the TV mirror image of the United States. Filipino voices are everywhere; cultural artifacts are taken seriously. The collision is that of electronic culture with folk culture. The local, in which colonized subjects speak, undermines the global.

While eighties theorists of postmodernism mourned our entrapment in the present, Deleuze and Guattari advocate the present-tense quality of history. The parallel of this tape with Deleuze and Guattari is close. *The Machine That Killed Bad People* is an *agencement,* with "lines of . . . segmentation, strata, territorialities; but also lines of flight, movements of deterritorialization." One line of flight is the New People's Army—a movement of deterritorialization, a claim for land reform, a class struggle. Set against this is an arborescent logic of hierarchy, of filiation, the clan system that owns the land and U.S. interests. *The Machine* is a rhizome that connects "organizations of power, and events in the arts, sciences, and social struggles."[13]

This is a revision of sixties countercultural protest movements and liberation struggles, the context of the first-generation video artists, a time of mobile and shifting alliances such as the women's movement, civil rights, arts activism, and the antiwar movement. This first wave of video understood the power and techniques of television, arguing that video should provide alternatives. Video was process, diversity, and heterogeneity; commercial or "beast" TV meant product, centrality, and homogeneity, with spokesmen speaking above and for us. As Michael Shamberg wrote in *Guerrilla TV:* "Because radio men have been unable to model a visual language, only abnormal modes of behavior are considered news. . . . A lack of a true video grammar . . . also means that the actual experience of being at an event can't be communicated and therefore isn't considered news."[14]

The "video freaks'" assessment of commercial TV, linked to official, government culture, was uncannily accurate and predictive. Akin to TV, "government is geared towards crisis management, to anticipatory response." Along with crisis and catastrophe, media celebrity was another earmark of product culture: "Abbie Hoffman thinks he's getting his message across by going on the Dick Cavett show, but as somebody . . . once said: 'The revolution ended when Abbie Hoffman shut up for the first commercial.'" "No alternate cultural vision is going to succeed in Media America unless it has its own alternate information structures, not just alternate control pumped across the existing ones. And that's what video-tape . . . is ultimately all about."[15]

The spirit of the tape reminds me of TVTV's brilliant and powerful "Four More Years," which was alternative coverage of the 1972 GOP convention, the year Marcos imposed martial law on the Philippines. The roving hippie reporters took their handheld video cameras onto the convention floor, charting a binary divide between the middle-class, suited conventioneers and the protesters outside the convention walls, with Vietnam Vets against the War, including the now-famous Ron Kovic, author of *Born on the Fourth of July*, chanting "Tricky Dicky's Got to Go," trying to shout down the GOP's Nixon slogan, "Four More Years." Along with charting an era that protested war and imperialism, the reporters interviewed the network stars as much as the politicians, while the networks statically recorded official history, remaining above events in their booths.

"Four More Years" became history of the eighties, of political events (the move to the right, fundamentalism, and Reagan, a star of the tape), and of TV style (and even TV theory, with a long debate on the real or simulated enthusiasm of youths for Nixon predictive of Baudrillard, a mid-eighties hand-wringing era that might, thank God, be over). Video guerrillas disavowed retaining any distinction between the real and the simulation. What is striking about "Four More Years," nineteen years later, is the tape's radical aesthetics, its vision of video's capacity to inscribe a history of the present that is valid and moving today rather than distanced and over.

"Four More Years" takes to positive ends Fredric Jameson's condemnation of network television: "The disappearance of a sense of history, the way in which our entire contemporary social system has . . . begun to lose its capacity to retain its own past, has begun to live in a perpetual present," with media figured as "agents" for our "historical amnesia."[16] Rather than amnesia, "Four More Years" inscribes memory akin to Benjamin's "conception of the present as the 'time of the now' which is shot through with chips of Messianic time,"[17] causing us to assimilate "the information it supplies as part of [our] own experience."[18] "Where there is experience in the strict sense of the word, certain contents of the individual past combine with material of the collective past."[19]

Fagin takes Benjamin's negative examples of information—"brevity, comprehensibility, and above all, lack of connection between the indi-

vidual news items" (so prescient a description of commercial TV)—
to positive ends. The very defining features of postmodernism for
Jameson—"the transformation of reality into images, the fragmentation
of time into a series of perpetual presents"—are Fagin's primary tactics for
this history of the present.[20] History is not over but ongoing. Neither is
history linear, chronological, or univocal.

Bakhtin's dialogic culture describes the tape's double-directed hybrid
tactics. Benita Parry suggests that the position of "hybridity" can "cir-
cumvent, challenge, and refuse colonial authority."[21] Against the centrip-
etal notion of TV-speak, Bakhtin prefers dispersity, plurality, and de-cen-
tering, without closure or identification. "The productivity of the event
does not lie in the fusion of all into one, but in . . . my nonfusion, in the
reliance upon the privilege afforded me by my unique position, outside."[22]

Popular culture, which is "free, full of ambivalent laughter . . . dispar-
agement and unseemly behavior, familiar contact with everybody and
everything," with respect for the "repertory of small, everyday genres," is
preferred to official culture, which is monologic: "Monolithically serious
and somber, beholden to strict hierarchical order, filled with fear, dogma-
tism, devotion, and pretense."[23] Guerrilla video versus TV news.

"Intonation" for Bakhtin is "at the boundary between the verbal and
the nonverbal, the said and the unsaid."[24] Intonation is directed toward
life and the listener as ally or witness. Thus, we engage in a dialogue.
Significantly for Bakhtin, the "other" is located not in the unconscious, as
it is for Freud and Lacan, but in the social, in language. Thus, expression
organizes experience rather than the other way around—a concept
highly pertinent to television. Also applicable to television is Bakhtin's
idea of "character zones"—"from . . . alien expressive elements into authorial discourses—ellipsis, questions, exclamations—characters' voices
intermingle with authors' voices."[25]

The Machine is not a monologic condemnation of U.S. imperialism,
what Parry calls "the eurovision of the metropolitan left."[26] The final two
scenes explode. The first is an interview with Father Gerry Cabillo, the
jovial land-reform activist: "We were always dictated upon. . . . We should
run on our own . . . self-determination . . . masters of our own destiny."
Immediately, Connie says: "Welcome back to the USA." She reads a letter,
discovered by accident, written by Lansdale to his father in 1951. After
writing about the World Series, he criticizes the Europeans, who don't

realize the importance of "oppression, communism, atheism. . . . It's really true, the fate of the world is in our hands, and we just have to round the Filipinos into shape. My advertising experience comes in handy. . . . Sometimes this war makes me feel like a kid again back in Detroit. Often it's games and pranks that work. . . . But at least it's a Christian country." It is Christmas: "It sure is festive—a bit too festive, almost pagan. Now I understand what McKinley meant when he said we had to Christianize them. Wait till next year. Your loving son."

For Bhabha, "the modern colonization imagination conceives of its dependencies as a territory, never as a people." Bhabha might call this "muscular Christianity and the civilizing mission, a vigorous despotism."[27] This is a boyhood dream, that of an adolescent male, the good son: "Sometimes this war makes me feel like a kid again back in Detroit." "P.S. Tell Mom to send some of her cookies." As this letter, imagined by Fagin, is being read by DeJong/Lansdale, it assumes a nefarious actuality. Off to the side, the fierce and malevolent machine, clanking violently, shuddering and bloody, is relentlessly, blindly smashing into the Filipino emblem.

When I saw the tape, the letter sounded like another era. However, Dan Rather's August 1990 interviews with young U.S. soldiers on ships sent to the Persian Gulf and Iraq reminded me of these youthful American words. While *The Machine* is specific to the Philippines, it also demonstrates that U.S. values continue to repeat themselves over time and continents. History continues to jump into the present, hanging over our heads like the sword of Damocles. Nowhere were "muscular Christianity and the civilizing mission" more operative than in the Bikini Atoll nuclear experiments—my last tale of catastrophe.

Steve Fagin
Machine Talk

As with many of the presenters at the conference, I have the problem of condensing a much longer piece—in my case a two-hour video, *The Machine That Killed Bad People.* The tape endures this fate in its own unique style, which, as is the California manner, I will "share" with you.

First of all, people get the wrong impression when seeing a segment of the tape. They presume, "Oh yes, I've seen a bit. I'm sure if I saw the whole piece all of this mishmash would be a seamless coherence." No such luck. The piece works in a fragmentary style, trying to emulate the way television constructs meaning through fragmentation. The viewer is held together, or in the language of theory "is constructed," in the manner in which the caramel holds the chocolate and peanuts together in a Snickers bar, only then to bind the same elements to your teeth. Second, the order of the fragments works as a complex chain of commands. One opens the mind like one cracks a safe—three to the right, two to the left, five backward, spin the dial, and "Open Sesame!"—the mind is open to suggestion. TV functions this way, opening up the phatic, dysfunctional channels of our minds.

It is this need for ordering that insists that the piece be two hours long. Most independent videos range from three to eleven minutes long, in order to deal with the normal exhibition context of the art gallery or museum. I truly see the piece as being as short as I could make it. I often boast that it's like Roger Bannister when he just broke the four-minute mile saying 3 minutes, 59.4 seconds: My tape is not two hours; it's one hour, fifty-nine minutes, forty-two seconds.

I should also point out that the piece is experimental, and by this I mean it's working on a question, exploring options. I see this as the responsibility of the independent arts. I must confess that this type of work is best when it comes out of a character affliction, not an ambition. One should never start off trying to be experimental; it ends up kitsch like

Dali. One should be like Raymond Roussel, an artist I've done a piece on, trying only to make "the most popular piece in the world," or be like Victor Hugo, or, in my case, Steven Spielberg, ending up shocked at people's incredulity.

A lot has happened since the piece's inception with the overthrow of the Marcos dictatorship in February 1986. As it was happening, I thought, "What extraordinary event am I watching?" The question mark heralds the crossing of a great historical divide: the transition from Chicago 1968 and the truly narcissistic baby-boomer motto, "The whole world is watching." I remember "watching" in Istanbul (pass the opium, please!) with about as much social engagement as I could muster, seeing friends of mine being beaten. The space traversed from Chicago to Manila lurches from empathy to interactivity. As my piece was being completed in 1989, the 1986 overthrow of the Marcoses (what's called the Edsa Revolution in the Philippines—the first revolution to be named after a traffic jam) was beginning to be perceived as the prototypical TV revolution on an international scale. The event was being reconstructed as the pilot episode for the second-most popular show of that season, "From China to Ceauşescu" with Ted Koppel as the series host. Only the Simpsons were more popular.

As a prelude to showing my piece, and to bring you back to those thrilling days of yesteryear, I will give you a series of suggestions on how one might have watched some of the telehistorical events that have occurred between now, November 1992, and the completion of the piece in December 1989, challenging the baby-boomer conceit that all events should be watched as if we were still in 1968 (even though I must concede my own nostalgia for opium in Istanbul).

I should make it very clear that I think the only history worth watching occurs on cable television, with Ted Turner emerging as a twenty-first-century Herodotus. I hold this to be immutable. I'll start with the most recent event, the presidential election, surfing stations. C-Span was definitely the station of choice, with Ross Perot dancing like Henry Fonda in *My Darling Clementine* into a visual sunset. Patsy Cline's song "Crazy" plays the whole time as people come in and out of frame—such a romantic gesture—but the gesture goes on and on, durational TV turning the charming into a repetition compulsion. I start off humming along to Patsy Cline's "Crazy" and end up trapped in a labyrinthine chase film. Patsy Cline has been transformed into Joseph Lewis, no longer "crazy for loving you" but just plain "gun crazy." I begin to wish C-Span would have commercials. I need to go to the rest room.

The campaign itself, having taken so long (sort of like an academic job interview), had to be watched on different stations at different times of day. In the morning, with coffee, the networks—but as an amendment to my prohibition against anything but cable news I say, like Lot leaving Sodom, "Listen, but don't turn to watch." The insipid patter of "Good Morning America" gives a bottom beat worthy of the brilliant Cuban bassist Cachao. In the afternoon one had to be mobile, catching the syndicated shows: "Oprah," "Donahue," "Geraldo." At night, the Arkansas Ornette Coleman—Bill Clinton—knew that it was either Arsenio on Fox or Rome itself, CNN. Even Bush figured this out, appearing on "Larry King Live" the Friday prior to the election.

Our next step backward comes to rest on Hurricane Andrew. Of course one would have watched the Weather Channel, but against the grain of its intention, without channel surfing. The Weather Channel, which I believe to be the most-watched cable station, is viewed on the average for thirty seconds per hit. The network's pacing assumes this, so they want people to switch the station. I must admit I watch this station only seasonably, in the winter, when living in California encourages my sadistic side to enjoy the Michelin snow reports from the East.

It is from the Weather Channel that I draw my model of history, much different from the Marxist dialectic (easterly winds) being assumed by many of the presenters in this conference. In my model of history, one is dominated by a bunch of gadgets, predictions that try to predict through means more folkloric than scientific. Once the storm is sighted and named, the process becomes a bit more ritualistic. The response of people involved in a hurricane is quite the opposite of what I would have assumed. No one panics. Instead, people's lives become meticulous. Maps, tracking devices, shortwave radios, inch by inch, step by step, but then the hurricane hits, and all becomes unpredictable. It stops, starts, jumps, and one just rides it out. I do think history works like this. We can know something is going to break, all the circumstances are right, but we cannot assume effects, only opportunities. Systems will hover off the coast, the Holy Roman Empire can last on the verge of collapse for five hundred years, gradually losing its holiness, its Romanness, its empireness, until all at once it collapses into chaos, a black hole.

Likewise, dictatorships like Ceauşescu's or Marcos's can hold onto power in their last stages for such a long period of time that it becomes a managerial style in itself: capricious and erratic, but with the logic-of-the-last-stages style of management. When things crack, like a hurricane hitting land, everything becomes unpredictable. Where is the power going to turn next? It is this moment in history, the contact with land, that I am interested in engaging; looking for a Northwest Passage but feeling like I'm going over Niagara Falls in a barrel.

Next event, the Rodney King riots. This was best watched on local cable. Again, since I'm in southern California, I was able to watch the local Los Angeles stations. Now, this event was a beautiful study of dissonance being recuperated. During this type of brought-to-you-live event, one becomes painfully aware of the training of the local newscasters. All they know how to narrate is a five-alarm fire. Regardless of the origin and direction of the event, it eventually seeps to this level. At first, everything is a bit off: the wrong person is being interviewed, dark figures are running in and out of the frame, passersby are contradicting the on-the-spot reporter. It is very interesting to observe how, over time, they turn it into one of the few stories they have been trained to tell, and when the eleven o'clock news comes on, it's all so comfy . . . another fire story. Logo, then traffic copter view of "raging flames," cut to center frame, well-lit summary of damage to retailers, and finally talk to an eyewitness for fifteen seconds, the camera cutting before anyone makes eye contact with the camera. The coverage from eight to eleven, however—what a difference! Random camera movements, people competing to watch it tilt and turn, a couch-potato game of pinball unraveling before your sour cream cherry–flavored bag of chips.

The Persian Gulf War. As stupid as it might sound, the only place on my eighty-three channel TV set I could find nonwhites being slaughtered for no apparent reason was on ESPN. The Buffalo Bills were killing "the grey and black." The Raiders were being slaughtered. The Bills were using their "hurry-up" offense, the score was around 60-3 after a quarter, and I switched back to CNN to the TV moment of the war that first Saturday, before live coverage was thereafter quarantined. There was an oral virus sweeping the airwaves, much more lethal than anything the Iraqis would ever release. It was during the coverage of a SCUD attack, the camera frantically scanning the sky in a manner much more disorienting than anything from Michael Snow's experimental film *La région centrale*. The newscaster, trying to talk through a gas mask, is looking like a character from a Soviet constructivist play, with costumes by Rodchenko. Bobbi Battista, hysterically shrieking into her knocked-askew-by-the-gas-mask earplug that they had overheard from Dan Rather's assistant that there was a gas attack. This roller-coaster ride of rumor and disinformation is circulating like an oral tear-gas attack, the best experimental theater I've seen in years. It was like a new installment of a Wooster Group theater performance. This was the last day this type of coverage appeared on the network. There were no more live SCUD broadcasts after that.

The last events leading back to my tape are the TV revolutions of '89: Berlin, Prague, Budapest, modeled after the Edsa Revolution in the Philippines. I must concede that this was the last great moment of the major networks, watching before bed, horizontally between one's toes. I'm sure there has been some type of study showing that Ted Koppel's hair really looks sexy when seen between one's toes. The thing I most remember about this coverage was the radical time difference among the performers. It was always daytime for the people onscreen during "Nightline," or they were about to have breakfast, being awakened in the middle of the night. Truly these events took place in a hybrid time more like a dream than waking life.

To the piece itself, *The Machine That Killed Bad People:* the piece grew out of an epiphany that, like all wisdoms of that genre, is now on the verge of becoming a cliché. While watching the overthrow of the Marcoses, it became apparent that there was no longer a conceptual separation among event, televising, and watching; the spatial separation had been imploded and now constituted a single complex multispatial/temporal event. During the Gulf War, many "well-meaning" people voiced their horror over the observation of this style of event: earth-shattering spectacle, televised, controlled by rumor and the intimacy of the frame. Television had revealed its disposition: a wanton creature not good for modern dance or "Masterpiece Theater," only good for assassinations, touchdowns, revolutions, and earthquakes. These are hypertraumas and dramas of the present tense.

I, unlike these well-meaning people, was not appalled by this observation. It seemed a squandered sentiment, as useful as being appalled by a thunderstorm. Instead of critiquing this mode of television, I wanted to study its scale and force and see if I could learn to ride, then change, its course. I saw the format as powerful, and I wanted to figure out how to use it and alter the affect, keep the intensity but change the meaning. Too many papers in this conference have talked of resistance to spectacle, putting the cross in front of the vampire or simply watching from the outside and saying "I told you so" over and over again, a rosary-stroking gesture that is often called *critique.* So I jumped in and tried to create a network of my own, trying to cross Bertolt Brecht with Ted Turner. I couldn't do any more harm than efforts to convert spring wheat into winter wheat: no one was going to starve to death because of my less than noble experiment. I wanted to tangle with this postmodern octopus, the CNN-ification of the planet.

Before showing some of the tape I would like to talk a bit about the different responses I've had to the piece among the Filipino communities. I've had basically two diametrically opposed responses. When I've shown it to intellectuals who have been raised in the Philippines, the response has been intensely supportive. There is an appreciation of the piece's effort to acknowledge a complex Filipino identity, where there is no essential Filipino waiting to be released from imprisonment in First World pop culture. The brilliance of Filipino intellectuals is their ability to perform their identity not by some form of raw expressivity but through subtle toning: irony, self-deprecation, and black humor allow them to resolve the seeming paradox of both embracing and liberating themselves from U.S. popular culture. Are Filipinos neocolonialized? The answer was, "Yes, then no," or "No, then yes," depending on the individual. So these sophisticates have been a source of great support for my piece. On the other hand, when the piece has been viewed by young Filipino American college students, they have been disappointed or even angered. Why all the emphasis on Filipino involvement with U.S. culture? Where are the pure Filipino values they wish to embrace? I try to indicate to them that the piece is about the extraordinary twists and turns of this involvement, what's called *the special relation,* that is the Filipino/U.S. liaison.

In regard to the formal strategies of the piece, the inspiration lies in work done in the thirties. If one figure had to be singled out, it would be the Portuguese American novelist John Dos Passos and his magnum opus *U.S.A.* In Dos Passos, the newspaper was seen as the complex site of how people construct their narrative relation to events through a patchwork quilt of visually simultaneous, self-canceling stories. Just look at the formal richness of a newspaper page: pictures, large and small typefaces, stories all over the place, obituaries juxtaposed with statistics about the comparative literacy in developing nations. What an experimental form in terms of its grammar, but the semantics are reductive and most often conservative. The form encourages the opening up of the imagination and then its contraction. This is the issue that interested me. I wanted to transform this type of experimentation done in the thirties to the narrative image site of the present: cable television. I worked off cable television formatting, trying to take advantage of its grammatical resourcefulness, the way things are told and how they're juxtaposed, and redress the semantic redundancy and conservativeness. If image grammarians were to study my piece in the twenty-third century, they would perceive it as typical.

I'm going to show parts from all four sections of the piece and then take questions. I'll take the questions à la Donahue and have someone go around the audience with a mike. It's that time of late afternoon when our appetite for truth has shifted: we no longer crave soap opera but the syndicated talk show. Our midday meal is dominated by melodrama, high tea by confession.

Steve Fagin
Excerpts from *The Machine That Killed Bad People*

Manila, 7 December 1972.

Thousands watched on live television as she was carried off, her beige terno soaked in blood. Dr. Robert Chase, a hand expert from Stanford University flown in to consult, said he believed the first lady survived due to her expertise at ping-pong. "She threw her arm up and danced back when he came forward, and that was part of her ping-pong capability."

Constance:

Weather.

Cloudy.

Metro Manila will be cloudy and will have rain showers. Light Northeasterly winds will blow. Forecast range of temperature: twenty-two to thirty degrees Celsius.

Eastern Luzon will have scattered rain showers due to the northeast monsoon. Eastern and western Visayas, along with Mindanao, will have occasional rains due to the tail end of the cold front. The rest of the country will be cloudy.

Sunrise today: 6:43; sunset: 5:24.

Ron:

Under the Marcoses this place was a kleptocracy. Imelda would go into Tiffany's on Fifth Avenue, a Unesco check made out to the Philippines neatly folded in one of her native bags, pick out a bangle, and as they wrapped the sparkler would demurely ask, "Would you take a second-person check?" They, seeing the Unesco signature, would nod ever so slightly as the check passed from her hand to theirs.

Now, like a character from *Dawn of the Dead,* she haunts the malls of Hawaii, one day joyously charging more than she can carry. The next day, playing a tortured credit-card Lady Macbeth, she repents for her purchases, returning more than she bought the previous day.

Home Shopping:

Hello Shoppers!

Welcome to "Some are Smarter than Others"!

Our featured shopper is Marcos crony Herminio Disini, who master-minded the fattest single contract ever landed in the Philippines: the Westinghouse nuclear power plant in Bataan, built on a site subject to tidal waves, five miles from a volcano and twenty-five miles from three geological faults. Disini was paid a commission by Westinghouse of $50 million. Disini companies became in charge of civil works, engineering, communication, and insurance. The original design of the reactor was defective and eventually cost $2.2 billion.

Remember to stay home and shop. If you ever want to get a taste of what it would be like if World War III broke out, go to a shopping mall between now and Christmas.

Ron:

Two hundred eighteen days, but no nights, the corpse was being held hostage by the living. They knew the Americans would be impressed, a trace of Iran. Both Donna Josefa Marcos, Ferdinand's mother, and Ninoy Aquino had the same embalmer, the wake's tour guide politely informed me. Such a small country. When I first arrived, I thought it to be my good luck. Drop the right name, doors, now even coffins opened. Everyone seemed to know one another, and they were so closely knit. Later I would realize, Right, that's what an oligarchy feels like. The wake now going longer than a miniseries but not quite long enough for syndication. The paid mourners, the mother in state, well lit, just enough flowers to fill the frame. The Right had become so accessible. Once arrogant and removed, they saw their last hope as American television. The Left, on the other hand, was cautious. Maybe their image would be seen by the vigilante death squads, perhaps you're in the CIA—oh yes, a concerned writer. Know an issue in a weekend, and show it in a thirty-second balanced featurette. The wake's hostess inquired, Would I like to meet the Marcoses' cook? Ferdinand's first-grade teacher? A child saved from drowning? As I stared into the coffin I thought of little. Being a method mourner, I thought of my grandmother's funeral, my grandfather shrieking as he threw himself into the open grave. Becoming professional, I insisted the camera should shoot directly into the casket. The guide smiled. The sequence was shot a second time. A retake. What did I expect? The corpse to blow its lines, to blink, to sneeze? Only the camera made death feel near. I went outside for room, and death washed over me. That night my dreams were flooded.

Ron Vawter in "Hotel Reporting," from *The Machine That Killed*

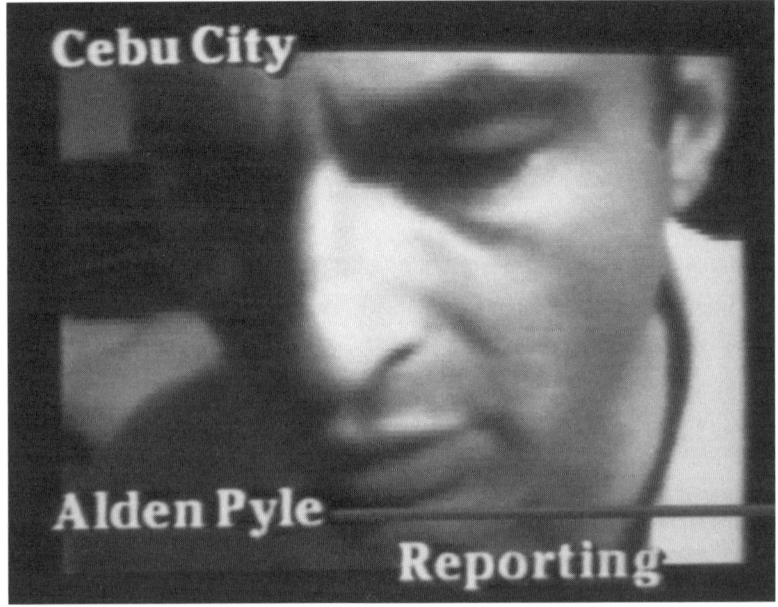

Vicente L. Rafael
Updates: Doubled Histories

In his video *The Machine That Killed Bad People*, Steve Fagin views the Philippines shortly after the People Power uprising in 1986. He fastens on to what Walter Benjamin, referring to another place and time, called "the pile of debris" whipped up by "this storm we call . . . progress." Fagin offers us a collection of chronotopes so that the country comes across as if it were the site of a series of redemptive possibilities stretching from Tiananmen Square to the collapse of the Berlin Wall. For this reason, it is not difficult to understand the wishfulness that pervades this work, a wishfulness that, as in the case of a dream, subsequent events show to have been productively misplaced.

What has happened? The New People's Army with its factionalized cadres, its numerous strategic blunders, its bankrupt and ideologically frozen party leadership, has cast into serious doubt attempts to locate them as vanguards in the struggle for what was once called *national democracy*. Indeed, the very notion of the *national*—in the sense of a bounded territory whose heterogeneous population can be contained within the sovereign power of the state—has lately come under pressure from the movements of hundreds and thousands of Filipinos seeking employment overseas. Along with Filipino immigrant populations in North America, Filipino overseas contract workers from Singapore to Rome have created enclaves of "Filipino-ness" constituted by the commodification of what passes for national culture.

What else? The Marcoses, both the living and the dead, have returned, as mother and son seek, however farcically, to rehabilitate the legacy of Ferdinand's demagoguery. And, as if on cue, the old oligarchy has joined with the newly rich to secure the reigns of the state, while the proliferation of religious fundamentalisms from the Opus Dei to a variety of born-again sects has created a culturally conservative climate cutting across social classes. Finally, the departure of the U.S. military bases at Subic and Clark through the combination of nationalist agitation and natural calamities has meant the loss of the most tangible basis of U.S. interests in this part of the Pacific and concurrently the loss of U.S. media attention on the Philippines. If it surfaces at all in the American press nowadays, it is usually as the latest example of yet another Third World country poised for NIC-dom, the newest site for global sourcing thanks to the liberal, free-market authoritarianism of the Ramos regime and his likely successor.

The Machine could not have recorded, much less forecast, these particular storm signals from paradise. Its primary project, as I understand it, is to call attention to the televisual grammar informing Western coverage of a certain already-known "Philippines" and to posit ways for perverting its enunciatory power. But, while mixing narrative genres, it also has a secondary aim: that of pointing out the historical particularity of colonial domination and warfare that makes possible the citing of an alternative history of the Philippines enfolded within the workings of the tape's visual apparatus. The first project, so dazzlingly conceived as to be spectacularly obvious to an audience here on this side of the metropolitan divide, in fact opens up to the second, less apparent because visually "impoverished," project. It is this latent aspect of the video that I would like to dwell on.

To think about the possibilities for seeing other kinds of histories: such is what I take to be the provocatively haphazard and fitfully articulated desire of *The Machine*. Unlike the more manifest and tightly scripted moments of its media critique, this other, more tentative moment is anchored neither to a specific figure (a newspaper reporter or a television anchorwoman) nor to a particular genre (the nineteenth-century novel or the twentieth-century shopping network). Rather, these alternative histories exist in between such tropes, either as extended and unedited "interviews" (where answers are given for which there are no questions) or as found footage (low-tech fragments and other documents of distraction that fall outside narrative temporality). Such scenes stutter their way through the visual framework, interrupting the interruptions inherent in the critical vocation of the tape. In doing so, they tend to suspend the trajectory of Fagin's writerly interventions with their seemingly unmotivated insertions of different languages, accents, and body gestures. In these moments, what emerges is a semiotics of hesitations, pauses, and exclamations at a remove from the perverse but still quite readable discourse of the video. There are numerous such instances. Let me just cite two.

First example. In the section entitled "Tourism," there is a segment on Alex Orbito, "travel agent and faith healer." As if to capitalize on the historical conjunction of tourism and therapy in the modern Westernized mind, Orbito sits in an office whose wallpaper of palm trees and beaches lends a hallucinatory sense to the difference between inside and outside. More interestingly, he speaks in a kind of English that verges on creolization: tonally assertive while grammatically and phonetically dissonant. He treats Anna O'Harra on his desk, seeming to penetrate her stomach and digging out bits and pieces of God only knows what. For the camera, he creates a spectacle of abjection where "healing" occurs without the mediation of medical discourse. The woman's body is not objectified into a set of symptoms and anatomical parts but instead submitted to what seems like the most cursory and ritually casual procedures. An anonymous set of hands appears here and there, but the general impression one gets is that everything just seems to happen so that in the end nothing really seems to have occurred at all. The rubbing alcohol applied to her stomach serves only to erase whatever traces the transaction may have left behind (and, for this reason, rubbing alcohol has long been a staple antiseptic in Philippine bordellos and massage parlors). That "nothing" has happened is confirmed by the patient herself, who cheerfully relates her new condition while Orbito looks away impassively, bored and unconnected to what is being said about him.

Here, a disjuncture appears between Orbito as the person who speaks and Orbito as the person who is spoken about, between, that is, the identity of the self and the circulation of its products and representations. It is a gap that was already figured in his speech, a difference internal to the speaking subject that, to my mind, is the symptomatic recurrence of the fundamental fissures and encoded violence brought about by the force of colonial history. Where the American woman feels "whole" after the treatment, able to go on with her life because able to consolidate her bodily state with her mental disposition, Orbito dwells in his doubleness, which is also a kind of duplicity, one inherited from a long history of colonial mimesis and collaborative violence.

Second example. A number of the found footage sections in the tape consist of the Marcoses' home videos, which to this day have yet to be systematically cataloged and made available to the public. From a North American perspective, there has always been something titillating about watching these tapes, as if one were seeing what was not meant to be seen: namely, the sight of the rich and powerful appearing foolish and vulnerable. Yet, from another angle, this titillation turns out to be without foundation.

In these home videos, Imelda, Ferdinand, and their children are captured belting out ballads in the vernacular and in English. Seen from the perspective of Filipino entertainment and political history, these moments quickly become recognizable. They are typical rather than embarrassing, as a Western media epistemology might have us believe. Power in the Philippines is historically indissociable from its dramatic performance rather than its rationalized administration. Political campaigns since the early twentieth century have featured variety shows, declamatory contests, celebrity endorsements, and singing and dancing. Ferdinand and Imelda were seasoned veterans of such antics. To stand in front of others—as in the amateur contest that figures in town fiestas and TV variety shows—and to take on another voice, one that entails speaking or singing in shifting registers, is to establish oneself as worthy of recognition. It is to set oneself apart in public and thus command, at least potentially, the prospect of deference from others. That is because speaking and singing in public can amount to displaying one's proximity to power, understood as the realm of potency and limitless aid, a realm that historically has stretched from the spirit world of pre- and post-Catholic beliefs to the military and financial capitals of Western Europe, North America, and Japan. This logic of power through performance—and its accompanying fantasies of patronage and reciprocal indebtedness—helps clarify the privileged position enjoyed by various important figures in the history of Filipino culture, figures whom the Marcoses themselves sought to embody simultaneously: the spirit medium, the mestizo elite, the nationalist politician, the Westernized technocrat, the provincial warlord, the glamorous movie star. These are all agents of hybridity who occupy and so control the points midway between the outside, and unknown forces emanating from the world, and the inside, and all too familiar material frailties and social antagonisms that compose the "underdevelopment" of myriad localities in the country.

The strangeness of these Marcos home videos has to do with their ability to restate the familiar in a technologically novel register and thus restage the basis of their power. They show the spectacle of those on top of the hierarchy performing and thus revealing their ability to dissimulate other voices, to sound and act otherwise, thereby confirming their capacity to command the technologies for reproducing and containing the contradictory desires for modernity *and* social hierarchy.

There is, however, an additional complication. These variant histories of another Philippines, one that is opened up by *The Machine*'s disassembling of television, can be read in terms of specific grammars of disjuncture (such as creolization). But doing so brings up the possibility of discerning still other moments barely available to a televisual gaze or to a mimicry-historiographic practice.

A final example. There is the footage of the attempted assassination of Imelda prior to 1972 that occurs in the beginning and close to the middle of the video. We see a black-suited man appear on a stage where Imelda is handing out prizes to farmers. He looks to his right, then reaches into his jacket to draw out a long knife. Lunging at Imelda, he hacks away again and again until her security guards overpower him. Imelda escapes with only minor injuries. Thanks to her skill at ping-pong, as her Stanford physician later explains, she is able to fend off her attacker's blows.

This scene is only a few seconds long. I recall seeing it while I was in high school in Manila. The local television news could do nothing but replay this segment over and over again. At least, this is my recollection of the event. It was as if television were reduced to a kind of ceaseless stuttering. Rather than controlling the representation of the event, the television appeared to fall wholly under its control. It was as if the news were possessed by a memory simultaneously unforgettable and unlivable. The sudden sight of Imelda being slashed again and again in murderous frenzy opened up the horrifying possibility—horrifying at least to those invested in the ordered representation of social hierarchy—that anything could happen: that an unknown assailant could, without warning and without reference to a prior order, come perilously close to cutting off a figure of authority. Thus did Philippine TV respond in a way that perhaps reverberated with the nation's reaction: repeating this scene, blurting it out uncontrollably, finding itself beside itself in mimicking those repetitious gestures of her assailant, gestures that Imelda herself repeatedly matched in order to fend off. *The Machine* sees this—or more precisely sees it again—and so relays something of a history of repetitions that shadows the storms of progress in the Philippines, hinting as well at the progress of storms yet to come.

■ ■ ■

Constance:

Essential items whose prices are reduced: coconut-based cooking oil, 5–10 centavos per kilo; sugar from 14 pesos per kilo to 12.90 pesos per kilo; evaporated and soya-based milk products from 8.60 pesos to 8.30 pesos per can; locally manufactured drugs and medicines by at least 10 percent.

Items whose prices are maintained at current level: poultry and hog products; imported medicines and drugs; canned sardines, school supplies, cements, and detergents.

Home Shopping:

Hello Shoppers!

This transcends the incredible!

Our featured shopper is Marcos crony Bobby Benedicto. His family fortune in sugar amassed through burning peasant villages and bribing local officials. They were the largest property owners in Negros and early backers of Ferdinand Marcos. Benedicto was made president of the Philippine National Bank, and under martial law only his newspaper and television station were allowed to stay in operation. All sugar in the Philippines was stored in his warehouses, insured by his company, and shipped in his tankers. Some of the profits of the sugar industry were used to finance the Negros police force, whose vehicles, instead of having the usual saint's image on the dashboard, displayed a photo of Mr. and Mrs. Benedicto.

Ron:

Here it is only the underclass that live in Asia; the upper class live behind armed gates. Entire communities: schools, fire stations, ranch houses with patios to barbecue, streets like Elm, Cherry, Main. They live in what they call villages like Connecticut and La Jolla. They say "the ultimate paradise." I call it "Stepford Paradise."

People Stop Marines:

The people had swelled at about 4:30 P.M. when rumors went around that the Marines would take the camp and that the crowd would be dispersed with tear gas.

General Tadiar denied it. "We do not have a single tear gas here," he said.

An hour later, a helicopter landed in the vacant lot, drawing people around it, chanting "Cory! Cory!"

Seeing it was impossible for his men to carry out their mission, Tadiar finally gave up and said: "I don't want to hurt these people; I'm also human just like you."

Tadiar then ordered his men to withdraw from the area. The standoff lasted a few hours.

(*Manila Times,* 24 February, p. 1)

At midnight, after two armored vehicles sped down the side of the square from the front gate, the tension mounted even higher. Shrill loudspeakers barked out repeated "notifications." Thick formations of soldiers in steel helmets were moving into the square from all sides. In the dark, we could make out machine-gun placements on the roof of the History Museum. The students crowded back around the Heroes Monument.

At 4 A.M. Sunday the lights on the square were suddenly extinguished. Through the loudspeakers, we again heard the order to "clear out." A sudden wave of anxiety passed through me, and a voice in my head said over and over, "The moment has come."

Then, [Taiwan pop singer] Hou Dejian and other hunger strikers negotiated with the army for a peaceful retreat of the students. But just as we were about to move, at 4:40 A.M., a barrage of red flares shot into the sky. Immediately, the square was brightly illuminated. I saw that the front of the square was full of soldiers. From the Great Hall of the People, a squadron of soldiers rushed out, dressed in camouflage, carrying assault rifles, and wearing helmets and gas masks.

The first thing that the charging soldiers did was to erect a row of ten or more machine guns right in front of the Heroes Monument. The machine gunners took a prone position, with their backs to the Gate of Heavenly Peace. As soon as the placements were established, a huge number of soldiers and military police appeared.

They were all holding electric cattle prods and rubber truncheons and some special purpose weapons that we did not recognize. They charged at us, breaking apart the formation in which we were sitting, beating us with all their might. Our ranks were broken into two groups, and they forced their way through the middle to the third tier of the monument. I saw about fifty students who were so badly beaten that blood completely covered their faces.

At that monument, the armored vehicles and additional forces that had been waiting on the square closed in on us, and we were completely surrounded by rows and rows of vehicles, leaving only a small gap in the direction of the museum.

At the same time, the soldiers and military police who had reached the third tier went about smashing all the students' printing and broadcasting equipment and dragged the students down from the steps. Even then we remained seated, holding hands and singing the "Internationale" and shouting "The People's Army will not hurt the people!" But, unable to resist the kicking and clubbing of such a large number of attackers, the students sitting on the third tier were forced down.

When they reached the ground, machine guns erupted. Some soldiers opened fire from a kneeling position, their bullets flying over our heads, but the gunners splayed on the ground were shooting right at the chests and heads of the students. When this happened, we could only retreat up the back of the monument. Then the machine guns stopped. But the beating of the soldiers above forced us back down. Then the machine guns started again.

At this time, workers and citizens, putting their own lives aside, took up bottles, sticks, or anything that could be used as weapons and rushed across to fight the soldiers.

The Student Association urged everyone to get out of the square.

At that point a large number of students tried to get out through the gap in the armored vehicles. But even this exit was sealed off. Thirty armored cars came crushing into the crowd. Some students died under the wheels, and even the flagpole in front of the monument was knocked down.

I never thought that the students could be so courageous. One group went to try to turn over the vehicles but were repulsed by bullets. Then a second wave, stepping over the bodies of those in front, rushed at the vehicles again, managing to topple one of them. Three thousand students, myself included, rushed out amid flying bullets through this opening toward the History Museum.

Those who survived joined citizens outside the museum who were running north. Seeing flashes of gunfire from the trees ahead, we turned around and ran south.

Tears streamed down our faces as we ran. We could see a second group of students trying to escape under fire, many of them falling. We all wept, and, weeping, we ran. Just as our group reached the front gate of the city, we were met by a large contingent of soldiers, all running from the direction of the Jewelry Market. When we met, they didn't shoot but began beating us madly with huge wooden clubs.

At this point, a crowd of citizens came rushing up the front gate and started fighting ferociously with the soldiers; they did this to protect us as we tried to break through in the direction of the railway station. The soldiers pursued us. By 5 A.M. the gunfire in the square was dying away. Afterward, I ran into a friend at the international Red Cross, and he told me that by 5 A.M. anyone who could escape had done so.

I will never be able to forget what happened when the students were shot down and others rushed to save the wounded and carry away the bodies. Some of the women tore off their clothes to bandage wounds until they had nothing more to take off.

A Qinghua University friend of mine from Jiangsu Province was bleeding heavily but still running with us until he could keep up no longer. He fell against my shoulder, saying, "Can you help me?" I was already supporting two injured women students, so I couldn't get to him right away. He fell on the ground, and the crowd trampled him. I still have the stains of his blood on my back. [*New York Times?*]

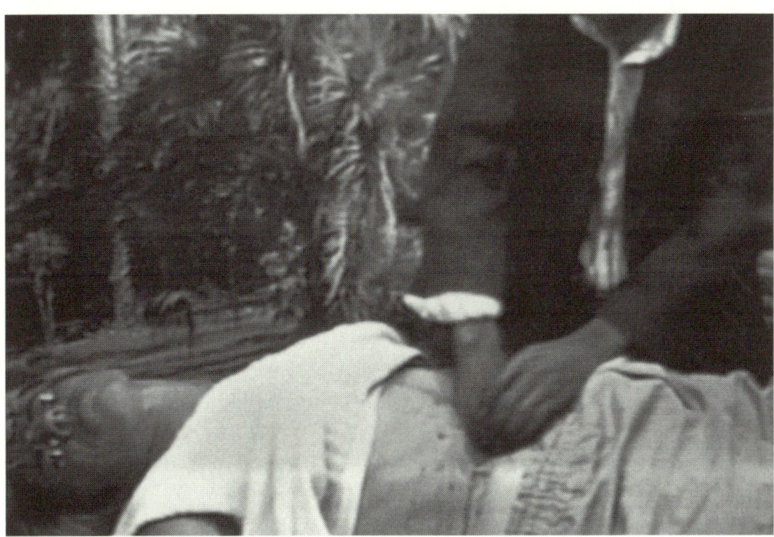

"Tourist Agent/Faith Healer," from *The Machine That Killed*

Minh-ha:

I closed my eyes as piss still dripped from his pecker.

The fall of a dictator.

The urine filled my nostrils, blocking the smell of the cartons of Chinese food ordered for two hundred, one hour before.

One hour later the Americans would swoop them away.

Ferdinand called for caviar and watched the black eggs as they were poured over the piss-stained green carpet.

He said, "Cory will think it's the odor of caviar."

He started to giggle.

Meanwhile, Imelda stood transfixed, burning papers, blowing the fire out before more than the edges were charred.

She read aloud from the remains,

"There will be a charge of $14,500 for a 9 x 10 painting that will take 2 1/2 months to execute. There will be an additional charge of $1,500 for persons added, but no extra charge for animals you wish to include in the painting.

Sincerely yours, Ralph Wolfe Cowan"

Ron:

There's a short story written at the turn of the century called "The False Messiah" or "The Great Film." It's about a film company who specialized in what was called actualization. Their catalog was chock-full of irresistible events, including, they would boast, the getting up in the morning of the president of the republic and the birth of the prince. But what was missing from their near-perfect catalog was a crime. Cinematic integrity would not allow them to reenact one, so they decided to perpetrate one themselves. They set about the crime by kidnapping three people—a rather eccentrically dressed younger couple and an elderly mustachioed man in dress clothes. Now they drugged and undressed them, opening the woman's bodice and leaving the man in shirt sleeves: these would be the victims. The other kidnap victim, who would be the criminal, was given a dagger and told that he must first revive them and then kill the couple; otherwise he would be murdered himself. He agreed and suggested that his character wear a mask. The crime was committed for the camera. Afterward, the camera still rolling, the assassin washed his hands, combed his hair, and brushed himself off. Finally, the camera was turned off.

The film company was quite lucky. Their victims turned out to be minor celebrities: she the wife of a minister of a small Balkan state and he the son of the pretender to the throne of a North German principality. The company came out with the film only moments after the story hit the tabloids. The police never believed for a moment that the film was an offering of the real crime, even though the film company boldly proclaimed it to be so. The film was a great success, and eventually the police arrested and then executed a quite innocent oriental. Once again the film company was in luck. They were given permission to shoot the execution, which they exhibited on a double bill with the crime.

Constance:

Manila, 7 December 1972.

Thousands watched on live television as she was carried off, her beige terno soaked in blood. Dr. Robert Chase, a hand expert from Stanford University flown in to consult, said he believed the first lady survived due to her expertise at ping-pong. "She threw her arm up and danced back when he came forward, and that was part of her ping-pong capability."

It was in Leyte that she, Imelda Roumaldez Marcos, had first heard of Europe. Brought by her widowed father to live in the family home, already nearly falling down. Her nun half sister told her the story of the opera singer Maria Malibran. As a little girl, her father, a famous tenor, had forced Maria to sing the role of Desdemona in Rossini's *Otello*. This would be her debut. Her father told her that if she didn't sing perfectly he would strangle her to death. The critical scene of the opera occurred, his hand on Maria's throat. She couldn't tell if it was Desdemona being strangled to death by her jealous husband or her own father trying to kill her. She sang perfectly.

Ten years later, Maria, now the most famous soprano in Europe, learns that she has but a few months left to live. She has only one request. Before she dies she wishes to play the lead in *Otello*.

Imelda arose, the morning after the assassination attempt, in the manner of the hysteric who, after a hectic day of being beaten, tortured, and defeated by her symptoms, awakens refreshed. She had dreamed of mermaids, but this image was replaced by a more troubled one. Huge stones took shape before her, carved with strange etchings. It was a temple and a tomb, a royal tomb. A white vapor rose up from one of the pillars. It took the shape of a queen, a miracle of beauty. The

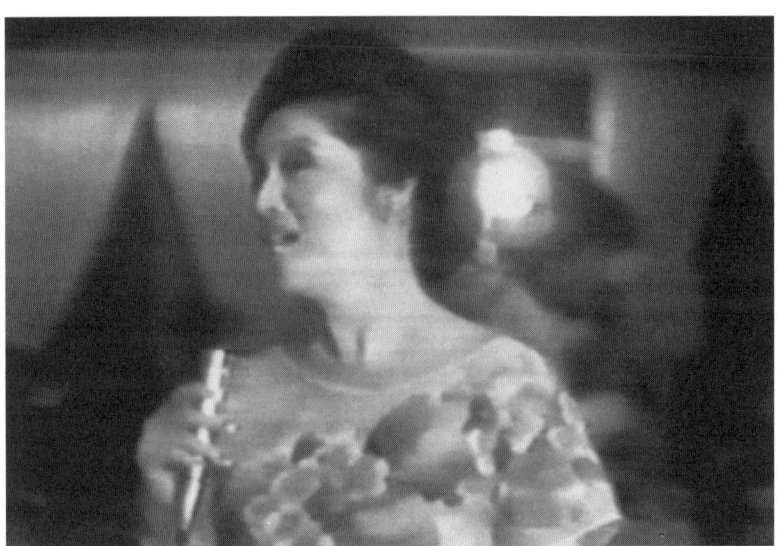

"Imelda Sings," from *The Machine That Killed*

woman smiled at Imelda and took her hand. Her hand slipped from the beautiful vision's grasp. Imelda tried to shout, but no sound came from her mouth. Instead, she heard loud voices calling to her. At this moment she rejoined the living.

Later in the day, still resting, watching the events broadcast in an endless loop on the television, she remained perplexed. Why had Ver's security, standing by, not rushed to her rescue? Ver politely explained that his men had wished to remain out of camera range to give her center stage.

It was the custom in the Roumaldez household to gather in the sala after supper for an evening of music. Don Vicente played the piano, one daughter played violin, and Imelda sang. After the Americans had retaken Leyte, several would gather to hear this pure voice soar over the accompaniment of the piano and violin. Eventually, this was brought to the attention of Irving Berlin, touring the liberated South.

Although her range of songs was more distinguished, from the Abelardo Kundimans to selections from *The Desert Song,* Imelda sang to Berlin "You Are My Sunshine." She had been told this was the anthem of the American liberation. Despite Berlin's praises, Imelda decided not to pursue a singing career.

Trinh T. Minh-ha
Voice-Over I

Air *(Your Tongue)*

And sensuality? Sensuality follows the listeners. For some, it delights, moves, awakens desire; for others, it sows doubt, irritates, and is finally rejected on the side of femininity.

From the depths of . . . , on the very surface, it tells all my secrets. I can't hear it without feeling exposed. Whose is it?

A voice. Over. I.

Voice: in the confines of this relationship with the body, from the inside out, between absence and presence, desire. The voice of the name appearing on the image is a fiction. The speaker, the news reporter, or the narrator has a fictive identity, for *I* is a fiction of identity. Not all of what is seen, heard, smelled, tasted, and felt is representable, for *I* represent not I. I read what I've been told, and, all of a sudden, I hear my own voice. *I* am (no) other than the eye *I* represent or the represented *I*. The tongue that falsifies must then be trimmed, cut, edited. Selectively staged. Tactically turned over. Dis-played aloud, always interrupted in its breath. A site of love, a tear on silence. Voice evokes rape. Unapproachable, it arouses sexual desires. Does it lie? No, identity and non-identity meet in the question asked; they interact in the same sound space. Perhaps it is too difficult to find the word in which it lies, and one goes on wondering which I in the impassioned eye? An *I* that reads, an *I* that hears, or an *I* you hear? What asserts itself over the eye, the image, the non-displayed silence would have to be both an absent presence and a present absence. The eye/I reading is finally more *I* than the I saying *I*.

A voice exists in voic-ing. On its materiality—physical, erotic, *and* uninhabitable—a world is being built in the projected intervals of image, words, music, and silence. Likely to suscitate disappointment and disgust is the ease with which one summarizes, explains, classifies, assimilates, neutralizes, impersonalizes, hence co-opts and destroys. Beg-in a-gain. I hear myself detached from myself in the space of sound time. There, something is uttered that has no head, no tail, and with each word emitted, I perceive myself faltering, sickened by the sound taking shape in the hollow of my throat. My, mine; often moved by an urgent desire, not so much to deform the world becoming sound becoming form through such a closed venue, as to simply let free. If only the words can (be let) ring or die. They can swell, I can make my body resonate, and perhaps inscribe: here one does not speak; one groans, moans, sighs; one breathes. Resists. Turns faint, inaudible. Lovers becoming sound becoming animals are so much alike. There is no longer I, but only Sighs, Sighs, Moans, Moans, Breaths. Nothing original, nothing personal, yet all intensely intimate. The unique, irreplaceably non-personal intimacy. Here, one can only gasp for Air as one finds one's way through the long, stuffy, densely packed corridor of intentional meaning.

Move your tongue over your lips.

Earth *(Your Lips)*

Voice has no memory. Free of context and of development, it reads blindly, understanding "everything of what others read but nothing of what it reads" (to quote myself quoted). *I* is always past. The eye of the voice is an absent eye, not yet subject nor quite object. In my own voice, I would stray away from meaning. Voice would slip into non-sense, coming closer to the scream, the laugh, the cry, the song. The onomatopeias of a loving body. It caresses, makes desire audible. Voice then, not in the words, but in their sounds, in the way it sounds and sculpts the space it traverses. A half-audible, half-silenced movement of lust, thirst, and hunger is projected, captured, to reveal not what cannot be seen, or what remains absent, but what seems not to lend itself to representation. Lov*ing*. When the non-representable finds its place in the relation of word, sound, silence, and image, or of timbre, tone, dynamics, and duration, meaning can only circulate at the limit of sense and non-sense.

One goes on hearing, eyes shut. Loses one's breath as time seems to come to a standstill. Here, where air is rarefied. . . . A swoon. All lights become dimmers. Insight, intuition, and other sensory faculties let go of their ingenuity, leaving room for an overfocused in-. Intensity. Less and less clear as the lips touch each other, less and less sharp as the sounds roll out, deformed in their contours, barely recognizable, and above all not-yet-not-quite finished. The voice keeps on drifting, incomplete, continually growing and coming into being, stretching beyond sense, beyond sight, beyond pleasure, toward uncertainty and un-desirability, toward its own peril. Own death. Breath.

A present without presence. A voice (re)recorded. A loss of subjectivity. What if what one hears as "true," "authentic," "personal," is nothing other than a ghostly projection, a dis-embodied sound of a body in love with its own sound? Swallow, and wet your lips. As meaning enters and settles down, beware, voice becomes conscious of its "significance," its role as holder of truth and of knowledge. Voice becomes Someone's voice. It centers. Carries a specific function, for it is there to inform, to state "facts," to *cover* the news, to give mean-ing to non- and not-yet-mean-ingful events. It fulfills its useful task and becomes *voice* all *over* again. *Over*tly situated, *cover*tly omniscient. Or is it the other way around? What makes it ring off-site? Oddly enough, what seems strange is when it sounds true. No doubt, it's all wet.

Water *(Your Saliva)*
And sensuality. Can anything sound drier? more senseless? S-wallow, clear y-our throat. The spit lands on the sidewalk, on the floor in a restaurant, on the train, in a bus, neatly next to one's foot

between two seats in a movie theater. It hardly *looks* inspiring. And yet. . . . Constantly darting and licking, the tongue continues its favorite activity, wetting the entire skin surface of the lips, cheeks, chin, and throat. Do you care for more (water)? Again, I insist: and sensuality? Your parched lips. Always in want of the moist that refuses to dwell, or spread. Sensuality doesn't belong to the visible or to the audible, it hardly articulates. It caresses. Sometimes one hears it too well; it overwhelms. Other times one solicits it in vain. It remains absent, barely there, already somewhere else. When it comes, it goes; it returns weeks after, unexpectedly. Creating a resonance more subtle than sound, more persistent than sight, it is a physics of the voice, comparable in precision and in intensity to the infinity of pentamerous rhythm.

Streams and rivers held internally are released and externalized in gradients. The voice heard is an aural glyph for the inner experience of pitch, volume, and rhythm. Without practice, it is easily silted over. One would then have to wash it clean to make it resonate anew. A waking up to sound and voice can open to an intimate love for the basic creative elements of music and the primary directions of creation—north, south, east, west, and the Middle or the empty center. Of the five intoxications to which one easily falls prey, as they say in many parts of Asia, music is the fifth, the four others being beauty, wealth, power, and knowledge. Music is both the source of creativity and the means to receive it. Your saliva heals and destroys. Gives life and dissolves it. Engenders, regenerates, moistens, softens, or insults. Certainly it arouses and calms, awakens or kills desire. The passion, the art of transmitting saliva. The science and the eroticism of breath. The violence-becoming-tenderness of that movement without memory between receptivity (in creation) and creativity (in reception). Attraction and repulsion are, in the end, all music.

Light *(The Way You Move)*

Voice structures both physical and narrative space. With it, desire is made audible, rhythmic. Breath is manifested as word, as
sound, as music, and silence is reintroduced into the image. The
voice renders, it doesn't reproduce. It works as a sound seer
whose rhythms translate less the realities evoked than the internal life of its own constitutive elements. Here, one is bound to
read blindly. Or to go blind while hearing oneself speaking. The
timbre, tone, and rhythm can enliven myriads of sensations—visual, tactile, spatial, temporal. Can you see it?

Some viewers-listeners never really cross this threshold, who
conceive the voice only as information and communication. They
do not hear. Have heard nothing. Caught in de-ci-phering rather
than in re-ceiving, they find meaning in the said, the all-too-vis-
ible. They? I. I too listen to myself speaking meaningfully when I
set out to represent (an)other voices. And I may forget a moment
of no-meaning, no-understanding does not necessarily hinder
understanding. The two, as Dogen reminds, are like spring and
autumn. In love with one another. Since the sky in its entirety lies
in a drop of water, it is often not in front of images that one
dreams. One encounters a voice and embarks on a journey of no
return. One hears it before one even becomes a spectator-listener.
A voyage is produced not by the vision or the sound projected,
but by a musical receptivity that allows one to tune in before the
event, toward the softness of a becoming-voice—a spirit in motions. In this twilight reverie, the ear is led, between sense and
sound, from "non-formed" to not-yet-formed words, from hints of
articulation to hints of inarticulation, from silent cues to half-
said, half-sung vowels and consonants. And the journey continues its course, exposing itself as site of transience and availabil-
ity, as play between rupture and rapture.

The complex harmonies make the voice hang in the image
space, which remains suspended in what it shows and says. A

long tone, for example, is not a boring one-line-event, but a mul-
tiplicity of moments shifting wildly between the raw and the
cooked. That darkness in voicing: an odor of bodily liquid, the
fragrance of a familiar breath. Melody loses its central role when
pleasure comes with the ability to travel through different tonal
places, to render a timbre in its fullness, or to explore the dynamics of overtones. Sensitivity to timbre and tone, over- and under-,
keeps one alert to the most subtle changes of light and color,
shades and hues. The tones with which you speak are so many
seeds disseminated in the space through which you move. Finally, one never stops listening to the rhythm of a voice, whether
consciously or unconsciously. If the rhythm doesn't work, the
voice doesn't work. Nothing comes together, nothing comes apart;
only the stagnancy and monotony of a spiritless utterance lend
themselves to one's reading and hearing. There are as many
voices as there are "souls," it is often said. One may be born to a
certain pitch, a certain tone, and a certain timbre, but what is
"natural" becomes "magical" when, in the manner of nature, it is
developed and cultivated. Perhaps, to practice the erotic science
of breath is to learn how to perform simple activities such as: to
make a sound, to say a word, to pause, to be silent. In other words,
to let one's breath find its rhythm, to let one's voice find its way.
Powerful in its vulnerability. Magical in its simplicity.

■ ■ ■

Ron:

She had almost never gone to the palace. Well, once that is, trapped by
her own hospitality. A visiting English friend had begged her, there
was this certain international pianist. As feared, she was eventually
cornered by Mrs. Marcos, who requested her to "come sit," her index
and forefinger insisting. Imelda asked petulantly, "Why don't you ever
ask me for a favor? I'll do anything you want." Experienced from
fighting off so many suitors, she replied, "Mrs. Marcos, why do you
care if I like you? You have all these other people." Imelda replied,
"These others appreciate my favors the first time, maybe the second or

third time, but by the sixth time if they ask for something and I might have to say no they will forget the five favors and never forgive me. You, on the other hand, who have never asked me for a favor, if you ask for just one, you will always be thankful."

Minh-ha:

American television would charge to the rescue. Save the fiasco in the editing. This has become instinct. Now they could only tell stories—they had lost the ability to untell them. They worked efficiently, and the points to be covered were obvious. Fifteen seconds each. The family portrait, a bit dog-eared, informal but quaint, children falling in and out of frame. The now pathetic despot, groping for the seal of his sovereignty, which sat right under his nose. He could still smell it. The moment of conflict: the savage watchdog Ver turning on his master, live television, calling for violence, as Marcos, near collapse, framed the charge of an original civility, trying one last time to fool the Americans. And a self-portrait, a journalist speaking out, insisting on The Truth. A minute soap opera, one minute covering the quaint, the pathetic, the heroic, and still fifteen seconds left over to pat oneself on the back. In the Philippines, something else was watched. The drama of duration.

267

"Save the Fiasco in the Editing," from *The Machine That Killed*

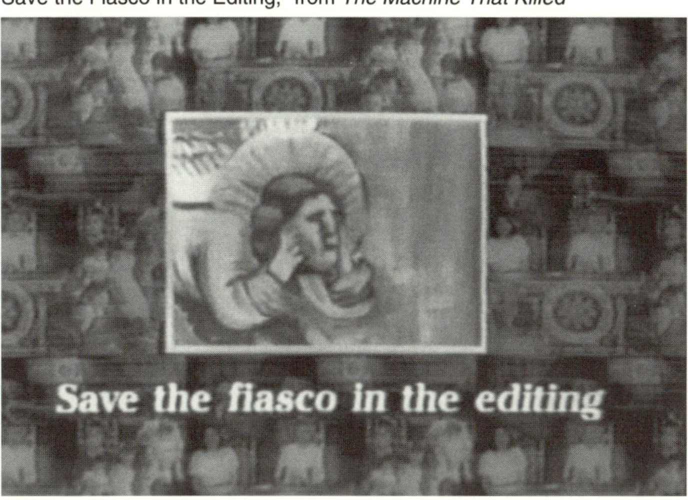

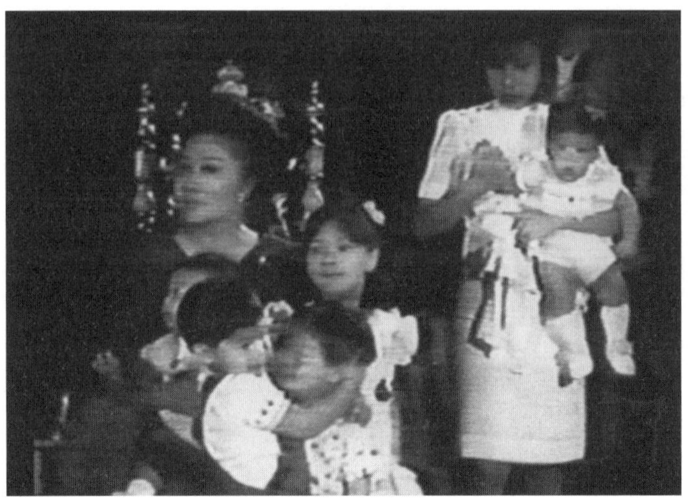

"The Family Portrait," from *The Machine That Killed*

The untelling of a dictatorship. They watched the whole fifty minutes. The little family tyrant repeating, obsessing, falling into aphasia, desperately looking around, clutching at the puppets of his power, holding on for a second, the moments the Americans would cover before he tumbled still again. They were watching a dead man, and every second was savored. TV had been reversed, and power now flowed upstream. A dictator under surveillance, television stripping the emperor bare, a whole nation watched a machine hand out its own justice, a spectacle toppled before the wrath of the real.

Home Shopping:

Hello Shoppers!

Our featured shopper is the Marcoses' favorite brother-in-law, Kokoye Roumaldez. Before the Marcoses came to power, Kokoye was unemployed. During the dictatorship, he was ambassador to Beijing and absentee governor of his home province, Leyte. In exchange for the release of Eugenio Lopez Jr., Kokoye was able to purchase $20 million in electric company stock for $1,500 from the Lopez family. In a book of essays on the Marcos dictatorship, a noted Filipino journalist devoted a chapter to the thoughts of Kokoye. All the pages were blank.

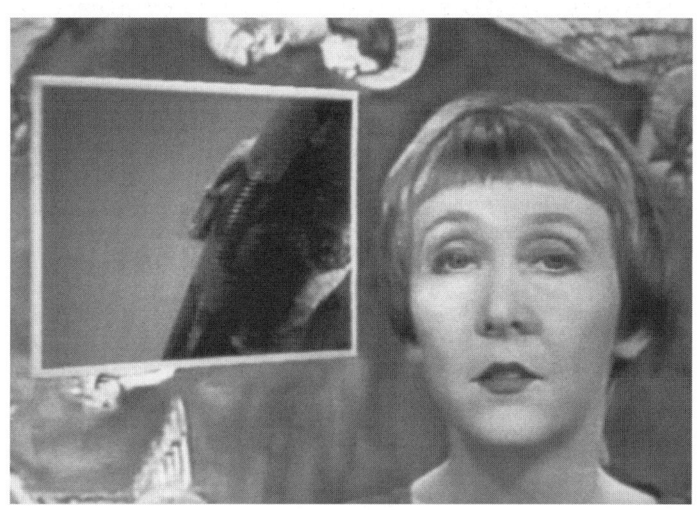

"Home Shopping," from *The Machine That Killed*

Constance:

20 July 1970.

Architecture, the social art. A speech delivered before the Philippine Institute of Architecture. Imelda Marcos began her address with the following story: The Roman emperor Hadrian, fancying himself to be an architect, once designed a large temple in which he placed an enormous statue of a goddess seated on a throne. He then sent for the famous Greek architect Appollinodorous, who was his slave, and asked him what he thought of it. Appollinodorous replied that it looked good except for one thing—that if the goddess stood up, her head would go through the roof.

Appollinodorous thus became the first, but not the last, architect to lose his job—and his head—for criticizing the ideas of his client.

It has been said of Imelda that she has the lips of Marilyn Monroe but the eyes of Caligula. Perhaps she is more like Emma Bovary, an ambitious girl from the provinces who had dreams that were symptoms of her century. The difference, Imelda's dreams came true. First as daydream, and finally as nightmare.

When criticized as being only a dreamer, she responded, "People say Mrs. Marcos is a great dreamer. Oh yes, I dream not only at night when there is the moon and the stars, but I dream more so during the daytime without the moon and the stars. But I don't just dream. I do it. I am an activist."

Manila International Film Center opens.
10 January 1982.

Standing in earshot of George Hamilton, Brooke Shields, and Sly Stallone—the Americans—a smartly dressed Filipino, his tuxedo being crushed by the eager crowd, whispered, "Imelda is truly like European royalty, Mad King Ludwig. They both suffer from edifice complexes."

The building of the film center was completed so close to the opening of the festival that the workers, still sweeping and cleaning, seemed to mingle with the international celebrities. Rich and poor rubbed elbows, as in an episode of Tati's *Playtime.*

Eight thousand workers had labored round the clock for 150 days to finish the Parthenon-like structure. During construction the roof collapsed, killing a hundred workers. Building went on, without stop; carpenters sawed off the protruding limbs of the dead. Others were simply entombed under the pouring concrete. Despite the passing of the moon and the stars, the odor lingered.

15 December 1897.

Ninoy's grandfather, then only a major, awoke from a deep sleep, his forehead dripping. As he turned he felt a cold numbness in his feet. He looked down, seeing his body from above, boxed and severed, split in the middle, toes still twitching. Smiling, he thought back to the magician's trick he had seen as a child, but there was no tuxedoed man with a saw in front of him, but a young Spaniard, sideburns shaved neatly. Wiping the tips of his Filipino body with chemicals. The previous day his head had been shaved. The sentence had been read on

Wednesday, and he was to be shot on Saturday. In between there was a general amnesty.

26 February 1898.

Alert.

Secretary of the Navy Long returned to his post well rested. The previous day, a bit tired, he had left a few hours early to take a nap. Undersecretary Teddy Roosevelt was told to simply take messages. Upon his return, Long was greeted with an explosion louder than the blowing up of the *Maine.* The undersecretary had acted.

Fifteen hundred troops had been added. Three thousand tons of coal moved. The entire Asian fleet, except for the monarchy, was sent full speed to Hong Kong. The department had been put on war alert.

13 November 1899.

The Yanquii in front of them, the hills behind. A torrential downpour washed the soil of tarlac from beneath their feet. Ninoy's grandfather, now a general, listened, head up, as Aqunialdo declared the fall of the first republic—they would no longer fight front to back or back to front. There would be no ground beneath their feet. They would become Rough Riders in reverse. Guerrillas.

9 October 1900.

Friend or Foe.

While the American troops were occupying towns and establishing municipal governments, the insurgents arranged a parallel organization, employing the same people who held office under the Americans. The towns were taxed, contributions and supplies collected, and recruits for guerrilla forces enlisted right under the nose of the American, General Arthur MacArthur.

11 November 1903.

One million dead.

The American congressman snickered, wishing to stay anonymous as he said, "They never rebel in Luzon anymore because there is nobody left to rebel."

Sports in brief.

26 November 1988.

Filipino squash bets clobber U.S. team.

The Philippine team defeated the United States last Saturday to win the 1988 Ambassador's Cup squash tournament at the Manila boat club courts. Ambassador Nick Platt struggled to win the first match 3-2 over Ron y Ribano, but the next three matches were easily bagged by the Philippine squashers, with Baloy Tiaqqui defeating Jeff-Taft-Dick.

Home Shopping:

Hello Shoppers!

Welcome to "Some Are Smarter than Others"!

Our featured shopper is Marcos crony Eduardo Cojuango Jr. Born to a wealthy landed family from central Tarlac that split into warring factions over his cousin Cory's marriage to Nenoye Aquino. His rise to power under the Marcoses was more modest than others because he started off on top. During the Marcos regime he was a roving ambassador for international corruption, amassing a personal fortune of billions of dollars through his many holdings, including a complete monopoly over the coconut industry. He was the largest private collector of small arms in the world, which were used by his Israeli-trained five-thousand-man private army. But Eduardo did not want to run the Philippines, merely to own it.

Constance:

26 November 1988.

Business.

Japanese investments to increase.

The Tokyo-based Asian Promotion Center on Trade, Investment,

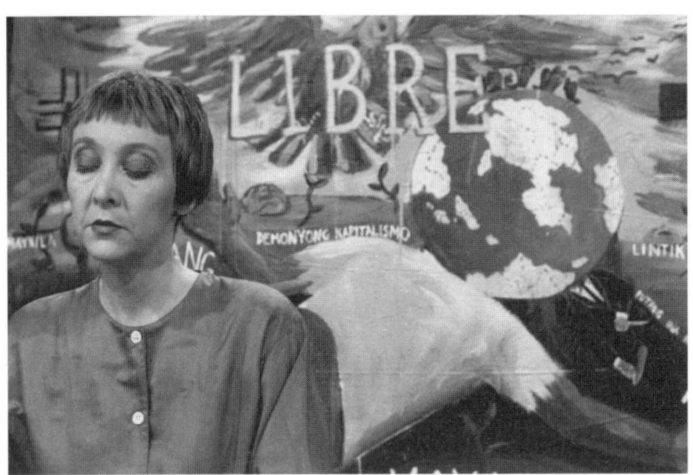

"Station Break," from *The Machine That Killed*

and Tourism has reported a shift in investment inquiries from Thailand to the Philippines since March 1988.

1943.

Bataan.

Not the battle but the movie; 1945, *I Shall Return.*

The sequel.

1988.

Back to Bataan.

The movies have been updated, colorized. Can you half colorize a movie? The Japanese are finally truly the yellow peril. The Americans, Robert Taylor and John Wayne, have lost their luster, their khaki colors mute against the vibrating chroma of the jungle. The color had taken away their camouflage.

Back to the Jungle.

After the war the jungle would transform itself. The Huk rebellion. Land reform. The people's war. Other Americans would come. In living color. Ugly Americans, cloaked in altruism. CIA.

Ninoy's father and the other leaders of the second republic were summoned to Japan by the emperor, MacArthur.

Collaborators.

They proudly refused to clean the prison yard of cigarettes. Theirs had been a struggle for independence. What difference to them if it came through the Japanese filter?

Back to the Philippines.

Returned to Manila as prisoners. Later they, the past and future leaders of the Philippines, would jest of being alumni of Mutinlupa. The old city, intramuros. Manila as they had known it was in ruins.

A few years later released but still awaiting trial.

Ninoy's father took him to the prize fight. The betting in the gallery was on Tirso, but at ringside Ortiz was favored. In what in the next day's papers would be called the fatal round, the fourth, as the referee counted eight over the fallen Tirso, Ninoy's father clutched his heart.

After the death, Ninoy's grandfather, the general, was summoned to the president's office and told that the dead man would be given all the honors due him. The proud general said to the president, "Nobody thought of giving my son any honors when he was alive. In fact, some thought him to be a traitor. I don't see, now that he is dead, he is less of a traitor. I will take my son back to Tarlac and bury him in my own way."

Despite the family's wishes, Ninoy's father was buried in Manila, as a hero.

Back to business.

The Asean Center, headed by Dr. Fumiya Okada, has said that the nature of investment inquiries has ranged from bigger projects like electronics, watch production, wire harness, resort development, development of industrial areas, construction of condominiums, to small ones like manufacturing, kotasu production, fruit juice processing, etc.

Ron:

She sat like a stuffed bird, perched, her blue eye staring right at me while her green one strayed callously over my shoulder. She told of sitting at a state dinner between Enrile and Ramos. Looking both ways, she didn't know which way to turn. As she hesitated, Enrile started to talk. She gasped, telling me, "Such halitosis. Who could stand having him as a president?"

Constance:

22 August 1983.

The tragedy of the twenty-first of August.

Marcos's trusted watchdog, General Fabian Ver, still lying on his back, his aids thinking him sound asleep, listened to their squelched laughter as they still again told that joke. "No, you have it the wrong way round. Gelman first committed suicide, then murdered Aquino." They laughed.

All that remained on the tarmac to mark the bodies were thinly drawn chalk outlines, Ninoy's partially obscured by a muddied footprint. The body of Gelman had been hastily removed, his blood both

"Smokey Mountain," from *The Machine That Killed*

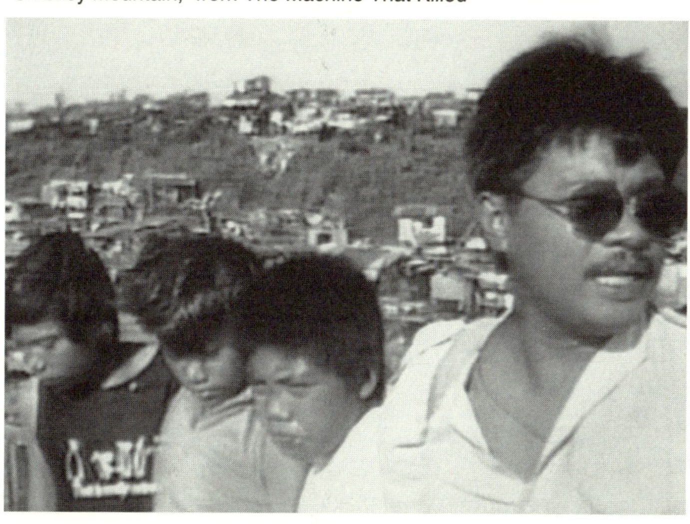

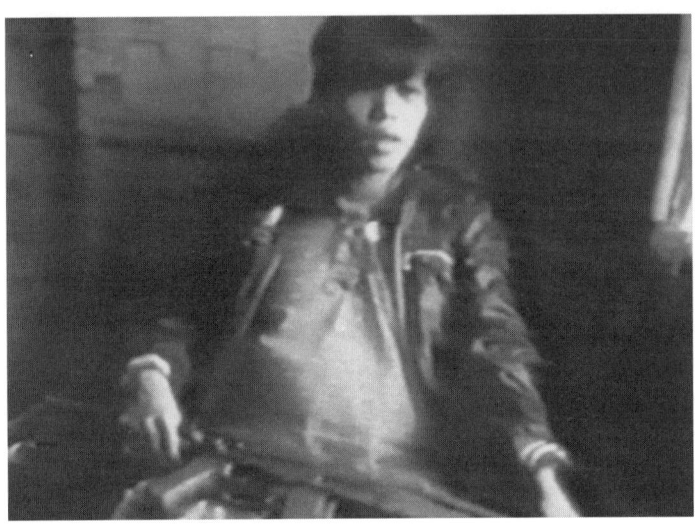

"The New People's Army," from *The Machine That Killed*

still wet and dried; eighteen bullets had pierced the body, entering both front to back and back to front. The Aquino corpse had but one bullet hole through the back of the neck. He had worn the same body armor as the American president.

General Ver turned onto his belly. He had dreamed of a battle, lasting not even a minute. Suspended in midair, their knives flashing. The slash in midair made thrice the damage as the one on the ground. He thought, "In the air they are angels, on the ground merely fowl."

He returned.

The saving grace of the assassination was that it had been so perfectly bungled. He imagined the American ambassador saying, "Surely the work of amateurs." He would nod and mumble not even a word but the letters NPA.

Cockfights.
The half sleep reminded Ver of blue grass.
Kentucky.

Trained in torture, by experts, he bristled at their taunts. "Nothing but barbarism," they would say. He would snicker and remind them that "the cock had lost to the eagle by one vote when THEIR republic had selected its national symbol."

As he lay there, eyes fixed on the ceiling, he lost control. The Romans had derisively called cockfighting the Greek diversion. The laughter had subsided. His aides, fallen silent, turned toward him to listen, and he overheard his own voice saying into this air, "Cocks are birds; it is we who have brought them down to earth."

Minh-ha:

Manila, 4 December 1989.

"Manila rebels still fighting. One hundred civilians are now reported dead in the most recent colonel's coup attempt engineered by gringo Honasen," the anchor grimly reported. Turning camera front, his co-anchor with great compassion says, "That's terrible. I hope we can expect something better from the weather."

Home Shopping:

Hello Shoppers!

Our featured shopper is Marcos crony Manuel Elizalde. Coming from a rum-distilling family, Elizalde was the secretary of Panamin (Presidential Assistance of National Minorities). The organization functioned as a front for family mining interests, and he exploited the alleged discovery of the pure Stone Age tribe the Tasaday, who were prominently featured in *Life* magazine and *National Geographic.* In 1984, Elizalde fled the country, taking with him millions of dollars in Panamin monies and twenty native maidens. He has recently returned to the Philippines, where he still supervises the Tasaday, allowing the pure Stone Age tribe to stay at his mansion in Manila as they shop for trinkets and lounge around the pool watching jungle movies. He is rumored to be considering produc-ing a show for Hong Kong television called "Lifestyles of the Pure and Innocent."

Constance:

Senate probes human rights violations.

The Senate voted to investigate the human rights situation in the country amid reports of continuing human rights violations even as four suspects were arrested in the Cebu massacre Tuesday night.

The military version of the event was contradicted by a survivor, Meredita Bitoon, twenty-three. She told the Associated Press that a few days before the attack a member of the vigilante group threatened them with harm because they were Communist sympathizers.

In the Senate, Senator Osmena said in a privilege speech that the Aquino government was guilty of benign neglect of human rights in this country. "To this day," he said, "not a single military officer has been brought to justice for violation of human rights." He said there was a disturbing resistance on the part of some military personnel to following due process, while rationalizing human rights violations.

This letter, dated 17 December 1951, was recently discovered quite by accident in an attic in Detroit, Michigan. At this time, it would be best to withhold the author's name. We can, however, tell you a bit about him. He was Oliver North's hero, and after his tour of duty in the Philippines he went on to Vietnam and, finally, Central America.

It has been said about him, no, about a character in a novel based on him, that he was determined to do good. Not to any individual, but to a country, a continent, a world.

Well, here's the letter:

Dear Dad,

Thanks so much for your letter dated 13 October. Sorry to be so slow to respond, but things take so long here, and I was off in the jungles of Luzon. But even there I heard that the Yankees had won the World Series. Most everyone here, even the Flips, root for the Yanks. It didn't surprise me that the Yanks had won, what else is new, but I was shocked to find out they had beaten the Giants. What the heck hap-

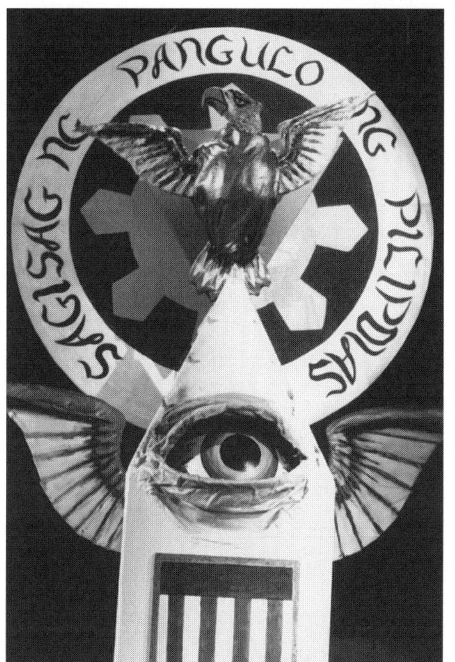

"Dirty Tricks," from *The Machine That Killed*

pened to the Dodgers? Well, your letter really filled me in on that. I must confess, I took a certain unsavory pleasure in the way you described the excruciating details. I, like you, wondered why Dresson had put Branca in, after the Giants had murdered him all year and Thomson himself had hit a homer off of him in game 1. My favorite part of your letter (even more than the overpunctuated rendition of Russ Hodges saying over and over again, "The Giants win the Pennant, the Giants win the Pennant, the Giants win the Pennant"; did it really need four exclamation points each time?) was the postgame interview with Dresson, him saying, without any punctuation in his voice, "I called the bullpen and they said Erskine just bounced a curve Roe ain't ready and Branca's throwing hard." He would have been better off consulting a numerologist. How can you put someone in, with the pennant on the line, who's wearing a big fat thirteen all over his back? Well, at least that turncoat Durocher lost the series.

As to some of your questions, yes, I'm still playing the harmonica, and no, I don't like the Europeans any better. They seem so tired and cynical. They don't seem to see the importance of all this. Oppression, communism, atheism: to them it seems like a mah-jongg game. I think they just come over to our officer's club because they think it's safe from the hand grenades. They are so easily amused, eating fried chicken and taking drugs. It's really true, the fate of the world is in our hands, and we just have to round the Filipinos into shape. My advertising experience comes in handy, and this seems to be the terrain that we can turn this thing around on. Magsasay is a bit stupid, but at least he listens and does what we tell him. And the song I wrote, "Mambo Mambo Magsasay," is all the rage.

Sometimes this war makes me feel like a kid again back in Detroit. Often it's games and pranks that work. I concocted this eye-of-God scheme, borrowing it from the Egyptians, a little ancient history never hurts. We would, in the middle of the night, paint these evil eyes on the houses of suspected Huks. It would really scare the Huk out of them. Also we have thought of a rather clever use of aircraft. We broadcast from the other side of the clouds, over loudspeakers telling the natives not to feed the Huks. This voice of God seems to work better than the Voice of America.

Well, I guess by the time you receive this letter it will be a white Christmas. Here in the jungle, it's just green and more green. But at least it's a Christian country. They really carry on about Christmas. It seems to start up a week after the fourth of July, reach full throttle Labor Day, and a crescendo level from Thanksgiving to Christmas Eve. It sure is festive—a bit too festive, almost pagan. Now I understand what McKinley meant when he said we had to Christianize them.

Wait till next year.

Your loving son,

P.S. Tell mom to send some of her cookies; the desserts here are just too sweet. Also around here you can't find any serious reading, only novels, plays, and poetry, so send me something, anything. I trust you.

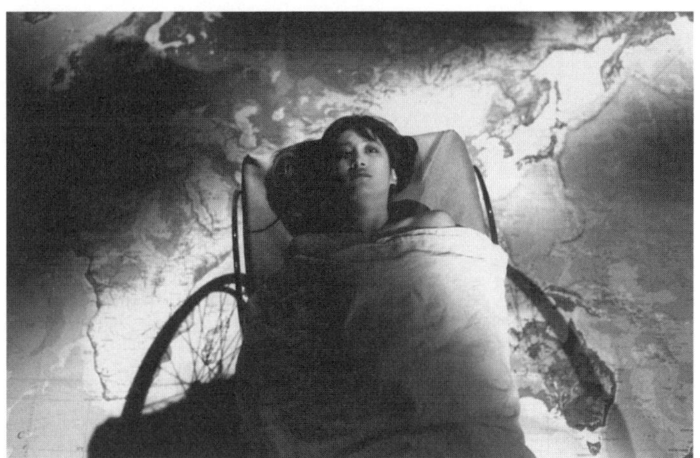

"Gurney Disco," from *The Machine That Killed*

■ ■ ■

Andrew Ross TV Guidance

Mission: Forty-eight hours of tolerant TV in twin formats.

Date: Long after the sweeps, 1995.

Conditions: Not of our own making.

Objective: To pass.

Station Identification:

> The Nivea Network, "Not a Cosmetic Society."
>
> Channel So-So, "Getting in Under the Wire."

The Nivea Network   **Channel So-So**

6:30 Professional Wrestling   **6:30 Latin Futbol Monthly**
An ambitious young doctor takes   Including Top Ten Goals.
on an ambitious young lawyer.

7:00 Bright and Early

(News and Weather.) Broadcasting this week from Scotland with hosts Maxine Fonda and Jeff Wang. Mel Gibson with his take on medieval Scottish culture. A team of psychics looks into Lulu's future. Joanna Lumley takes her turn in an open-face coal mine. Rab C. Nesbitt on the new fall fashion. Tom Nairn and Stuart Hall dissect how home rule will affect black British politics. Musical guests: The Alexander Brothers and One Dove.

9:00 Tosser and Dipthong

More cat-and-dog adult cartoon capers as these tireless tykes are haunted by their past lovers. Guest voices include Tina Turner as Phosphorus, Joe Piscopo as Plantagenet, Ossie Davis as the Litigator, and Billy Ray Martin as Sister Enchilada.

9:30 Chris Marker's Mountain Bikes

Over hill and dale in the Appalachians.

7:00 Bonjour Vitesse

(News and Weather.) With Holly Schroeder and Flip Cromwell. Author Brendan Baghead discusses his biography of Valerie Solanas. Sally Cantor on her new Broadway play *Breaking with the Bronx*. Mike Tyson presents his new philosophy. Jesse Young checks into cyberspace with the Blue Spartacist movement. Musical guests: Nasal Passage and Ol' Dirty Bastard.

9:00 Workout with Wassily

A violent finale in the swimming pool.

9:30 Top Sex Trips from the Stars

Lessons in the art of love. Meg Ryan on rimming techniques. S/M scholarship from Denzel Washington, a resisting bottom, and Keanu Reeves, a hair slave. Auto-cunnilingus—Susan Lucci shows how.

10:00 Judy Pushkin
Scheduled topics: men who date only muscular women; female ejaculation.

10:30 Arcadio
Scheduled topics: husbands who flirt with their brothers-in-law; what to do in a drive-by.

11:00 Lime Tree Walk
Flip and Lucy have reached an understanding: there will be no more secrets. Deadly revenge in the offing for the Contessa. Marcia is snubbed in Uncle Nick's will. Monica shows up at Damian's press conference and spills the beans. Josh calls the police after he discovers that Faye has been stalking him. Lucinda puts the pieces together and pays a visit to the farmhouse where she first saw Millicent Mapplethorpe.

11:00 Cartoon Forum
Virtual reality brings together Quick Draw McGraw, Top Cat, Bullwinkle, Scooby Doo, Popeye, and Olive Oyl for a discussion about the representation of minorities in cartoon history. Donald Duck responds to Mattelart and Dorfman. Xuxa moderates.

11:30 TV Trivia Trauma
Tony Danza quotes from Gramsci in which episode of what? Which of Charlie's Angels was the muff diver? What was the name of George Jetson's cousin? Laverne and Stimpy—what's the connection?

12:00 The Wild Cyberthing
Linda Evangelista launches an in-

12:00 Ivory Towers
Professor Schindler's tenure case

teractive wildlife show. Computers help us learn how it feels to be preyed on. A polar bear teaches its cubs how to hunt. A cheetah stalks a gazelle, and you are the gazelle.

12:30 *The Water* (1974)
Slovenian New Wave classic, recreates the charged atmosphere of workers' vacation hotel on shores of Lake Idrac in the early sixties. Filmed in moody black and white, and purportedly directed by Catalan novelist in exile Miguel Muntades. Not for the restless.

is on the rocks, and she is forced to court the support of Dean "the Whig" Buttercup, her secret admirer. Rosie Marquez believes that she has solved the Manitoba Monk Conjecture but is distracted by pressure to join the Latino Coalition's campaign to have the Manifest Destiny Pavilion renamed as Bufadora Plaza. In the meantime, Clark and Fenimore are plotting the downfall of the Penn State fencing team. Patty takes her history TA to task for asserting that the origins of World War I were economic in nature.

1:00 Question Time from the Houses of Parliament
Sitcom pilot about English public schoolboys marooned on the rain-swept Westminster Islands. They mistake their new home for a sovereign nation-state, only to find that there is no writ-

ten constitution. Bedlam ensues as they debate how to stop the natives from eating them alive.

2:00 The World Tomorrow
Back after a five-week absence. This week's topic: cold fusion. Is it worth the money? Richard Feynman moderates a discussion with tennis idol Pancho Gonzalez, bowler-hat maven Patrick McNee, and infomercial queen Ali McGraw.

2:30 Whitecoats
Breckman operates in mid-flight on Tricia's collapsed lung. Vengeful Maurice wins back Diana and begs Brimley to get dirt on the new intern. Birkin has a bad fall, and it is feared he will never have the full use of his legs again. Frank learns of Sara's long-standing dislike for the woman he plans to marry. As predicted in the gardener's dream, Hannah delivers a child with twelve fingers.

3:00 The Lysenko Interview
The man from Kiev goes ten rounds with the fragrant Naomi Crump, who describes herself as "a very complicated and often homicidal person." Crump recalls her Panamanian childhood, ranges

2:30 Social Darwinism Today
In Alaska, a grizzly bear feasts on spawning salmon. In Dresden, the Deutsche Bank cleans up. In Rio, the favelas are on fire again. A new generation of Rockefellers explains the links between these events. Pat Riley mediates with flair, if not passion.

3:00 The Lumbar Support Club
Weekly look at the world of health.

over the highs and lows of the Carter administration, and lionizes her struggle to find good roles.

3:45 Worlds Apart

"Losing Europe." Classic episode from the 1972 season. Princeton antiwar protester (Nastassja Kinski) falls hopelessly in love with a Florida arms manufacturer (Klaus Kinski). She agrees to become a state terrorist, assisting Foggy Bottom in Luxembourg's "dirty war" in return for the amnesty of her imprisoned Spartacist lover (Bernd Kinski). Unconvincing Southern accents, but a stylish reminder of the "golden age" of the docudrama.

4:15 Get a Life, Charlie

Johnny Boy owes the bartender

3:20 *The Professional Jew* (1984)

Long-winded horse opera about over-the-hill desperadoes and a dandified lawman. In the two incongruous subplots, a kick-boxer rabbi is hired to guard a homicidal drug kingpin, and a Canadian Mountie is sent to quell a Cree rebellion. Quirky when not downright confusing. Cast includes Martin Landau, Morgan Freeman, Bette Midler, and Mickey Dolenz.

big-time, Saint Francis is back running numbers, Teresa loses her lease but wins a part in the new Gangrene Babies video.

5:15 Khalid
Scheduled topics: Bobby Brown and Aliyah. Was age nothing but a number?

6:00 American Vampires
Top business executives interviewed by Phylicia Rashad on the secrets of their success in overcoming compassion, fellow feeling, and class revulsion.

6:30 News and Weather

5:00 Gourmet Astronaut
Biff Shoptaw takes us into food orbit: watercress cream soup; vegetable terrine; hake steak in green sauce; braised rabbit; tortellini stuffed with scallop mousse; stonecrab salad; baked alaska.

5:30 The Restless Pursuit of Profit
Fourth of a lively thirteen-part series about capital accumulation. This week: the response of tycoons to antitrust legislation and the 1913 introduction of income tax. Introduced and narrated by Carroll O'Connor and Julie Andrews.

6:30 News and Weather

7:00 Last Chance

Perky Australian comedy-drama: Liz likes to dress up as a trades-man. This week she is a plumber, and it's Rosalinda whose U-section is blocked. Bruce gives his tenants another chance.

7:30 Manfred

It's vacation time. Manfred wants to go to Acapulco. Lillian prefers Oaxaca. Where do they end up? Kansas City—in high tornado season.

8:00 Grains of Sand

The question must be asked: Who is Rachel's father? Nikki turns her attention to Angie. Jacob decides on an exorcism for Luke. Lance is subpoenaed to testify against Mon-signor Clancy. Alicia learns about Omar's past as a gourmet chef. Rozalla and Frankie have their first date—in a laundry. Hamish is exposed—he never went to law school, and he's really a woman.

7:00 There Goes the Undergrowth

Mort Downey Jr.'s comeback (short-lived, we predict) as host of anarchic game show. General knowledge about gardening, interspersed with Hollywood Babylonia. Winners get to choose plastic surgery.

7:30 Femmes Fatales

The nation's favorite babes be-hind bars. Is this the last seasonor just the season finale? Julie has a dream with real-life consequences. Yvonne shaves her eyebrows. A touch of arson in Block H.

8:00 911 Is A Joke

Top-rated sitcom about police bru-tality. Sonny takes an early-evening stroll and winds up in a Ninth Pre-cinct cell, paralyzed from the waist down. Inspector Garcia plays Barney in the Christmas panto-mime. Strong language. Homopho-bia. (Repeat.)

8:30 Rock Against Rape

Jack Nicholson hosts a star-studded benefit from Giants Stadium for In-ternational Women's Rights. Rod Stewart, Ice Cube, Dolly Parton, Dr. Dre, Paula Abdul, Shabba Ranks, and the Rolling Stones. Lady Di in attendance. (Highlights only.)

9:00 *I, Cleaver* (1986)

A bored, bourgeois housewife (Pia Zadora) takes a part-time job in a slaughterhouse and discovers an inhibition-relieving drug that turns loose her bestial alter ego. Few of her fellow workers are spared. Stale dialogue. Not for vegetarians or the bourgeoisie.

9:30 Ball of Wax

Morag's HIV test is negative. The Snyder farm burns to the ground, and Comstock Ken's mortgage application is denied. Dr. Massimo's diary, retrieved from the plane wreckage, reveals a callow deed. Gina discovers that she is not the apple of her vain stepmother's eye. Darryl decides on his disguise as a drum majorette. Keesha and Mik-hail find love in-flight, heading for a not so warm airport welcome from Interpol.

10:30 Carmen Brando Poses the Question

Crypto-rodent Elliott Abrams and celebrity felon Manuel Noriega are in the hot seat. Comedy from Kandy Kandinsky. Musical

10:30 Positively No Propaganda

This week: "Catholics and Sex," an offhand review of the church's repressive history, with Robert De Niro and Richard Chamberlain, and some inappropriate cameo commentary by Jim Carrey. A

289

guests: The Gangrene Babies.

11:00 Liberal Guilt
A self-help magazine for the wretched of the earth. This week: race or class? Harnessing the po-wer to choose. (Brought to you by Sears.)

11:30 *Beat No Retreat* (1966)
What to do if you discovered your late husband wasn't the astronaut he pretended to be. Angela Lansbury turns sleuth and ends up running a child pornography ring. Romantic weepie with few surprises, beyond the obvious. Strong language. Cold War ideology.

12:00 Bass and Drum
Funkologist Tung Twista checks suckas claiming to be pimps who end up being simps. Illustrates with tight grooves. Smooth Maniac and Panther Posse are in the house.

12:30 Sociological Imagination
"Religion or Rights." The Limbo

downer, but may save young lives.

11:00 Governing at a Distance
"Out in Court." Gay lawyers come to terms with the politics of identity in courtroom life. Featuring a mock trial in which the legal status of "queerness" is debated. Fine example of the New Documentary, bad hair day for most of the cast/producers.

11:30 Beyond the Beltway
A young Republican swell exchanges roles with a single mother in West Virginia. A circus family arrives in a small New Hampshire town.

12:30 States' Rights
From Alexander Hamilton to Newt Gingrich. Politically correct docu-

Club is back with another low-tech series about civil liberties in an age without the need for consent. The agony of an ordained minister committed to keeping his faith as well as his drug addiction.

1:00 *Flatbush Palindrome* (1987)

Lighthearted, offbeat comedy about a nightclub singer who bets her drummer that she can make his overprotective brother into a popular crooner. She wins but falls for a wife cheater she fell for once before. Stars Pam Grier, ably supported by Frankie Avalon. Some continuity problems.

2:15 **Infomercial of the Week**

Kathy Lee Crosby considers the case for Autopander (TM). A new way to beat genital chafing, or some old snake oil? Jocelyn Elders provides lucid testimony.

mentary about how Washington elites have exploited populism to further their interests. Narrated by Bob Newhart.

1:00 **Dance Girlfriend Dance**

"Hidden" cameras capture the after-hours moves at the Velveeta Club. MC Bonny Donahue hosts a Miss Blasé contest. DJs include A Man Called Sanchez and Della Stallas.

2:00 *Don't Count Me Out* (1980)

Elaborate spine-chiller masquerading as a tearjerker about a boy and his stallion. "Jacko" Corazon relishes a role (turned down by Danny De Vito) as Trainer Vic, whose African American sidekick (Danny Glover) sacrifices his life to preserve the endangered white family unit. Unusual kitchen layouts. Strong language. Animal brutality.

2:30 Let's Make a Meal

Feasting for insomniacs with ebullient hostess Lather McLachlan. On the menu: strawberry soup; cock-a-leekie; tuna tartare; quail with mushrooms and red wine sauce; lobster and saffron; Sacher torte.

**3:00 *The Puce Fuselage*
(1975)**

Elizabeth Montgomery is woefully miscast as a small-town prostitute trying to quit. Danny De Vito saves this doomed teleplay through his Emmy-winning role as the sympathetic coach of an all-American football star who falls in love with a wheelchair-bound boy. Memorable score by someone smart.

**3:30 *Barefoot Contestants*
(1972)**

Gothic hide-and-seek saga. Two sisters—one wheelchair bound, the other her sadistic jailer—have second thoughts about their codependency when a cynical TV weatherman who resembles their dead father decides to move in next door. Tuesday Weld at her very best as the game-show host. Cameo appearance by Gene Autry as a racketeer with far-fetched sexual tastes.

**4:00 *Hostage to the Clock*
(1973)**

Low-calorie thriller starring Meredith Ponsonby-Smythe. Schizophrenic vixen arrives at an exclusive New England ladies' college, the water supply is poisoned, a Maoist cell is exposed, and a POW back from Vietnam is brought in to assess the situation. Suggested by actual events. Sexual situations. Victorian ideology.

5:30 A Personal Journey with José Feliciano Through the Warner Brothers Archive

In this last segment, the cult performer and cinéaste analyzes the effects on film genres of the breakup of the Hollywood studio system.

6:00 Anna Domini

Anna is ill, but it's all a ruse to get Sasha to stay home. The fun begins when Mario revises his will after he encounters the spirit of an ancient Egyptian royal in the Metropolitan Museum and undergoes hypnotic regression. (Crucial repeat.)

6:30 Yesterday's Dish

How does food go out of fashion? Walter Matthau dons his apron and his thinking cap to consider "The Case of Fondue."

5:30 Justice and the State

Veronica Webb interviews political prisoners without household names.

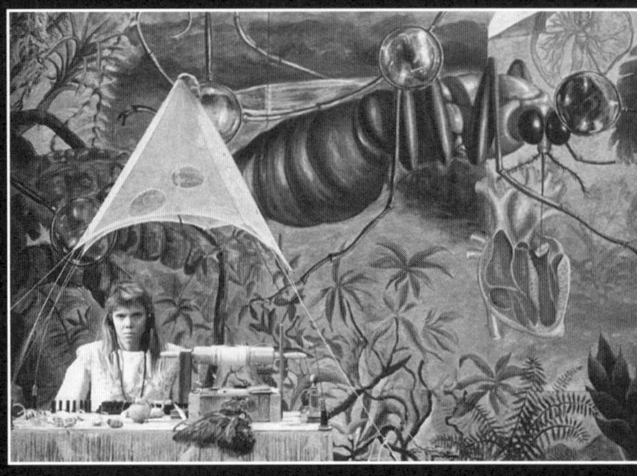

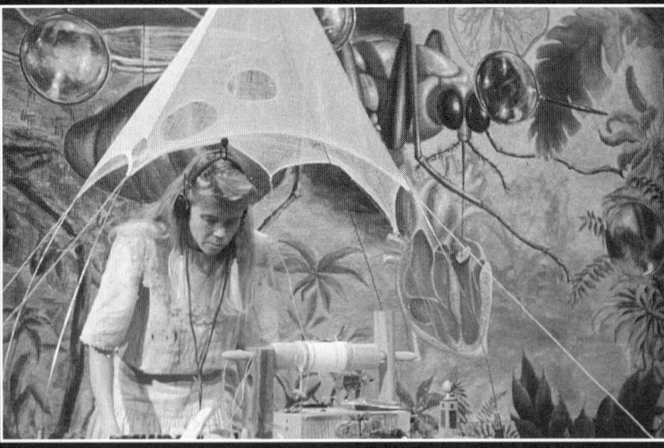

Melissa Smedley in "Radio Propagation,"
from *Zero Degrees Latitude*

Ivone Margulies
Confessions of a Quiet American: Fagin's Anemic Aesthetics

Inside the box, the world—or the power-to-be-a world—
is condensed: it's the size of a conventional package, a gift,
it's power made handleable. The viewer might be led
to believe then, that the world is in his or her hands.
—Vito Acconci

The title of Steve Fagin's third tape, *The Machine That Killed Bad People* (1990), brings to mind, most immediately, a children's morality play, a clear picture of good and evil. Even after watching the tape's intricate distribution of guilt and responsibility in the Philippines during Marcos's fall, this association persists. The title hangs over the tape's simulation of TV's infotainment, suggesting a deliberately naive alternative to the quandaries of postmodern evasiveness. Fagin's early tapes, on the other hand, are themselves symbolic apparatuses engaged in a purely textual circulation of meaning. Obsessively interested in discourses around the interpretive apparatus, he illustrates the impossibility of stable reference through elaborate examples taken from art and psychoanalysis. He sets the stage as if for a child's play on the play of signifiers. The monitor surface is equated with an intellectual's version of a playpen.

With *The Machine That Killed Bad People* Fagin blows up his box of tricks in a mimicry of TV. His poetic endeavors are magnified when placed in dialogue with the more familiar setting of TV, and his progressive engagement with the external world suggests the need to articulate a drama of good and evil. As Fagin engages the dense political realities of the Philippines or Ecuador's colonization by North American evangelical doctrines (in *Zero Degrees Latitude* [1993]), his tapes activate a moral agency. Given the shift in Fagin's work, from the private quality of Cornell-like boxes of textual *mise-en-abîme* to tapes that explicitly engage a social and political reality via documentary footage and rhetoric, the allegory of a moral/

optical machine seems relevant. To this purpose I turn to an unlikely approximation—Rossellini's film *The Machine To Kill Bad People* (*La macchina ammazzacattivi*).

The Machine to Kill Bad People is an uncharacteristic Rossellini film from 1948. Instead of manifesting his typical "faith in reality," the film starts with a credit sequence in which cutout figures are manipulated over a paper set surrounded by curtains. In this filmic fantasy a still-photography camera is magically endowed to still, under its spell and click, any character deemed guilty by the photographer. The procedure is indirect and complex: one needs to reproduce the culprit's photograph in order to punish. The viewfinder is initially selective in the moral landscape it designs. Later on this corrective camera takes on its own momentum, and Celestino, the photographer, indiscriminately aims at any minor offender. Rather than reflexive, the centrality of photography in this film is predicated on a paradise-hell paradigm: good people naturally move, while those who are mean or socially unjust freeze in sculptural limbo. For a filmmaker who, in *Stromboli* or in *Europe 51,* so intently makes an instrument of redemption from the act of turning one's eyes to the real world, this film, in which the camera becomes a punishing agent, shows Rossellini's perverse Catholic underside. In *The Machine to Kill Bad People,* after a fit of self-righteousness the photographer cannot stop himself until the entire town, including he himself, is "judged": he commits himself to stillness by turning the photographic camera on himself. The film ends with the discovery that it was the devil who promoted such a radical destruction.

Rossellini's parable of an adjudicating crisis, figured through a punishing apparatus that cannot discriminate, is curiously related to the disseminatory bent of Steve Fagin's early work: *Virtual Play: The Double Direct Monkey Wrench in Black's Machinery* (1984) and *The Amazing Voyage of Gustave Flaubert and Raymond Roussel* (1986) are signifying machines that take a life of their own. They create their own circuit, and their explicit strategy and underlying theme are the obfuscations of language. The curtain and veil rather than the window are the videomaker's favored modes of display. On the other hand, the general direction of prodigality posited in Fagin's collages distances it from the efficient morality of the neorealist filmmaker's ultimate belief in original, unadulterated facts. Fagin's moral machine follows a more complex route than Celestino's devilish camera, but, as I will suggest, it also aims at Fagin himself. Both by contrast and by contamination, the figuration of an artist's world is of necessity questioned once Fagin ventures, with *The Machine* and *Zero Degrees*, into documentary practices.

In his first tapes Fagin's preferred collage format evens out information, scrambling his alignments. He deploys the series of narratives informing, for instance, the gossip subtext of psychoanalysis's theater of intimacy or undermines the authenticity of personal confessions through fake postcard texts. The allegorical nature of the videomaker's textual as well as visual reconstitutions of the fragment is apparent in his taste for images that preexist as cultural and aesthetic objects. He states that his emphasis lies in "laying out, restoring things to their place, not interpreting."[1] Fagin's addendum is a visual and aural spread of the questions asked elsewhere by Foucault, by Roussel, by Flaubert, by Deleuze and Guattari. He unpacks these theories, but his is a pseudoanalysis. One does not find out much about a post-Romantic imagination, but one does get intrigued by the drive animating this inquiry.

Fagin has claimed that the reduced scale of his images—cutout figures, miniature toy figures, pop-up books, postcards, and playing cards—was his "way of engaging the body actively." Tableau configurations formed visibly as bric-a-brac of domestic proportions state their marginal status through the videomaker's *povera* procedures: the hand of the narrator arranges little doll-size collages, moves in sign language, and conducts finger-puppet dialogues with a tape recorder. These underground Méliès *féeries* become somehow more physical. The scaling down of objects for human manipulation creates a world in which all references are evenly available. Fagin's flat surfaces with textured collages of miniatures and other cultural artifacts recall the shift performed by Rauchenberg's collages. Leo Steinberg describes how the artist's transformation of the vertical confrontational axis (common to both Old Masters and modernist art) into a flatbed surface plane, a working ground and a surface akin to a switchboard, created a "painted surface" that "is no longer an analogue of a visual experience of nature but of operational processes."[2] Turning knobs make any and every kind of image and information equally accessible, a desired de-hierarchizing effect in Fagin's playhouse world. On the other hand, the manageability and scale of video suggest a dialogue with that other scaled-down world in a box, the TV and its own "power-to be-a world."[3] This dialogue stops short, however, of any sense of communicative or informational purpose. Fagin proposes a parallel universe. By using all the world as a children's play set, Fagin provides an image of the video as an unthreatened haven where the play of signifiers is quite safe from alien influences. It is in this sense that Fagin's early videos are conceptual art pieces. For all their juxtapositional energy, the ideas circulate in an airtight compartment. Rather than TV's precarious composite of reality, a fragile order where different forms of address can eventually negate each other's reality, Fagin creates a twilight zone world, perfect in that all its elements pertain to the same class and could be part of a well-edited text anthology on copy and dissemination. The concerted focus on issues of representation, refracted by discourses that continuously suggest the impossibility of organic unity—Roussel's machines or Flaubert's *Bouvard and Pecuchet*—presents the artistic enterprise itself as somewhat manic in its certainties. The highly theoretical reach of Fagin's links, as well as their concentrated focus, shapes a well-oiled machine: in perfect functioning it exacts distance. Formally and thematically Fagin's collages return, like the celibate movement described in Duchamps's *Large Glass,* to the master circuit of signification foreseen by the artist. His tapes are "mock journeys" whose effect, in the monitor space as well as in the solipsism of a looped discourse on reproduction, is doubly claustrophobic. There are no autonomous progenies, and the potential chain of associations seems to be entirely anticipated by the videomaker.

In *The Machine,* Fagin refines his collage procedures. He articulates with an incredible dexterity several orders of address and appropriates the heterogeneous nature of TV rhythm and texture in its various modes of advertisement: news announcement, weather report, shopping channel, reportage, and sensationalist TV faith healings. Fagin's perverse creativity sparks, for instance, when in staging the shopping channels' glitz he smuggles in information-*qua*-gossip about power and corruption in the semifeudal Philippine oligarchies. When, however, he simulates the informational scattering of TV through a surface mimicry of its eclecticism, he faces a formidable challenge: the closer he is to his model, the more seamless is the result of his enterprise. And again, although Fagin enlarges the range of his engagement, he creates a new totality, a flawless machine. Appearances and timing guarantee a perfect simulation of TV's void and constant variety. In this machine the glitches are intentional and built-in. They neutralize alterity by an all-too-perfect fit within a deconstructive vortex.

Zero Degrees Latitude clarifies what is wrong with perfection. The tape is composed of two radically heterogeneous approaches to image and sound. The first of these presents the tape's subject matter—evangelical conversion in Ecuador—through the familiar investigative possibilities of documentary. The sound is direct, the format is vérité, and for extended portions of the tape we witness a respectful interest: the reality of different registers of need and belief is questioned by the invisible cameraperson whose voice (Bertha Jottar's) we hear. The second set of images and sound is a series of tableaux portraying a white woman in front of a painted backdrop (the mosquito mural). The woman, dressed in an early-century fashion, is engaged in reading the Bible. She also at times seems to speak in tongues, and her body rides or moves extravagant installations made of wood, cord, nails—a weaving hobbyhorse compound, an agricultural-sailing-boat *dispositif,* a feeding-hanging attachment. A broom structures the sail; a rake structures the main axis of a pedaling machine moved by the woman's swimming motions as she hangs suspended by lines. These machines are outrageous and inefficient, and their motions lead nowhere. They are symbolic artifacts with no pretension to science or productivity. The scope of the woman's attention and the self-absorbed nature of her drive are figured by the circular quality present in the machines' arbitrary motions. This movement is also, significantly, the background for a subjective voice-over reading of a diary. Throughout several of these vignettes the videomaker creates a character, a male evangelist (one assumes, from the diaries' content, from the Summer Institute of Linguistics), who at some point in history was presumably stepping over the same roads trailed by Fagin's camera and tape recorder.

The presence of these two very diverse forms of representation in *Zero Degrees* invites a question about the effects of their awkward coexistence in this tape, a démarche that clearly departs from Fagin's media coverage in *The Machine.* Instead of a series of different notations that broadcast TV's ease of channel change, *Zero Degrees* is sparse and insists on two single poles—the "real" world and the fabricated reality. Their purposefully cumbersome contact allows Fagin to parade his investment in moving from the solipsistic discourses of his two early tapes toward that something else that might set in motion, with likely and welcome friction, a machine that might otherwise grind to a halt.

The rough quality of this pronounced stutter, the passage from one system of visual and aural imprint to another—more dreamlike in its artificial scenery and also more poetic in its verbal associations—imposes an unstable spectatorial position, an impatience regarding the issue of agency. In a tape that is generated around the revisions of the 1492 discovery of America and that explicitly directs our attention to the North-South vector of colonization, the interest in Fagin's position is not an empty question. The extreme sparseness of *Zero Degrees*'s configuration of a problematic needs to be seen already as a partial positioning. The difficult relay between the two sets of images present in the tape, different both in look (natural versus artificial) and in the nature of their engagement (with the world and with "fiction"), imposes a retroactive reading of Fagin's ambitions for, as well as skepticism of, artistic creation.

The first image from *Zero Degrees* aligned with the South is that of a single eye, which the camera first tapes out of focus and which eventually fills the monitor with a staring gaze. The direct address to the camera, maintained for a certain duration, forces one to stand, momentarily, as the object of a reverse inquisition. This eye seems all-knowing, and we who watch fall under a judging scrutiny. This subjective response to direct cinema's objective neutrality is not the only way Fagin calls documentaries into question. In another image, this time from *The Machine That Killed Bad People,* we witness an operation performed without anesthetic or surgical instruments, and we watch as the healer opens an incision by hand and pokes his hand in a woman's belly as if looking for a known shape in a woman's handbag. We also see his hand caressing the wound as he undoes and sutures the hole. That we indeed see all of it checks our belief in our own vision. This is a figuration of a real unconstrained by reality's logic but submitted to us through the directness of a real-time image. This sight answers other "trick" profilmic images, for instance, that of a magician performing for an audience of children in Dziga Vertov's *The Man with the Movie Camera,* an image later revealed as part of cinema's necessary illusions. With Fagin there is no unmasking *qua*-promise of truth. Instead, the faith healing in *The Machine* assumes the tone of a riddle about visibility and evidence. The direct cinema camera cannot show the mechanism, the link, that sutures the woman's belly.

In *Zero Degrees* we witness a return to the theme of the *curandero,* the town healer. Sitting by his family, he describes how he borrows animistic forces in order to heal. When he calmly talks about his dealings with the demons, he seems to acknowledge that he is surrounded by the pressure of a puritanical rule. Against the evangelist proscription of drinking he claims he needs a few drinks to make his head dizzy and initiate his work. He also enhances the status of his healing as a profession by stating, for instance, that he spent six years in contact with animals. "He graduated," mocks his nephew.

From *The Machine*'s spectacular scene of faith healing to the rather vapid account of healing in *Zero Degrees*, one notes the inscription of a significant difference. *Zero Degrees* promotes an anemic aesthetics. In the latter tape the *curandero* and not the healing is the focus. Instead of the shock tactics of the spectacle of vision betrayed, we witness the banality of a system of belief that needs to stand its own against the pressure of a modern, puritanical, foreign potency. The revelation about the years spent in the lake with animals and demons has thus a paradoxical and even unconvincing function of authentication. Likewise, what becomes increasingly embarrassing, as we watch and assume the camera position, is the blatant attempt to please a foreigner, the effort to do one's homework—apparent in the boatman's description of the improved professionalization brought about by the Summer Institute of Linguistics (the front for evangelism in Central America) or in the proud faces of those who sing hymns and say by heart verses from the gospel in Quechua (their own language) to the camera.

Fagin's insistence on the social constraints of belief grants to the sustained return of the camera's gaze a pressing and emblematic value. That this native resistance is problematic is in turn made clear when Fagin zooms out, allowing us to see the radio. For, when the camera reframes, we notice that the intensity of this man's staring eye is not so focused. The man's attention is actually divided between what he sees and what he listens to; he is intent rather on the sounds coming out of his radio, which he proudly raises close to his ears. At one point in *Zero Degrees* a progressive indigenous Catholic priest explains that the radio is the main means of communication forming the basis of the evangelization of Latin America. What is curious, he remarks, is that these radios, given as gifts to anyone who converted to evangelism, transmitted only two channels, both controlled by the evangelical churches. Conversely, in the studio set we listen to a single channel reminiscent of Fagin's earlier textured monologues: the drone-like confessions of the male voice-over suggest an inward radio, a process of self-baptism. A process of conversion is rehearsed in the swaying motions of subjectivity of the evangelist preacher.

Because it is invisible, sound stands—within Fagin's subtle economy of display—in place of a direct presentation of links. The figure of the ventriloquist in *The Amazing Voyage* is an example of this attempt to veil causes; the faith healing in *The Machine* another. Yet within the colonizing vector of the narrative of *Zero Degrees,* Fagin's zooming in on the radio held by the man whose eye we've faced insists that the waves of the radio, out there, everywhere, are the unseen mechanisms of penetration. The tape suggests that, for the sound to better circulate, the eye has to remain semiclosed. Several instances reveal how the focus on sound and inner voices depends on keeping one's eyes closed. And, while the white woman's somnambulist disposition echoes, from a clean and dreamlike setting, the Northern contours of this willed blindness, the more alienating effects of evangelical conversion are revealed in the documentary sections assessing the alternatives as well as the economic bonus of evangelism. The parallels are inevitable and suggest an unwitting division of labor. Fagin promotes this critical contamination through a hint of what is permissible—a form of daydream drunkenness in the North but not in the South (where the evangelical preachers proscribe alcohol). These very distinct sets of images and aesthetics frame each other: the documentary enterprise stumbles with, as it comments on, the sense of closed circuitry associated in the tapes both with a poetic excess and with a Northern entitlement. The very association of a formal privilege with a character so markedly identifiable with a preacher from the American South becomes, within *Zero Degrees*'s questioning of colonial economy, an issue.

This assertion might be a hypostatization of the ethics animating this project. Bearing in mind the direction of Fagin's former talent, the drastic contrast between the better-known territory of juxtapositional mastery and the new, but otherwise familiar, repertoire of vérité interviewing in *Zero Degrees* leads to a more basic question. If Fagin's most creative and fictional figurations are loosely identifiable with a certain image of the North American white male, present at times as an army veteran, an evangelist preacher, or a journalist, what is the relevance of the notion of character in his work? What is the author's kinship to this particular character for it to warrant such an outpouring of creative attention?

The characters I wish to discuss share significant features. Their private, authentic core is substantiated through letters and diaries. Their rhetoric meshes baseball gossip with nationalist bravados against communism and clichés about Europeans and "them." The basic themes of these rev-elations relate to strong American values, be they gung-ho militarism or evangelization or even, in the case of the artist-reporter, the problematics of social engagement.

The first character is mentioned in the last scene in *The Machine That Killed Bad People.* The reporter Connie sits on a stool beside a metal hu-manoid, a little hut from which a rocket-like shape emerges with a big staring eye. Recalling the dollar bill's masonic symbol, this mechanical puppet flaps its arms, blinks repeatedly, catches on fire. As an eagle at-tached to this machine bites the puppet's (Prometheus-like) shoulder, it starts to spurt red paint, and the "blood" quenches the fire. This miniallegory for imperialist America, proceeds in its successive phases of "despair," "rage," and self-destruction, as the reporter mentions before reading a letter from December 1951 "discovered quite by accident in an attic in Michigan." "It would be best to withhold the author's name. We can, however, tell you a bit about him. He was Oliver North's hero, and after his tour of duty in the Philippines he went on to Vietnam and, finally, Central America. It has been said about him, no, about a character in a novel based on him [Graham Greene's *The Quiet American*], that he was determined to do good. Not to any individual, but to a country, a continent, a world. Well, here's the letter. Dear Dad, . . ." The second personal account revealing a character is the evangelist's diary. It is voiced at times by a man with a Southern accent, at times by the woman in the studio in *Zero Degrees.* "Why is it I remember all the pitchers on a team that batted .313? Cherry would tease, "Only a Protestant could root for something named the Saint Louis Browns. . . . When I married Cam, I knew his first love was the Lord, but I didn't imagine his second was base-ball.'" The third example of Fagin's national portrait is introduced through a visual approach that contrasts markedly with the rest of *The Machine.* The wandering movements of Leslie Thornton's camera, focus-ing on unexpected areas of the actor Ron Vawter's body or the room, produce a grainy image whose obscuring effect adds perfectly to the sense of subjective cornering that the journalist's verbal and written reports re-veal. As the reporter is introduced, writing on the last days of the Marcoses' rule in the Philippines, other, parallel events of historic magni-tude are introduced. At one point we listen as he discourses with a certain angst on facts about Marcos's family—"that's what an oligarchy feels like," "the wake now going longer than a miniseries." Then, in a next segment, reading on the killings at Tiananmen Square, as we ourselves try to focus on blurry headlines and newspaper typeface, Vawter's face emerges, as he softly cries. It was with the Tiananmen Square events that the West for the first time broadcast, on such a massive scale, visuals that were informationally nil. Instead of the Chinese drama, American TV presented diagrams of the journalists' hotels and their relative position vis-à-vis the unfolding of events. Fagin's amazing prose, as well as Thornton's myopic close-up aesthetics, inscribe this portrait of liberal angst socially. By dint of an association with the events in China, the brilliance of a creative act (the prose, the visuals, and Vawter's performance) is related to a blocked reportage, an obstructed communication.

The cost of privileging art over reporting can be felt in other works by Fagin. This aesthetic economy destines inventiveness and artistic expression to the pathos of the *incommunicado*. These personal accounts clothed as documents can thus be seen as allegories for Fagin's balancing act as an artist. Fagin's characterization of the artist as linguist (in *Zero Degrees*) or the romantic fleshing out of a character through textual disjunction (in *Zero Degrees* and in *The Machine*) is a signature of sorts. More important here, the love for baseball or a midwestern American origin (similar to the videomaker's Chicago) is intended as a giveaway sign for the affinity between the artist and a problematic national identity.

I suggested earlier that the move to realist representation and documentary rhetoric was a comment on the circuitry of the author's poetic machines. This move, dramatized in *Zero Degrees*'s peculiar structure, implied the need to introduce an ethical dimension, a more conclusive positioning of the author as an artist and as a progressive American. The characters described above create an intricate circulation of morality. They provide the answer, provisional as it might be, about Fagin's share in a national portrait.

The videomaker engages these characters with a vengeance. He grants them a composite subjectivity, textually conflating author and character. These personages' express function is then to contaminate the notion of a (politically) correct authorial position. In these constructs the videomaker aligns himself with the white male character by granting him a surplus expressivity, an extra textual power. The obviousness of this compensatory mechanism is meant in turn to be telling. Fagin proclaims his investment, purposefully problematizing his artistic progressivism once he moves South or East. It is finally the very allure of Fagin's poetics that, standing as the artist's blatant excuse, casts a shadow on his all-too-powerful, privileged characters. That Fagin stills his progressive stance, investing himself in the persona of an interventionist American, is only part of his feat in *Zero Degrees*. This quiet revelation attests to the subtlety and complexity of Fagin's self-questioning as an artist.

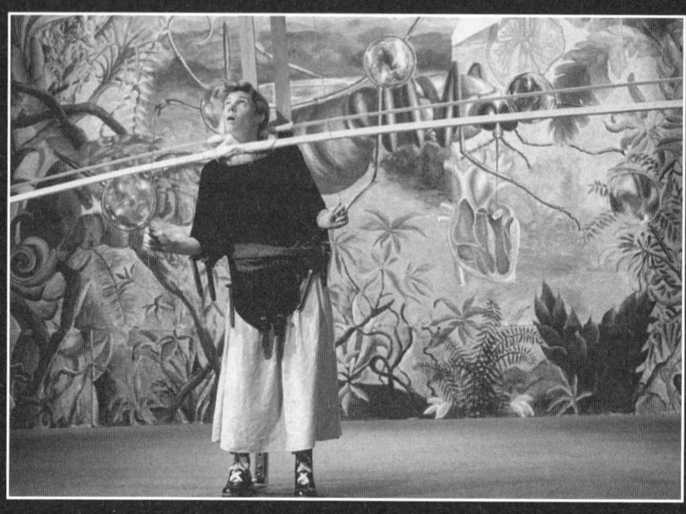

"Death of a Salesman," from *Zero Degrees Latitude*

Steve Fagin
Voice-Over from *Zero Degrees Latitude*

Dixie Davis

Rasty Wright

Elam Vanglider

Jockey Kolp

Shucks Pruett

Urban Schocker

Why is it I remember all the pitchers on a team that batted .313? Cherry would tease, "Only a Protestant could root for something named the Saint Louis Browns." She knew I would turn red as an Injun, but continued, "When I married Cam, I knew his first love was the Lord, but I didn't imagine his second was baseball." I have wondered if she would have married me at all knowing it had been my first, well at least as a boy, my heart broken by the Browns. They had scored a hundred more runs than the Yankees, Williams had even out-homered Ruth thirty-nine to thirty-five. Still they lost, by one game, on the final day. Who would have thought the day of judgment would be ruled by an umpire, jerking his thumb upward toward the heavens, condemning to eternal damnation a prone and dirt-covered Babydoll Jacobson. Babydoll spat Red Man on the umpire's trouser leg as I scribbled out *stealing* on my scorecard. Unlike Lazarus, the Browns would never rise again.

5 June 1957

Fifty-five years later, I hear "sacrifice" and am pushed past the once savage Dayuma, a miracle clutching at the curtain. Ralph Edwards greets my eyes with the words, "The founding father of the Summer Institute of Linguistics." I fall into a trance and think: "134, 246, .420, 18, and 51."

"Sisler," I mumble in front of thirty million television viewers, and I twinge as Ralph howls, "This is your life Rachel Saint." I see a finger pointing at her, then me, as a vanishing idiot card reads the word *Wycliffe.* The new card says, *Uncle Cam, camera right,* and in capital letters *SCHOFIELD.* I read: Revelation 13:18.

Here is wisdom. Let him who has a mind calculate the number of the wild beast, for it is the number of mankind, and its number is 666. I tremble as I try to drown out the question I silently ask myself for the 999th time. Such numbers, was he a man, a beast, or perhaps a god?

Tuesday, 22 December 1992
The hand is always cold, the sheets wet, and my lips dry as the voice whispers.

Revelation 10:10 and 11
And I got the tiny scroll out of the hand of the messenger and devoured it. And in my mouth it was sweet as honey. And when I ate it, my bowels were made bitter. And they are saying to me, "You must prophesy again over peoples and nations and tongues and many kings." I awake, or imagine I awake, to the sound of the sea. But the air feels stale, and I drift. The voice returns and whispers loudly, "A place where dead men meet on the tongues of living men."

The voice hands me a yellowed pamphlet, a playbill, whose frontispiece reads "Morosco Theater, New York City, February 10, 1949." Music is heard. The curtain goes up before us; at first, only partly visible, is the salesman's house. We are aware of towering angular shapes behind it, surrounding it on all sides. Only the blue light of the sky falls upon the house and forestage; the surrounding area shows an angry glow of orange. An air of dream clings to the place, a dream rising out of reality. The salesman slowly walks into the light from stage right. He is dressed in a dark gray business suit, felt hat under his arm, and carries two sample cases. He is very tired and confused. A flute is heard in the distance, soft, beguiling, memorable. He hears it but is not aware of it. It plays a tinny melody of grass and trees and the horizon. He is sixty now, his emotions are, in a word, mercurial. He crosses stage left, unlocks the door, and enters the kitchen. He puts the cases down and sighs. They are heavy. He feels the calluses on his hand, then slams the door.

I close the booklet and am now truly awake. 4:00 A.M., and I think of Guatemala, *cakchiquel,* my first Bible translation, laugh, then say, "Being a door-to-door Bible salesman in this country really has its ups and downs." Take a breath, "Oh well, the best salesman still is the Bible in the mother tongue. . . ." My pause is broken by the sound of *cakchiquel,* a chorus of Indians miming my American accent. "Only two thousand tongues to go," shifting to English, parroting me as they lecture, "Why boys, when I was seventeen, I walked into the jungle and, when I was twenty-one, walked out, and by God I was rich. . . ." I have an appointment in *ketchikan,* Tuesday week.

Wednesday, 23 December 1992
Other breeding birds of prey include the diurnal short-eared owl and the nocturnal (and infrequently seen) barn owl. The bright red vermilion flycatcher is widespread in the highlands. More frequently seen is the drabber Galapagos (large-billed) flycatcher.

Revelation 21:1-4
And I perceived a new heaven and a new earth, for the former heaven and the former earth pass away, and the sea is no more. . . . And he will be brushing away every tear from their eyes. And death will be no more, nor mourning, nor clamor, nor misery. They will be no more, for the former things passed away.

JAARS
Larry Montgomery: great pilot, lousy salesman. Even with the military connection, the Jungle Aviation and Radio Service wouldn't have gotten off the ground. I would begin my sales pitch with a real jug handle: "Imagine Isabella Godin des Odonais wandering, lost, barefoot, filthy, deranged, and almost naked in the jungle, separated from her husband, a chain bearer to the equatorial measurement expedition, for

twenty-one years. Long since forgotten, she appeared without fanfare at Andoas, brought by twelve Indians, each wearing two small chains of gold around his neck. After hearing of Isabella's impending arrival in Cayenne, her husband, the last remaining member of the grand geodesic expedition on the South American continent, could not wait. In a canoe he hurried to meet the ship and was soon climbing on board. She looked blankly into her husband's blue eyes and greeted him in a matter-of-fact manner, but he understood not a word. She speaks only Quechua."

At this point I change speeds; I throw nothing but heat, imagine it had been Rachel Saint lost without JAARS, her miraculous work with the Aucas only a mirage. Envision her wandering in a jungle, its heat causing her soul to shrivel. She sees only desert, a land not blessed by God. Pausing, letting it wash over them, I quote from Luke: "What man of you, having a hundred sheep and losing one of them, is not leaving the ninety-nine in the wilderness and is going after the lost one 'til he may be finding it?" With JAARS we could save her.
STRIKE THREE for the Lord.

■ ■ ■

310

Constance Penley Out in Left Field

We feel . . . it is part of God's plan to at least begin
to crack the tribe for an entrance of His word.

Zero Degrees Latitude: It takes a while to get one's mind around the idea of Steve Fagin out in the jungle doing fieldwork, although it's not as if he's never been in the jungle before or never conducted interviews. In his earlier *The Machine That Killed Bad People* he did, after all, travel from Manila to distant jungle loca-

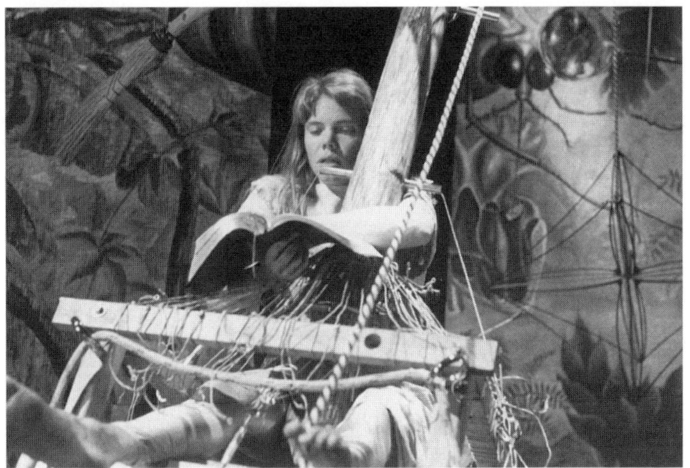

"Sunday Bible Reading in Mosquito Heaven," from *Zero Degrees Latitude*

tions to document indigenous rituals (surgery performed with bare hands!) and interview a range of Filipinos on contemporary political and cultural issues. But that video wove together its more ethnographic elements with fictional characters and events and the styles of other forms of video such as network news and cable home shopping. The editing thus ensured that the field documentation and interviews were no more privileged as truth bearing than the obviously fabricated fictions or the language of the other forms of video. *The Machine That Killed Bad People* invites us to understand Philippine politics and everyday life as much through the aesthetics of the Home Shopping Club as the verities of documentary.

But *Zero Degrees Latitude* really looks like ethnography. Weird ethnography, maybe, off base, but ethnography. The video consists largely of interviews with the inhabitants of small villages in Ecuador. The interviews attempt to solicit information about a specific cultural instance, the way the indigenous Ecuadorans responded to the tactics and theology of evangelical missionaries (the Wycliffe Bible Translators, or WBT) who came in the name of science (the Summer Institute of Linguistics, or SIL) to convert them to Christianity. *Zero Degrees Latitude* is not, of course, without its fictional or staged moments (this is, after all, a Steve Fagin video), but the ethnographic segments are given more screen time than are the video's signature machine dreams, of which more later.

Another indication that, with this video, Fagin wanted to explore the pleasure and efficacy of using the camera to capture something of the reality of the lived world—the documentary impulse—is his original, and ultimately unfulfilled, wish to have Joel DeMott and Jeff Kreines shoot the Ecuador footage. DeMott and Kreines spent most of 1983 in Muncie, Indiana, shooting their banned film *Seventeen,* a grim, stunning portrait of Middletown USA by two people who, in Fagin's words, "still believe in documentary." Although *Zero Degrees Latitude* does its fair share of deconstructing documentary (now de rigueur for any self-respecting poststructuralist artist-ethnographer), especially in its display of native informants' skill at playing to the camera, setting their own agendas, and deftly resisting the too obviously hoped-for answer, that's not the point of the video. The point is to show how the WBT/SIL attempted "to crack the tribe for an entrance of His word" and the way this colonizing invasion was rejected, negotiated, and transformed by native Ecuadorans. That's why Fagin wanted significant amounts of the footage to be shot by people who still believe in documentary. Although one sometimes suspects that Fagin's documentary impulse may arise more from a technologically utopian, modernist desire to boldly go where no eyeball has gone before than from the gritty will to capture raw reality, he nonetheless wanted *Zero Degrees Latitude* to be about *something*—something other than its own process, its own epistemological status.

We hear the story of the WBT/SIL from a variety of sources. The Marxist agitator for land rights calls evangelism "a hypnotization of the indigenous" and the missionaries' God "a capitalist God. A dollar God." The convert insists that evangelical culture and indigenous culture are one and the same—food, music, everything. Another convert says the evangelicals were concerned only with "civilizing people" by teaching them to read the Bible and learn useful occupations "such as carpenter, mechanic, teacher." Yet another believes that evangelism has helped her live through sadness and pain with the thought that "I have been crucified with Christ and I no longer live, but Christ lives in me." A former evangelical tells how he gave up teaching the gospel to work with boas and other animals, in an effort to tap into other demonic powers. This evangelical turned *curandero* also boasts that he sent his sons to university, in defiance of the missionaries' wish that the indigenous stay indigenous by learning only enough to read the Bible and nothing else. A man sitting in a church twists backward in his pew to whisper to the camera an explanation of the range of groups seen in church that day:

> Those who sit here are good Christian followers and believe in the Gospel. But the others over there are somewhat more distant from Christ and the Church, and those sitting in the back come only to hear the word of God and decide if they wish to follow Christ. Although they've been baptized by water, they await baptism through the spirit of Christ. Now those standing in the corner are church leaders who are observing people's behavior so that later they can better communicate Christ's message to them.

We learn about the evangelicals and their relation to the indigenous Ecuadorans through what are apparently the words of William Cameron Townsend, the founder of the WBT/SIL. But, in the video's play-by-play recounting of Townsend's missionary endeavors, the events of his life are filtered through the popular texts of American male myth, from John Ford–like westerns to *Death of a Salesman*. Here, "Cam" is a Bible- and baseball-loving evangelical who irresistibly puns on the meanings of *sacrifice*.

From this unseen male voice we get fleeting, elliptical references to JAARS, the Jungle Aviation and Radio Service, which rained missionaries and radios on the people below; the ridiculed and sometimes dangerous life of a Bible salesman; former Mexican president Cardenas, who inexplicably served as Cam's best man; a dream of a western in which a one-eyed man tells Cam, "You have trod on the wretched of the earth to seek your salvation!" and another dream of being introduced by Ralph Edwards to thirty million television viewers.

All the missionary's somewhat obscure words and stories are heard over the spectacle of machines, fantastic and fantastically beautiful machines that are both scary and funny. These are not bachelor machines for constructing paranoid, narcissistic interiorities, but socioreligious combines built for plowing and navigating the fields and waters of the Lord. Fashioned and performed by Melissa Smedley, one such combine is at once stocks, cross, and mast, to which she either is bound or has lashed herself. Another consists of her body stretched across a mechanical device that allows or forces her to rake, row, and read at the same time. In the third, called in the credits *Radio Is Propagation,* she appears as a crazed lady evangelical attached to a radio-like machine sending and receiving waves that are channeled through her body. The background for these machine dreams is a tropical mural of a giant mosquito pushing its proboscis into a sliced-open, sectioned heart.

As for the video's heart, it's right there, practically on its sleeve. Even when admiring the idiosyncratic intensity of the characters who were the WBT/SIL missionaries, *Zero Degrees Latitude* clearly sides not only with the indigenous peoples but more exclusively with the Indians who rejected conversion and chose militant social organizing instead. The militants' interviews, conducted in front of maps and a monitor showing the funeral of a fellow agrarian rights activist, forcefully present their arguments. So, too, the camera treats favorably and at length the man who gave up evangelism for native healing and sent his sons to university. The camera tends to stay on the converted, however, only until they start sounding a bit crazed, make a revealing slip, or break off awkwardly to escape a line of questioning that has proved too difficult. The man, for example, who said there were no differences between indigenous and gringo food admits on camera that, although the food is the same, income determines how it is prepared. We already know from earlier interviews that the indigenous people who took up with the evangelicals are better off financially than the nonconverted or the ones recruited to Catholicism, so the question of whether there is a difference between the foods is more than a cultural one; as soon as the man answers, he recognizes that he has given a disclosive answer to a loaded question and becomes even more eager to break away from the interviewer.

What would be the value of telling an even thicker story about this encounter of evangelicals and indigenous peoples, one that would give us more of the fears and wishes, motives and desires, of all the parties? Before asking this question it is important to say that, in paying equal attention to the work of symbolic systems and material conditions and their historic interplay, *Zero Degrees Latitude* comes closer than perhaps any other moving-image ethnography to the kind of qualitative, dialectical, writerly anthropology so brilliantly proposed by Michael Taussig in *The Devil and Commodity Fetishism in South America*. In that book Taussig tells the story of how the plantation workers and miners of South America adapted the Christian idea of the devil to comprehend and resist the capitalist proletarianization crushing down on them. After demonstrating in great detail how rural people in Colombia and Bolivia represent as "vividly unnatural, even evil," capitalist relations of production that have come to seem natural to us, Taussig shows us that understanding this confrontation between capitalist and precapitalist cultures is instrumental in helping us recognize the workings of the "phantom objectivity with which capitalist culture enshrouds its creations."[1]

In *Founders of Men or Fishers of Empire? The Wycliffe Bible Translators in Latin America,* David Stoll calls the WBT/SIL "a spectacle of dedication and technology that invites endless speculation,"[2] which is an equally apt description of *Zero Degrees Latitude.* Let's take the invitation to speculate (perhaps not endlessly) that Fagin's video offers to begin to dream a kind of visual anthropology that could, in Taussig's words, "provide us with some critical leverage with which to assess and understand the sacrosanct and unconscious assumptions that are built into and emerge from our social forms."[3]

At one point in *Zero Degrees Latitude* the interviewer, walking alongside the man who claimed there was no difference between indigenous and gringo food, is trying to get him to describe the parts of traditional culture that the evangelicals pressured the indigenous people to abandon. He answers by saying that "there are some traditions that upon conversion to evangelism we have abandoned. . . . Going to dances, for example. . . . Drinking in order to get drunk. . . . These traditions have changed." No more dancing and drinking! any viewer will think on hearing this. Isn't it just like those prissy, joyless missionaries to want to stamp out the Ecuadorans' pleasure-loving lives! But listening attentively to the man's explanation, both how he says it and what he says, and adding some knowledge of the history of conversion in Latin America appreciably thickens the story. First, he says, "*we* abandoned," thus at least claiming agency for the indigenous people and subtly stressing that it was a choice. Dancing and drinking to get drunk he describes as *traditions* that have changed. But where did these supposedly indigenous rituals come from? Landowners, with the Catholic church's complicity, who preferred a drunken, illiterate, and indebted labor force, a system threatened by Protestant abstinence, literacy, and thrift—all qualities that the indigenous peoples could adapt to defy their oppressors. From here, we would be able to go to the vital insight of what a double-edged sword evangelism through literacy and technology training can and has been. Because the WBT/SIL often taught literacy in Spanish along with the native tongue to those they had chosen to be leaders, this opened the door to reading other books besides the Bible as well as writing all kinds of other texts. And, according to David Stoll, the indigenous people quickly learned how to use the radios rained on them by JAARS to communicate back to the missionaries their demands for goods and supplies in return for agreeing to be converted through education and training. It is not surprising that crucial segments of the indigenous Ecuadorans figured out how to use evangelism against itself, for Taussig illustrates the long history of native South Americans and black slaves ingeniously tapping into the revolutionary and egalitarian spirit of early Christianity to defy the modern church in its own devil's pact with the ruling classes.

Thickening this story, along the lines that *Zero Degrees Latitude* makes possible, would likely require introducing one of the critical players, radical Catholicism, evangelism's main rival in capturing the hearts and minds of the indigenous people. As Taussig shows, the earlier people who resisted the church did not do so by harking back to primitive lore and magic; instead, they subsumed Christianity into indigenous symbolic systems to create a new social imaginary, one built on a necessary defetishization of the relations of production: "In the colonial situation the zombies and spirits change to reflect the new situation rather than the precolonial spirit world."[4] Our thicker ethnography might then put some pressure on the Marxist in *Zero Degrees Latitude* who claims that the Quechua-speaking people have abandoned their belief that God is within nature—"in the mountains, the snakes"—either under the pressure of evangelism or because lapsed evangelicals have turned to other gods, with the result that "people who are not evangelized here don't believe in God or anything." But how likely is it that people would subscribe to no belief structure whatever? The admittedly utopian ethnography pointed to here, a denser and more dialectical ethnography, would allow us to listen perhaps differently to the speech of the indigenous peoples, to learn more about the belief structure of the nonconverted *and* the converted.

It's also the case that, if we want to understand what evangelism has meant to the Ecuadorans, to then be able to say what they have *done* with it, we need to acknowledge the way its initial appeal was indeed appealing. Thus far, those writing and thinking within the field of cultural studies have been reluctant, to say the least, to consider the homegrown U.S. religions as popular culture. The "cultural dope" theory of cultural consumption still reigns when it comes to religion, that well-known opiate of the masses. But if we think of these religions—ranging from Mormonism and Spiritualism to Christian Science and Scientology—as popular culture, then we must ask the same question of them that we would ask of other realms of massified culture that attempt to recruit us as consumer-subjects: to what popular pleasures, everyday desires, intellectual curiosities, and utopian possibilities do these religions speak—admittedly within the aim of containing and codifying those yearnings to serve their own institutional needs? If such a question could be posed, then we would also want to follow up on what it means for an indigenous man to say, "With regard to tradition, there are some that upon conversion *we* have abandoned." We can either dismiss this man as "hypnotized" or try to understand the kind of claim about human and social agency that is being articulated here. In one of the machine dream segments later in the video, a woman is *wearing* the Rube Goldberg–like machine that is at once stocks, cross, and mast, with iron nails and bells hanging from her body. In her first encounter with the machine, it wasn't clear whether she had been lashed to the mast or had bound herself to it. Here, we think she is trapped in the machine but then see that she is pulling the ropes that move the machine, manipulating the machine as it encases her. This same double notion of agency, as both being done to and doing, could reasonably be applied to the Ecuadoran converts we see in the video as much as to the native militants or fictionally depicted missionaries.

We can also proceed in a way that will "provide us with some critical leverage" to learn about our own social forms if we can thicken the description of popular religion's relation to science. The two richest stories that have been told about the WBT/SIL, Stoll's book and Fagin's video, assume that the evangelical leaders tried to acquire for religion the aura of scientific authority by cynically, dishonestly, and hypocritically wrapping themselves in the mantle of science. As the story goes, the missionaries gained entry by persuading government officials, military leaders, and community members that they were linguists coming to study the indigenous language and the native habitat of the speakers. Once in, they began proselytizing and converting as many of the indigenous as possible, often with the silent approval of the government and the military, who knew what the "linguists" were up to all along and were grateful for any help the missionaries might give them in convincing people to leave coveted and valuable land that could then be confiscated. But it is too simple a story to see the religious relation to science as purely superficial and instrumental, if not entirely devious. A central and enduring feature of the homegrown U.S. religions is the scientific impulse that has fueled all of them. And it's not just the ones, from Christian Science to Scientology, that make apparent their scientific identifications; it's many others as well, including Mormonism, Seventh Day Adventism, and even the Nation of Islam, with its theological invention of a scientist who created white people, the mutant results of an experiment. The story that is usually told about these religions is that they are viciously irrational and destructively antiscientific. But what if the story is that they don't hate science, they love it, and love it so much that they think science is too important to be left to the scientists? If the telling of the story starts from the recognition that most of the U.S. religions are also popular science cultures, then the critical issue won't be that of tearing away the false mantle of science to reveal the purely religious motives that lurk beneath, but that of trying to understand the power of a popular theology that offers the possibility of a human and ethical relation to science and a zest for experimentation as well.

Even Creationists call their efforts to resolve the biblical and scientific accounts of the origins of the universe "creation science" or "Bible science." As Christopher P. Toumey shows in his ethnography of creation science study groups, *God's Own Scientists: Creationists in a Secular World*,[5] the members find science compelling and are far less opposed to science than to what they see as the arrogance of the nation's scientific-educational establishment, a view shared by many outside conservative Christianity. Toumey also points out that within the study groups the Creationists are much more open than they are in public about discussing the logical flaws in their theories and debate constantly the nature of scientific authority, a question too often suppressed among official scientists.

To understand the SIL then as merely a "front" for the WBT is to misconceive the way science and religion are inextricably bound up with one another in U.S. religions. A final plot turn that could be added to what is becoming a story both thick and convoluted is the role of women in these popular U.S. scientific religions, most of which were founded and/or heavily staffed by women. *Zero Degrees Latitude* aptly puts the women missionaries on center stage, in the machine dream segments and in the dialogue: "Cam" can tell his story of the WBT/SIL only by also recounting the adventures of intrepid missionary Rachel Saint, whose work educating an indigenous woman was the source for *The Dayuma Story*, WBT's all-time best-seller and the book that got Saint, and a reluctant Dayuma, an appearance on Ralph Edwards's "This Is Your Life!"

The interest here lies not in heroicizing the women participants in these religioscientific cultures but rather, as with Willa Cather's 1907 biography of the eccentric and spellbinding Mary Baker Eddy, in recognizing how these much derided and zealously debunked communities—now ranging from Spiritualism to Biosphere 2—can function as alternative cultures for women, as unique popular sites of sexual, social, and scientific experimentation.

To understand is not, of course, to forgive. Protestant evangelicals such as the ones featured in *Zero Degrees Latitude* have done a great deal of damage to the indigenous peoples of Latin America. Especially harmful are the practices arising from the evangelicals' particular brand of millennialism, which equates the Kingdom Come with a thoroughly evangelized and prosperously capitalized world and sees as the anti-Christ progressive social movements, such as those theorized and enabled by liberation theology. But, in any case, a greater comparative and historical understanding of these popular scientific religions could only help, whether one is trying to reform, reshape, or reject the ideas and strategies of the evangelists, and no matter where they might be plowing the fields of the Lord.

What difference does it make to understanding the Ecuadorans' encounter with the evangelicals to recognize how the WBT and the SIL embody and make apparent what I argue elsewhere is a deep structure of U.S. culture: the copresence of a strong belief in religion and an equally powerful one in science?[6] So, too, what can we learn about that encounter by recognizing the major role that women have played in the alternative U.S. popular cultures that have been devoted to experimenting with living and acting on these two simultaneous beliefs? And, to put it the other way, how can that understanding give us critical leverage on our own "sacrosanct and unconscious assumptions"? These are the questions I am left with as I read Taussig's provocative book and look at the extraordinary promise of *Zero Degrees Latitude* in helping us conceive new ways to describe and explain the world.

■ ■ ■

Christmas Eve, 1992

Christmas always makes me think. Pictures, they reappear like magic: before the ceremony, former Mexican president Cardenas, my best man, takes a boutonnière from the bride's bouquet, somewhere in the middle of the pile, my Texas hat and Mexican briefcase in focus, all the rest out. And the snapshot I always save for last: the banner, Arkansas, "Camp Wycliffe 1936 To Translate the Bible in Every Language Upon the Earth . . ." and what I can't see any more but know by heart, Romans 15:20, "Yea, so have I strived to preach the Gospel, not where Christ was named lest I should build another man's foundation. But as it is written, to whom he was not spoken of, they shall see: and they that have not heard shall understand." Surrounded by all the boys: Miller, Pike, Gene, Elvira, and Ethel, her face worn thin by the aging of the picture.

At Wycliffe I had a vision, the foreground, John Ford's West, Henry Fonda sitting, no, balancing himself on the single leg of a chair, back and forth, left foot, then right. The background, it's Tombstone, not Dodge. There should be a half-built church, but instead I see a pale horse. And his name that sits on him is death, and hell followed with him. And power was given unto them, and they reach out and slay the living, Henry Fonda and the dead, his darlin' Clementine, bashing them with the beasts of the earth. Then the black vision cries out in the voice of a one-eyed man, "You have trod on the wretched of the earth to seek your salvation."

■ ■ ■

Excerpts from *Zero Degrees Latitude:* Voice from Ecuador

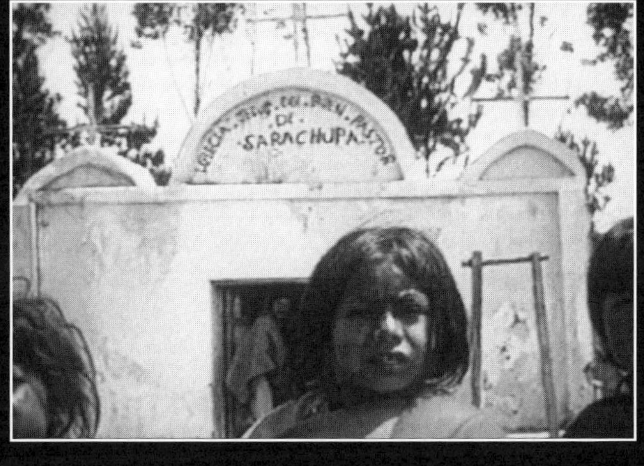

Before the baptism in Sarachupa, from *Zero Degrees Latitude*

■ ■ ■

Bertha Jottar Diary

Landscape

Why didn't we videotape more of it? It wasn't postmodern enough for us? Video is too flat to capture it? The horror of it was too surreal? My first encounter with the Andes; I had such a stereotypical image of them; they were going to be the good mountains, like the Alps were in my childhood imagination. I was expecting a beautifully green landscape with llamas jumping from hill to hill. *Pero ni. . . .* What devastation! We were literally in a desert, sand dunes decorated by pine trees. It was too shocking to videotape. For me, somebody from a very big city, Mexico City, this was not a filmable horror of political atrocity; it was not representable; I understood how to frame the slaying of a political leader or the clubbing of student demonstrators, also images from my childhood. Still, my detachment from the land, at least this image of it, has everything to do with my spatial distance from indigenous communities. Even though I am very committed, I don't know how to photograph this image of exploitation. It would have been less shocking to me if they would have executed an indigenous liberation theology priest in front of our very eyes. These Andean desert lands are the result of an idiotic reforestation plan by Ecuador's central government. As Miguel Ángel said, the government's plan was to improve the land by chopping the eucalyptus trees, but their choice, pine trees, soak the water out of the soil; they are like poison to the land.

We had came to this duned area for an evangelical baptism; Pedro was presiding over it. Not lots of water during the ceremony, but plenty of sodas *y muchos Cuyos para cenar.*

script interruption

The Perfect Ethnographic Moment

What a drag. Here we are in the middle of a community meeting, in the dunes of highland Ecuador. The meeting was so different than we had imagined. Quite frankly, I don't know what we expected, but not this. So low-key, polite, and lightweight. As Steve would say, "way boring." A circle of women and men, their hats on, just sitting on the sand, and it is so foggy. So what do you do when you get there, after accepting their kind invitation to videotape? The material is not what you want. Do you videotape or not? I guess out of respect for them, and after all it's only videotape, not film, you shoot. Not surprisingly, no miracle happens; the footage is so documentarily predictable. Portraits of women looking either at the camera or away from it, the modest interchanges of the town meeting. Oh, the problems of documentary, the assumptions of transparency and neutrality, for "reasons of the good documentary," sort of like "reasons of state"; this material could have been well edited, just used in order to "show" the community meeting. But is that our purpose? Or is it to try to find a way to construct a mechanism to disidentify from the "transparent" event? Yes, use it, but how?

Carnitas

Today I had to make a political choice while recording. We wanted to interview an indigenous woman who was evangelist. We had already interviewed or exchanged information with various, very bright, indigenous men, but still no luck finding a woman who would talk. We were at the market in Colta, and because of my fetishistic relation to jewelry, I moved next to a young woman selling velvet material. I asked her if I could interview her for the camera; to facilitate the interview Steve purchased some material, my favorite. I immediately honed in on the jewelry she was wearing and asked about her glass necklaces: Was there any particular reason to combine blue and white beads? Why glass and so many of them? Did all of this have any religious significance? Every time I asked her a question, her husband answered for her. As the camera operator, I thought to myself, "Should I pan to him while he answers for his wife?" I did it once and decided not to do it again. The interview became a bit tense; I continued to address my questions to her, and when he answered, I kept the camera on her, recording her silent glances. *Hartada,* in a *chilanga* way, I said to him, "Let her talk." Well, to be honest, I had to eat my embarrassment; I had just wanted to know about the necklaces, but she seemed quite disinterested; also I could never quite figure out how much Spanish she actually understood. Meanwhile, a few stands from the inadequate interview, Steve was eating his fifteenth pork *carnitas* plate. "Just trying to keep out of the way," he said, as he avariciously scanned the footage I had just shot.

Articulado

"Articulate," the gringos say. That is one of the frustrations of some of my friends. The gringos seem so amazed that a "person of color" can talk: "She is soooo articulate, and she expresses herself so clearly!" they say. It's that exclamation point at the end that bothers me. Well, Delfín Tanasca *era bien articulado! Qué claridad* when we interviewed him.

"The problems that we have come from 500 years ago. . . . But with the coming of the Protestants, or perhaps evangelization, as it is called. Perhaps, in the name of ridding us of who knows what: drug addiction, perhaps alcoholism, or whatever. Instead, evangelism has functioned as a hypnotization of the indigenous. . . . The fact is that this Protestant religion is not one of a true God but rather a capitalist God. A dollar God. It sees a God of money, an individualistic God, a God who divides. I think that the God of Protestantism is only a God of capitalism and power seeking." Steve and Delfín's relation was a bit testy. Steve kept insisting

Delfín shorten his answers. Steve said, "Either you cut the length of your answers, or I will in the editing." Eventually they worked out a compromise, but after Steve finished with his questions, it got really interesting. Delfín grabbed the mike and said, "Now it is my turn to interview the director." All his questions were right on! About economic and military U.S. sponsorship in various regions of the world, about the situation of Afro-Americans in the United States, etc.

Steve is a very clear and progressive thinker, a good match until Delfín asked him about Native Americans' involvement in the continental indigenous events surrounding the Five Hundred Years of Resistance. Steve had to admit he knew nothing about U.S. indigenous mobilization.

As we did with many of the activists we interviewed, it was agreed to send Delfín VHS copies of the unedited footage he was in. Of course, he could recycle it as he wished.

Cuyo

When I taped the *cuyo en el mercado de* Colta, I did it to honor Steve. I zoomed in on the hands of an indigenous woman holding, almost strangling, *el cuyito aprisionado*. This shot would, in the final tape, be our private joke. What a surprise when I figured out that Steve had not figured out that the sweet, semistruggling *cuyo* he had been so amused by was the same *animalito* he had so happily digested the evening before in the house where Pedro had led the evangelical baptism. *Qué raro*, Steve was so shocked when he put it together that a *cuyo* is a guinea pig, not a pig that looks like a guinea hen. After having seen Steve chew, with *tremenda alegría*, devouring the head of the animal (something that my dentist would not suggest with my "non-European teeth"), why was he so *infartado*?

Nahum and His Mother

The mother. How to talk to her, *esta indígena,* citizen of the Amazon, this woman who had given birth to five children? Her oldest son was an artist, the middle one a politician, and the youngest one, Nahum, a great orator, although still a boy. He, unlike the others, seemed to have or be developing a critical distance from his culture. Nahum explained to us what it meant for people to sit in the front, middle, and rear of the *parroquia.* Those in the first row were so close to the pastor, they were there to pray, to cry, to talk to the Lord. But the middle rows, those occupied by the youngsters like him, had a more complex agenda. Maybe to gossip, to talk to a pretty girl. And those in the back, the elders, listening to what everyone else was saying, listening to the mix, so they could judge. But wherever one sat, they participated through sound: whispers, songs, prayers, and gossip filled the space. This was an aural space, not a visual one; the empty white walls, so different from the neighborhood Catholic church of my youth in Mexico City.

I start thinking of the crucifixion scenes, *las tres caídas* during *el camino al calvario* I used to contemplate. The procession of Christ, his being whipped on his way to the *cruz.*

The mother, how to talk to her, *esta indígena,* citizen of the Amazon, woman who had given birth to five children? I went for a second walk with her, the wife of the first indigenous man who worked for the Summer Institute of Linguistics in Limoncocha. I was recording her with the camera, my magnifying glass. But her relationship to me was different from when we were surrounded by the rest of the family; she was no longer being "shy" about talking or something I read as such. Or no longer "not being shy enough" about her flesh, letting us tape her in her underwear after the storm. Oh well, it's probably that I'm beginning to identify with the codes of what is proper and what's not; personally none of it gives me a problem. We just walk for a long time, and she just talks about her *males,* her physical pains, about the "gringos" who used to live in Limoncocha, and about her relationship with God. "In Quechua please, may I say it in Quechua," she said. She told me her favorite vesicles from the New Testament. I wondered if she noticed that I didn't understand a word that she was saying. Would that matter to her? It didn't matter to me; it was about her relationship with God. Something that would fall beyond my understanding regardless of what language it was spoken in.

Again

I have embarrassed myself again. That was tough, beyond pain. We had been driving through the Andean dunes for an hour. I mean, I had already driven from Río Bamba, that makes it two hours total, shaking in this suspensionless Jeep; I always wondered what a spin in a washing machine would feel like, and now I know (I wish this skill counted on my résumé). We finally stepped out of our capsule; we had arrived at our destination, a small *parroquia* with one house nearby. We looked like those clowns that pile out of the car in the circus, but these clowns had sand inside their underwear! I shift over to my professional gear; unwrap the camera, clean it, and run to the ceremony that had already started. I squeeze into the ceremony, between two children; my luck—only room for one foot; my other foot would vanish into a hole if I place it down. Luckily enough, I have experience standing on one foot, traveling in Mexico; everything counts in life. You can place one foot over the other, like when I used to travel by bus from Atotonilco to Pachuca Hidalgo. Or just pretend you're a flamingo in a crowded lagoon. At least here I don't have to worry about falling down, there is no empty space to do so. Anyway, to avoid the pain, I imagine that I am a knot.

Next an interview with Pedro. Steve insists we do it walking; I'm sure he doesn't notice it's on sand. He says, "Do the questions while you walk and shoot," and I think, another talent that has little room on my résumé. I was so distracted; holding the camera, walking backward on the side of a sand-covered mountain, I began to fear falling, not just down, but off the mountain entirely, and I become a bit distracted. I start mixing up the differences between Catholic and Protestant appellations in my questions. I just hope Steve will cut out all my fuck-ups. Why would he use an eight-minute single-take interview anyway? He doesn't need my questions, right? That is my *consuelo* because I am asking things assuming they won't be used in the final cut; some of the questions are quite empty.

Finally, back at the hotel in Río Bamba, and I'm able to fall down, on the bed, but only after putting on some sandless underwear.

Jatarichi

"Jatarichi," from San Juan. That is the name of the first song on the Andean folkloric tape by Duchicela that we listen to over and over again while we drive in the jeep.

This song follows us, or should I say haunts us. Once you listen to it the melody never leaves you. It is a looping phrase in a four- or two-bar rhythm. The melody of the song is a loop; it never changes (not to my ears), but the harmonization of the instruments shifts in sweet variations. It shifts from voice to multiple flutes, accompanied by guitars, mandolin, violins, and *quenachos*.

It's Christmas, and I hear this same song from every carnival truck. Despite the evangelists' taboo on festivities and dances, this melody is the spine of all religious services we hear. Nahum says: "Evangelists are those who praise God with such faith within them, that they don't drink, dance, smoke, they don't do nothing!! Because the Bible says they're not supposed to do it if they want to be Gods' children."

In the *Navadades* parade in Colta, the nativity-costumed

trucks had bands blaring "Jatarahci," with the saxophones taking the upper hand in these arrangements. Sometimes an amplified keyboard would silence everything. In public transportation the flutes are the most predominate, perhaps because they are higher in pitch and can be heard over the traffic. In the *Parroquias*, in Colta as in Nahum's Limoncocha, the service had two *guitarras* and one big drum, a *bombo* of unshaved *chivo* skin of white color with brown spots. In the Colta *parroquia*, the children's voices took the lead; they screamed at the top of their lungs; maybe it was for the camera? But in this religious musical context, technology comes into play, to capture the performative.

There is a man holding a boom box next to me in the Sarachupa baptism. It was as if he were holding a camera; he was pointing the machine toward the baptism and later at the chorus, following Pedro's hand orchestration. He apparently didn't understand the function of the recorder, but oddly his presence made me feel more at ease: I was not the only one; we were technological comrades. After the ceremony, we set the camera up outside the Sarachupa *parroquia* to videotape people exiting; the man and his recorder appeared, accompanied by a scratchy sound which served as his aura. It took me a while, because I was looking through the camera, to locate the source of the sound; finally I moved into the boom box faithfully playing "Jatarachi." His machine had its own arrangement, dominated by tape hiss. It was now a transculturated, translated musical text. I speculated that this playing back of his recording somehow functioned in the ceremony as a memory trace of the already recorded version of the song these people had heard over the evangelist radio station. Like on the show, the music functioned as background for a voice in Quechua talking from the New Testament. Unlike the Dulchicela interpretation of "Jatarachi," which emphasized the orchestration of the violins, various types of flutes (Andean and European), mandolin, quena, guitar and a very metallic sound, perhaps coming from a *batería*. The voice in Dulchicela's version is just expressive of *dichos,* and *upah*! But basically it's the instruments that talk to me. While in the Sarachupa variation the instruments recede, giving room for the voice of God, in Quechua, to fill the vacated space.

For the First Time

Steve had often talked of a book about the massive indigenous conversion to Protestantism, Sheldon Annis's *God and Production in a Guatemalan Town.* He had mentioned how the book had tried to demonstrate the shift in the community's values through analyzing the women's weavings. What were the differences between the Catholic and the Protestant weavings, and what different values did they manifest? This story returns to me as I try to collect my thoughts after seeing the finished video for the first time. The piece strikes me as weirdly put together; then I get it, or at least know where to look. Yes, it is the weaving together of the piece that is its secret, the way the elements are stitched together. It is a weaving that combines the everyday with the abstract. But also there are two sides to the carpet. On one side, the indigenous: cultural translation, initiation, acculturation, appropriation, syncretism, and shifting identities. In short, the everyday reinvention of culture through religious experiences and beliefs. But what about the studio footage? Clearly it is the inclusion of this footage that makes the work typical of Steve and a very eccentric addition to the work done on the Five Hundred Years of Resistance. So many other "well-meaning" pieces had been done that began and ended with the same punch line, "The white man has committed atrocities against the pure indigenous peoples of this continent." *Sin nombres? Zero Degrees Latitude* understands that the results of history are sometimes simple but that its causes are always complex. The piece tries to interweave the lives and thoughts of indigenous people with the fantasies of their Protestant neocolonizers, but not the North Americans' fantasies of the indigenous or of conquest, rather their dreams of their own everyday actions. Isn't that what the "good Protestant" is supposed to be thinking about anyway?

For us to understand a culture's "will to power" we must understand the way they dream their ordinary actions as well as their extraordinary goals. So we are given a Protestant vision, recast into an Orientalist fantasy turned onto itself. The Protestant missionaries are both the subject and the object of the fantasy, "Orientalizing themselves." As one would expect, the results get a bit out of their control.

For me, however, it is the passage from the imaginary space (the studio) to the equally rhetorical space of the *vérité* footage in Ecuador that makes the piece special. But this is not a seamless passage; it is so unlike *The Machine That Killed Bad People;* here we are supposed to see and think about the awkward stitching, not just admire the carpet. The piece is a patch quilt. Although the combination is ungainly, it is still powerful. I must confess when seeing the piece for the first time, I eagerly anticipated how he had depicted the real places I had been to; I left appreciating the conceptual place he had constructed. A good translation wouldn't have been enough.

The Second Time
Dear Melissa,

Your radio station, the one constructed in the studio for Steve's tape, speaks to me once more. As you or your character said: "They are out there . . . they are out there. . . ." The radio waves strike me as having an indulgence, like the indulgence of the voice of God. A particularly perverse version of this voice, one read through the New Testament, that is the translation of the New Testament spoken in Quechua.

Like radio waves my mind jumps rapidly, to Nahum's mother walking in a saturated Amazon. I slip into a pothole. So much for "gringo efficiency"; nevertheless, I continue taping as she says, "I have been crucified with Christ and I no longer live, but Christ lives in me" (Galatians 2:20).

Somehow, I feel your radio station speaks to me as those evangelical radio stations spoke to the indigenous people of Ecuador. Miguel Ángel Dexell told us during our interview: "I remember when I was fourteen years old. . . ." He talks about the combination of novelty, it being a gift, speaking to them in their "mother tongue." The radio helped create a new listening public, an aural community, a born-again indigenous body connected through sacred waves in Quechua. A community no longer connected through spatial or grammatological relationships or political commitments but through the disembodied, the aural, coming from a sacred "other" land, a land of a sacred "other." The radio heralds, like a false Gabriel, the supplementation of the Catholic mode of colonization: racial, linguistic, and spatial hierarchization, radically shifting the regime of belief/colonization. We have seen or, should I say, heard the second coming, and it is a performance not based on vision and presence but on absence and aurality. Although it has been disembodied, it still walks the earth, or has souls, indigenous ones with radios attached to their ears, walking the earth in its name.

Your radio station, Melissa, or Melissa/Isabella, in fact all your indulgent machines hearken to some perverse heaven on earth. What a Protestant version of heaven, so heavy on the labor and so short on the pleasure. Still, I must confess, the Catholic still in me notices your ecstasy, and this mesmerizes me.

Besos,

Bertha

Zapatistas

Que desencanto, today I saw a "work in progress"; frankly, I missed the progress, a documentary film by two famous leftists. It is amazing to see, once more, the unquestioning belief in documentary and its conventions. The belief in the image as given, not as constructed. People and genres can be unthawed like something from the deep freeze, brought to you by Birdseye. *Que desperdicio* to have a camera in front of *Sub-comandante* Marcos and "capture" him. He appears as the predictable, *el caudillo*— once more—walking through the green landscape, "thinking" while smoking his pipe! An idealist and ideologist picture, a cliché, "the revolutionary" *Que Hueva.* But worse still is the confusion between the Zapatistas themselves and other Latin American guerrilla movements. Two of the important distinctive char-acteristics are the Zapatistas' use of mass media and their prioritization of indigenous rights over any simple-minded class-only-based notion of overthrow of the state. The need to negotiate the complex space between demands and communication in the contemporary transnational political arena has been addressed by Marcos. "That nose behind the black wool mask became the center of attention for the national and international media. But the need of translation from indigenous culture and the national and international culture provoked the need for this nose." The issue is not simply resolved because he is not indigenous, but we must understand why he wasn't indigenous.

But, of course, the Zapatistas' awareness of mass media strategies comes also from having learned from the struggles of other indigenous people across the continent. I remember our conversation in Ecuador with Miguel Ángel Dexell, one of the leaders of the Consejo Nacional Indígena from Ecuador (CONAIE). Miguel Ángel understood the way the national media in Ecuador had sabotaged the initially successful 1990 indigenous national uprising, whose purpose was to claim the fertile land promised them

by the agrarian reform. He talked to us while showing us one of
the videotapes they had recently made to draw attention to their
struggle: "This is a shot taken here at Chimborazo! What they're
carrying is Osvaldo Cubi's body, who was killed the second of
June, during the uprising. . . . This is the one that took place in
1990, and it is not really the first one, due to the fact that we've
always had uprisings here . . . several uprisings in which [we]
have rebelled against the unjust, oppressive, and marginal treatment that has been imposed on [us] throughout the ages."

I learned from Miguel Ángel that the national media in Ecuador simply did not cover their uprising. The only documentation
of the massive demonstrations, sit-ins, hacienda takeovers, and
speeches was made by the indigenous peoples themselves. But
where to broadcast them? We still live in a world where the peri-
odic indigenous uprisings in Latin America basically go uncovered by the international press.

Four years after this uprising in Ecuador, the Zapatistas were
able to mobilize a sharp and selective control of the international
media and through them the Mexican public. The Zapatistas initially—after a spectacular New Year's Day takeover of the tourist
center, San Cristobal de las Casas—would not talk to the na-
tional/*Televisa* news; they shrouded themselves in mystery, using
the silence usually imposed on them to their advantage. They
would wait for CNN. CNN seeing itself, as always, like the cavalry
charging to the rescue, took the bait; for the record, they arrived
two days late. The Zapatistas were able to speak through them to
the Mexican national audience, using the pressure caused by the
Free Trade Agreement to keep the Mexican military at bay—no
human rights violations for external consumption. I'm sure if the
Free Trade Agreement hadn't been going into effect that very day,
throwing international/U.S. focus on Mexico, the uprising would
have suffered a very different news fate.

When Steve and I arrived in Ecuador at the end of 1991, it was a moment of reflection for the indigenous movement; they were thinking about the results of the 1990 uprising. Foremost on their minds was how to control one's image in the media. They knew a real victory needed a media prelude. We were allowed into communities because we were seen as affiliated with media production and they wanted to learn about it. They had questions we could answer and equipment we might leave them for their use. There was only one occasion when we were denied access; it was in Chimborazo, at a community meeting organized by liberation theology leaders. Despite Delfín Tamasca's warm introduction we were not allowed to tape. I thought it was because Steve was a "gringo," but he thought it was because we didn't have a Catholic agenda. . . . *No me acuerdo.*

The indigenous recuperation of the land, *Pache Mama,* is the primary concern of their struggle. The narrative of the nation, as Miguel Ángel had explained, begins with the egalitarian redistribution of *Pache Mama,* the center of indigenous civilizations. Now the Zapatistas are using mass media in order to rewrite the narrative of this hemisphere. To reclaim it for justice. This is why when President Zedillo sent the military to imprison *Subcomandante* Marcos, the people at the rallies in Mexico shouted in unison, "We are all Marcos." In contemporary America, the continent, those of us who rally against neocolonialism have to say, we are all behind that mask. We must struggle in Quechua, Chilango, Tzotzil, Tzetzal, Boricua, English, Spanglish, etc., etc., etc., yes, even in Latin. CNN promises to be there, *¿y nosotros?*

■　■　■

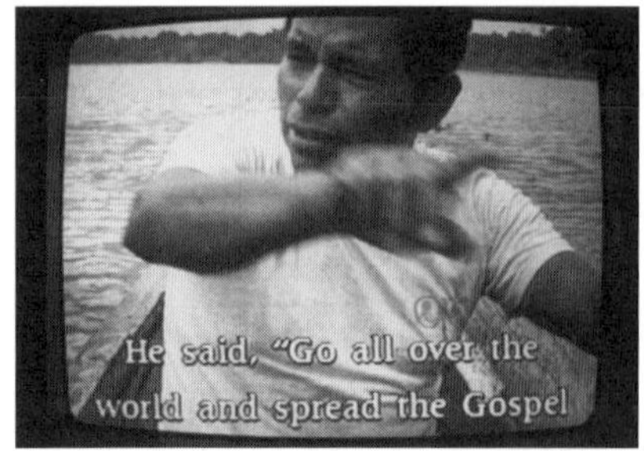

Saqueo: the first convert in Limoncocha,
from *Zero Degrees Latitude*

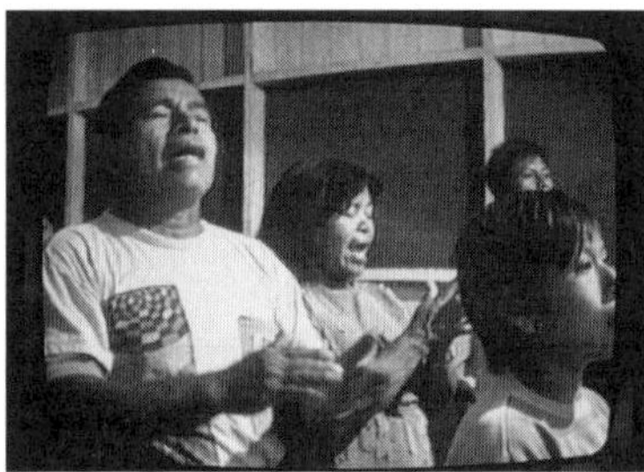

Saqueo and Rosa singing in Quechua,
from *Zero Degrees Latitude*

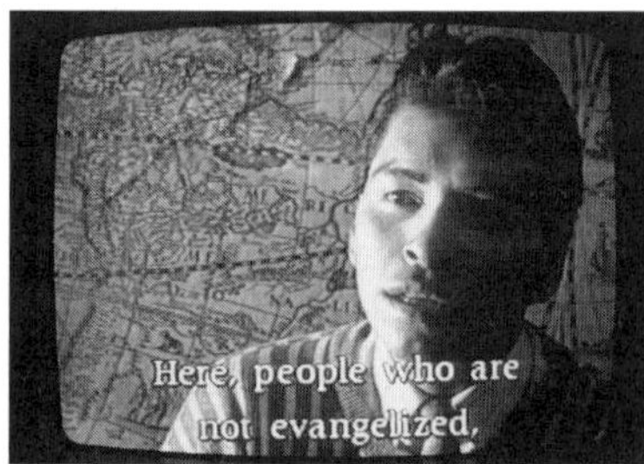

Johnson, son of Saqueo and Rosa in
Quito, from *Zero Degrees Latitude*

338

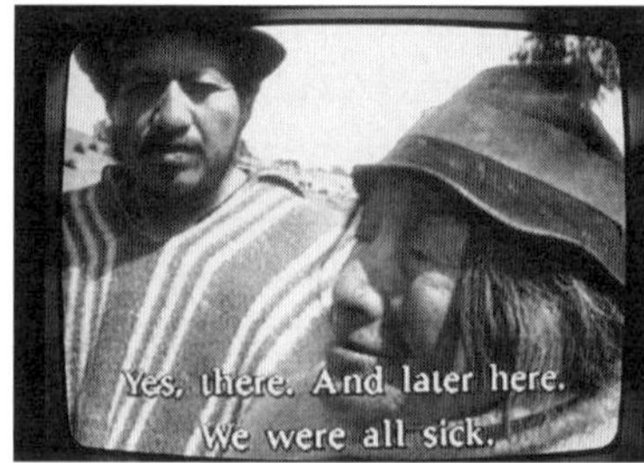

Silverio talks of healing, from *Zero
Degrees Latitude*

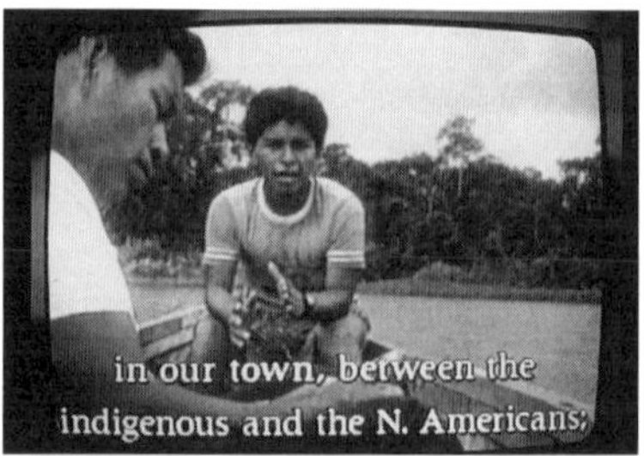

Nahum and his father on the lake, from
Zero Degrees Latitude

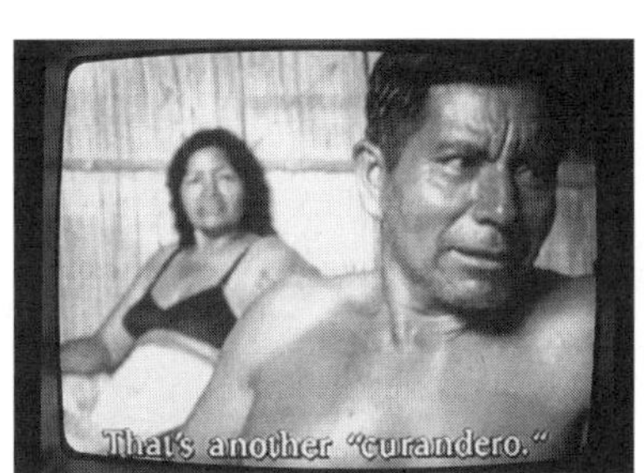

Juliana and Miguel Ángel in the Andean highlands, from *Zero Degrees Latitude*

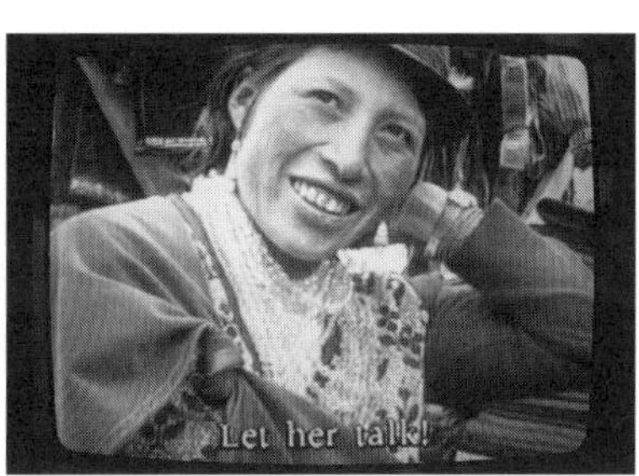

Colta: Interview at the market, from *Zero Degrees Latitude*

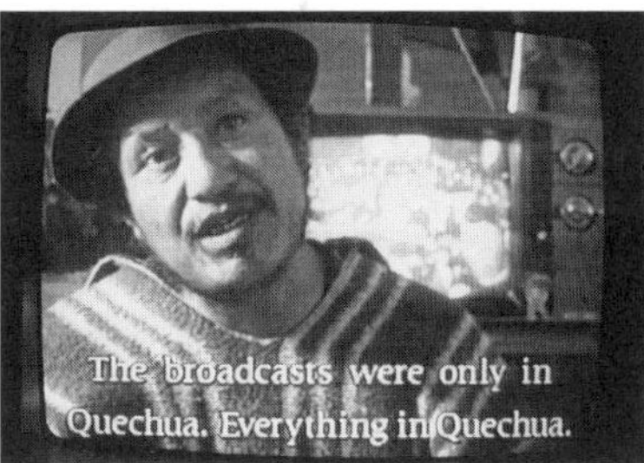

Miguel Ángel talks of the first radio, from *Zero Degrees Latitude*

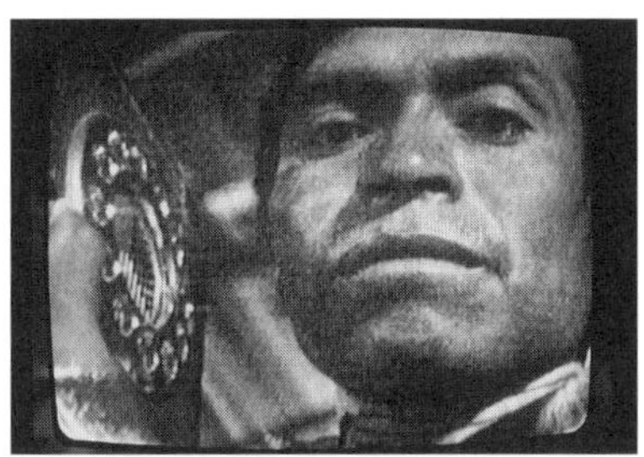

Sarachupa, man with the boom box, from *Zero Degrees Latitude*

■ ■ ■

Delfín: God—the Pachecama, as we call him now—Pachecama is the world's caretaker, and we are his children. Nature must be distributed very carefully. That was, and still is, the indigenous people's thinking. But with the coming of the Protestants, or perhaps evangelization, as it is called. Perhaps, in the name of ridding us of who knows what: drug addiction, perhaps alcoholism, or whatever. Instead, evangelism has functioned as a hypnotization of the indigenous. A hypnotization of the indigenous. The fact is that this Protestant religion is not one of a true God but rather a capitalist God. A dollar God. It sees a God of money, an individualistic God, a God who divides. I think that the God of Protestantism is only a God of capitalism and power seeking.

Pedro: Traditions and legends—some of them, around thirty years ago—have definitely been lost because we considered them a sort of negative action against the Christian man. Parties and dances, for example, or alcoholism, for instance. And we considered them negative. If somebody told you, "You have to make a decision: either live with your native indigenous community that is not Protestant or with a Protestant community that is nonindigenous but 'urban,' which, or what, would be your inclination?"

Bertha: [Speaking to two musicians who had been playing guitar during previous part of conversation.] Thanks. . . . What are your names? . . . Your name?

First musician: My name is José Julio Crollo Rivera.

Second musician: My name is Reino Punieyra Quilemu.

Bertha: Very good. And where are we? What's the name of this place? Ah, Sarachupa. . . . Thanks.

First musician: You're welcome.

Bertha: Thank you.

Pedro: In other words, it's like any decision. To live with Protestant people or non-Protestants or, in other words, Catholics as we call them. It's all the same: urban or rural living. The only influencing factor, all of a sudden, could be due to some economic situation where one suddenly needs to change his mind, isn't that so?

Delfín: I come from a high altitude and an arid climate, a community dedicated exclusively to agriculture. A community in conflict. Well, now it is also organized, although several problems have arisen in the last four years. But that's not only in this community but rather in several other indigenous communities around this province also.

Bertha: What's the community's name?

Delfín: San José de Mayorazgo. I'm Delfín Tenesaco, from this community. It belongs to a town called Guamote.

Saqueo: The New Testament says that when Christ was here, he said, "Go all over the world and spread the Gospel to all creatures. He who believes shall be baptized and be saved." That's what the paragraph from the New Testament says. To abide by this commandment as I understand it, I have preached the gospel within my community and to all the surrounding areas.

Johnson: I have a personal relationship with God. I believe in God and talk with God. I lead a very good personal life with God, but I also believe that there are those other evils, but I don't have faith in them. Since I believe in God, I don't think "those things" can affect me.

Nahum: Those who sit here are good Christian followers and believe in the gospel. But those others over there are somewhat more distant from Christ and the church. And those that seat themselves in the back come to hear the word of God in order to decide if they wish to follow Christ. Although they've been baptized by water, they await baptism through the spirit of Christ. Now those standing in the corner are church leaders who are observing people's behavior at church so that later they can better communicate Christ's message to them. . . .

Saqueo: [Praying in Quechua.] I deliver everything into thy hand and ask that you help us this night, that you help us with everything in our lives. Everything I deliver into thy hands and ask you to save us from all things, in the name of your son, Jesus Christ. Amen.

Nahum: Who, me? Well, in essence, we believe that the devil has power. It heals but has minimal power—a little less than God, the gospel says. Because the devil can also heal anything that serves his purposes. If the person—the *curandero*—has the power of the devil, he can heal because he has faith in the devil's strength to help him heal any illness.

Rosa: One day. A house. A place. Well, we're going to enter there. For that reason here, or in any circumstance, when I'm sad, when I'm crying, when I'm in pain, quite a bit of pain, I continue praising the Lord, praising the Lord to this day, with my fifty years. I am now fifty years old and continue to live with Jesus Christ in me.

Bertha: What do you call it?

Rosa: I want to quote a verse, in Quechua.

Bertha: OK, sure. Let's go for a walk. . . .

Rosa: [In Quechua.] "I have been crucified with Christ and I no longer live, but Christ lives in me." Galatians 2:20. "For the wages of sin is death, but the gift of God is eternal life in Christ Jesus our Lord." Romans 6:23.

Bertha: Were the people from the Summer Institute of Linguistics [ILD] here?

Rosa: Yes!

Bertha: But were they white?

Rosa: Yes. Gringos, they were the gringos.

Bertha: And do you accept the gringos in your community if they are evangelicals?

Rosa: Before there were none. Later on, people from Rionaco arrived.

Bertha: Who arrived first, the ILD people or you folks?

Rosa: The ILD.

Bertha: Were they gringos?

Rosa: Yes.

Bertha: But would you live among them?

Rosa: Yes. [Addressing someone else.] Watch out!

Saqueo: They were concerned with civilizing people. Training them in occupations such as carpenter, mechanic, teacher. I'm a teacher, trained by the ILD. And they taught other courses, too. And because of it people here in Limoncocha became better trained. Here in Limoncocha we have native evangelical pastors, native teachers, native carpenters, native orderlies, all of them trained by the Summer Institute of Linguistics. This was their main goal when they came to Ecuador.

Bertha: It is said that to talk about traditions such as dancing, clothing, or food is one thing but that it is an entirely different matter to talk about the system of beliefs that stands behind those traditions. So, then, to what degree is this system of beliefs being affected or influenced?

Johnson: In reality, the system of beliefs of the indigenous communities, those of the Oriente, in which the Quechua-speaking people are also represented, have always been ruled by the belief, for example, that God is within nature, in the mountains, the snakes, etc. These traditions have been left behind. And I cannot specifically tell you whether this is due to evangelization or if their falling out of practice has caused them to detach themselves completely from believing in other gods. Now, for example, people who are not evangelized here don't believe in God or anything.

Nahum: Evangelicals are those who praise God with such faith that they don't drink, dance, smoke, they don't do nothing, because the Bible says they're not supposed to if they want to be God's children and get to where Jesus Christ is.

Miguel Ángel: This is a shot taken here at Chimborazo! What they're carrying is Osvaldo Cubi's body, who was killed the second of June, during the uprising.

Bertha: Could you please tell us something about how this uprising for land rights got started?

Miguel Ángel: Well, what must be pointed out on this matter is that people are interpreting it as being the first uprising. That's what's being said. But this is the one that took place in 1990, and it is not really the first one, due to the fact that we've always had uprisings here. And above all, here in Chimborazo, there's a very peculiar thing. People here, according to the history that we have, have had several uprisings in which they have rebelled against the unjust, oppressive, and marginal treatment that has been imposed on them throughout the ages.

Delfín: Talking about this land over which the agrarian reform is drawn, the reform never served the interests of the *indio.* The agrarian reform has only served, or, rather, has only benefited, the landowners as, for example, in the case of the haciendas. What they accomplished with this law is an expulsion from the more fertile parts of the land, up to the high and barren plains, or the distribution of arid or rocky areas, or whatever has less value, right? But it was nothing less than the expulsion of the indigenous peoples, or, in other words, they pushed them out. That's all the agrarian reform did. And that's how it went.

Juliana: Hold it there! Don't tire yourself. That's far enough.

Bertha: Where?

Juliana: I lived here with my little sister.

Bertha: Where? Quechuanish?

Juliana: We lived there, where the tree is. That's where we lived.

Bertha: Where the tree is?

Juliana: Yes, there. And later here. We were all sick. Then we came down and started to live here. We were living there, we came down from that hill where we were living. We were getting sick, getting sick, getting sick.

Johnson: As far as the Summer Institute of Linguistics's own customs were concerned, they wanted to influence us, but we didn't have the resources to apply what we learned. They had their boats with engines and used them to cross the lagoon. If it took us forty-five minutes to an hour to cross the lagoon, it took them two or three minutes.

Nahum: When the Summer Institute of Linguistics was here in Limoncocha, between the years 1955 and 1982, there was a division in our town, Limoncocha, between the indigenous and the North Americans; and the division was marked by the airstrip. The airstrip divided us. On one side the Quechua speakers, and on the other side the North Americans.

Bertha: Whose culture are you talking about?

Saqueo: The tribe's own culture. They gave us the knowledge of the Bible; they taught us to read and write in our own language so that we could get jobs and have a sound basic education. That's what the ILD was interested in.

Nahum: This whole area belonged to the ILD. They had all sorts of services provided for them. They had everything within reach. Their lawns: all nicely mowed, neat, and well maintained. The streets: very clean; they didn't want to see any garbage around here. They had electric power with lights for the streets and inside their houses as well.

Bertha: I'm asking you if you knew that the Summer Institute of Linguistics was supposed to be exclusively linguistic and anthropological but not evangelical? Did you know the mandate of the institute?

Saqueo: Yes.

Bertha: What happened when you tried to send your son to the university?

Saqueo: When I wanted to send my son to the university, they didn't want me to do it.

Bertha: Why?

Saqueo: Because. . . . I don't know what they thought, they thought something, they thought the indigenous had to stay indigenous. To live at their indigenous level. If one were to move to the city, then one might change and try to be like the white people. The ILD did not like that. They said, "We have come to help the indigenous people become educated enough that they can lead their indigenous group." That's what they wanted, and that's why they didn't want my sons to go to the university. But in spite of all, my wish was to educate them further, so I sent my son to Quito. My first son attended the university for two years, and my fourth son, Johnson, completed six years at the university. Now we are serving our community.

Nahum: "The deceivers. Walking around the world are many deceivers who do not acknowledge that Jesus Christ came into the world as 'true man.' He who thinks that way is a deceiver and enemy of Christ."

Silverio: So let me say that before I became a *curandero,* I was an evangelical, preaching the gospel. Later on I stopped preaching the gospel and started looking for another type of job. I tried to obtain a demon that could give some powers. I started working with animals, such as boas and other types of animals, in order to obtain such powers.

Nahum: "A new heaven and a new earth. I saw a new heaven and a new earth: the former had ceased to exist."

Salesman: Do you want to cure yourself of whatever ails you? Do you have headaches, liver, or kidney pains? Altered nerves, or a heart condition? For five hundred sucres you can buy this healing elixir in Quito. Go to Quito, to Santo Domingo Los Colorados. Come to 29th of May and to San Miguel Streets, and buy it!

Silverio: So the demons gave me the power. As I said, I've lived with these demons for quite some time now. They followed me during the night, blowing their powers onto me, over my hands and head. And after six years passed, they gave me the power to heal.

Nahum: He graduated at that time. Yes, it's almost like when you graduated from school. Like graduating from a university.

Silverio: Yeah, the same thing exactly! But there's a series of steps one must follow in order to continue. Oh, yeah! You must keep right on studying and learning. [. . .] That's another *curandero.* Oh, I see what you mean. Because I worked in what you call *champalear.* Uh huh.

Rosa: Witches blow these things like darts. What are they? Look, over there.

Nahum: This one? What my uncle did. . . . I'd better get over here, this will look better. What my uncle did before becoming a *curandero* was to heal those that were afflicted with spells cast by other people. He worked doing something we call *champalear.* When their affliction was on certain parts of their body. . . .

Bertha: You cured them from the sorcery only at night, right?

Silverio: Yeah, whenever he's going to cure someone from something, he does it at night, never during the day.

Nahum: He cures them at night.

Bertha: And how do you know what ails them?

Silverio: Like I told you, before doing anything, first, one must have a few drinks. For instance, I would have a few drinks and wait till my head got dizzy. Then different . . . demons! Demons. Then I would have visions of the person being afflicted with a sorcery that was causing a particular damage. Then I would know who the person was who cast that kind of disease. Then I would know and tell the patient: "So-and-so is causing you this damage." That way we were able to know. Once I knew the who, the what, and the where of the disease, and once I could see which evil spirit was inside, then I would see it and tell the person that in order to cure them I needed to prepare this and they needed to do this. . . . Then I could cure it.

Bertha: Where did you learn this tradition?

Silverio: Learned exclusively from Satan himself. Yes. For years I lived in the nearby lagoon, in the water with the demons. I lived in the lagoon. Throughout that time, during the more than four years that I lived in the water with them, asking them for their powers, and after a period of years, I was empowered to heal, easily, by just running my hand across their body, like this, and they were healed within a half hour or an hour. Entirely healed.

Bertha: Oh, so you're evangelical?

Man in marketplace: Yes, I am. Are you?

Bertha: Who me? No, I'm not. I'm just helping to do these interviews.

Pedro: Yes, the evangelical church.

Bertha: . . . evangelical church. Now tell me what happened today at the evangelical church.

Pedro: There was a celebration dedicated to the child.

Bertha: What child?

Pedro: The Marcos David Roldán child.

Bertha: Uh huh, I see.

Pedro: It was his baptism today.

Bertha: Oh, how nice!

Pedro: Yes.

Bertha: Now talk to me about the songs you were singing. Are they traditional songs or religious ones?

Pedro: Religious songs.

Bertha: I see. Now, when were they translated into Quechua?

Pedro: They've been translated some fifty years ago, here in Ecuador, by the Ecuadoran Biblical Society.

Bertha: I see . . . and the Bible that you're reading, is it in Spanish or in Quechua?

Pedro: Both in Spanish and in Quechua. . . .

Bertha: I noticed that some people were reading from one book and you were reading from a different one. What were they reading?

Pedro: The same Bible, but different versions. One is the *Dios Habla Hoy* [God Speaks Today] *Bible,* others have the *Holy Bible,* which turns out to be somewhat difficult in Spanish, and others are Quechua Bibles. As a matter of fact, there are two Quechua Bibles: a small New Testament version and a larger version that includes both the Old and New Testaments in Quechua.

Bertha: Now, the manner in which you handled today's ceremony. Does it have any traditional Quechua characteristics or. . . .

Pedro: Please, can you repeat the question?

Bertha: Yes. . . . Is the ceremony you performed today exclusively evangelical, or does it have any traditional forms?

Pedro: It is exclusively what evangelism is about.

Bertha: I see. Now tell me. The songs they were playing sound a bit. . . . Well, in my opinion, they sound Ecuadoran.

Pedro: Yes.

Bertha: What then? Do you combine the evangelical with the Ecuadoran songs?

Pedro: Of course! They are all Ecuadoran songs played in different rhythms.

Bertha: Ah, very good. OK. We're leaving now. [To the little girl.] Miriam! Come, let's go! . . . The kid's restless already. Were you baptized this way?

Pedro: Which of us?

Bertha: You. Were you baptized like an evangelical?

Pedro: Me? No, not me.

Bertha: I see. . . . And when did you convert to evangelism?

Pedro: I converted to evangelism when I was sixteen years old.

Bertha: Sixteen?

Pedro: Yes.

Bertha: Now, describe the process for me. When did it happen? Where and why?

Pedro: Well, some evangelical pastors' preaching motivated me into converting to evangelism.

Bertha: And where did these priests come from?

Pedro: No. Pastors [woman reaffirms word]. Pastors from the same community I belong to. . . . In other words, from within our people . . . our own race.

Bertha: And what about your parents? Were they evangelical or Catholic?

Pedro: No, they're Catholic.

Bertha: And what did they say when you converted to evangelism?

Pedro: There were a few problems with my parents because they agreed with whatever was Catholic and did not want me to become an evangelical. [Woman affirms with *aha.*] A few problems, yes, but later on, my *testimonio* made them more accepting, I believe.

Bertha: Tell me a little bit more about how you go about mixing traditions . . . Ecuadoran food and music, for instance, with religion?

Pedro: Well, there's nothing different about our food and what's evangelical. It's the same food—that which God gives us. In other words, it's the same as any indigenous people's food, but it is prepared according to one's income. But one cannot say the evangelicals eat better or worse than Catholics—nothing like that! With regard to tradition, there are some traditions that upon conversion to evangelism we have abandoned.

Bertha: For instance? . . . Give me an example.

Pedro: Going to dances, for example. We don't organize dances anymore. [Woman affirms with *aha.*] Drinking in order to get drunk or something; we don't do that anymore. These traditions have changed.

Bertha: No. . . . [Begins to leave.] I want to talk with the lady.

Pedro: Sure. . . . Thanks.

Delfín: I think there's another intention regarding those that follow, the followers of these evangelicals. The evangelicals have inflicted a lot of fear over the last five hundred years, in the name of saving souls. . . . So recently the incoming evangelicals (Protestants) have scared people even more with the idea that these human souls are going to burn in hell. That they're going to burn. This fear they've transmitted to our people through videos, filmstrips, radio, books, brochures, magazines, etc. They have placed this fear deep in the hearts of these indigenous people (their converts). Therefore, the so-called evangelicals want to save the soul. And how are they going to save the soul? Instead of going to hell, they want them to go to heaven—isn't it so? They want to save their souls, and they don't want them to perceive that what must be saved is the unjust society that is of THIS world.

Bertha: Is it religion—is it part of religion? . . . [To a woman.] What's your religion?

Woman: Evangelical.

Bertha: Oh, you're evangelical.

Woman: Yes; and you?

Bertha: Me? No, I'm just helping to do these interviews. [Man acknowledges.] Oh, and about the colors. Are they related with evangelicals as being blue and white? How does it relate to evangelism?

Husband: No. It has nothing to do with it. You just put out some different ones.

Bertha: Uh huh.

Husband: They're not related.

Bertha: Oh, they're very pretty. Have you been evangelical for long?

Husband: Yes. There's quite a few of them, here in Ecuador.

Bertha: Let her talk! I've been wanting to ask you, What's your name? What is it?

Woman: My name? Mercedes.

Bertha: And how many children do you have?

Woman: Two.

Bertha: Two children? Girl or boy?

Woman: One girl, and one boy.

Bertha: Did you baptize them?

Woman: Yes.

Bertha: As evangelicals?

Woman: Yes.

Bertha: And were your parents Christians or evangelicals?

Woman: Evangelicals.

Bertha: I see, evangelicals. Where you both live, is everybody evangelical?

Woman: Yes.

Bertha: Where do you live?

Woman: In Colta.

Bertha: In which *cantón*?

Woman: In Cantón Colta, the Columbé Parish.

Bertha: The Columbé Parish?

Woman: Yes.

Bertha: And are there a lot of evangelical churches there?

Woman: Yes.

Bertha: Do you both really like evangelism?

Woman: Yes.

Bertha: What do you like about evangelism?

Woman: The study of the Bible.

Bertha: Studying it? And don't you study the Bible with other religions?

Woman: No . . . but with them also.

Bertha: And do you study the Bible in your language, or . . . do you read it in Quechua?

Woman: In Quechua. No, in both languages: Spanish and Quechua.

Bertha: Very good . . . Spanish and Quechua. Well, thank you very much for allowing us to chat with both of you.

Miguel Ángel: I remember when I was fourteen years old: one of the Cantón Colta communities that I lived in had radios. This was quite a surprise for me since I didn't know what a radio was. It looked like a simple wooden box. It was very simple. But to hear it talk and emit music was something quite surprising! There were times when they had music and then began talking about God. More than anything, the most attractive thing was that they were giving them away. But only those who promised to commit themselves to God would get them— that was the message: to get a radio one had to make a firm commitment to serve God. That's the first thing I remember about evangelism. That's how they spread it.

Bertha: But who brought the radios?

Miguel Ángel: The radios were given by the evangelicals, and as it was understood, they were from outside our area—the gringos, they said. So the gringos had a radio station in Quito—HCJB—and later another one called "The Voice of Majipamba," which is here in Cantón Colta. They used these two stations back then to broadcast their message to these communities. The odd thing about these radios is that one could only tune in these two radio stations and no others. That's the issue. And the broadcasts were only in Quechua. Everything in Quechua.

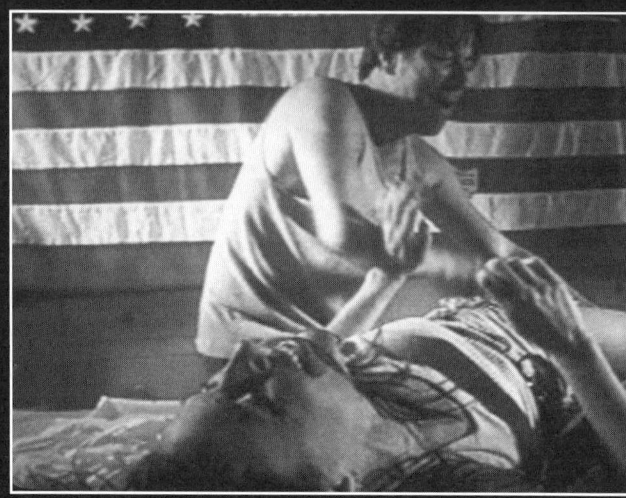

"I'm Hungry," from *Memorial Day (Observed)*

Bill Horrigan
Ohio Impromptu

Since the unknown is not identifiable, the speaker himself gradually loses his identity, his name, his face, everything the other person is unaware of and does not need to know. What remains is only the story. . . . Instead of taking in the story he is being told, he will grasp at the qualities he believes the story reveals. And once a person is endowed with qualities he is no longer unique; qualities we share with everybody. It is better to be only an anecdote than to be a person with qualities.—Hannah Arendt

Despite the effort to do so never to my knowledge having been publicly ventured or expended by anyone else, the soul-scouring lassitude descending on Columbus, Ohio, during summer holiday weekends is registered once and for all in *Memorial Day (Observed)*. No matter that this was achieved not by Columbus having been made, for the duration of the shooting, into a Hollywood-by-the-Scioto; the physical location of Hollywood, where the piece was in fact shot, evidently lends to the efforts of those who toil there, in some cases (in this case, for instance: the case of Steve Fagin, who is nothing if not conversant with the Hollywood cinema's language both surpassing and preceding understanding), a genius gift of American movies, which is a tenderness extended on behalf of belief. Hence *Memorial Day (Observed)*, which has various aims, has as one of its premise-forming best aims that of simulating in dramatic terms a place and an occasion, the actual terms of whose place and occasion being through almost pure contingency known long enough and well to this commentator.

This is being written on Independence Day in Columbus, Ohio. The holiday was actually "observed" on 3 July, yesterday, and was officially expressed by "the largest fireworks display in the Midwest," a claim maintained about itself by every city in these parts with more than a quarter million people (but speak that, along with much else relating to civic self-regard, in a whisper, as queries addressed to civic behavior come to be heard as well-poisoning or garbled *schadenfreude*). Today, what happens is that the television news shows all replay highlights of the fireworks as the lead story (the second and third stories invariably concerning fireworks-related casualties: this year, a policeman got run over by a truck of drunk fireworks spectators, and a "West Side" (Columbus-speak for Appalachian, the city's blithely referenced native workforce) youth shot his mother in the face with a roman candle when front-lawn partying "got out of hand"), and tonight they rebroadcast the ephemerally bombastic spectacle in its entirety.

If life-altering dramatic cataclysm is what's wanted, look much further than this Columbus, the discreetly quotidian character of which native son James Thurber definitively evoked when he recalled that, while growing up here, the most riveting moment came "the night the bed fell on my father." Every several years Columbus attempts to grab a place on a hazily imagined national or international stage by authorizing the presentation of an invariably quarter-baked spectacle of one sort or another (flower extravaganza, UN summit, etc.); inevitably, said event happens, to the tune of deafening civic hyperbole, and the "outside" world coasts on, serenely hearing impaired (or maybe just attention deficit) to the heartland's squawking.

We'd all feel a whole lot better if our rulers would just stop yelling about all this and let us get on with our lives. Otherwise, it's just an embarrassment and, anyway, impossible to really explain to friends living somewhere else. We probably shouldn't say that we just want to be left alone, even though it's true, because when we are left alone, we just end up whining about it. (Sort of like this, honestly.)

It's also like this, just like this, all across the republic, I think . . . the unraveling throughline of many, many lives, lives coming to a halt (full stop? that's the sole prerogative of illness) only when the life of work is brought by decree or tradition to a weekend-plus intermission. And what happens then, on these days like today, which Peter (whose forty-third birthday two weeks ago I just this moment remembered) used to describe in syndromatic form as DWMs (days without mail)? As always, there is a national ideal to honor: Independence Day (in Minneapolis, it was jokingly/not jokingly referred to as Codependence Day, a reclamation as true now as it was in 1984 when Richard and I, like John Cheever's *The Swimmer*, wandered through Kenwood, attached to each other by drink, debt, and the experience of near-fatal biking escapades, in search of any of our colleagues who might be at air-conditioned home for us that holiday; one friend was home, but her backyard was on fire, which we then photographed), which should encourage us to appreciate the enormity of what our eighteenth-century begetters wrought (hard to do, of course, lacking a vast historical sympathetic imagination to fully glimpse any other world [come home, Coriolanus]). It can be accomplished in rhetoric, of course (it's today's story on page 1, where the anecdote-bedecked nation-minded ideal, "bereft of anyone to please, it withers so, having no heart . . ." [Philip Larkin, referring to something else]), and in drama: on today's "Guiding Light," for example, the annual Bauer family Fourth of July cookout occurred, as it has since apparently the advent of recorded speech, and watching that was soothing because for a few moments the treadmill heartache of the characters' lives (Roger is scheming to abort Holly's wedding; Blake is distraught over Holly's not inviting her to go wedding-dress shopping with her; Ed Bauer is shouldering on with the cookout despite Eve's tragic death and Michelle's relegation to the limbo of offscreen space [she's in "Europe"]; etc.; I could go on) was awkwardly but finely interrupted, in order for Ed to give a speech to his friends expressing their collective appreciation of being American, which, he said, meant that we live in a nation in which citizens are able to make choices about the course of their lives. Probably not (but maybe, albeit lightly) coded political speech, Ed Bauer's invocation of "choice" at least had the virtue of specifying the register, which is a behavioral one, in which it would be possible to force thoughts worthy to entertain as deference to the observed day's holiday status.

Meaning, you live as we choose, not as you must; or, maybe, she lives with the choices she doesn't know she's made. Or maybe they don't understand why the Bauer family cookout on "Guiding Light" is the only Independence Day observance they know with certainty will occur, to their satisfaction.

J.J. and Sidney, in *Memorial Day (Observed)* (the names if not characters derived from 1957's *The Sweet Smell of Success*, J.J. Hunsecker being Burt Lancaster as a vicious Winchell-style Broadway columnist and Sidney being Tony Curtis as a conniving shill, both sprung from the imagination [surprisingly corrosive, late in his career] of Clifford Odets), are holed up in what I imagine to be Clintonville, a Columbus neighborhood directly north of the university: spanning east and west sides of High Street, block upon block of single- and two-family houses from before both wars, on tiny lots, some on modest bluffs and some running down toward the miniature Olentangy River, and home turf, stereotypically, to unreconstructed hippies now bewilderedly ravaged by the onslaught of their "passages." Sprawled like Fassbinder's Petra von Kant and consort on a vast low bed, Old Glory dressing the set and, in the foreground (perfect) the upper right corner of a TV set showing a baseball game (a Fagin signature flourish, this persistent trope grounded in the disappointment accruing to a lifetime whose boyhood was spent as a native Cubs fan), Sidney and J.J. fight about food, of course (like Steve, of course: when he visits Columbus, the daily quest [urban Chicago Jewish] becomes that of locating "interesting restaurants," and as this demand is addressed to someone [suburban Chicago Irish: our souls may be blackened, but thank God we don't have bodies] constitutionally content forever to subsist on any version of humanly tolerated kibble, confusion and failure typically ensue [but no one goes home hungry]). J.J. and Sidney, aware that they've escaped the fate of living-in-tragedy (in contrast to their cinematic forebears, the puppet-like protagonists of the cinema Fagin loves, as authored by Ophuls, Minnelli, Manckiwiecz, Sirk, Ray, this studio-coerced body of chamber plays given rosy flesh by the likes of Ava Gardner, Dean Martin, Montgomery Clift, Liz, of course, Gloria Grahame, Lana Turner [Lana Turner last week dead, of throat cancer; and praise, for once, to the *New York Times,* for according her death notice no more or no fewer column inches than those given the notice of the same day's death of the inestimable Barney Simon, co-founder of South Africa's Market Theater (and uncle, by the way, to Jason Simon, who produced the, to me, most valued Fagin-directed video sequence, which is that of Ron Vawter, captured by Leslie Thornton's Fisher-Price pixelvision camera in a room at the Gramercy Park Hotel, for *The Machine That Killed Bad People* [this very article, what's being written now, was "commissioned" with a request or an invitation for it to address this sequence, but as love ("love"), mine, for Ron prohibitively intervened (Ron who said in Amsterdam three days before he died that his heart had been broken, but not by AIDS; and Ron whose company I had last enjoyed courtesy of Steve, when I was house-sitting in La Jolla, during the week that John Cage died [remembered as such only because I answered the phone at eight in the morning, and heard a woman, since identified, sobbingly asking for Ron, who with Greg was sleeping; and Ron was roused, took the call, sighed, hung up, said Cage was dead (the rest is silence, Ron said: same as it ever was), waited as coffee was made, sat on the patio beneath the bougainvillea reading Nicholas Mosley (*Accident*), and showed me his decaying toenails (Philoctetes: the body uprising and spiraling downward), which toenails we then photographed])])]), nonetheless are sketched as humans bound to appetite, satiable as indiscriminately by Buckeye Donuts (Satan's en-chantments) as by Chi-Chi's ("A celebration of food!") or by Wendy's (one franchise on every block corner; Columbus is after all Wendy's foun-tainhead, and the breezily sketched background for founder Dave Thomas's autobiography, the mandated uplift attached to which having to do with the possibilities for aiming high even while grazing low).

Manic when not lethargic, J.J. and Sidney venture outdoors for an airy scene change, which repairs not in the slightest the wound of being in Columbus while not being Cuban. One of them (it could be either) asks, "Why should you be happy when I'm not?" which then registers as a troubling puzzlement. Well, why *should* you? Ohio is a "whole big state," they acknowledge, with endless attractions: is today the day for going to the zoo or for at-home toenail painting? You have to choose. Maybe if you're not as happy as I am, it's because *you've made that choice.* (Who did? Was I in the room at the time?) J.J. and Sidney, anyway, he with his Catholic boy conspiracy rant (the great John Fleck) and she with her hula-hoop dreams (Fallon, who's great), conform intermittently to an ideal of the couple, meaning that together they're more substantial than either one is as a solo act and that, as a live-in bonus, there's always an-other agent available there in the same room or across the bed sufficiently endowed with the capacities for thought, speech, and action to validate the vast driftfulness one or the other of them at most moments feels im-pending. Hence J.J.'s head-on send-off, adrift like that of the patriarch Minafer major in *The Magnificent Ambersons* ("first there was the sun . . ."), turns into a lament, piercing in its inability to say aloud the exact formula of words such as would make anything change, offering instead an actionless diagnostic prayer verbatim from DeTocqueville, here anticipating of all people Scott Fitzgerald: "They can never attain as much as they desire. . . . At every moment, they think they are about to grasp it. . . . They are near enough to see its charms, but too far off to enjoy them. And before they have fully tasted its delights, they die."

(But not from love.)

Americans dreaming of a place in the sun, J.J. and Sidney, these video creatures alive for thirteen minutes, are as "alive" as any of the inhabitants, historical or imagined, in Fagin's preceding epic video productions.[1] Commissioned by KCET, Los Angeles's public television station, as part of a creative project on notions of democracy, *Memorial Day (Observed)* actually is constructed to function as a short, to be shown before the station's broadcast of *The Sweet Smell of Success,* and, in its way, the video short is as moving as the feature film in its declension of a certain mode of American desperation; it is, at any rate, Fagin's least ironic work to date, opting for an honest resolve in the face of recondite private doubts.

(Rant deleted here about irony—irony is/as disease.)

The streets of Columbus on our Independence Day seem deserted; I live next to a large park, and there's no one visible over there today. I went to the corner decaf house, and the owner was there and no one else (the owner is from Zaire, which means exactly what?). What do people do? Where do people go? We hear ourselves asking these questions all the time, but, as we mainly ask each other, there's seldom a new answer. We talk to our friends with children, and they talk as though they have no children, but, then again, they're our friends, and so of course they know nothing we don't ourselves know. Friendships want a certain ignorance.

On the phone this morning to San Francisco while sitting on the front porch, I began to describe the curious lack of any detectable comradely activity here, only to look up and see a man in a fully appointed Batman costume strolling vigilantly past the house. I reported this to San Francisco; at once addled and jaded, San Francisco responded by invoking the haiku-like allure (men, birds, fog) of his own adopted landscape, where the simple act of concentrated looking is, for some, an endlessly absorbing routine. It's taken six years now for Batman to go strolling past my house, and, although in truth I can't say I've been six years waiting for precisely that vision to descend, I do wonder (idly? no, not idly: precisely not idly) if it will be six years again before I discover where he was going and why he was on my street while en route there, because at the time (and also before and also after) no one else was on my street, except, obviously, me, on the porch, seeing if not (though who knows? obviously not me) being seen, except maybe for last night when the fireworks downtown, on our Independence Day, were launched high enough aloft into a north-blowing wind to endow their trail ends with still sufficient force almost to illuminate our house and those on its porch, in the accident of their descent.

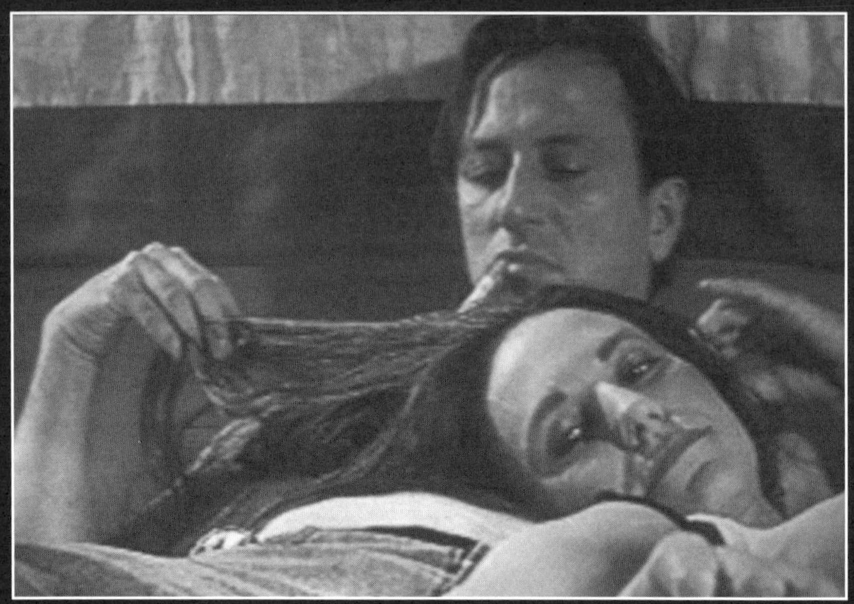

"Sidney and J.J. Try to Relax," from *Memorial Day (Observed)*

Steve Fagin
Excerpts from Voice-Over
from *Memorial Day (Observed)*

They can never attain as much as they desire. It perpetually retires from before them, yet without hiding itself from sight, and in retiring draws them on. At every moment they think they are about to grasp it; it escapes at every moment from their hold. They are near enough to see its charms, but too far off to enjoy them; and before they have fully tasted its delights, they die.—Alexis de Toqueville, *Democracy in America* (1840)

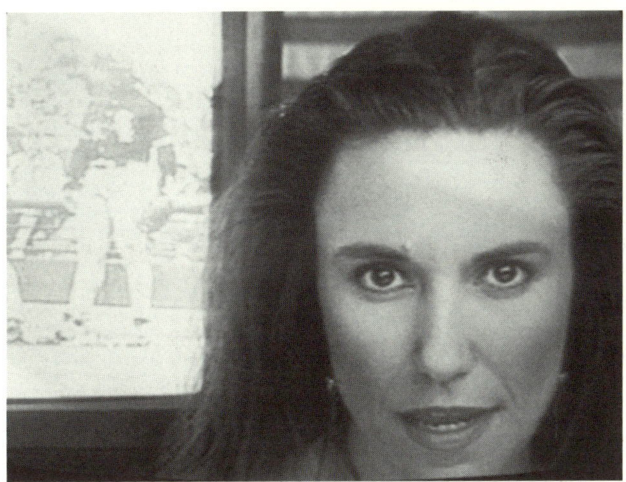

Fallon in "I Could Never Love You," from *Memorial Day (Observed)*

i could never be with him, well maybe, if i imagined us in a movie.
a place in the sun.
i'm elizabeth taylor and he's montgomery clift.
my sister she's shelley winters. all bloated, lying at the bottom of a lake.
montgomery clift sweats, basting in his own confusion.

me, i stare with my violet eyes into the black and white camera,
trusting the cuts to produce my emotions.
i know we live no longer in tragedy but hope it is not yet farce.

the soundtrack
it's piercing,
the radio unravels him, as the motorboat buzzes round and round.

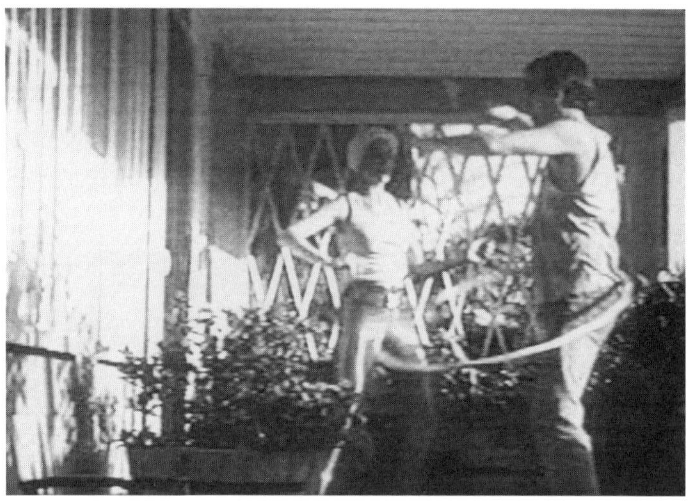

"I'd Rather Be Cuban," from *Memorial Day (Observed)*

i'd rather be cuban
columbus didn't come here

i'm very spanish, ava gardner in the barefoot contessa, and he,
he's el barbaro, beny moré, fred astaire from the waist up
but from the waist down, strictly not kosher
it's all in the hips
i dance son, he prefers guaguanco
he gives me his handkerchief and warns, don't cross your clavé
we repeat our dance
i bark, capitalism is just a rat race

he shrieks his montuno, socialism in cuba is a herd of lemmings

hurling

themselves into the sea,

i add, don't wait for don johnson to catch you.

he tunes me out and moves only the toes of his feet, i hear los van van

and

elio reve

he points his cane at the quinto, i look away

although his body stays young his face turns old as he says, it isn't

just

aragon,

castro fiddles and we burn.

the yellow of occhun fades into the red sea

ava and beny dissolve into blackness and i see a star, no a

constellation.

desilu, and say

maybe, i'll just marry cuban.

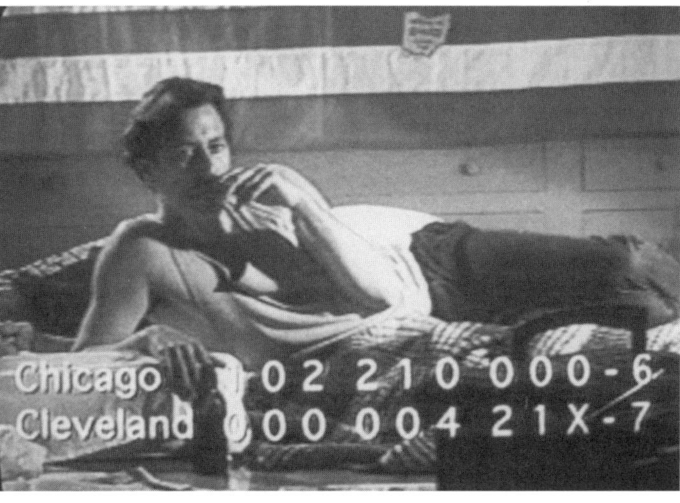

John Fleck in "They Can Never Attain as Much as They Desire," from *Memorial Day (Observed)*

John Welchman
Faces, Boxes, and *The Moves*

"Traveling (Video) Cultures"

How can we speak of a "traveling video"—an activity of moving-image production that makes and imagines movement: relocations, migrations, translations, the flows of information, the projections of fantasy, the hard "realities" of location, the vicissitudes of the voyage, the stubbornness of adventure? How can we mark a space for representing or ordering *the moves* (to insist on their specificity and plurality)? There is much to move around. For such an attempt should not be unaccountably obsessed with the strictures of location or the prophetic immanence of "dwelling" (of which Heidegger has become the poet and master).[1] Nor should it succumb to the different inertia arising from the logic of a postcolonial morality that sometimes refuses the possibilities, empowerments, and pleasures of moves—whether by selves, others, or the others of others. The refusal of encounter is not a solution to the problem posed by "forced locations," by encounters with no account, by repositions that are blind to their motivations, consequences, or disruptions. The problem is in moving itself.

For a travel is always, simultaneously, a transgression and a surrender. It is always marked by desires and needs. It is always a rupture formed of several violences to place—the separation or splitting off from "home"; the vector or passage between or through; and the continuous intrusion of arrivals. A "traveling video" would take place in an arena whose outsides are made up of travesties of *the moves:* the immanence of dwelling, the morality of localism, the imaginary fissions of pure "flow," the vertigo of transgressive surrender, and the perverse ambition to "represent." I want to suggest that the video work of Steve Fagin—while often, perhaps necessarily, getting caught on the ropes of all these demarcations—has nevertheless struggled with unusual passion and energy to move away from their confinements to image conditions inside the arena.

This "inside" is dense and compacted. Not that Fagin produces precious or hallowed objects of displacement (as in some aesthetic, "installational" *moves* developed in the art world). Rather, a primary consequence of Fagin's weave of moving images is that its complexities and folds, its structures of reference and provisional asides, its dialogues and diversities, will confound the partial and reductive allocations of a critical narrative, just as they might saturate or overflow particular spectatorial horizons. There is a kind of sumptuary risk in this plurality: for even as the running on of references is multiplied to excess, as they move apart and together in serial sequence and metaphoric overlay, their hatching and warp might open too many little depths, puncture too many apertures-for-knowing in the little box of sound and light where video comes from.

The following remarks will suggest some of the ways in which Fagin has staged and overcome this risk; how he has balanced profusion and restraint, hears and theres, dreams and ideologies, heres and theirs—how he has produced a vision of *the moves*. As a way of bringing the more specifically and intimately referenced contributions to this book up against another set of contexts, I want not so much to offer them another description or analysis as to draw his videos alongside various understandings of relocation and "travel" as they have been played out in three recent discussions and sites of production: in so-called postmodern anthropologies (especially in the new "visual anthropologies"), in aspects of postwar film and experimental video, and (briefly) in the art world. In conclusion I will suggest how his visualizations of encounter produce what I want to describe as a kind of "postphysiognomy" of place. Faces, boxes, and *the moves*.

A "traveling video," then, might pass by a similar range of incitements, revisions, old dangers, new pleasures, and recontested politics as those confronted in what James Clifford has described as "traveling cultures."[2] Clifford argues that such cultures have arisen in relation to a number of "travel conjunctures" focused on the transition from anthropological "informants" to "hybridized," postmodern countertravelers—those traveling in their own way and among their routes (which might include "ours"), who are encountered (on the way) by the sense-making machines of "advanced" anthropologies. This transition is predicated on the shift from "informants" and static research to "participant observation" (after Malinovsky)—a sort of dignified getting down with the natives, which went on to include the technics of living and language immersion (like a second baptism into the new life of the other culture). But "participant observation" itself, still offered a form of "co-residency" rather than travel, one in which the anthropologist (who might also be a filmmaker and would almost certainly be a photographer or draughtsperson) sought a one-way exchange of homes with the native settlement—an "exchange" based on the anthropologist "moving in" for long periods, probably uninvited, and usually unannounced. Such behavior, of course, has no reciprocal issue in the West, it being—for the most part—quite inconceivable that even a family member could stay in Western-style domestic space for months or years without mutual negotiation or clearly specified invitation.

The place of classical anthropology is thought by Clifford as one of the sides that rope off his mobile arena of "traveling cultures": for "fieldwork" must be understood "as a special kind of localized *dwelling*" undertaken by "homebodies abroad" (p. 99) who invest in complex imaginary relations to local languages, rituals, everyday life, etc., which they *observe.* The vectors and machines of travel are ignored in this account, capital cities and national contexts erased; and the originary home of the researcher, and the many sites and operations of translation (mostly between languages, but also between customs, manners, religions, etc.), forgotten or marginalized. The control system of the anthropological experiment is thus incubated from the contaminants of social and political context—either local, national, or global (in respect of the peoples/places involved).

Searching for a renegotiation of this problem, Clifford suggests that the people who used to be positioned as "informants" might instead be seen to "write" and "travel" culture back. The new anthropology turns home truths into away provisions. It looks, for example, at beaches, shores, and interiors, not at "autonomous" islands, or cut-out communities; it affirms the "multiple authorship" of other cultures, not their definitional reduction to a singular ethnographic trait or dominant language group. It will encounter conflict and nonconsensuality, rather than smooth its "results" into a homogeneous form or cumulative pronouncement.

As we will see with the emergence of a discourse of "visual anthropology," Fagin's position in relation to the representation of "traveling cultures" is neither illustrative nor instrumental. That is, his videos cannot be simply inscribed within the new anthropologies or even—more abstractly—within their transdisciplinary paradigms. Yet they clearly cut across the suggestions, desires, and investments of such para-academic discourses. Their location, if you like, is to travel through the materialized thought of "traveling cultures," being only what anthropology has never been—even in its newly imagined future. A measure of this virtual intersection is found in the places in Clifford's text where the possibilities of "traveling cultures" are imagined in the form of projects, itemizations, or parentheses. One of his roll calls of specific subject positions usually marginal to the concerns of anthropology reads like a crossover cast list from Fagin's *Zero Degrees Latitude:* "missionaries, converts, literate or educated informants, mixed bloods, translators, ethnographers, pilgrims . . ." (p. 101). With the single—and notable—exception of "ethnographers" themselves (who do, in fact, have an offstage presence in the piece), these are the people seen, encountered, interviewed, researched, simulated, imagined, and videoed in Fagin's most recent work. It is thus that his representations might find a provisional definition as one of the "new representational strategies" or "notes for ways of looking at culture (along with tradition and identity) in terms of travel relations" (p. 101) that Clifford recommends. While Clifford's discussion goes on to privilege (although also to problematize) the category of "ex-centric natives" or "traveling 'indigenous' culture-makers," Fagin is more concerned about the ways that cultures are traveled to and around—both historically and televisually—and how these representations circulate and are exchanged and overlaid.

It is significant that in thinking through these representational strategies Clifford begins, not with postmodern anthropological *writing* (whose problematics and possible reformulations he has discussed elsewhere),[3] but by addressing particular kinds of overlap between traveling cultures and filmic representation. His delivery of "traveling cultures" to the (privileged) threshold of cinema allows us cross over into "traveling film" and again to "traveling video."

Clifford alludes to three positions, which considered together can form a preliminary matrix for the working out of a critical "traveling video." First, he outlines "the story of dwelling-in-travel" located around the Moe family, a Hawaiian performing group, within whose migrations, he suggests, the possibility that a filmwork-in-progress about the family would be able to deploy excerpts from the "home" (really "road-home") movies made by traveling family member Tal Moe. Second, Clifford introduces a film by Bob Connolly and Robin Anderson, *Joe Leahy's Neighbors,* which follows the movements and hybrid sociality of a mixed-blood inhabitant ("the sort of figure who turns up in travel books, but seldom in ethnographies") of the New Guinea highlands.

He turns, finally, to a historical antecedent of "traveling film" in the "ethnographie vérité" of Jean Rouch, noting in particular his *Jaguar* (1953–67), which unfolds as a journey between Mali and the "Gold Coast" in West Africa, "a wild, picaresque swoop through Francophone Africa,"[4] an "ethno-fiction" of "social change and displacement" narrated and "performed" by three young Songhay men. In the touching of film and ethnography the work of Rouch makes a crucial gesture—both historically and critically.[5] An autodidact who conjugated the moving image with aspects of later surrealism and the camera-eye theories of Dziga Vertov, Rouch produced a "participatory cinema" in which—most obviously in the films of migration and travel, including *Jaguar* and *Moi un noir* (about a dockworker in the Ivory Coast port of Abijan)—the maker would embark on an interactive journey with the film's "subjects." He would record "found" situations by improvisational means. And it is in this sense that he has been seen by his sympathetic critics as a "cinematic griot," as a participant anthropologist who finally "became part of contemporary Songhay cosmology," but equally as a maker of images who merged with his camera in a moment of epiphanic unity that somehow answered to the native rituals of "possession" that obsessed him.[6] In this reading Rouch is made over as a "radical empiricist for whom lived experience is a primary component of fieldwork" and whose visionary-real camera actions constituted a kind sympathetic magic or "artistic anthropology" actually capable of "solving" "ethnographic mysteries."[7]

Such devotions have the merit, at least, of showing how Rouch stands at the apogee of the ethnographic tradition of "participation"—becoming a borderline subject of his places of relocation—yet at the same time clearly reveal that Rouch's substitution of coproduction for "participation" transgressed the disciplinary bounds and counterinteractive moralities that still dominate the pursuit of academic, and even "para-," anthropologies. The relatively recent history of "visual anthropology"—for which Rouch's films constitute a favored set of representations, although not always uncritically—is a case in point. Most of the earlier accounts of ethnographic film establish, or subscribe to, rigid exclusionary models that proscribe clear bounds and limits in the specific and privileged association of "scientific" ethnography and film. Karl Heider, for example, sketches a categorical defense of "ethnographic integrity" from which all "errors" of "cinematic aesthetic" must be refused or purged. Ethnographic film must dissociate itself from "jump-cuts" and "subjectivity"; it must zealously pursue an utter minimization of anthropological "presence," and it must indulge in no "artifice" of any kind—it must have nothing at all to do with the bastard lineage of "Flaherty's igloo."[8]

Departing from this purist position, much of the subsequent debate in the emergence of "visual anthropology" has been variously preoccupied with sullying the transparency of the ethnofilmic image, engaging on the way, little by little, developments in seventies and eighties film theory, Derridean-influenced spacings between "visuality" and "textuality," and a whole range of renegotiations with modernist and colonialist authority collected from the endgame of postmodern and postcolonial theory.

Here, again, the work of Rouch marks a necessary moment of pause in the recent call, purportedly taken up—or exemplified—in the very different projects of Robert Gardner and Trinh T. Minh-ha, for a "move within anthropology from representation to evocation."[9] This call, and other, "progressive" suggestions from younger anthropologists (and others) concerned with the visual field, often seems both to leap too far (into the celebrated unknowability of "the poetic") and to fall too short. Crudely put, the problem is one of *combinations* and multiplicities (although emphatically *not* of the "surrender" to them or of any abandonment to some postmodern "euphoria of exchange").

A line of postures, between the too much of the poetic and the too little of anthropological stricture, is another measure of the profuse balance achieved in Fagin's work. For in a sense Fagin's videos are stacked like dream works in the unconscious of even the more radical exponents of visual anthropology, from which—somewhat in the manner of Clifford's text—they occasionally escape in the compressed form of lists and slips and asides. In this condition they are what is desired but never quite stated; or, alternatively, what is thought but never quite produced. It soon becomes clear that Fagin has worked like a video-spider making webs from the little catalogs and possibility strings that Clifford and others have built into a tentative pocket Larousse of "traveling cultures."

One of the corners thus webbed over is the place of historical travel and its kinds, how histories of movement (migrations, evacuations, tourism, adventure, emergencies, refugeeism, pilgrimage, and so on) are invoked, and how they merge and interfere with the structures and experiences of "home" in the present (when and if there is one). In another little list—of "letters, diaries, oral history, music and performance traditions" (p. 107), Clifford opens a fresh parenthesis onto the supporting discourses and resources of traveling knowledge and confession that fed into Fagin's earlier videos that dealt with historical literary travelers such as Flaubert and Roussel.

Zero Degrees Latitude, even through its title, speaks to the perils of diminishing return as visual anthropology thinks the dangerous question of correlation between "documentary" and "fiction." As Dai Vaughan puts it: "Some people would argue that any distinction between documentary and fiction diminishes rapidly to zero as film increases in complexity."[10] *Zero Degrees Latitude* offers an ironic allegory of the zero complexity in the question of latitude and reach between site, archive, and imagination.[11] In this condition it forms a dialogue with the carefully thought attempts of Trinh T. Minh-ha to negotiate between the possibilities (and demands) of "documentary" and "fiction," not by making recourse to conventional antagonisms ("being merely 'anti-'"), but by questioning the "specialized, professionalized 'censorship' generated by conventions." This results, not in the denial or negation of such "categories and approaches," but rather in an "extension" of their reach in projects that continuously work at their limits or edges.[12] Moving through what Judith Mayne refers to as this "resistance to categorization"[13] and Trinh T. Minh-ha herself describes as a "desire not to simply mean," she underlines a commitment to "stories, songs, music, proverbs, as well as people's daily interactions."[14] Such "stories" include "Western writers" (such as Bachelard, Cixous, Heidegger, and Eluard) as well as local traditions: "for the place of hybridity is also the place of my identity."[15] As Benjamin argued of his project on Moscow, there is an effort here to put "theory" in a kind of vivid suspension within and around the processes of traveling-writing-(filming). It is not, and cannot ever be, forgotten, but, equally, it is never a privileged "safe place" of pronouncement separated from experience—or confusion.

There are several contributions to questions of ethnography and the techniques and strategies of visualization—as there are in the rethinking of anthropology at large in which Clifford has figured so prominently—that shift discussion (and imagination) in a direction that I am claiming

Fagin and a small company of others have already begun to move. These include the work of several imagemakers and theorists who have worked in Australia, such as Eric Michaels[16] and David MacDougall. MacDougall engages with the "complicities of style" that might attend an "intertextual cinema." Such a cinema would traduce the monopoly values of older ethnographic film: it would speak to multiple voices in multiple cultures and deploy multiple codes. In a gesture that runs in the opposite direction to the occasional film theory written or spoken by the "antitraveling" Federico Fellini (for whom the face functions as his leading fetish of "home," the dwelling place of national emotivity), MacDougall poses a number of restraints to Western points of view fixed in the moving image, notably "the assumption that characters will assert their personalities and desires visually, in ways that can be registered in close-ups of the face."[17] This and related suggestions about the Western encoding of the close-up, which have a theoretical point of origin in Béla Balász's emotive hyperfacialization of the filmic world,[18] offer a useful "corrective," but it should not become a stricture. The films of Trinh T. Minh-ha show the way to a reimagination of Western-non-Western "reassemblages" of the face,[19] while Fagin's videos suggest a different, but related, concern with the physiognomies of location.

To move from the reasonable suggestions of MacDougall to the videos of Steve Fagin is to move from the collision of "two texts of life" (in MacDougall's terms) to interactions in a global-social space that are more desiring, more abstract, and more layered. It is to move from the anxious influence system that flickers between "texts" to the catastrophic encounter of discourses or systems and clusters of flowing texts. Thus, *Zero Degrees Latitude* is inscribed across a hybrid fusion of (local) religious worldviews, merging missionary, evangelical Protestantism (overlaid with cold war calculation) with a syncretic native Catholicism and various local religions and "animisms." It might be that Fagin would also fear MacDougall's fears: the consequences of "cultural relativity run wild" or "mirrors within mirrors and unending nesting boxes," but such threats of signifying entrapment or abandon are for him an incitement to representation—just as they are recognized to be part-conditions of the unequal exchange between cultures, capital, and powers. As Trinh T. Minh-ha has shown (and written), it is possible, and necessary, to make "commitment from the mirror-writing box."[20]

Sketches

As *Zero Degrees Latitude* begins, the camera moves in on an old-style map of the Americas, written over with pseudoarchaic calligraphy. We zoom in on the equator as it passes through Ecuador. This is not an allegory, or at least not quite. Steve Fagin is a maker and surveyor of maps, but his are maps spun together from travel machines, visual codes, and a stout-hearted roll call of fragrant travelers, connoisseurs of displacement, and virtual mountaineers. He is mapping, making space, listening to it. He is coiled up around it. Just as there are cartographic connectivities suggested in our fin-de-siècle telegeographies, in non-Western spirit worlds, and among the written-down trade winds represented by the adventure colonists, so Fagin gives and takes his video spaces, with spirit and virtuality, adventure and social inscription, so that they are always spaces making meanings, place part objects that simultaneously refer to and refuse an assemblage of "bigger pictures."[21]

Fagin's maps stack up like a "magic encyclopedia" of travels (the phrase is Walter Benjamin's, ventured in relation to the folds, layers, and epiphanies of his library)—of removes and displacements. Their leading figure is the "amazing voyage." But his voyages (and amazements) are of many kinds, spaced out in the posthallucinogenic world beyond the magical mystery tour, where they are aligned in three merging experiences: literary travel, ethnographic travel, and cinematic travel. Some of these goings are oneiric or imaginary, done in rooms with the blinds down (like Roussel); some follow the move across missionary positions or media displacements; others shunt to and fro inside the brackets of language or under the cover of travel surrogates like photographs, movies, and TV.

We see traveling TV, video on the road, home-made runarounds, and Flaubertian escapades, in which visual delicacies substitute for the writer's sonorous periods, even passages of modified exotica (as in the Ecuadoran Amazon). There is studio travel, in which the prop and the backdrop substitute for places and bring them wildly home, and editorial travel of unimaginable splices and mergers. There is the lustful, dusty stasis of archival travel and the moral travel of purpose and commitment. All are driven forward by a percussive assemblage of machines of travel. Think of the chamber-bound Tinguelyesque confection that stomps forward by the inch in the studio sequences of *Zero Degrees Latitude* and the intimate-text/fragment-image machine of the postcard. Or think of the satellite Trojan Horse of television, whose monitor-face is neither quite perspectival nor just a black-and-white surface system, but a jukebox of Poppy colors and struggling, little dimensions. Think, again, of the real-delusional travel of the dream and the vectoring machines of the walk, the run, the pursuit, the drive, the crossing, and the flight.

All these are driven forward under the parallel time harness of genres and codes: the real space probe time of the documentary, where the camera is taken in, lofted into an "authentic" site. We are in a breakwater or on a hill walk, where it enframes the candid explosions of a religious physiognomy. The throwup, throwaway loop of vérité, the soliloquy, and the voice-over are the personae of Fagin's hyphenated generic miscegenation.

Then there are the codes of travel itself, and Fagin depends on them and rips them off in equal measure. For he tilts against the grandiosity of the odyssey, the bigotry of the pilgrimage, the picturesque voyeurism of the tour, the inconsequentiality of the strolling *flâneur,* the abstract mission of the adventurer, the unmagic encyclopedism of the ethnographer, the terror of the runaway, the bar codes of the reporter, the grandstanding of the modern aerialists (the pilot, the balloonist, the cosmonaut), the banality of the commuter, and the contrasensuality of virtual travel (by the hacker or the cybersurfer).

And there are the travelers, the crew of persons (verifiable, invented, found, and imagined) who inhabit mondo Fagin. We meet a guest list of circa-end-of-the-century voyagers, including Gustave Flaubert, Roussel, Lou Andreas-Salomé, Rimbaud, Walter Benjamin, Jules Verne, and Pierre Loti. These negotiants with the onset of the twentieth century meet with a more generic cast of mildly millennial types obliviously living out its opposite end: TV reporters, CIA operatives, presidential entourages, missionaries, camera operators, a young woman lost in the jungle.

But all "this is not a nomadology."[22] It doesn't desire so much abstract subversion, and its multiple instances (codes, persons, histories, image types) take the place of multiple theorizations. Fagin's discretionary universes of cross-culturated travel transform the stolid interiority of TV's chamber into a rainbow net of movements. They are studies, or *ébauches,* that meet the as-yet "sketchy" demands for "a comparative cultural studies approach to specific histories, tactics, everyday practices of dwelling *and* traveling."[23]

Filmic Homebodies and Countertraveling Selves

These locations within and around the theory-practice represented in some "postmodern ethnographies," or the recent and progressively more persuasive discussions developed in "visual anthropology," speak only to one particular intersection of Fagin's work. As we begin to think through other connections and refusals, we reveal a series of projects whose sites between contemporary developments in the cultural politics of the art world, experimental film and video, cultural, postcolonial and gender studies, stand as one of the most intricately formatted assemblages in recent practice. As each weave is measured and tied, very little is given away or assumed without being closely thought through among the many levels of video production—script, "location," theory, "performance," historical context, editing, sound, and screening and reception (to abbreviate).

The place of these formats, their scales and redemptions, might also be posed in relation to both canonical and experimental film or video traditions. Again, the question, "travel," as problematized by Clifford and others, provides a point of entry. For it is not only traditional anthropology that "has privileged relations of dwelling over relations of travel."[24] Variously formulated investments in the static conditions of "home," "dwelling," and "origin" have also marked film production in the postwar years in ways that are instructive for any consideration of *the moves*.

How, then, can we think Fagin's place in relation to cinemas that take on, or passively contest, the effects of travels and displacement? This question needs more consideration than is possible here; but I want to offer a few "points of departure." Fagin's work is clearly remote from the quasi-allegorical, historic montage of D. W. Griffith's *Intolerance* or later, epic reconstructions of all-world narrative legends in Hollywood drag. But Fagin's "traveling video" also looks and sounds against the interiorizing closures loaded into mainstream and experimental film, from the postwar U.S. comedies of "social relevance" to Woody Allen, from Antonioni's colorfully decomposed suburbs to Fellini's Italian labyrinths of home, from the interiorities of John Cassavetes' *Faces* or Aleksandr Sokurov's nineteenth-century Russian interior city to the in-your-face closure of Michael Snow's loft.

Of the several instructive possibilities here, the comparison with Federico Fellini is especially revealing. For among Fellini's films, and in his miscellaneous commentaries on and around them, we encounter a summa of precious investments in the conditions of "home," national identity, domestic tourism, and the contratraveling self that mark the limit term antitheses to Fagin's hybrid relocationism. Such vigorous attachment to location and origin is by no means an exclusive characteristic of the coproduction Italy-Fellini-character-auteur. It marks the works of Antonioni, Cassavetes, Bergman, and other New Wave filmmakers in the sixties; and it extends the long history of modernist disquisition on the postures, anxieties, and dilemmas of the alienated modern self.

In the "family-centered, domestic, work-a-day world" inhabited by Cassavetes' obsessively scrutinized protagonists, for example, local, interior space seethes with endless permutations. As Raymond Carney puts it, "there is nowhere to run to" outside the hard-ended parentheses of constant emotional adjustment: for "if characters run off to construct and temporarily inhabit imaginative worlds 'worlds elsewhere,' they and their creators only care about experience insofar as it can be brought back home to those who stay at home. That the American sublime can be domesticated is indeed the dream of America."[25] Here even other worlds that are "imaginative" and "temporary" cannot be grasped by a neo-sublime subtracted from the landscape and the outside only to be reconvened around a suburban dining-room table.

Antonioni offers us a more literal view of the lost cartography of elsewhere. In *Red Desert* Guiliana sits on the floor at the height of her obsessions, with a map of South America (showing Patagonia) on her lap: "Who knows," she laments, "if there's a place in the world where we would be better off." The map slips. And the globe dissolves: for the only nonsuburban territory that unfolds are dreamscapes of distraction, social dismemberment, and placelessness. Places that are only memories or desires, the middle-class evaporation of the social necessities of emigration, the modernist obsession with the labyrinth of the inner self, and isolated, ego-centered voyaging—all are remaindered in Antonioni's lusciously painted cuticles of film as the map of somewhere else falls away.

With Fellini, that which simply slips and fades is radically disabused. For he is the engineer of a face–travel machine whose interiority is the obsessional obverse of Fagin's physiognomy of relocation and cultural encounter. Fellini is emphatically not a traveler, in film or in life: "I dislike traveling, and am ill at ease on journeys. In Italy, I can manage it: curiosity is aroused, I know what there is behind all those faces, voices, places. But when I'm abroad this bores me: I no longer know what anything means, I can no longer make anything out, I feel excluded. All the same, there is always an atmosphere of travel around me. Arrivals and departures, farewells and welcomes. I love this movement around me. My friends are fellow travelers."[26]

In a condition where the nontraveling subject is orbited by surrogate satellite travelers, we traverse a Felliniocentric universe that circles around the xenophobic imaginary of the creative artist. While he adores local transport (especially trams and bicycles), Fellini cannot endure the thought and experience of international transit: for such movement is discomforting, alienating, difficult, obscure, and exclusionary. Travel's trouble is that it gives rise to situations that contradict originary experience; the face-to-faces it envisages are blank and empty because they are not formed in the bonds of identity, nor can they be satisfactorily controlled or manipulated or even adequately decoded by the privileged spectator who demands empowerment over them.

For Fellini, the film man who wishes to "penetrate—how shall I put it?—as a tourist without being involved,"[27] there are certain conditions: the cinematic self, the "ready-made" faces of character actors, memories, dreams, and vivid epiphanies. Fellini will order these ingredients with the passionate abandonment of a syncopated tourist. All the places in Fellini's filmic mind converge in the memory-driven dreamscape present of his Italy and the amniotic "hovel of Theater 5" at Cinecittà: "Whenever there I am protected from falling off the cliff by the capacious net consisting of my roots, my memories, my habits, my home: in sum by my laboratory."[28] Fellini knows only home travel and imaginary home-style transit. He even distinguishes his incestuous intimacy with "Italian reality" and its "systems of representation, among newspapers, television, publicity, winks of an eye, and the syntheses of images common to us all," from the experience of middle European émigré Jews, such as Milos Forman and Roman Polanski, who can "absorb like vampires the history, culture, memories of others."

Just as Fellini has his nontraveling companions, who travel on his behalf simply by virtue of being with him, so Fagin also, although inversely, looks across to a small band of fellow travelers (who are never quite there): Jean Rouch (in West Africa); Trinh T. Minh-ha (in Africa, China, and Vietnam); Chantal Ackerman (in Russia); Chris Marker (in Guinea Bissau, Siberia, and Japan). His work makes perhaps its closest approach to Chris Marker's films, video essays, and fictional cine-novellas—from

Lettre de Sibérie (1958) and *Sans soleil* (1982) to *The Last Bolshevik* (1993).
Both have made visual lacework with the old-style parameters of the voyage, explored the conditions of encounter with other places and the limits, pleasures, shocks, and fantasies that attend the making and editing of
moving images away from home.

But Marker puts in something more and leaves out something that is
rather less. Marker offers a more mannered performance of the symbolic
self, emanating from a visual scene that is by turns oblique and definite.
This "less," or omission, has several elements: it is underlined (like the
poetic "more" of visual anthropology) in Marker's suggestion that the
image might be a madeleine—the dissolving memory taste of Proust,
even if this little bite is piqued with "humility" and fragile "power" as he
also claims.[29] And it is written through Marker's clearly marked (if am-
biguously performed) positions as the diarist, the narrator, the writer-
poet, the activist, and the "founder, editor and writer" for Éditions du
Seuil Planète.[30]

On the other hand, there is a "more" caught up in a web of fabrications
that fictionalize the subject positions of the Maker-Marker. These include
exotic, invented, biographical details: Marker refers in one place to "we
Brazilians" and elsewhere to the we who might have been born (for dramatic effect) in Ulan Bator rather than a Parisian suburb. All these dispersed personae—with their ineffable origins and unflappable presents—
are quite distinct (perhaps generationally so as much as anything else)
from Fagin's measured noninterventionism of the self. The aura encoded
in Marker's vague, sometimes ironic, aggrandizements is entirely foreign
to Fagin's finesseful dissociation from almost all visible or sounded (and,
therefore, literal) self-inscription. Marker, in other words, simultaneously
surrenders to the poetry of the other place and reins himself back with an
intrusive, confessional, believable, diary-documentary voice. As a result,
his pieces are strangely, pleasurably, but also easily sutured, joining together the imaging of intangible others and the Fantastic Travels of
Mandeville, with a lyrical yet foot-firm, anecdotal, walk-and-talk-about
"I." It is almost as if, as has been said of Rousseau (and we have seen of
Fellini), "places are so many figures of himself."[31]

From the White Cube to the Rainbow Net
Fagin's video box (if not all that's in it) also stands somewhere at the end
of a long tradition of cubing the world. The linguistic "mirrors" and vi-

sual "nesting boxes" that threaten the discourse of visual anthropology dwell in Fagin's monitor-sized globe like fallen angels. But they also enframe it, for the box is the parentheses, or brackets, of video as it offers a dwelling place to a moving world.

At the head of the twentieth-century destiny of the cube, the minimalist neocubism of the sixties, epitomized in the boxes of Donald Judd, offered body- or artwork-scaled cubes that masqueraded as assertions about the specificity of the object as it was coproduced by the experiences of an active viewership whose perceptual fields they variously interrupted and extended. Of the several softnesses that fell against the synthetic sides of the untitled minimalist container, the most significant were not the cushiony surfaces of pop but softness of life itself. Cubic life was an art life that touched the world strangely in places where no one could really see. The comforts of this life were threatened, not so much by the simulated softness of vinyl or the soft time of surrealism, as by the softness of bodies and the un-time of the reinvented category of happenings and "real life."

But Fagin's solitary box fights for its very existence in a world where the cubed image has become either ferociously engorged through multiplication, miniaturization, installation, or has fallen into tragic enigma—two positions that often form a single switch. Its extension in singular depth contends both with the superficial lateral spread of the TV image in the monitor environments of "video art" and with the snapshot metaphoricity of recent "photo installations." In the work of Alfredo Jaar, for example, the quasi-reportorial photographic image has become a means of bearing political "witness"—most recently in Rwanda, Uganda, and Zaire (following visits in August 1994). The results of this art as witness, shown at Galerie Lelong in New York (May-June 1995), are ordered in archival minimalist-type boxes, which can't (or shouldn't) be opened. This gesture has its measure of effectiveness, but it follows the logic of the "taken" memorial image to its ultimate destiny in silence and withdrawal. The tragedy of the photographic *ars memoria* is sufficient to deny its visibility (although it can be *read*, and thus "imagined," in the form of remaindered captions). Travel as tragedy-without-seeing is one quite logical product of the destiny of politically predetermined visuality. The result is a mummer box, a pantomime cube covered by an art-world blindfold. As such, it takes its place alongside other species of altar-piece frontality and single-image iconicity, which offer little more than facades for the decorative sojourn of ideas and places. There is something inevitably religious (but not quite revelatory) in these lay-bys, for they function either as graves for graven images, headstones for marking, or moments for ritual reflection.

Face-to-Place

... does the city possess its own facade? At which moment
does the city show us its own face?—Paul Virilio

The geographies and displacements, commitments and pleasures, layered together in the videos of Steve Fagin remind me before anything else of the concentration, intensity, and spiraling periods of Walter Benjamin—whose historical voice is filtered through the male narrator in *The Amazing Voyage*. It's not just that they both partake in the joys of the fragment, in browsing, details, cities, arcades, libraries, love quests, disenchanted political engagement—among a myriad shared likes. Nor that their modes of production share passions for the nostalgias of the nineteenth century, the image machines of mechanical reproduction, and the abandonment of wandering between places. Rather, there's something that is lodged in the foundations of their often baffling architectures of ideas, passions, places, and positions: a certain dedication to what I want to call the face of the world as it's caught in *the move*.

Above all, the space measured between Fagin and Benjamin converges on the face. Fagin offers a sustained glimpse of what Benjamin identified in the production of theory, and history, and of what he defines as the basis of the photographic image—its revolutionary aspect. Benjamin's writings are sustained by three crucial forms of facial enunciation. The first is located in the general drift of his thought toward the articulation of a "materialist physiognomics." The second is more specific and is caught up in the several instances of the *face city* as they are inscribed in Benjamin's strangely luminous "city portraits." The third (the most literal and perhaps the least susceptible of critical elaboration) is founded on several kinds of *identification* of Benjamin with the face—both in his own essays and fragments and in the critical literature discussing them. In this third form, which culminates in Derrida's suggestive formula, the Benjamin *front,* the writer somehow merges with his (self-)portrait or his face—which is his self, his song, and the desire and failure of the revolution, all at once. It is his critical epiphany.[32]

In its three forms (its recto, verso, and sides) and their necessary intersections, the face lies at the center of Benjamin's converging projects on the origins and social philosophy of modernity. It is one of the chief "routes" along which the writer might travel "to attain" something much desired: what Benjamin termed "a heightened graphicness (Anschaulichkeit)."[33] It is a meeting point for Benjamin's attempt to provide a solution to the problems of historical materialism through a montage of citations and subjective-countersubjective musings. For only in this way can a face be known. The fragments he constructed are the facets that make a facade, the ruinous architecture and the architectural ruins of the face of the modern. The face is aligned with the focal length of Benjamin's dreams. Its parts are made up of their colors: profane illumination and mimetic experience; the critique of history and myth; and his ultimate, the dream—the dream of the nineteenth century from which we must awake.

In one of the few discussions of Benjamin that take some account of the social coding, metaphoricity, and subjective intensities of the face, Rolf Tiedemann points to his desire to use the face as a means to "recover," to gain an impress of, "the ever more rapid obsolescence of the inventions and innovations generated by capitalism's productive forces." Such a recovery would brandish "the appearances of the unsightly [rag pickers, prostitutes, streets, etc.], *intentione recta,* the physiognomic way: by showing rags, as a montage of trash."[34] The face is an instrument that when read by its commentators renders visible something of the marginal and unconscious effect of capital and its movements.

It is with these thoughts as a backdrop that Tiedemann identifies the central effort of Benjamin's work as a "material physiognomics": "Benjamin did not set out according to ideology critique; rather he gave way to the notion of materialist physiognomics, which he probably understood as a complement, or an extension of Marxist theory. Physiognomics infers the interior from the exterior, it decodes the whole from the detail, it represents the general in the particular. Nominalistically speaking, it proceeds from tangible object; inductively in the realm of the intuitive."[35] This coupling of the materialism of one history with the form and scope of another reveals a shape, a corrective, and a compulsion in Benjamin's understanding of the inherited past. But we should resist any intimation of a vulgar symptomology, a kind of facial determinism that sees the countenance as a mere scene of inscription for the crow-footed march of historical reality. The face is a multiplex screen of histories, causes, and selves. It is a machine that simultaneously manufactures difference and mills identity.

Tiedemann argues further that the transition from the first to the second drafts of his *Passagen-Werk* project (which was an effort "to safeguard his work against the demands of historical materialism") preserved "motifs belonging to metaphysics and theology . . . in the physiognomic concept of the epoch's closing stage." He continues in order to provide further arguments for Benjamin's concretion and specificity, modeled on the illuminations of the face:

> The abstractions of mere conceptual thinking were insufficient to demystify . . . [capitalism's "abhorrent" effects], such that a mimetic-intuitive corrective was imposed to decipher the code of the universal in the image. Physiognomic thought was assigned the task of "recognizing the monuments of the bourgeoisie as ruins even before they have crumbled" (V:59).—The prolegomena to a materialist physiognomics that can be gleaned from the *Passagen-Werk* counts among Benjamin's most prodigious conceptions. It is the programmatic harbinger of that aesthetic theory which Marxism has not been able to develop to this day.[36]

The face becomes an emblem of that still point of presentness Benjamin argued was needed by historical materialism for its effectiveness to be made known. For Tiedemann, Benjamin "speaks in direct theological terms in his interpretation of the modern as 'the time of hell'":[37] "The point is that the face of the world, that enormous head, never changes, certainly not in what is the newest, that this 'newest' remains the same in all its parts. This constitutes both the eternity of hell and the sadist's desire for innovation. To define the totality of the features by which the modern expresses itself means to represent hell."[38] Benjamin's final face is the giant, demonic face of the world whose expressions—and attendant interpretations—are the very countenance of hell. Throughout Benjamin's writings the face will reappear haunted by this satanic prototype. But when he returns to the *Passagen-Werk* project in 1934 he writes of its "new face," his own turn to a thought that was more sociological and political. The new face of social possibility replaces the fetish character of commodities, the phantasmagorias and lusters laid over the beguiling faces of the nineteenth century.

Part of this face, a special landscape face, is also underlined, he claims, in allegory, where "the observer is confronted by the *facies hippocratica* of history as a petrified, primordial landscape. Everything about history that, from the beginning, has been untimely, sorrowful, unsuccessful, is expressed in a face—or rather a death's head."[39] And the face has yet another special home in the photographic image, in the course of a description of which Benjamin offers one of his most celebrated physiognomic metaphors: "At the same time photography reveals in this material the physiognomic aspects of visual worlds which dwell in the smallest things, meaningful yet covert enough to find a hiding place in waking dreams, but which enlarged and capable of formulation, make the difference between technology and magic visible as a thoroughly historical variable."[40]

If these moments of discussion constitute the armature for a "materialist physiognomics," the clearest profile of the face arrives for Benjamin (as it often does for Fagin) with the reception and experience of a foreign city—the Naples he wrote about in 1925, Moscow (1927), Marseilles (1929), and his book project *Berliner Kindheit um Neunzehnhundert?* As Peter Szondi notes, "It is metaphor that makes Benjamin's city portraits what they are. It is the source of their magic and, in a very precise sense, their status as poetic writing."[41] But if, as Szondi asserts, "the metaphorist's glance proves to be that of the theologian's,"[42] we should give priority, not as he does to the displacements of the "name" or the "glass globes in which snow falls on a landscape" (Benjamin's "favorite objects"), but to scrutinizing the chief of all Benjamin's many metaphors of the city, the one that defines it first and foremost as a *portrait,* and more particularly as a *face.*

It is Szondi's contention that Benjamin's *Städtebilder* (city portraits) are combines of memory and memoir, forms of childhood knowledge layered with its travesties. The face of one's own city is in this sense the face of the mother, at first seen as a mere extension of one's own body and then as a traumatic object outside the self. The foreign city is both a return to this fantasy ("foreign surroundings do not just replace the distance of childhood for the adult; they turn him into a child again")[43] and its opposite, a scene of pure difference, of exaggerated otherness, where the subject can wander without recognizing his own origins and familial scenes. As a scene of the pleasure of nonrecognition, this city offers the face of a stranger. Sometimes it is the face of erotic desire, as opposed to the face of maternal love. But it can rarely be the face of a companion, friend, confidant, a close face, as the foreign city is by definition distant and of short acquaintance. The home city is a face of becoming, change, transition, passage; the foreign city is a theater set for the play of desire and a short-circuit back to the traumas of the early self.

When the face of the city as desire is passed over by a paternal mask that presents the city as authority, order, and serial repetition, the liberatory play of the desired, pleasured faces of the child and the lover are dissolved. Such is the case with the Moscow's burgeoning image cult of Lenin, which Benjamin details in the final pages of his essay "Moscow," but which were sprinkled throughout the entries in *Moscow Diary*: "In corners and niches consecrated to Lenin, they appear as busts; in the larger clubs, as bronze statues or reliefs; in offices, as life-size half-length portraits; in kitchens, laundry rooms, and storehouses as small photographs."[44] Benjamin's attention to the face of city life merges here with the religious efficacy of the saintly face and the usurpation of this sign by the personality cults of totalitarianism. Not only do the *figures* of Lenin take over the "corners and niches" traditionally reserved in the *izbar* or village wooden house, for the worship of icons, but they also invade key material and generic orders of visual representation, specifically itemized by Benjamin as "busts," "bronze statues," "reliefs," "life-size . . . portraits," and "small photographs." Benjamin catches the suffocating domination of the state as a face (the ultimate territorial metaphor of the face, one fit to compete with the Face of God) even more immediately when he notes that, "since the selling of icons is considered a branch of the picture and paper trade, these booths with pictures of saints tend to be located near paper goods stands, so that everywhere they are flanked by pictures of Lenin, like a prisoner between two policemen."[45]

Two unfathomable faces obsess Walter Benjamin in his *Moscow Diary* written in the winter of 1926–27: the face of Asja Lacis and the face of Moscow—the close-up, nearsighted, scrutinized, miniature city invented in Benjamin's incessant browsing and looking down, a city of shelves and gutters and toys. Benjamin notes the "desperate details" of his courtship with Asja ("a Bolshevik Latvian from Riga"), whom he had met on the island of Capri in May 1924 and encountered again in Berlin later in the same year and in Riga in 1925 and to whom his *One-Way Street* is dedicated. He is seduced, distracted, and perhaps appalled by her face, which is the object of Benjamin's intensest scrutiny: "I barely hear what she is saying because I am examining her so intently."[46]

Between the face of the object of desire and the tumultuous physiognomy of the quasi-revolutionary city, Benjamin catches the drift of his cross-identities.[47] For the intensity of the double face of *Moscow Diary* offers a refuge from theory and a concomitant outpouring of immediacies and sensations. The face of Moscow is a substitute and composite of Benjamin's faces. The dominance of the face provokes a relinquishment of abstraction and "theory." While a major incentive for his visit was various "literary obligations" to "render" "the 'physiognomy' of Moscow" (which resulted in four publications in early 1927), it was, as Benjamin noted, the "situation" of Moscow that most concerned him, its revolutionary present, its composure, texture, and contemporary expression. In a letter to Martin Buber of 23 February 1927, written after his return from Moscow (having nearly completed the "Moscow" essay for *Die Kraetur*), Benjamin spells out the countertheory represented by his Moscow projects:

> My presentation will be devoid of all theory. In this fashion I hope to succeed in allowing the creatural to speak for itself: inasmuch as I have succeeded in seizing and rendering this very new and disorienting language that echoes loudly through the resounding mask of an environment that has been totally transformed. I want to write a description of Moscow at the present moment in which "all factuality is already theory" and which would therefore refrain from any deductive abstraction, from any prognostication, and even within certain limits from any judgement—all of which, I am absolutely convinced, cannot in this case be formulated on the basis of "spiritual" data, but only on the basis of economic facts of which few people, even in Russia, have a sufficiently broad grasp. Moscow as it appears at the present reveals a full range of possibilities in schematic form: above all, the possibility that the Revolution might fail or succeed. In either case, something unforeseeable will result and its picture will be far different from any programmatic sketch one might draw of the future. The outlines of this are at present brutally and distinctly visible among the people and their environment.[48]

Allegory, photography, cities, and selves, even the projects of materialism and of "history" itself ("to write history means giving dates their physiognomy"),[49] are each caught up under the auspices of the face. At its furthest reach the metaphorization of the face of the world merges with the fetishistic Romantic imaginary traversed by Novalis's thousand "portal[s] to the universe": "anything that is strange, accidental, individual. . . . A face, a star, a stretch of countryside, an old tree etc. may make an epoch in our inner lives."[50] But this is a Medusa's head of social physiognomy, whose infantile gaze and allover erotic allure are sometimes indulged but elsewhere carefully resisted—on behalf of their respective histories—by both Benjamin and Fagin. Neither wish to deny the inner life, and both are at times thrillingly overwhelmed by it (Benjamin in Moscow, Fagin in his first two tapes). But what they labor to achieve is some measure of the vivid social conjunctions of their presents, points of merger and rupture and pleasure in the discourses of social becoming.

I offer the face, threaded through the subtle machinery of Benjamin's thought, as a measure of the parametrology of the moving image, as a necessary complement to the propulsions of travel, distance, and unknowledge. It is not a coincidence that the (different) reimagination of faces is crucial to the projects of several film- and videomakers whose paths we have already crossed. For Fellini, the face was the absorptive surface of cinema itself; the black hole with white walls that collapsed film into the ceaseless imagining of passionately found character-subjects. For Trinh T. Minh-ha, the face has an opposite centrality as the measure of a daring "poetic" extension and simultaneous critique of ethnographic knowing, a showing of the instability of identity itself. For Chris Marker, as with one of the three aspects of Benjamin's thought, the face stands in a condition of allegorical, portrait-like representation: it stands-in. Marker described *The Last Bolshevik* as a film that "attempts to trace the portrait of this generation through the portrait of a friend." Although crossed with stars and lovers, this was also Walter Benjamin's effort in his *Moscow Diary,* written in the winter of 1926–27, a few years before Medvekin was sending his "reality-shows" all around the Soviet Union in railroad cars.

For Steve Fagin, as for Benjamin at his most persuasive, the face has a more sustained metaphoric presence. It is a "real" metaphor that reaches between the social abstraction of theory and the instantiation of geographies and places. It stands for the vivacity of encounter, the shape and feel of a territory, even the welling up of desires and poetries. But it is seldom literal and rarely fetishized. It can be sighted in the feet of Imelda Marcos, the hats of the Ecuadoran highlanders, the scattered sexuality of Lou Andreas-Salomé, or an anagram by Raymond Roussel. It is a place of making known by intensity, by visions and sounds, movements and unfaded references. It offers an *almost* magic making over—in the box— of the face-to-face as a face-to-place.

Notes

Victoria Gill: Foreword

1. The quotations herein are "outtakes" from the interview with Steve Fagin that forms the introduction to this book.

2. Stuart Hall, "Cultural Studies and Its Theoretical Legacies," in *Cultural Studies,* ed. Lawrence Grossberg, Cary Nelson, and Paula A. Treichler (New York: Routledge, 1992), 277–94.

3. Daniel Pennac, *Comme un roman* (Paris: Gallimard, 1992); the translation here is my own.

Maggie Morse: "Waking and Shaking"

Margaret Morse's "Waking and Shaking," a review of Steve Fagin's *Virtual Play: The Double Direct Monkey Wrench in Black's Machinery—Dedicated to Lou Andreas-Salomé* (distributed by Video Data Bank, the Art Institute of Chicago), originally appeared in the November 1985 issue of *Afterimage.*

1. Fredric Jameson, writing specifically of Lyotard's project in his critical preface to Jean-Francois Lyotard, *The Postmodern Condition: A Report on Knowledge,* Theory and History of Literature, vol. 10 (Minneapolis: University of Minnesota Press, 1984), xix.

2. Fredric Jameson, "Postmodernism and Consumer Society," in *The Anti-Aesthetic,* ed. Hal Foster (Port Townsend, Wash.: Bay Press, 1983), 122. Referring to a specific poem in order to extrapolate a characteristic of postmodernism, Jameson adds, "Their [the sentences of the poem] referents are other images, another text, and the 'unity' of the poem is not *in* the text at all but outside it in the bound unity of an absent book" (p. 123).

3. *Pastiche* and *schizophrenia* are the main characteristics of postmodernism developed by Jameson in "Postmodernism and Consumer Society."

4. Quoted in H. F. Peters, *My Sister, My Spouse: A Biography of Lou Andreas-Salomé* (New York: Norton, 1974), 270f.

5. Rudolph Binion, *Frau Lou: Nietzsche's Wayward Disciple* (Princeton, N.J.: Princeton University Press, 1968), 32.

6. Peters, *My Sister, My Spouse,* 270f.

7. The essays have retained the regard of contemporary critics; her fiction, very popular in the period, is now devalued. Binion uses her stories as a basis for his psychoanalytic investigation of Lou in *Frau Lou.*

8. Lou's essays on Ibsen are considered among her best work.

9. See Jameson, "Postmodernism and Consumer Society," 118ff.

10. See Mikhail Bakhtin, *The Dialogic Imagination* (Austin: University of Texas Press, 1981), and others of his works.

11. See esp. Pat Mellencamp, "Postmodern TV: Wegman and Smith" (paper delivered at the Society for Cinema Studies conference in New York, June 1985). Note also Craig Owens, "The Discourse of Others: Feminists and Postmodernism," in *The Anti-Aesthetic,* 57–82.

Leslie Dick: "Lou: A Superficial Look"

1. Paul Rée killed himself in 1901, finally—or possibly he fell accidentally to his death from an icy cliff. (Sixty years later, the innkeeper's daughter claimed to remember that he had been suffering from diarrhea and that he fell while defecating.)

2. Elisabeth's husband, Bernard Forster, killed himself in 1889 by taking poison in a hotel in Paraguay. By this time Nietzsche was irreversibly insane, as an effect of tertiary syphillis, and he died in 1900.

3. Victor Tausk killed himself in 1919 by shooting himself in the head while tied up in a noose so that he would hang himself when he fell.

4. Dorothy's husband, Robert Burlingham, killed himself in 1938 by jumping out the four-teenth-floor window of his New York apartment.

Vivian Sobchack: "The Occidental Tourist"

1. All Fagin quotes come from "An Interview with Steve Fagin" by Peter Wollen, which is reprinted in this volume.

2. Raymond Fielding, "Hale's Tours: Ultrarealism in the Pre-1910 Motion Picture," in *Film before Griffith,* ed. John Fell (Berkeley and Los Angeles: University of California Press, 1983), 126.

3. Ibid., 118.

4. Michel Foucault, *Death and the Labyrinth: The World of Raymond Roussel,* trans. Charles Ruas (Berkeley and Los Angeles: University of California Press, 1986), 52.

5. Cited in Fielding, "Hale's Tours," 129.

6. Foucault, *Death,* 52.

7. Stephen Kern, *The Culture of Time and Space: 1880-1918* (Cambridge, Mass.: Harvard University Press, 1983), 212–13.

8. Foucault, *Death,* 86.

9. John Ashbery, introduction to Foucault's *Death,* xxvi.

10. Clifford Irving, review of *The Adventures of Baron Munchausen* (Terry Gilliam, 1989), *Premiere* 2, no. 9 (May 1989): 102.

11. Kern, *Time and Space,* 96.

12. Irving, review, 102.

13. Margaret Morse, "Waking and Shaking," reprinted in this volume.

14. Foucault, *Death,* 11.

Peter Wollen: "An Interview with Steve Fagin"

This piece is an edited transcript of an interview, conducted in the spring of 1987, concerning Steve Fagin's two feature-length videotapes. *Virtual Play: The Double Direct Monkey Wrench in Black's Machinery* (1984) is a video essay on representation, narrative, and love humorously woven through the life of Lou Andreas-Salomé, the turn-of-the-century romantic intellectual who captivated, among others, Freud, Nietzsche, and Rilke. *The Amazing Voyage of Gustave Flaubert and Raymond Roussel* (1986) is organized around the lives and writings of two solipsistic, indulgent, maternally obsessed personalities who, as it has been said of Balzac, "saw nothing and remembered everything." The mood of the tape fluctuates between vaudeville and opera, and the narrative unfolds in the form of letters, diary entries, and postcards—all fictitious. Both tapes are distributed by The Kitchen and Video Data Bank.

Constance DeJong: "For Steve Fagin"

1. Steve Fagin quoted from "Interview with Steve Fagin" by Peter Wollen, included in this volume.

Mellencamp: "Disastrous Events"

1. These quotations are from the text, Fagin's words that accompany the piece.

2. Stanley Karnow, *In Our Own Image: America's Empire in the Philippines* (New York: Random House, 1989). Karnow, a foreign news correspondent, is another version of Lansdale.

3. Ibid., 422.

4. Ibid., 423.

5. The kinship structure in the Philippines is not analogous to the Western notion of family. It involves a very extended family and an ethical commitment to kin that supersedes other structures. Along with land ownership, politics are determined by kinship structures. The custom of "favors" is another difference.

6. Homi K. Bhabha, "The Other Question—the Stereotype and Colonial Discourse," *Screen* 24, no. 2 (November/December 1983): 23, 29.

7. Homi K. Bhabha, "Sly Civility," *October* 43 (Fall 1985): 75.

8. Graham Pechey, "On the Borders of Bakhtin: Dialogization, Decolonialization," *Oxford Literary Review* 9, nos. 1/2 (1987): 69.

9. Karnow, *In Our Own Image*, 348.

10. Benita Parry, "Problems in Current Theories of Colonial Discourse," *Oxford Literary Review* 9, nos. 1/2 (1987): 44. Parry compares the formulations of Bhabha and Gayatri Spivak and reminds us that for Frantz Fanon, whose writings she is employing, "a native context initially enunciated in the invaders' language culminates in a rejection of imperialism's signifying system. This is a move which colonial discourse theory has not taken on board" (p. 45). It would appear that communication scholars' "anti-imperialism" thesis regarding media in the Third World has, to a degree, heeded Fanon's analysis and has indeed taken this work on board, however, not from the point of view of the colonized in the studies quoted in the prologue.

11. Karnow, *In Our Own Image*, 375.

12. Ibid., 373.

13. Gilles Deleuze and Félix Guatarri, *On the Line* (New York: Semiotext[e], 1983), 2, 12. See also their *A Thousand Plateaus: Capitalism and Schizophrenia* (Minneapolis: University of Minnesota Press, 1987).

14. Michael Shamberg, *Guerrilla TV* (New York: Holt, Rinehart & Winston, 1970), 33.

15. Ibid., 14, 29.

16. Fredric Jameson, "Postmodernism and Consumer Society," in *The Anti-Aesthetic: Essays on Postmodern Culture,* ed. Hal Foster (Port Townsend, Wash.: Bay Press, 1983).

17. I repeat these quotations by Benjamin—partially as a comparison with Jameson's assertions. Benjamin formulates an experience of the present as thoroughly inflected by history.

18. Benjamin argues personal experience inflected by memory, or living in the present *and* remembering the past, as a both/and logic that combines the intellect with affect; it is beyond the grasp of the intellect and more than sheer emotion. His theory of personal experience is a both/and logic and is thus pertinent to my argument and women.

19. Jameson, "Postmodernism," 159.

20. Ibid., 158, 125. The latter is, of course, his famous formulation.

21. Parry, "Problems in Current Theories," 42.

22. Tzvetan Todorov, *Mikhail Bakhtin: The Dialogical Principal* (Minneapolis: University of Minnesota Press, 1984), 108.

23. Ibid., 178.

24. Ibid., 46.

25. Mikhail Bakhtin, *The Dialogical Imagination,* ed. Michael Holquist (Austin: University of Texas Press, 1981).

26. Parry, "Problems in Current Theories," 51.

27. Bhabha, "Sly Civility," 75. See also "Of Mimicry and Man: The Ambivalence of Colonial Discourse," *October* 28 (Spring 1984).

Ivone Margulies: "Confessions of a Quiet American"

I would like to thank Mark Cohen for his incisive comments.

1. All Fagin quotes come from "An Interview with Steve Fagin" by Peter Wollen, which is reprinted in this volume.

2. Leo Steinberg states that the flatbed picture plane—which "makes its symbolic allusion to hard surfaces such as tabletops, studio floors, charts, bulletin boards—any receptor surface on which information may be received, printed, impressed"—presents a "special mode of imaginative confrontation," one that expresses "the most radical shift in the subject matter of art, the shift from nature to culture" ("Other Criteria," in *Other Criteria* [New York: Oxford University Press, 1972], 84).

3. Vito Acconci, "Television, Furniture, and Sculpture: The Room with the American View," in *Illuminating Video: An Essential Guide to Video,* ed. Doug Hall and Sally Jo Fifer (New York: Aperture, 1990), 125.

Constance Penley: "Out in Left Field"

1. Michael T. Taussig, *The Devil and Commodity Fetishism in South America* (Chapel Hill: University of North Carolina Press, 1980).

2. David Stoll, *Fishers of Men or Founders of Empire? The Wycliffe Bible Translators in Latin America* (London: Zed; Cambridge, Mass.: Cultural Survival, 1982).

3. Taussig, *Commodity Fetishism.*

4. Ibid.

5. Christopher P. Toumey, *God's Own Scientists: Creationists in a Secular World* (New Brunswick, N.J.: Rutgers University Press, 1994).

6. These ideas are discussed at much greater length in my *Popular Science and Sex in America* (London: Verso, 1996).

Bill Horrigan: "Ohio Impromptu"

1. I wanted to insert something here about the status of video within a prevalent "art world," but then became hopelessly or more hopelessly sidetracked in advance into a rant about this year's Venice Biennale, which in some respects accorded video, in installation form, a conspicuous pride of place, only to have that accommodating gesture backfire when the result was installations lacking any sort of ethical conviction whatsoever, aside from the dumb/smart joke of Fischli and Weiss, who decided that video was . . . well . . . just television (a lot of television). Full throttle into a metarant here, I wanted also to say something about Venice in general (although it would be impossible to compete with the huffy report from the first non-Italian director of the Venice Biennale, Jean Clair, recently opining in the *Art Newspaper* on the city's scandalous decline: "Even as late as the Fifties, great figures in the art world used to meet in the grand cafés which have now been given over to the tour operators. As part of their all-in package they include a drink at Florian's. Florian's is now a disaster area"—so much for Venice (Preserved); never myself having heard of Florian's but getting the general idea, we were simply grateful to have enjoyed free Bellini's at the Bauer-Gruenwald), but less about the Biennale than about the successful quest to find Frederick Rolfe's tombstone (but not Ezra Pound's), and about the folly of our then trying to contact Jean-Luc Godard (he's in Switzerland; isn't that like right next to Italy?) to invite him to produce, yes, a video installation, the ultimate anticipated fax response being that J-L. G. "has no time"—yeh, right, as though *we* have time. Well, this, or some of this, is what I was going to say here.

John Welchman: "Faces, Boxes, and *The Moves*"

1. See, esp., "Building, Dwelling, Thinking," in Martin Heidegger, *Poetry, Language, Thought,* trans. Albert Hofstadter (New York: Harper & Row, 1971), 142–61. Here he writes, for example, that "to say that mortals *are* is to say that *in dwelling* they persist through spaces by virtue of their stay among things and locations" (p. 157).

2. James Clifford, "Traveling Cultures," in *Cultural Studies,* ed. Lawrence Grossberg, Cary Nelson, and Paula Treichler (London: Routledge, 1992), 96–116 (including responses). Future references in text are to page numbers.

3. See James Clifford, *Writing Culture: The Poetics and Politics of Ethnography,* ed. James Clifford and George E. Marcus (Berkeley and Los Angeles: University of California Press, 1986).

4. Basil Wright, *The Long View* (New York: Knopf, 1974), 502.

5. The fullest account of Jean Rouch's "ethnographic film" is Paul Stoller's *The Cinematic Griot: The Ethnography of Jean Rouch* (Chicago: University of Chicago Press, 1992). See also the 1989 special issue of *Visual Anthropology* on the cinema of Jean Rouch.

6. See Stoller, *The Cinematic Griot,* 6, 162.

7. Ibid.; see chap. 11, esp. p. 202.

8. See Karl Heider, *Ethnographic Film* (Austin: University of Texas Press, 1976). "Flaherty's igloo" is a reference to the "home improvement" sanctioned by Robert Flaherty when he

had an igloo artificially enlarged during the shooting of *Nanook of the North* so that he would have room to film the domestic activities inside.

9. See Peter Ian Crawford, "Film as Discourse: The Invention of Anthropological Realities," in *Film as Ethnography*, ed. Peter Ian Crawford and David Turton (Manchester: Manchester University Press, 1992).

10. Dai Vaughan, "The Aesthetics of Ambiguity," in ibid., 105.

11. For a discussion of the relation between anthropology and fiction film in India, see K. N. Salay, "Visual Anthropology and Indian Fiction Films," in *Journal of Social Research* 29, no. 2 (1986): 1–41.

12. See "Professional Censorship" in Trinh T. Minh-ha's *Framer Framed* (New York: Routledge, 1992).

13. Judith Mayne, *Woman, Native, Other: Writing, Postcoloniality and Feminism* (Bloomington: Indiana University Press, 1989), 137.

14. Trinh, "Professional Censorship," 148.

15. Mayne, *Woman, Native, Other*, 129. In *Naked Spaces*, the soundtrack of three differentiated female voices offers a triple register of commentary—local/traditional; personal; and voices imbued with "Western logic" (see pp. 127–28).

16. Eric Michaels, *Bad Aboriginal Art: Tradition, Media and Technological Horizons* (Minneapolis: University of Minnesota Press, 1994).

17. David MacDougall, "Complicities of Style," in *Film as Ethnography*, 94.

18. See Béla Balász, *Theory of the Film: Character and Growth of a New Art*, trans. Edith Bone (New York: Dover, 1970), esp. chaps. 7 and 8.

19. In the question of the representation of the faces of others, Trinh T. Minh-ha has made an especially powerful intervention, going so far as to reverse MacDougall's suggestions. Her films are in a special sense both centered and decentered on the envisioning, particularizing, fracturing, and metaphoric relocation of faces, a process that she foregrounds in the selection of stills that illustrate the film scripts and interviews in *Framer Framed* and the cover of her collection of critical writings *Woman, Native, Other.*

20. This phrase is the title of the first essay in Trinh T. Minh-ha's *Woman, Native, Other* . . .

21. For a wide-ranging discussion of the political, symbolic, and social relativity of "maps," see Denis Wood, *The Power of Maps* (New York: Guilford, 1992). I am here indebted to pp. 194–95 of this discussion.

22. The phrase is again from Clifford's "Traveling Cultures." While I think I understand the motivation for what has become the quite generalized (almost always underspecified) demonization of a set of ideas developed most notably by Gilles Deleuze and Félix Guattari in the two volumes of their *Capitalism and Schizophrenia*, I would also suggest that there is much that is radical and challenging in this discussion. For a (now dated) summary of different formations of nomadological discourse (in anthropology, in literary travel writing, and in critical theory), see my column "Here, There and Otherwise" in *Artforum* (January 1989).

23. Clifford, "Traveling Cultures," 108.

24. Ibid., 99.

25. Raymond Carney, *American Dreaming: The Films of John Cassavetes and the American Experience* (Berkeley and Los Angeles: University of California Press, 1985), 301.

26. Federico Fellini, "Miscellany I—'I'm a Liar, but an Honest One,'" in *Fellini on Fellini*, trans. Isabel Quigley (London: Eyre Methuen, 1976), 53–54.

27. "Rimini, My Home Town," in ibid., 32–33.

28. Federico Fellini, *Comments on Film,* ed. Giovanni Grazzini, trans. Joseph Henry (Fresno: The Press at California State University, 1988), 115.

29. Chris Marker, *Immemory* (proposal, January 1994), 3, cited in Bill Horrigan, "Another Likeness," in *Chris Marker: Silent Movie* (Columbus, Ohio: Wexner Center for the Arts, 1995), 9.

30. A "series of travelogues that blended impressionistic journalism with still photography," Museum of Modern Art, Department of Film, notes for "Chris Marker: A Video Selection," 1.

31. J. B. Pontalis, cited in Georges Van Den Abbeele, *Travel as Metaphor: From Montaigne to Rousseau* (Minneapolis: University of Minnesota Press, 1992), 120.

32. See Jacques Derrida, *The Truth in Painting,* trans. Geoff Bennington and Ian McLoed (Chicago: University of Chicago Press, 1987). In addition to Derrida's proposal of the Benjamin *front,* several other writers and critics develop some account of Benjamin as a physiognomy. See Theodor Adorno, "A Portrait of Walter Benjamin," in *Prisms,* trans. Samuel Weber and Shierry Weber (Cambridge, Mass.: MIT Press, 1981), 229–41; and Winifred Menninghaus, "Walter Benjamin's Theory of Myth," in *On Walter Benjamin: Critical Essays and Recollections,* ed. Gary Smith (Cambridge, Mass.: MIT Press, 1988), 292ff.: "To reconstruct Benjamin's use of the term 'myth' is to present a comprehensive portrait of his thought" (p. 293). Menninghaus also refers to "the physiognomy of Benjamin's thought" (p. 293).

33. Rolf Tiedemann, "Dialectics at a Standstill: Approaches to the *Passagen-Werk,*" in *On Walter Benjamin,* 265.

34. Ibid., 270.

35. Ibid., 279.

36. Ibid., 281.

37. Ibid., 273.

38. Ibid., 280.

39. Walter Benjamin, *The Origins of German Tragic Drama* (London: New Left Books, 1977), 166.

40. Walter Benjamin, "A Small History of Photography," in *One-Way Street and Other Writings,* trans. E. Jephcott and K. Shorter (London: New Left Books, 1979), 243–44. Also cited in Michael Taussig, *Mimesis and Alterity: A Particular History of the Senses* (London: Routledge, 1993), 24, where Taussig emphasizes the tactile nature of physiognomy, not its facelikeness. Later in this study (p. 81) he discusses Darwin's encounter with the Fuegians, who imitate the ship's crew: "It's as if the Fuegians can't help themselves, that their mimetic flair is more like an instinctual reflex than a faculty, an instinct for facing the unknown—and I mean *facing.* I mean sentience and copying in the face of strange faces. Note the way they are painted, especially the face, especially the eyes. Note the grimacing of the face that sets off a chain reaction between sailors and Fuegians."

41. Peter Szondi, "Walter Benjamin's City Portraits" (1962), trans. Harvey Mendelsohn in *On Walter Benjamin,* 26. Szondi notes further that, "as Proust himself came to realize, metaphor aided him in his search for lost time" (p. 28); "metaphor helps Benjamin paint his city portraits as miniatures, much like his preferred form, the fragment" (p. 28).

42. Ibid., 30.

43. Ibid., 22. Also: "a foreign city can fulfill its secret task of turning the visitor into a child

only if it appears as exotic and as picturesque as the child's own city appeared to him" (p. 23).

44. Benjamin, cited in ibid., 25.

45. Benjamin, cited in ibid., 26.

46. Walter Benjamin, *Moscow Diary,* ed. Gary Smith, trans. Richard Sieburth (Cambridge, Mass.: Harvard University Press, 1986), 7, 8, 21.

47. The face of Moscow and Asja's face are not the only faces that obsess Benjamin while he is in the city. Despite his explicit disavowal on failing to meet a friend, Gnedin, at the Proletkult Theater that "it is inconceivable that exhausted as I was, and given my poor memory for faces, I didn't recognize him in his coat and cap" (ibid., 88), Benjamin catalogs a dozen or more facial encounters. Of the poet and activist Alexandr Illich Bezymensky he writes that "the most curious thing about him is his long, apparently unarticulated face with its broad planes. His chin is far longer than any I have seen, except for the one on the invalid Grommer [Jakob Grommer, an assistant to Einstein who suffered from acromegaly], and it is barely cleft" (p. 14); of "the stationer who sits in hiding, enthroned behind her silver crates, an oriental veil of tinsel and cotton-wool Father Christmases drawn across her face" (p. 23); of the face of Joseph Roth "all creased with wrinkles and [with] the unpleasant look of a snoop" (p. 30); of "the physiological configuration of a small canvas by Marie Laurencin— the head of a woman, her hand extending into the painting, a flower rising out of it— [which] reminded me of Munchhaussen and made his former love of Marie Laurencin obvi- ous to me" (p. 86); and of the German consul general with his "coarse . . . face . . . only superficially etched with intelligence" (p. 92). In relation to the unparticularized faces of the crowd he indulges in an exoticist fantasy: "The degree to which the exotic surges forth from the city is always astounding. I see as many Mongol faces as I wish every day in my hotel" (p. 104). And, when he reads to Asja, it is, of course, "the section about wrinkles in *One-Way Street*" (p. 15).

48. Ibid., 5, 6–7. Benjamin reiterates these sentiments on p. 47, where, in conversation with Reich, he notes that "mere convictions and abstract decisions were not enough, only concrete tasks and challenges could really help me make headway. Here he reminded me of my essays on cities." And again on p. 114, when back in Berlin.

49. Benjamin, cited in *On Walter Benjamin,* 67.

50. Novalis cited in Werner Spies, *Max Ernst: Collages: The Invention of the Surrealist Universe* (New York, 1991), 11.

Contributors

Gregg Bordowitz is a filmmaker and writer living in New York City. His recent films include *Fast Trip, Long Drop*, and an adaptation of Nickolai Erdman's play *The Suicide*. He is currently working on a screen adaptation of Tony Kushner's play *A Bright Room Called Day*.

Constance DeJong is an award-winning author who has made performance a natural extension of her writing. She has toured extensively in the U.S., Canada, and Europe presenting oral adaptations of her published texts. She has also collaborated with Tony Oursler on a number of works, including: *Joyride TM* (1988); *Relatives*, which was performed in twenty international cities as part of the 1989 Whitney Biennial; and, with Tony Oursler and Steven Vitiello, *Fantastic Prayers*, an interactive project for the DIA Center for the Arts.

Leslie Dick is author of two highly regarded novels: *Without Falling* (1987) and *Kicking* (1992). A collection of short stories, *The Skull of Charlotte Corday and Other Stories*, was published in London in 1995. She was visiting lecturer in Women's Studies at Vassar College and a Mellon Fellow in criticism at California Institute of the Arts. Her work has appeared in various magazines and anthologies, notably *Interview, Semiotexte, Now Time, The Seven Deadly Sins, Sex and The City, Serious Hysteria,* and *Other Than Itself: Writing Photography*. She currently teaches at California Institute of the Arts.

Barry Gifford has received awards from PEN, the National Endowment for the Arts, and the American Library Association. His nonfiction has appeared in *Esquire, Cosmopolitan,* the *New York Times*, and *Rolling Stone*. His novel *Night People* was awarded the Premio Brancati, Italy's national book award. His fiction has most recently been anthologized in the *Norton Anthology of Literature*. He has also written several screenplays, most recently "Lost Highway," a film directed and cowritten by David Lynch.

Victoria Gill is a freelance editor, French translator, and literary paramedic. Her most recent publication is a poem in the baseball anthology *Diamonds Are a Girl's Best Friend* (1995). She lives in San Francisco and is currently at work on a crime novel.

Bill Horrigan is Media Curator at the Wexner Center for the Arts at Ohio State University.

Bertha Jottar is a videomaker from Mexico City. She lived on the Tijuana/San Diego border for eight years, and was a member of Border Arts Workshop and a founding member of Las Comadres. She is currently a Ph.D. candidate in Performance Studies at New York University.

Ivone Margulies is Assistant Professor at the Department of Theatre and Film at Hunter College (CUNY). She has written on American avant-garde film, and is the author of *Nothing Happens: Chantal Akerman's Hyperrealist Everyday* (1996).

Patricia Mellencamp is Professor of Film and Cultural Theory in the Department of Art History, University of Wisconsin at Madison. She has published several books, including *High Anxiety: Catastrophe, Scandal, Age, and Comedy* and *Indiscretions: Avant-Garde Film, Video, and Feminism.*

Margaret Morse is Associate Professor of Film, Video, and New Media at the University of California at Santa Cruz. She has published widely on subjects ranging from aerobics, art, death, food, and freeway driving to memory, obsession, and the z-axis. Her book, *Virtualities: Television, Media Art, and Cyberculture* is forthcoming from Indiana University Press.

Constance Penley is Professor of Film Studies and Women's Studies at the University of California, Santa Barbara. Her most recent book is *Nasa/Trek*. She is a founding editor of *Camera Obscura*, the author of *The Future of an Illusion: Film, Feminism, and Psychoanalysis*, the editor of *Feminism and Film Theory*, and coeditor of *Technoculture*, *Male Trouble*, and the forthcoming *The Visible Woman: Imaging Technologies, Gender, and Science*.

Vicente L. Rafael teaches in the Department of Communication, University of California, San Diego. He is the author of *Contracting Colonialism* (1993) and the editor of *Discrepant Histories: Translocal Essays on Filipino Cultures* (1995).

Mark Rappaport's recent films include *Rock Hudson's Home Movies* (1992), *Exterior Night* (1994), *From the Journals of Jean Seberg* (1995), and *The Silver Screen/Color Me Lavender* (1997).

Andrew Ross is Professor and Director of the American Studies Program at New York University. His books include *Real Love: In Pursuit of Cultural Justice* (1998), *The Chicago Gangster Theory of Life* (1994), *Strange Weather* (1991), and *No Respect* (1989). He is also the editor of a number of volumes, most recently *No Sweat: Fashion, Free Trade, and the Rights of Garment Workers*.

Vivian Sobchack is Associate Dean and Professor of Film and Television Studies at the UCLA School of Theater, Film, and Television. Her work focuses on film theory and its intersections with philosophy and cultural studies, genre studies of American film, and studies of electronic imaging. Her books include *Screening Space: The American Science Fiction Film* (1987) and *The Address of the Eye: A Phenomenology of Film Experience* (1992), and her articles and reviews have appeared in journals such as *Quarterly Review of Film and Video*, *Artforum International*, *Camera Obscura*, *Post-Script*, *Film Quarterly*, and *Representations*.

Trinh T. Minh-ha is a writer, filmmaker, and composer. Her more recent works include the books *Framer Framed* (1992), *When the Moon Waxes Red* (1991), *Woman, Native, Other* (1989), *En minuscules* (1987); and the films *A Tale of Love* (1995), *Shoot for the Contents* (1991), *Surname Viet Given Name Nam* (1989), *Naked Spaces* (1985), and *Reassemblage* (1982). She taught at the Dakar Conservatory of Music in Senegal, and at universities including Cornell, San Francisco State, Smith, and Harvard, and is presently Professor of Women's Studies and Film at the University of California, Berkeley.

John Welchman teaches in the visual arts department at the University of California, San Diego. He is coauthor of *The Dada and Surrealist Word-Image* (1989), author of *Modernism Relocated* (1995), and editor of *Rethinking Borders* (1996).

Peter Wollen is a filmmaker, video maker, script writer, short story writer, exhibition curator, critic, theorist, and professor who lives in London and Los Angeles and is currently Chair of the Critical Studies Program at UCLA's Department of Film and Television. His latest critical collection is *Raiding the Icebox: Reflections on Twentieth-Century Culture* (1993).

Library of Congress Cataloging-in-Publication Data
Talkin' with your mouth full: conversations with the videos
of Steve Fagin / Steve Fagin, editor.
ISBN 0-8223-2055-x (alk. paper).—ISBN 0-8223-2069-x (pbk.: alk. paper)
1. Fagin, Steve—Criticism and interpretation.   I. Fagin, Steve.
PN1998.3.F34T36 1998   791.43'0233'092—dc21   97-23874 CIP